THE SALMON RIVERS of SCOTLAND

By Derek Mills

Salmon and Trout
Introduction to Freshwater Ecology
Scotland's King of Fish

THE SALMON RIVERS of SCOTLAND

Derek Mills and Neil Graesser

CASSELL
LONDON

CASSELL LTD.
1 Vincent Square, London SW1P 2PN

Copyright © Derek Mills & Neil Graesser 1981

All rights reserved. No part of this publication may be reproduced, stored in a retrieval system, or transmitted, in any form or by any means, electronic, mechanical, photocopying, recording or otherwise, without the prior permission of Cassell Ltd.

First published 1981
First edition, second impression 1984

ISBN 0 304 30492 1

Printed and bound in Great Britain by
Mackays of Chatham Ltd

To our mutual old friend
the late
'JOCK' MENZIES

Contents

	Preface	xi
1	The Life History of the Salmon	1
2	Fluctuations in Salmon Stocks	9
3	Salmon Fishing	14
4	The Salmon River	24
5	The Tweed District *Tweed, Ettrick, Yarrow, Teviot, Till, Whiteadder*	28
6	The Forth–Teith System *Forth, Teith, Leny, Allan, Devon*	40
7	The Tay District *Tay, Loch Tay, Dochart, Lochay, Lyon, Garry, Braan, Tummel, Tilt, Isla, Ericht, Almond, Earn, Eden*	48
8	The North Esk, South Esk and Bervie	71
9	The Aberdeenshire Dee and Cowie	78
10	The Don	85
11	The Ythan and Ugie	89
12	The Deveron	93
13	The Spey	96
14	The Lossie, Findhorn and Nairn	102
15	The Ness District *Ness, Loch Ness, Oich, Loch Oich, Garry, Moriston*	108
16	The Beauly District *Glass, Farrar, Beauly*	116
17	The Conon District *Conon, Bran, Orrin, Black Water, Meig*	122
18	The Alness, Allt Graad and Balnagown	133
19	The Kyle of Sutherland *Carron, Einig, Oykel, Cassley, Shin, Evelix*	136
20	The Brora and Fleet	148
21	The Helmsdale	153
22	The Berriedale, Langwell, Dunbeath and Wick	157
23	The Thurso	161
24	The Forss, Halladale, Strathy, Naver and Borgie	165
25	The Kyle of Durness and Cape Wrath *Hope, Dionard, Kinloch, Polla, Grudie, Daill, Kearvaig, Shinary*	173

26	The Rivers of North-West Sutherland	180
	Inchard, Laxford, Duart, Inver, Kirkaig,	
	Polly, Garvie and Oscaig	
27	The Kanaird, Ullapool, Broom and Dundonnell	188
28	The Gruinard and Little Gruinard	193
29	The Rivers of South-West Ross	196
	Ewe, Kerry, Badachro, Torridon, Applecross,	
	Balgy, Shieldaig, Kishorn and Carron	
30	The Outer Hebrides, Skye, Mull, Arran and Islay	204
31	The Loch Alsh, Kintail, Mallaig, Shiel and Morvern District	229
	Ling, Elchaig, Croe, Shiel of Duich, Glenmore,	
	Glenbeg, Arnisdale, Guseran, Inverie, Garnach, Morar,	
	Ailort, Moidart, Shiel, Aline and Rannoch	
32	The Lochy District	241
	Lochy, Spean, Roy, Arkaig, Loy, Nevis,	
	Leven of Kinlochleven	
33	The Orchy, Awe, Creran, Etive, Kinglass, Coe, Euchar, Nell and Oude	247
34	The Kintyre District	259
	Add, Barr, Lussa, Machrihanish, Breackerie and	
	Conie Waters, Carradale and Claonaig	
35	The Fyne, Kinglas, Aray, Shira and Douglas	266
36	The Ruel, Eachaig, Loch Lomond, Falloch, Leven, Endrick	272
37	The Gryfe, Irvine, Garnock, Ayr, Doon, Girvan and Stinchar	279
38	The Solway Rivers: 1	290
	Luce, Bladnoch and Cree	
39	The Solway Rivers: 2	296
	Fleet, Dee and Urr	
40	The Solway Rivers: 3	302
	Nith, Cairn, Annan and Border Esk	
	Epilogue	313
	Appendix: *Annual Close Times Applicable to the Salmon Rivers in Scotland*	319
	Bibliography	322
	Index	325

Maps

The Salmon Rivers of North Scotland	16
The Salmon Rivers of South Scotland	20
The Tweed River System	29
The River Tweed following	36
The Rivers Forth and Teith and their major tributaries	46
The Rivers Tummel and Garry and the Tummel-Garry Hydro-electric Scheme	51
The River Tay following	52
The upper tributaries of the River Tay and River Earn and the Breadalbane Hydro-electric Scheme	53
Salmon Pools on the River Lyon from Roro Bridge to the Tay	59
Salmon Pools on the River Tummel	64
The River Dee following	84
The River Don	86
The River Spey following	100
The Rivers Garry and Moriston and the Garry–Moriston Hydro-electric Scheme	112
The Rivers Beauly and Glass and the Glen Affric, Strathfarrar and Aigas–Kilmorack Hydro-electric Scheme	117
The Rivers Conon, Black Water, Meig and Bran and the Conon Basin Hydro-electric Scheme	125
The Rivers Oykel, Cassley and Shin	141
Salmon Pools at the Cassley Falls	143
The River Brora	149
The River Helmsdale	155
The River Thurso	163
Salmon Pools on the River Naver	171
The Salmon Rivers of North-West Ross	190
The Gruinard Rivers of Wester Ross	195
The Salmon Rivers of the Outer Hebrides	206
Salmon Pools on the River Lochy	242
The Rivers Awe and Orchy and the Awe Hydro-electric Scheme	251
The Salmon Rivers of South Argyll and the Sloy–Shira Hydro-electric Scheme	268
The River Cree	294
The River Nith	305
The Rivers Annan and Esk	310

Preface

Over sixty-five years have elapsed since the last edition of Augustus Grimble's book on the salmon rivers of Scotland was published in 1913, while an even longer time has passed since W.L. Calderwood produced his book on *The Salmon Rivers and Lochs of Scotland* in 1909. Since then there have been two world wars and a major change in Scotland's social and industrial life which, with the development of the North Sea oil resources and membership of the EEC, is still in the process of further change. If these two eminent anglers were to return to cast a line on their beloved rivers they would find striking differences in the conditions they had previously experienced. Hydro-electric and water abstraction schemes have altered the régimes of many of these waters, while afforestation and industrial developments have influenced their physical, chemical and biological characteristics. An increased urban population with a greater amount of leisure time, together with a large influx of overseas tourists, has seen the rivers visited more regularly and their salmon stocks the quarry for an ever-growing number of anglers from both home and overseas.

Because the works of Calderwood and Grimble have been such a mine of information for almost three-quarters of a century but now, because of so many radical changes, are so sadly out of date, we felt it would be of value to many if we produced an up-to-date account of what forms an important part of Scotland's heritage. If our rivers are to survive as salmon waters then developers and planners, biologists and engineers, foresters and farmers, as well as sport and commercial fishermen, must be aware of the present state of our rivers and their salmon stocks, so that developments can proceed cautiously in the future, benefiting from the mistakes of our forebears. As a result of our accumulated knowledge on the *King of Fish* over a period which has seen more rapid changes than any other period in man's history we are now in a position to do this.

We had the anglers very much in mind while preparing this book and hope we have made it easier for them to explore new waters with a greater knowledge of their quarry and of the factors which influence its survival.

Throughout the preparation of this book we have been helped by very many people who have gone to endless trouble to provide us with information on the rivers they know so well. Were we to mention individually all those who have given us help, be they individual proprietors, district fishery boards, commissioners or angling associations, we would produce a list which would inevitably be incomplete, as so many people 'behind the scenes' did so much to make our task easier. We now take this opportunity to express our grateful appreciation to all of them. Miss Jannet Grant of Cassell does, however, deserve particular mention for the considerable work and care that she has put into editing the manuscript.

I (D.H.M.) would also like to thank the Travel and Research Committee of the University of Edinburgh and The Carnegie Trust for the Universities of Scotland for generously awarding me grants to help with the costs of field work.

Edinburgh and DEREK MILLS
Rosehall NEIL GRAESSER
November, 1980

NOTE:

Gaelic and local names referred to in this book are spelt according to the Ordnance Survey maps. In certain areas, variations from these spellings may occur.

1

THE LIFE HISTORY OF THE SALMON

With rare exceptions, the salmon depends on two distinct environments for the successful fulfilment of its life history. The first is a freshwater environment in which the reproductive and nursery phase of its life cycle occur and the second is a marine environment for its main feeding phase, during which rapid growth is achieved.

The salmon enters the river at all times of the year; if it has spent two, three or four years at sea before returning to freshwater it is known as a 'salmon' and, depending on the time of year at which it returns, is called a spring, summer or autumn fish. If the salmon has spent only a little over a year at sea before returning it is termed a 'grilse'. Quite often there is little difference in the size of these fish, but their age can be determined by examining their scales, which lay down rings in a seasonal pattern.

On approaching freshwater the salmon stops feeding and will not feed again until it returns to salt water as a spent fish or kelt, which may be six months to a year or more later. Fortunately, this phenomenon makes little difference to the angler as salmon, for some inexplicable reason, take anglers' lures into their mouths although not feeding. Once in freshwater the salmon will migrate upstream at varying speeds depending on the time of year, water temperature and stream flow.

The time of entry of the main runs of fish varies from river to river. Some rivers such as the Tweed, Tay, Findhorn, Spey, Inverness-shire Garry and Ness have early runs of spring fish while others, such as those on the west coast of Scotland, may have very few spring fish with the first large runs of fish only starting to enter the rivers in June and July as grilse and summer fish. Again there are rivers such as the Tweed which have a large run of autumn fish which continues well into December.

In the past a great deal of work was done in describing the characteristics of salmon of individual rivers from the results of studies of their scales. More recently the Salmon Research Trust of Ireland has undertaken the rearing of fish of known ancestry and their subsequent tagging, release and recapture. In these experiments fish derived from spring fish parents have returned as spring fish and those derived from grilse parents have returned as grilse. However, it was found that spring fish do not invariably breed spring fish nor do grilse invariably breed grilse, although the majority of smolts derived from grilse have returned as grilse. It was also noticed that there is a tendency for smolts of spring fish to return as grilse, and a similar situation has also been observed in hatchery-reared smolts in Scotland.

Probably one of the most intriguing aspects of the salmon's life history is its homing instinct. According to Izaak Walton, the return of a salmon to its parent river had already been established by 1653 by 'tying a riband or some known tape or thread in the tale of smolts and catching them again when they came back to the same place usually six months after'. However, the tagging experiments carried out on the River Tay in 1905 and 1906 by the late P.D.H. Malloch of Perth were among the first serious marking investigations carried out anywhere in the world.

Many theories have been put forward to explain the way in which salmon find their way back to their parent river. The most generally accepted theory is one derived from the work of two Americans which demonstrates the importance of stream odours in the orientation of fish. This theory is not a new one, and almost a hundred years ago the eminent fisheries naturalist Frank Buckland suggested that salmon were assisted by their power of smell to find their way in the ocean, and also to find their parent river.

Another interesting aspect of homing instinct is that in which fish reared in one river, or in a hatchery fed by one river, and then released in another river, sometimes very far away and often under such conditions that they will leave this second river almost immediately, have returned to the river in which they were released. This indicates that the memory of smell of the home water is imprinted a few days before entering the sea or on their downstream migration and not during their early river life.

A host of factors are said to be responsible for the entry of salmon into rivers and their subsequent upstream migration. It has been found that fish move out of tidal waters into fresh water at dusk and that light change might be the operating factor. There is also evidence that fairly strong onshore winds induce salmon to concentrate in the river estuary and eventually ascend. Peaks in the tidal cycles representing daily increasing differences between high and low tides also seem to be effective in concentrating salmon on the coast and initiating a run into freshwater. It has also been shown that water temperature is of great importance to fish movement in the spring, and until the water temperature reaches 42°F there is little upstream movement of fish over obstacles.

Upstream migration is undoubtedly associated with thyroid activity as the salmon becomes sexually mature, and it has been suggested that the alternating periods of activity and torpor which characterise the behaviour of ascending salmon may be due to variations in the activity of the thyroid gland. Although floods have always been associated with major upstream movements of salmon there is increasing evidence to show that salmon move upstream at very low flows and often during periods of darkness.

The adult male and female salmon change in appearance after entering freshwater and as spawning time approaches. Some of the bones of the salmon grow substantially and a new set of breeding teeth appears. The bones that increase their size and acquire new material include the main bones of the jaws, this being particularly noticeable in the male which develops a hooked lower jaw or kype.

Spawning, or egg laying, starts in the late autumn. Some fish lay their eggs in November, but those which have entered the river late in the season may not deposit theirs until January or February. By the time spawning commences salmon will have occupied suitable spawning grounds, which consist of silt-free gravel in areas extending from the upper reaches of the watershed down to tidal level. The salmon does not lay many eggs, relatively speaking; how many depends on its size. The number ranges from 2,000 to 15,000. A high fecundity is not essential because the eggs are well protected in nests or redds under several inches of gravel. After spawning, most of the males die, but a relatively small proportion of the females return to spawn a second time.

The eggs hatch in late March or early April and the alevins make their way up through the gravel to emerge as fry four or five weeks later, when their yolk sac has been absorbed. At the end of their first year of life the fry are known as parr and they remain in this stage until the spring of their second, third or even fourth year of life, depending on stream conditions, when they turn silver and become smolts. At this stage they migrate to sea, the migration being triggered off by one or more environmental factors. The progeny of one fish do not necessarily go to sea in the same year or return at the same time and this phenomenon gives obvious survival advantages to the species. A varying proportion of male parr attain sexual maturity before leaving the river and it is considered that the presence of ripe male parr in the spawning grounds is to ensure fertilisation of the eggs in case of inadequate fertilisation, or lack of fertilisation, by the adult male.

Once the smolts have entered the sea little is known of their movements, although with the advent of the Greenland fishery in 1957 much more is now known about the sea life of the Atlantic salmon. This has been due to the recapture, off Greenland, of fish tagged as smolts and kelts in Canada, England, Ireland, Scotland, Sweden and the United States. The sea food of salmon consists chiefly of fish, such as capelin, herring and sand-eels, and large zooplankton organisms.

The most important marine predator of salmon is the grey seal. They do considerable damage to the fish and to the nets. On the basis of the number of seals seen by fishermen in the vicinity of the nets when they are being fished, it has been estimated that 147,888 salmon and sea trout were killed by seals on the Scottish east coast from 1959 to 1963.

The adult and juvenile stages of the salmon are particularly vulnerable in the relatively confined areas of rivers and streams, and their predators can be listed as follows: (a) Fish: pike, perch, chub, eels and trout; (b) Birds: cormorant, shag, black-headed gull, goosander, red-breasted merganser, heron and osprey; (c) Mammals: otter and mink.

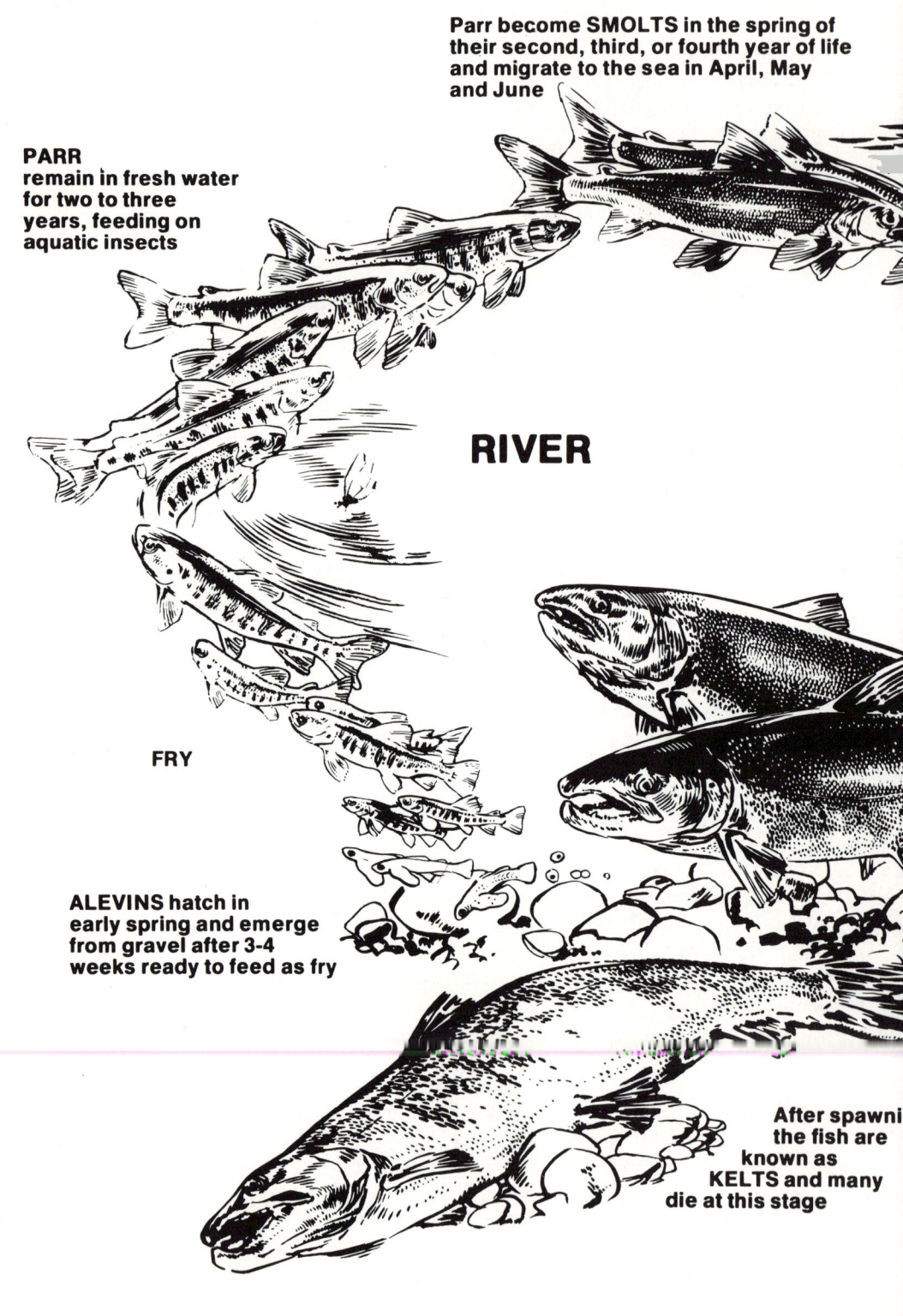

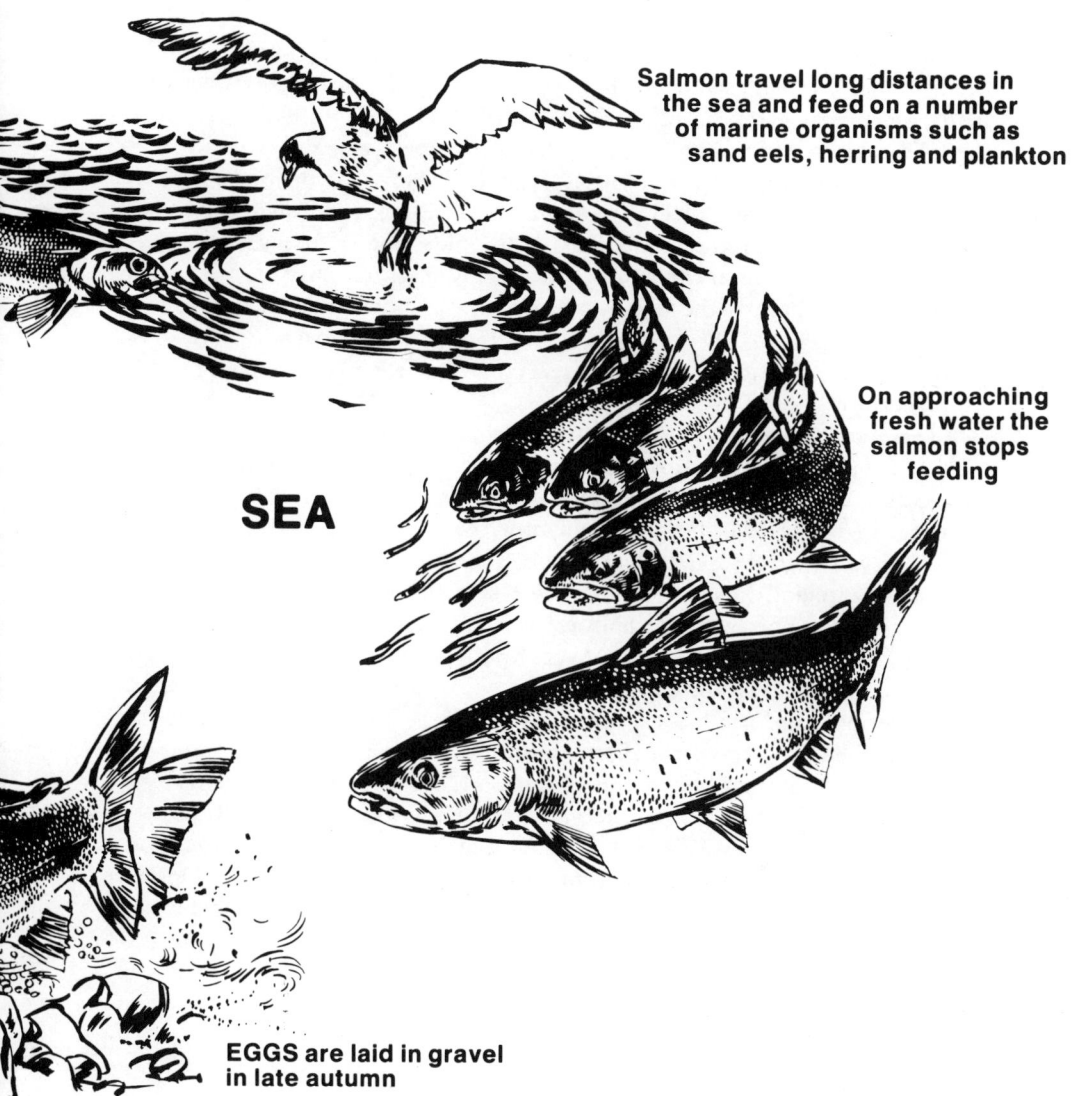

Life cycle of the salmon (from: Mills, 1971 and 1979)

Both pike and trout can be serious predators of salmon fry, parr and smolts. For example, it was estimated that 10% of the smolt run on the River Bran, Ross-shire, was eaten by pike in 1959 and 1961.

The salmon is subject to a number of diseases, some of which can be responsible for very high mortalities. The diseases include furunculosis, Dee disease, kidney disease, ulcerative dermal necrosis and vibriosis. Furunculosis is a particularly well-known disease of salmonids, and salmon suffering from the disease show a variety of external symptoms ranging from congestion of the fins to haemorrhage at the vent and furuncles. At other times there may be no external symptoms. The disease has been recognised for over sixty years as a cause of death during the summer, especially when the rivers are low and water temperatures rise to 55°F.

There are many reasons for believing that ulcerative dermal necrosis, or UDN for short, is the same disease as the 'salmon disease' which occurred towards the end of the last century. The diseases spread from one river to another in the same order and the symptoms were remarkably alike.

UDN was first observed in epidemic proportions in a number of rivers in south-west Ireland during 1964 – 1965. During 1966 the disease spread to the Lancashire, Cumberland and Solway river systems. By the end of 1967 the disease had spread to all east coast rivers from the Tweed to the Nairn with the exception of the Forth and Tay and, on the west coast, from the Solway Firth to the River Ayr. In 1968 cases appeared in the Forth, Tay, Ness and Conon river systems. The progress of the disease up the east coast of Scotland resembled that in Ireland, in that, for no apparent reason, one river might remain clear of the disease while its immediate neighbours were seriously affected. It has been suggested that it is possible that sea trout may have contributed to the spread of the disease as these fish move from estuary to estuary. In the rivers Deveron and Spey sea trout were seriously affected for almost two weeks before any diseased salmon were observed.

Commercial fishing

In Scotland the methods of commercial fishing for salmon along the coast are fixed engines or fixed nets, chiefly the bag net and the stake or fly net. The bag net is commonly used on rocky coasts and consists essentially of a trap made of netting to which fish are directed by a leader, that is a line of netting placed across the route the salmon usually follow as they move along the coast. The salmon swim towards the leader but cannot get through and instinctively turn seawards. Swimming along the leader they are led into the mouth of the net and through a succession of compartments into a final chamber or fish court. Stake nets, known as fly nets or 'jumpers' depending on their construction, are used on sandy shores and consist of walls of netting erected on stakes in the sea-bed which act as leaders to approaching salmon. At intervals pockets or traps are inserted to take the fish that are directed along the leader. Unlike bag nets, they are not floating but are fixed to the ground throughout their length. Fish taken by these nets and the bag net are trapped, and not caught in the meshes, and are usually alive when removed.

Fishing within estuarial waters and the rivers themselves is by net and coble only. The net is loaded on the coble and attached to it is a rope held by a fisherman on the shore. The coble moves across the estuary or river, shooting the net as it goes. Its course is roughly a semicircle, finishing on the shore from which the boat started out. The ends of the net are then hauled in and the fish removed.

Brief but strong mention should also be made of a drift or gill net fishery which developed off the east coast of Scotland in 1960. This drift net fishing was a new technique which had no parallel in Scotland and, until the Prohibition Order became effective on 15 September, 1962, drift net fishing for salmon was lawful outside the 3-mile limit. The drift net consists of sections of monofilament netting about 10 feet in depth suspended from a corked headrope and is either not weighted at all at the bottom or only very lightly weighted. Each section of net measures about 100 yards in length. Although drift netting and fixed hang nets, and other modifications of the drifting gill net, are now illegal under the Sea Fisheries Conservation Act of 1967 and subsequent statutory instrument orders, it is still carried out on both Scottish coasts. In 1976 and 1977 this method of fishing became widespread on the east coast and was of great concern to Salmon District Fishery Boards and other salmon conservationists.

The effects of man

The hazards affecting Scottish salmon stocks while in their marine environment have been stressed above and it is obvious that stricter control is necessary if these stocks are to maintain their present levels let alone increase. However, the salmon also experiences many dangers in its freshwater habitat, both in the juvenile and adult phase. Fortunately these are more easily controlled but there is no room for complacency as many of man's activities are insidious and there should be greater awareness of their effects. The majority of these effects in Scotland occur as a result of forestry, agriculture, hydro-electric development and water abstraction.

One of the main agricultural practices which has an adverse effect on spawning and nursery streams is land drainage. Land drainage causes a quicker run-off of water with an associated increase in bank erosion. This results in the transportation of a heavy silt load from the upper areas of streams and the deposition of this elsewhere in the river with a consequent covering of spawning and nursery areas. Land drainage is also associated with forestry and there is some concern over the likely effects of the transport of gravel and silt from drainage channels into neighbouring rivers.

Silt also occurs in rivers from erosion due to overgrazing, muir burn and crop production on steeply sloping land. In Scotland sheep cause a great deal of erosion by destroying the ground vegetation through grazing. They also contribute to the instability of hill ground and river banks by creating innumerable tracks and narrow paths and by using small knolls and irregularities in the ground and river banks for protection from the weather; these places are gradually worn down until a shallow soil profile is exposed which later increases in width and depth.

Muir burn may contribute to erosion and to landslides in certain types of terrain. Muir burn is the age-long practice of rotational firing of heathland, particularly on hill land, to prevent tree regeneration and especially to promote new growth of ling heather which provides part of the diet of sheep and grouse. The firing is usually carried out in the spring as a basic part of moorland management.

In many water supply schemes large rivers, such as the Tweed, may have their upper tributaries dammed to form reservoirs. The water in the reservoir is then piped to the city, which may be a considerable distance away. The formation of reservoirs may result in the flooding of spawning and nursery grounds and also the barring of salmon to spawning areas upstream of the reservoir. The Fruid Reservoir, for example, on one of the Tweed's upper tributaries, has flooded some spawning and nursery ground and, because there is no fish pass in the dam, salmon are prevented from reaching the remaining spawning grounds upstream of the reservoir. The storage of water also affects the flow of the river for some distance downstream until other tributaries join the main channel. Usually on migratory fish rivers a compensation flow is agreed upon by the authorities, with increases in flow to form 'freshets' when fish move upstream to spawn.

Hydro-electric development involves dams, reservoirs, power stations, tunnels and aqueducts, all of which may have effects on the well-being of migratory fish. These adverse effects include: (a) ascending fish: delay from low water flows, diverted flows (resulting in straying of 'homing' fish), delays at dams, passage through reservoirs, flooded spawning grounds; (b) descending fish: limited nursery areas, passage through reservoirs, predator accumulations in reservoirs, delay at dams and mortalities at screens and turbines.

The life of the salmon in Scottish rivers in modern times is therefore very much more different now compared to that of nearly 75 years ago, when the last book on the salmon rivers of Scotland was written. This will be very apparent as the reader turns the pages of this book.

2

FLUCTUATIONS IN SALMON STOCKS

In all animal stocks there are annual fluctuations in population numbers as a result of changes in breeding success, survival of progeny, mortality of adults and change in environment due to factors such as climate, exploitation, pollution, disease and predation. The salmon is no exception and most anglers are aware that the seasons are not the same in terms of fishing success, but an assessment of fish stocks (particularly from angling, and even commercial fishing, records) is not completely reliable. In the terrestrial environment it is certainly easier to assess stocks of sporting mammals (red deer) or birds (grouse and pheasant) visually, but in the aquatic habitat one is working almost blind, as one is relying on the ability to catch fish to assess their numbers.

Catching ability, as anglers and commercial fishermen are aware, is influenced by climate, river height, the behaviour of fish and a host of other factors. It is also affected by weekly and annual close seasons. For example, a run of fish entering the river at the weekend during the weekly close time will be missed by the nets at the river mouth, and a subsequent flood will disperse the fish throughout the river system before the anglers can take their toll, while autumn runs are never culled by the nets which have started their annual close season before the arrival of the late-running fish. Again, stocks of fish in a river may be large but climatic conditions may affect the rods more than the nets, and the angling records for a beat of the river may indicate a poor stock of fish while the commercial river net records may show the opposite. For example, the remarks column for the spring of 1924 in the angling records of a large estate on Tweed, with a famous beat on the lower reaches, states: 'River very low with severe frost, good catches at net stations. Salmon net catches at Berwick (15/2) had best catches for 40 years.' The spring (February–May) catch on that beat was only 16 fish, while in the years on either side the beat had catches of 94 and 75 fish. This might suggest that the fish were waiting to enter the river and were just not available to the rods. However, severe weather could also directly influence angling catches, and on the same beat the remarks for the 28 and 29 March, 1901, state: 'Twenty-two degrees of frost on 28th. Snow lying. Very cold south-east wind on 29th with snow blizzards about 6 p.m. River very low. Plenty of fish but taking badly.' Was it the low temperature affecting the fish's desire to 'take'? One wonders, particularly after reading the remarks for April in that year: 'Latter part of April very fine and warm. Good quantity of fish but taking badly.' One is tempted to ask if it

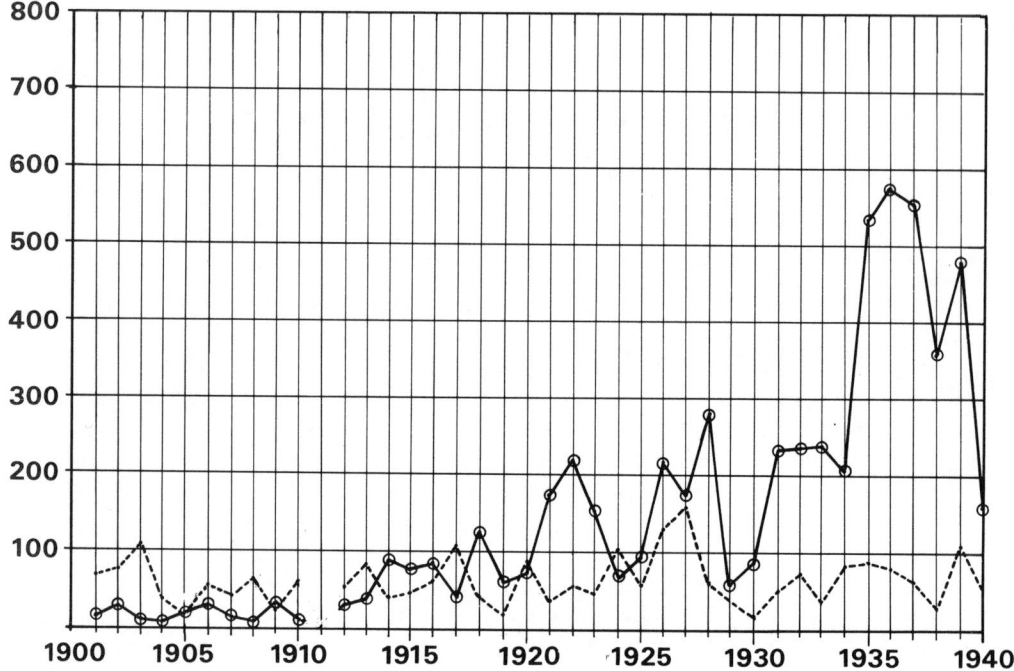

Graphs of the spring and autumn rod catches on one of the lower beats of the Tweed, 1901–1979

is not the concentration of fish which prevents 'taking', as a fish moving out to intercept the angler's lure will lose its secure position in the pool to another fish.

These thoughts are noted to indicate how difficult it is to assess objectively the stock of fish in a river on angling experience alone and even by visual observation, as in some rivers fish do not 'show' in the spring.

Factors affecting 'catchability' are not always appreciated when the fisheries biologist attempts to put some order into angling and commercial records by referring to 'fishing effort', that is the number of rods or rod/hours, or number of nets or net/days. Certainly this reduces the variability, but all the same the fishing effort, and efficiency, by two individual rods fishing for an hour can be very different, depending on whether they are fishing all day in a flood or all day under drought conditions, and on their individual prowess. Net fishing effort may be difficult to assess for similar reasons and may be complicated by changes in mesh size and the type of material with which the net is made.

Even an assessment based on escapement by judging the intensity of spawning by redd counts can be difficult and is dependent, among other things, on the river height at spawning time.

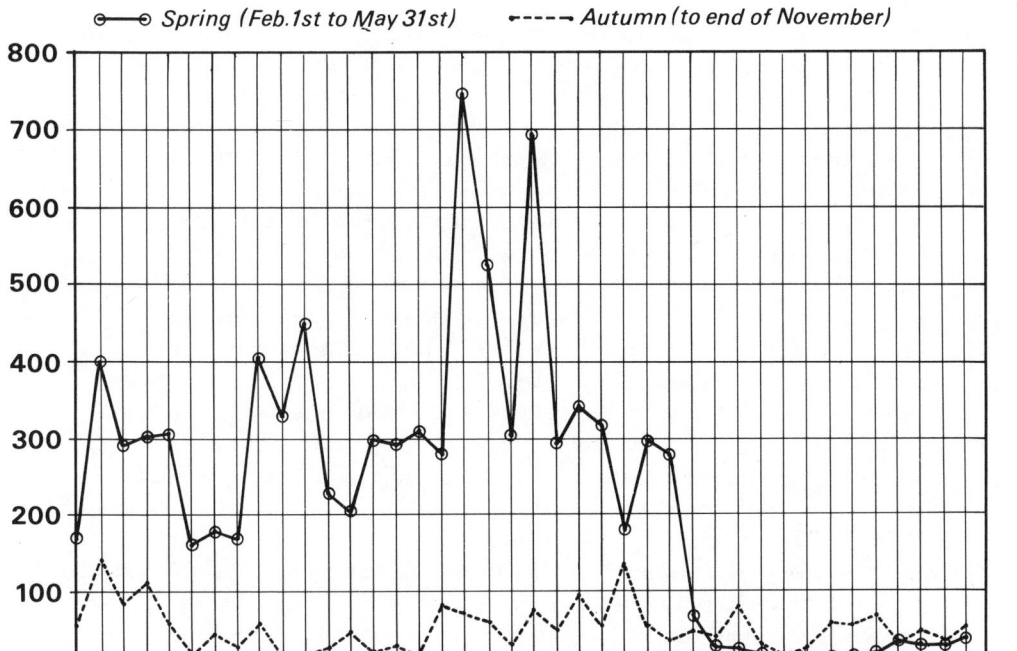

Little more need be said to show how difficult it is to make an objective assessment of how many fish are in the river when one is fishing and whether it has been a good season for the fish, although the angler will be in no doubt about it himself!

However, there are well-documented records of trends in the salmon stocks and a number of eminent salmon biologists, among them Huntsman, Hutton, Lindroth, Menzies and Went, have shown, from annual commercial landings of salmon, that there are marked fluctuations, some of which could be attributed to environmental conditions.

In addition to the existence of long-term trends and fluctuations in salmon stocks generally, there are also well-marked trends in the time of year that fish ascend the rivers. Some rivers which were previously renowned for their spring fish have gradually become noted for their autumn runs, and others have lost their early run and have stocks of grilse and summer fish only.

In certain cases these changes are cyclical and Tweed illustrates this very well. In the late nineteenth century, from about 1860, the autumn catches of salmon far exceeded those of the spring months. This state of affairs lasted until about 1904, after which there was a period of about 25 years when the spring and autumn catches were very similar. Then the catches of spring fish started to increase and the autumn catches to dwindle. By 1961 there were signs of a return of the autumn run followed six years later by a marked decline in the spring fish catches, and since 1967 the spring fishing has been relatively poor but the autumn fishing excellent. This cycle is well illustrated in Figure 2 which depicts the graphs of the spring and autumn rod catches on one of the lower beats of the Tweed for the period 1901—1979.

In recent years some rivers have lost their runs of spring fish and now have stocks which consist predominantly of grilse. This is particularly true of some Scottish rivers which have been harnessed for power generation, such as the Conon, the Black Water and the Shin. A logical reason for this change is cited by Dr Jones in his book *The Salmon*, when he refers to the Shannon in Ireland and the work of Dr Went. After the Shannon was harnessed for power it lost its big salmon when the spawning beds of the large fish were made unusable. The large fish, therefore, presumably spawned in grilse spawning areas and the resulting parr developed grilse tendencies, with the result that the Shannon is now primarily a grilse river. This explanation could certainly apply to the Shin where the upper spawning grounds have been lost through difficulty in fish ascending and descending the fish pass at Lairg Dam. It would not explain the situation on the Conon, and on the Black Water the stock is maintained artificially by fry planting, albeit with grilse progeny.

There have also been changes in the movements of salmon in the Tay–Tummel–Garry system. The spring runs have decreased since 1950 and the summer and autumn runs of salmon, as opposed to grilse, have increased since 1959. Gardiner (1971), who carried out this study, says in his discussion: 'It is tempting to speculate that the changes in migration time in the Tummel are a consequence of the hydro-electric developments. However, there is no direct evidence for this, and it must be remembered that similar changes have been described for rivers unaffected by damming as well as for the country as a whole. Menzies and Smart (1966) observe that early runs of salmon in Britain have declined, and that more adult 'salmon' – as distinct from 'grilse' – now appear in summer and autumn, providing figures from the North Esk (Angus) since 1925 as an example. They also state that the maximum of the grilse run entering rivers at Aberdeen and Montrose is later, and that this run now continues longer. Such variation has not been attributable to climatic factors. Commercial netsmen in other parts of Scotland have observed similar changes, and in most cases the August and September catches suddenly started to increase after 1958.'

Although this change is not attributable to climatic factors it is difficult to see how this marked increase in summer salmon and grilse in Scotland was not in some way related to the wet summer seasons in the 1950s, when probably a greater escapement of these fish led to competition on the spawning grounds to the detriment of the spring fish.

It is obvious that there should be many more investigations into the seasonal changes in the movements of salmon, much more intensive monitoring programmes of environmental conditions in rivers and also a closer scrutiny of oceanographic data by salmon biologists. Lastly, there should be greater access to catch records. It is only since the passing of the Salmon and Freshwater

Fisheries (Scotland) Act, 1951, that salmon catch statistics had to be submitted annually to the Secretary of State, but these cannot be made public for ten years from the year in which the catch was made. Further complications in the interpretation of catch records now arise as a result of the illegal salmon drift-netting operations off the Scottish coast.

3

SALMON FISHING

Salmon fishing in Scotland is nearly an all-year pursuit. In the spring it is confined almost entirely to the east coast rivers, part of the south-west corner and one or two rivers on the north coast. Apart from a few exceptions there is no real spring run in the north-west and west coast rivers and those of the Outer Isles, although an occasional early fish may be taken. Spring anglers are allowed to use bait or fly on most rivers, apart from those north of the Cromarty Firth where by proprietors' agreement angling is confined to fly only.

The earliest rivers open to angling are north of the Cromarty Firth. Some of these open on 11 and others on 12 January, the Brora being an exception to the rule in opening on 1 February. On the rivers south of the Cromarty Firth, the Tay is the first to open, on 15 January, most of the others being open between then and 1 February. The North and South Esk are the latest in opening on 16 February (see Appendix).

Some of the larger east coast rivers still have a winter run of salmon which enters between late November and January and is spread throughout the river system by the time the fishing season opens. Other rivers rely on the real spring run with fish being scarce during the opening weeks of the season, until March heralds the arrival of the first significant runs.

By the middle of May the rest of the rivers begin to benefit from the summer run, which increases rapidly through June and July by which time all the Scottish rivers are fully stocked with salmon, grilse and sea trout.

Many rivers close on 30 September and others on 15 October, but there are a few which remain open until the end of October to take advantage of the autumn run. The Tweed, renowned for its autumn fishing, does not close until 30 November.

Although sea trout enter most Scottish rivers, the west coast rivers are the most famed for this species, although there are exceptions. The Deveron, Spey, Ythan and South Esk all have good runs. The sea trout fishing on the west coast is not confined to the rivers and many of the lochs hold good stocks of this sporting fish with Lochs Maree, Stack and Dionard being among the most famous.

There have been many changes in salmon fishing methods over the last fifty years. Spinning, for instance, has seen the change over from cane rods of 11 feet or more equipped with easy cast or centre pin reels, silk lines and wire traces to lighter and shorter glass rods with fixed spool reels and nylon lines. Spinning baits have changed from the old leaded and painted canvas minnows or silver and gold preserved natural sprats to, firstly, metal Devon minnows and then, latterly, wooden minnows, some weighted and some not. More recently metal spoons of all shapes and sizes, mostly originating in Scandinavia, have been added to the armoury. The modern spinning equipment allows a complete novice the chance of catching a salmon on his first outing and he can become a proficient 'bait fisher' in a comparatively short space of time and with the least possible effort. It is also possible to cast a spinner a far greater distance than a fly and therefore cover a larger area of water.

Fly fishing has also seen many changes with the introduction of spliced split cane rods and lighter glass fibre rods and now carbon fibre rods, instead of the long greenheart rods of 15–20 feet and steel-centred split cane rods, commonly nicknamed 'barge poles', of the olden days, although it is doubtful whether these rods have improved distance casting there is no doubt that they have reduced the effort required. Lines have also changed dramatically from dressed silk 'Kingfisher' lines to various forms of sinking and floating lines. The cheaper nylon has replaced the silkworm gut of yore, which needed soaking before use, and has greatly reduced the number of fish lost due to breaks when a 'granny' or wind knot appeared in the cast on a windy day.

Tube flies of all shapes and sizes have replaced the large single hook flies on up to 9/0 and 10/0 hooks, which require a stiff rod not only to cast them but also to drive the hook home. Now with a treble hook attached to the tube fly it is possible to cast them and securely hook a fish on a comparatively light rod. If a treble is bent or broken it can be quickly replaced, whereas with a single or double hook or Waddington-type fly if a barb is broken the whole fly has to be discarded. There is therefore no more economic fly to use than a tube fly dressed in various sizes, although it is perhaps not so aesthetically pleasing to use as the conventionally dressed fly.

Summer fishing has gained very largely through the radical improvement to equipment in exactly the same way as spring fishing. Once again the lighter rod, better casts and small tube flies have revolutionised this type of fishing. The floating line requires special mention. It has saved the toil of greasing the line on some occasions and degreasing on others, with the inevitable annoyance of getting grease on the cast or fly and having to carry French chalk to correct this. Now, either one carries two reels, one with a floating and the other with a sinking line, or a reel with interchangeable spools which can be used at one's discretion if conditions change quickly.

Spinning equipment can nowadays be quickly adapted to fish prawn, shrimp, natural minnow or worm at the angler's discretion according to the various states of the river.

The angler coming to Scotland to enjoy a fishing holiday has a very wide choice open to him both for the type of fishing and for the time of year. The lower reaches of the Tweed, Tay, Dee and Spey are probably the most suitable

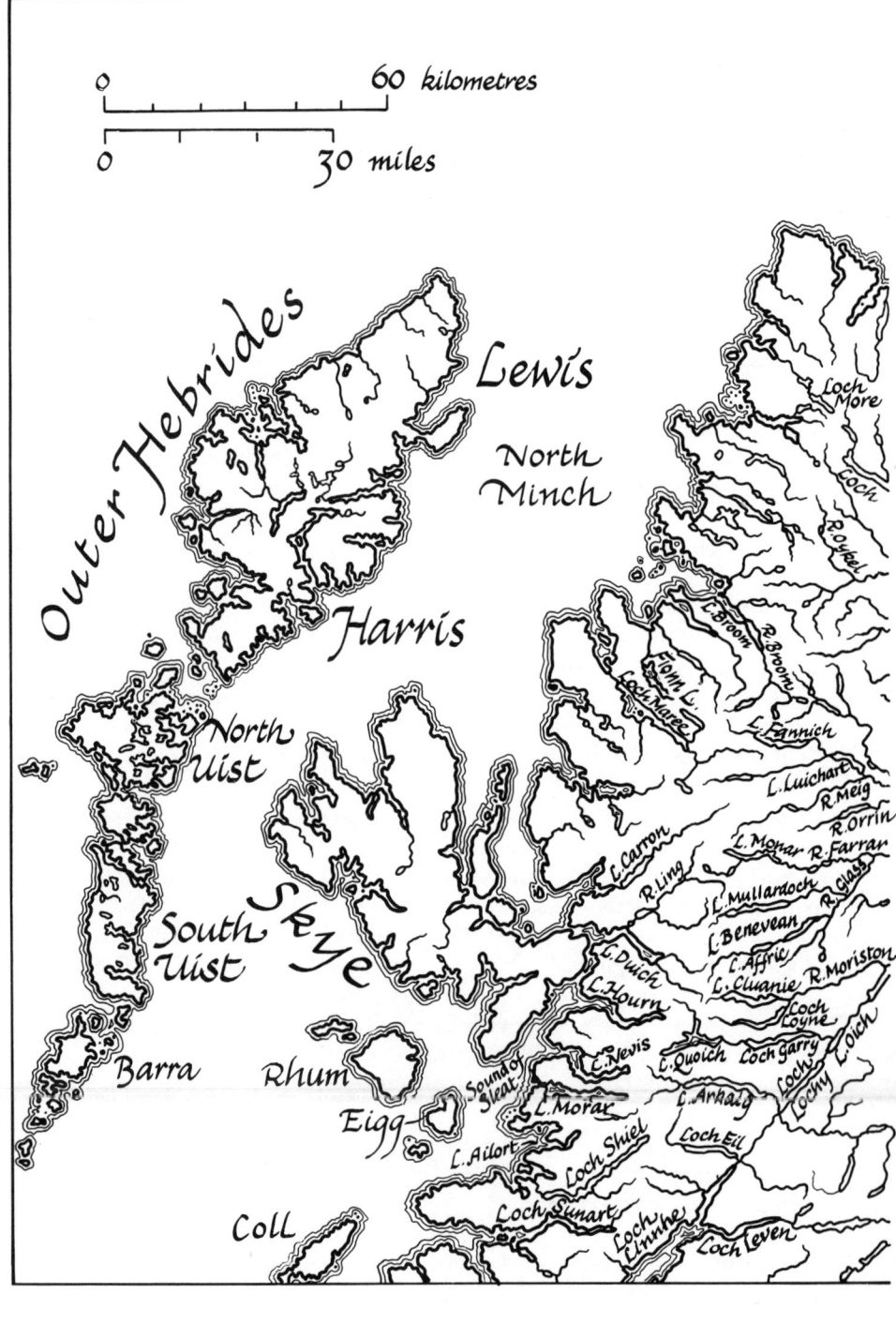

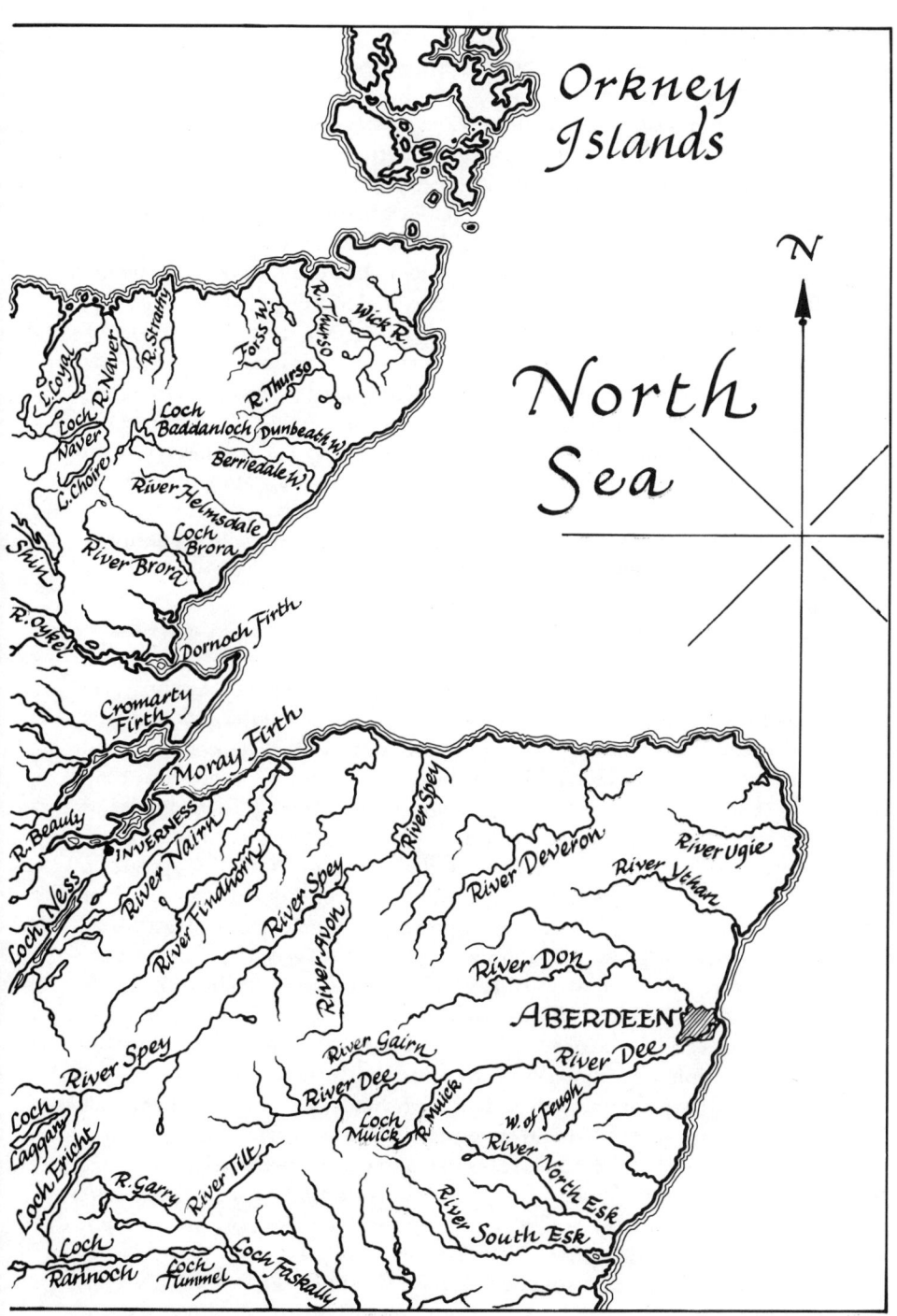
The Salmon Rivers of North Scotland

of the larger rivers for the angler wishing to fish in the early part of the year with either fly or spun bait and who is prepared to either wade or fish from a boat. Among the medium-sized rivers, at the same time of the year, the Annan, Deveron, Findhorn, Inverness-shire Garry, Moriston, Nith, North and South Esk and Teith are among the best where fly or minnow can be used. For those anglers preferring to fish where fly only is permitted, then the north-east and north coast rivers are the answer and the rivers for good spring fishing are the Brora, Carron, Cassley, Helmsdale, Naver, Oykel and Thurso.

For the summer months there is a much wider choice throughout the whole of Scotland and it really depends whether the angler enjoys fishing the large east coast rivers or the smaller west coast rivers amidst the splendour of the west coast scenery. Wherever one fishes during the summer one risks the possibility of low water conditions and the added hazard of midges. However, one always has the chance of catching sea trout at night no matter how bad the water conditions are. It would be very difficult to select a particular river, on either coast, as being better than its neighbour during the summer and it is far more a matter of luck in chosing a week when conditions are favourable.

For the angler who prefers to fish in the autumn, or cannot take his holidays until late in the year, then without doubt the Tweed is the river *par excellence*, and angling continues until 30 November.

It is not proposed to tell the reader how to fish for salmon as there are many books which do this and readers are recommended to delve into those. It would be unfair to recommend any particular one as quite often the authors have experience in one type of salmon fishing and not in another. However, perhaps it is worth mentioning one or two of the more controversial points in salmon angling, as there are two which perhaps influence an angler's success more than the many others. Firstly, at what depth should one fish one's fly or lure, and should one try to hang one's lure over a lie? If one accepts that the blindest point for a salmon is directly above its head, due to the position of its eyes, then an object directly above the centre of its head is at a point of extreme vision of either eye, if it is seen at all. The lure hanging over a lie is therefore least likely to succeed in attracting the fish than a lure moving away from either eye. Regarding depth, an object swimming above a fish is contrasted in the fish's vision against the sky, which is lighter than surrounding rocks and vegetation. If the object is level with the fish, or slightly above, then the contrast must be with bank vegetation or rocks and, according to the clarity of the water, can be greatly reduced. If the object is lower than the fish it is arguable whether it can be seen clearly, but this is dependent on the depth and clarity of the water below the fish. It would, therefore, seem to be preferable to fish a larger object fairly near the surface, to allow for better contrast against a lighter background, rather than a smaller and heavier object at a greater depth, when there must be a doubt whether the object is visible at all.

Secondly, when a salmon takes one's lure should one strike and, if so, when? Undoubtedly this is the most controversial issue in the art of salmon fishing

SALMON FISHING

and one which can, in the final minutes of a blank day, bring success or failure. The 'non-striker' will argue that a loose loop held by hand and released when a fish takes, enables the fish to turn with the fly in its mouth, and, when the angler tightens on the fish, it is then hooked firmly in the hinge or 'scissors' of its jaw. In theory this sounds logical but in practice it does not take into account that when a fish shuts its mouth on the lure it may feel the hook and eject it, nor does it take into account the fish which takes the fly while moving upstream and never turns. Both these situations happen frequently and can be witnessed when fishing pools from a height, when the take is clearly visible.

The angler who advocates striking will argue that if a fish has the lure in its mouth it is obvious that one should strike in order to drive the hook past the barb. If the fish turns on the fly he will feel a pull and, by striking normally, hooks the fish in the 'scissors', across the tongue or in the lip. If he strikes when sited high above the pool he normally hooks the fish in the upper jaw. If the fish takes while moving upstream, the angler will feel a hesitation or stop of the line and when he strikes he normally hooks the fish at the back of its throat or on the lips. There seems to be no doubt that the 'non-striker' will kill more fish if the fish does everything according to the book, but will miss the chance of killing the one which quickly ejects the fly or comes upstream. It stands to reason that the 'striker' has a chance of catching every fish, but occasionally will pull the hook out of the mouth of a fish. Nevertheless, on balance, he is more likely to hook more fish because there are no wasted chances. Once his line stops or he feels the pull the fish must have the fly in its mouth and, provided he does not hesitate, the fish has no time to eject the fly. The hesitant striker will probably miss more chances than the 'striker' or 'non-striker'. Having said that, it should be stressed that there is no substitute for experience, and after the novice has missed a few fish from either striking too soon or failing to strike he should have adopted a timing of his own which guarantees success but which may be difficult to describe!

Flies are always an extremely interesting subject in salmon fishing. This is mainly because there is little doubt that they never have, except in the smallest sizes, been designed to imitate their namesakes. The question must then be asked what do they imitate? There is little doubt that the old spring flies between No 4 and 10/0 could only imitate a small fish, with the jungle cock feather (which most regular patterns carried) representing the eye of the fish. The regular patterns such as Black Doctor, Mar Lodge, Jock Scott, Thunder and Lightning, Red Sandy, Silver Grey, Dusty Miller, Green Highlander and the Torrishes all carried them, as did many more of the old favourites. There were a few that didn't have jungle cock such as the Childers, Garry Dog, Brown Turkey and Silver Doctor. These, however, were the exception rather than the rule.

The smaller size of salmon fly, from 12 to 5, could also pass as a small fish if fished quickly but, when fished on a greased line and almost floated over the pool is more likely to imitate plankton, the drifting life in the sea which makes

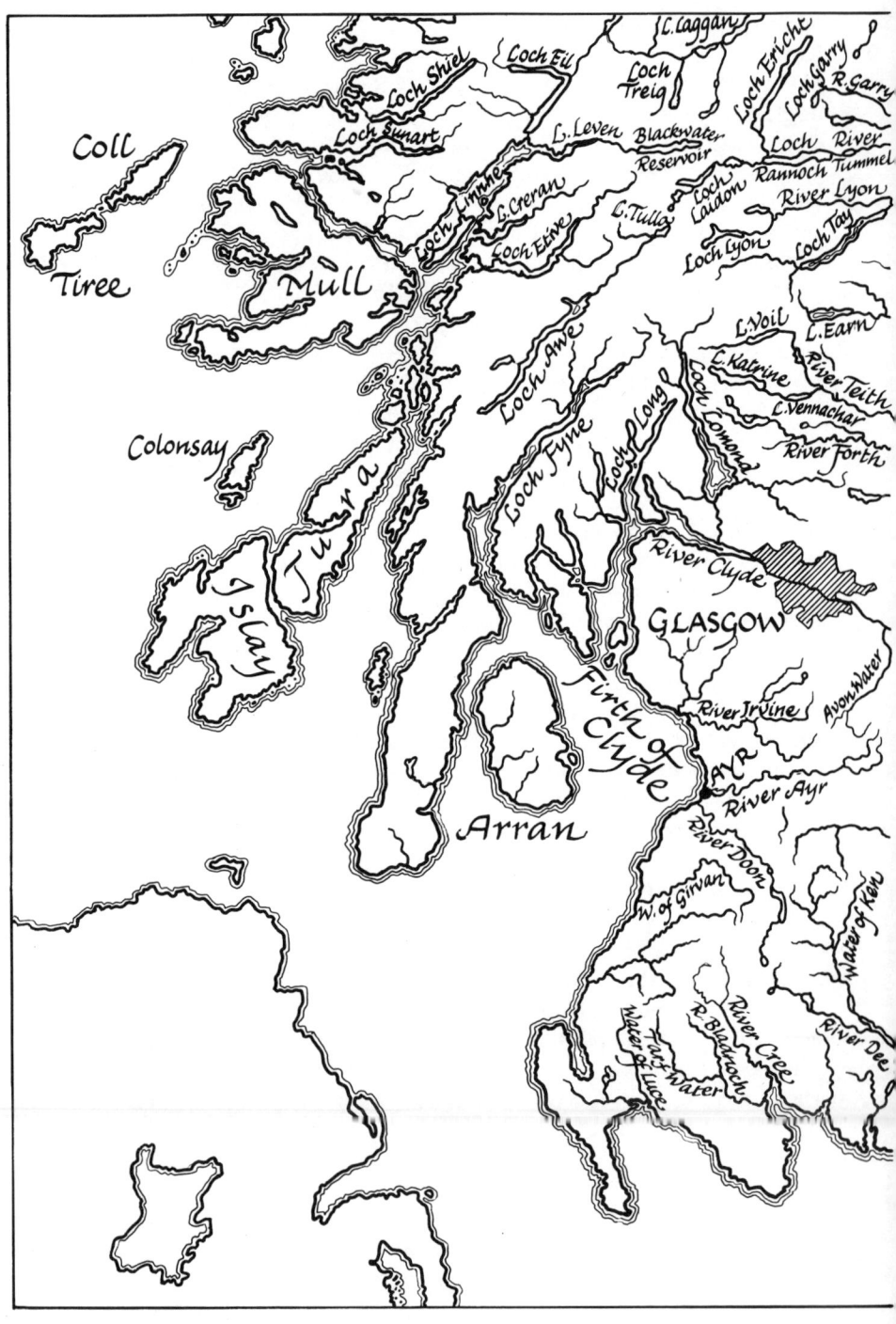

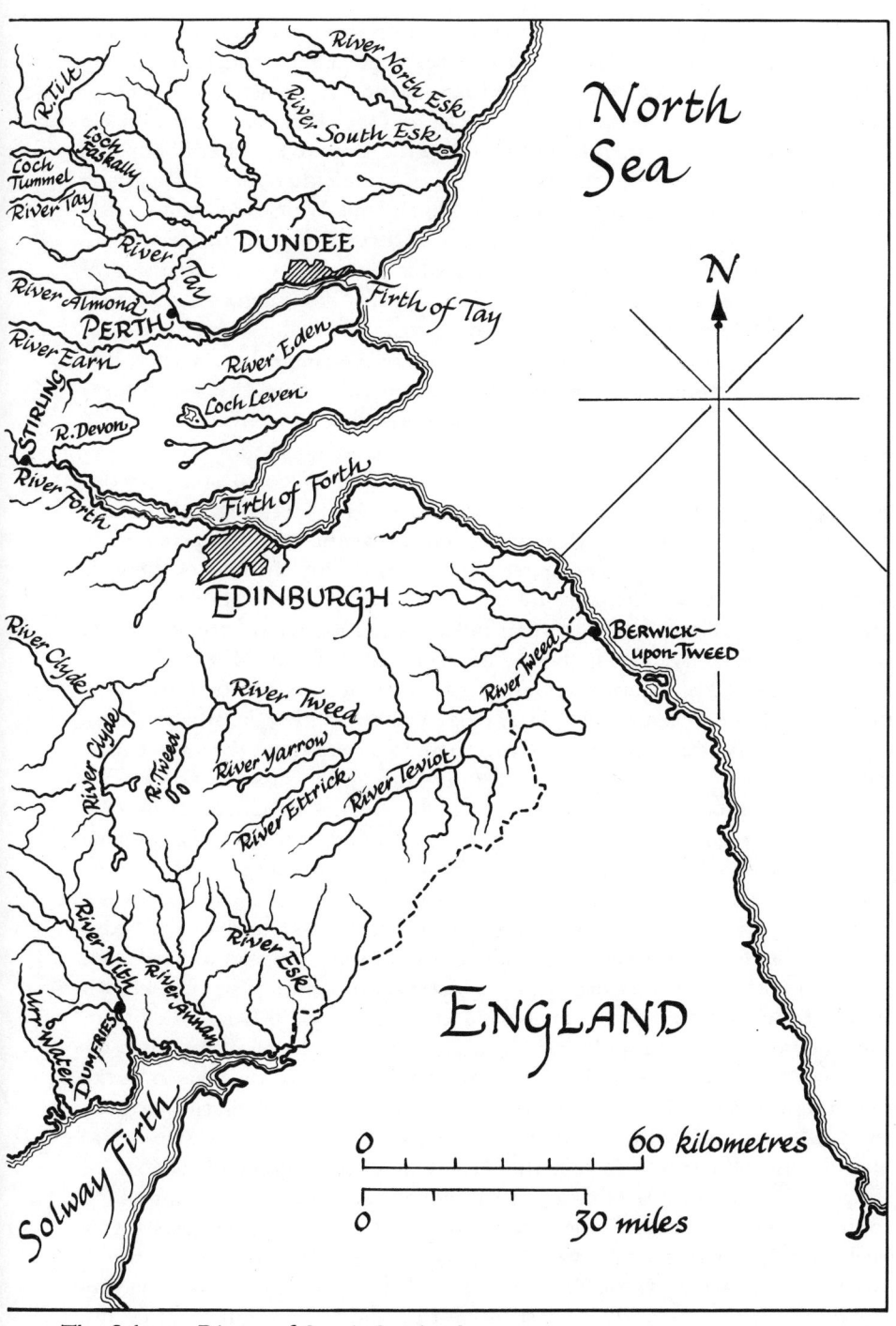

The Salmon Rivers of South Scotland

up an appreciable part of the salmon's marine diet. It is interesting to note that of these smaller summer patterns few of the regular ones had jungle cock. Among the best-known are the Blue Charm, Lady Caroline, Logie, Sweep, March Brown, Brown Turkey and Silver Blue. One of us once went to fish a beat on a famous river in July and the old ghillie looked at the fly box and selected a No 8 Silver Grey and as he tied it on he quickly removed the jungle cock feathers, remarking as he did so: 'That's a grand fly provided you remove its ornaments in the summer-time.' On going further into the matter during the day, it transpired that he did not worry what pattern he used at that time of the year provided it was the right size and that if it had jungle cock feathers these should be removed. With jungle cock hardly obtainable today his actions would not be popular now. Furthermore there are some flies, such as the Shrimp, which would just not be right without their jungle cock and some anglers swear by a small tube fly which they feel fishes more effectively with a single jungle cock feather tied in.

It is interesting to note how the hair-winged flies have almost superseded the feathered patterns in recent years. Part of the reason for this is undoubtedly the cost of the material, but there is no doubt that the hair flies give a more life-like action to the fly. The Garry Dog was probably the first of these. It originated on Tweed when a fly-tier met the local minister walking his dog. He fancied the colour of the dog's hair and asked permission to snip off some of the hair to tie a fly, saying he would name the fly the Minister's Dog. However, as the dog's name was Garry, they thought on reflection it would be more appropriate to name it the Garry Dog. The Bucktail, a Canadian fly, also followed shortly after and for some time these two were about the only regular patterns of hairwing fly used until the Hairy Mary and Stoat's Tail appeared in the 'Top Twenty'. After this nearly all fly dressers produced their own variations of regular patterns with hair wings. The tube flies also became increasingly popular in all sizes, and varying types of hair were tried. The latest development has been the long-tailed flies with the hair or feather overlapping the hook by at least the same amount as the length of the body. These are extremely effective flies in all heights of water and can be used from one to six inches in length according to water temperature. The best-known are the Blue Elverine (with a feather), Tadpole and Collie Dog (made from collie dog hair). The Tadpole and Collie are most effective in water temperatures over 45°F, whereas the Elverine fishes best on the west coast rivers in the summer time. Both the Collie and the Tadpole are used widely in the northern rivers where no spinning is allowed. The Tadpole, with its red head and maroon and yellow body and a plain black wing of collie dog hair, is good all the year round whereas the Collie, with either no body or a silver one and a long collie hair wing, can 'kill' the occasional fish in water temperatures below 40°F, but is best in warmer water. It is likely these three patterns represent sand-eels upon which the salmon feeds so avidly in the sea. The savage way salmon take this type of fly is most interesting and is often quite unlike any other 'take' of an ordinary pattern of fly, many fish being hooked right at the back of the throat.

4

THE SALMON RIVER

It would be fair to say that any river in the temperate regions of the world with an adequate supply of good quality water, no natural barrier to prevent the free ascent of fish and fast flowing gravelly upper reaches or tributaries has the potential to support salmon. The stock of a salmon river will then be almost entirely controlled by three factors, other than that of commercial netting and wholesale poaching, which are: (a) the amount of spawning gravel available in the main river and its tributaries; (b) the feeding capacity of the nursery areas; (c) the existence of good holding pools for the sanctuary of the adult fish either ascending the river or waiting to spawn.

At one time migratory fish inhabited nearly all Scottish rivers, although, for reasons given above, there were some which never supported salmon until man intervened. However, as the industrial revolution progressed there was an ever-increasing demand for water to meet the needs of new industries and a growing population. Pollution, water abstraction and obstructions soon affected some rivers. Those worst affected became untenable for salmon and sea trout which quickly became extinct in rivers such as the Clyde, Leith, Leven (Kinross-shire), Esk (East Lothian) and Almond, Avon and Carron (West Lothian). In other instances rivers such as the Doon, Forth, Irvine and Nith were threatened to a varying degree.

However, from the mid nineteenth century onwards the danger to salmon stocks was realised and various Acts were passed to remedy the situation. The major Scottish Fisheries Acts passed at that time, which safeguarded Scotland's salmon rivers, were the Tweed Fisheries Acts of 1857 and 1859 and the Salmon Fisheries (Scotland) Acts of 1862 and 1868. Later Acts, such as the Rivers (Prevention of Pollution) (Scotland) Acts of 1951 and 1965 and the Salmon and Freshwater Fisheries (Protection) (Scotland) Act of 1951 have reinforced the conservation measures set up earlier.

But let us look more closely at the essentials that a salmon river must have:

(a) Water

(i) Quality: The river can have all the water it requires to meet the needs of migratory fish but it could still be of no value to salmon if the water is of poor quality. The quality can be affected by a number of causes, such as poisons from agricultural and industrial processes and the action of bacteria on organic matter, leading to de-oxygenation and to suspended solids. Many salmon rivers have been affected by organic pollution from domestic and industrial wastes and the Don in Aberdeenshire is one where efforts are still being made to reduce pollution from pulp mill wastes.

An interesting example of the subtle effects of water quality is to be seen in the case of the Welsh rivers Ystwyth and Rheidol. The distribution of salmon in the Ystwyth is at present severely restricted by the high concentrations of zinc in the water coming from the disused lead mines in the upper reaches of the river. The neighbouring River Rheidol, however, has been greatly improved as a salmon river since the level of zinc has been reduced and it is now a commendable example of salmon reinstatement after pollution control.

A polluted estuary can effectively prevent a river from harbouring salmon and the estuaries of a number of the one-time salmon rivers in England, such as the Thames, Tees and Trent, became so polluted that the salmon stocks were eliminated. Only now are rivers such as the Tyne beginning to hold salmon again, as pollution is controlled.

Polluted headwaters – the productive part of the river for young fish – can also limit the value of a river for salmon. In the late 1950s the Miramichi River in New Brunswick was seriously affected by DDT from forest spraying operations and the young salmon populations were drastically reduced in some tributaries. In recent years some of the rivers of southern Norway, such as the Tovdal, have lost their salmon through the water becoming too acid. This was the result of sulphur dioxide polluted air making the rain and snow very acid and consequently reducing the river water to an intolerably low pH value of less than 4.5, at which level the water will not support young salmon.

(ii) Quantity: An adequate supply of good quality water, particularly in times of drought, is essential. A wide catchment is beneficial as the larger the catchment the more chance there is of some rain falling somewhere on the catchment and thereby allowing for a plentiful supply of natural freshets. A loch of reasonable size is also of great benefit to a salmon river, not only to stabilise the flow of the river but also to act as a large holding pool during low water conditions. This means that the fish are protected to a large degree from poaching or disease. The fish are also able to remain safely in the loch for long periods while they wait for the autumn spates to draw them up the small tributaries where they spawn. On many of the smaller west coast rivers the loch plays an essential part as a sanctuary during low water flows when, without it, adult salmon and sea trout would find it difficult to survive in the small burns that form the headwaters of these rivers, which themselves dwindle to insignificance between floods.

High altitude on the catchment is also a source of useful water reserves as the winter snows melt slowly through the early summer months.

(b) Pools and Falls
(i) Pools: The existence of good deep holding-pools, where fish can rest on their ascent of the river, is essential. In these they can reside for long periods while

waiting to spawn. In times of drought they are able to sink into the depths to avoid the scorching sun rays and they can seek shelter from predators among the boulders or rocky ledges. Long, deep, canal-like stretches of the river are also useful for holding fish and serve more or less the same role as a loch.

(ii) Falls: Natural falls, provided they are surmountable, are a useful check to fish ascending a river system and prevent overcrowding of the headwaters. Falls, according to how formidable they are, hold fish back at low water temperatures. Fish will normally ascend a small fall at temperatures of 40°F or more, larger falls at slightly higher temperatures but the most formidable falls are only surmounted at water temperatures of 52°F and above. A good example of this type of situation is demonstrated on the Cassley in Sutherland. Some falls, while surmountable to fish in the early part of the season, may become less so as the spawning season approaches and the fish become gravid.

(c) Spawning Areas

These are essential commodities controlling the productivity of a river. Salmon eggs are normally planted 6–9 inches deep in the gravel and there must be a steady flow of water through these nests of eggs (redds) during their incubation and while the alevins are in the gravel. It is also essential that the gravel is free of silt to allow this flow to pass unhindered over the eggs. Ideal spawning fords are normally found in gravelly areas at the head or tail of a pool and this pool acts as a reservoir for water to percolate through the redd. Side streams often provide very useful spawning fords and even the smallest burns can accommodate several pairs of fish. It must be realised that the entire act of making a redd is done by force and suction as the hen fish flaps her tail on the gravel surface. The speed of the current at the depth she is spawning is, therefore, an essential part of this process, not only to remove the debris but also to assist in moving the gravel to cover the eggs as they are laid in the hollow. After the last pocket of eggs is covered a hollow is left in front of the redd (which is now a mound of gravel) and this is the tell-tale evidence which the experienced eye can recognise, enabling a redd count to be made at the end of the spawning season.

(d) Feeding Areas

Once the alevins emerge from the gravel as fry they start to feed on the nymphs and larvae of aquatic insects and, depending on the type of stream in which they have had the fortune or misfortune to be placed as eggs, there will be a greater or lesser abundance of their food. The amount depends on the frequency of spates which may wash away many of the less tenacious insects and the stability of the gravel which, if set in motion by the spates, will dislodge and crush these food organisms. The fry in this situation will live a meagre existence and those that survive to the parr stage will continue to grow slowly and may reach the modest size of 5 inches after three or four years, after which they gain their well-earned freedom as smolts and go to sea for better fare. The

THE SALMON RIVER

situation described is that of a poor nursery area, but typical of many Highland burns which, with their low water temperatures and poor feeding, determine a long river life for the young salmon. The richer nursery areas in the main river and the lowland spawning streams have the advantage of more stable conditions and a greater supply of food material. It is, therefore, not surprising that a potentially good salmon river in all its other attributes is just not going to 'make the grade' if its physical characteristics are against its providing a reasonable larder for the young salmon. Judicious modifications to the river banks and the provision of groynes may help to stabilise the habitat and so improve the feeding areas. A small addition of nutrients in the form of sewage or agricultural effluent can also do wonders!

(e) Angling

A good salmon river — to an angler — is one which yields a generous supply of fish to the rod and so two equally good rivers, as far as physical, chemical and biological characteristics are concerned, will not have the same rating if one yields twice as many fish as the other. This can be the case and there are many rivers in northern Sweden where salmon do not 'take' at all. So perhaps we should also insert a final attribute to our list of features which make a good salmon river and add the ability to yield salmon to the angler. How well our Scottish rivers meet these requirements will be seen in the ensuing chapters.

5

THE TWEED DISTRICT

Tweed

There can be no more romantic and historic area of Scotland than the Borders. It is the setting for many tales by such famous novelists as Scott, Wilson and Buchan, and every town, village and hillside has an association with some historic event over the years of turmoil and bloodshed, as raiding parties from either side of the border clashed. It is also the birthplace or one-time fishing grounds of many well-known anglers such as John Younger, Tom Stoddart and William Scrope, all of whose written works are so much a part of treasured angling literature today.

This border river is the only one in Scotland, when reference is made to it, which does not have the definite article placed in front, and it is referred to with respect and affection simply as 'Tweed'. A Highlander may find the smooth rolling, grass-covered hills too gentle for his liking, and the landscape slightly monotonous when compared with the rugged mountain scenery of the north. Be that as it may, the border valleys and streams have a tranquillity found nowhere else in Scotland and, as John Buchan says in his book *Scholar Gipsies*, 'It is a fact of some celebrity that a man from Tweedside loves his native valleys with a love so indiscriminating that it will admit no rival,' and in the *Songs of the Edinburgh Angling Club* (1858) a verse from 'The Tweed' goes as follows:

> 'Let others discourse of the smooth-winding Tay,
> Or tell of the charms of the swift rolling Spey,
> Of the Dee and the Don, the Forth and the Clyde;
> But I love the fair Tweed as a bridegroom his bride.'

Tweed is 96 miles long and rises in Tweed's Well, only a few miles from the Devil's Beef Tub near Moffat where the Annan starts its course and also not so very far from the source of the Clyde. There is an old Scottish rhyme which goes:

> Annan, Tweed and Clyde,
> Rise a' out o' ae hillside,
> Tweed ran, Annan wan,
> Clyde broke its neck o'er Corra Linn

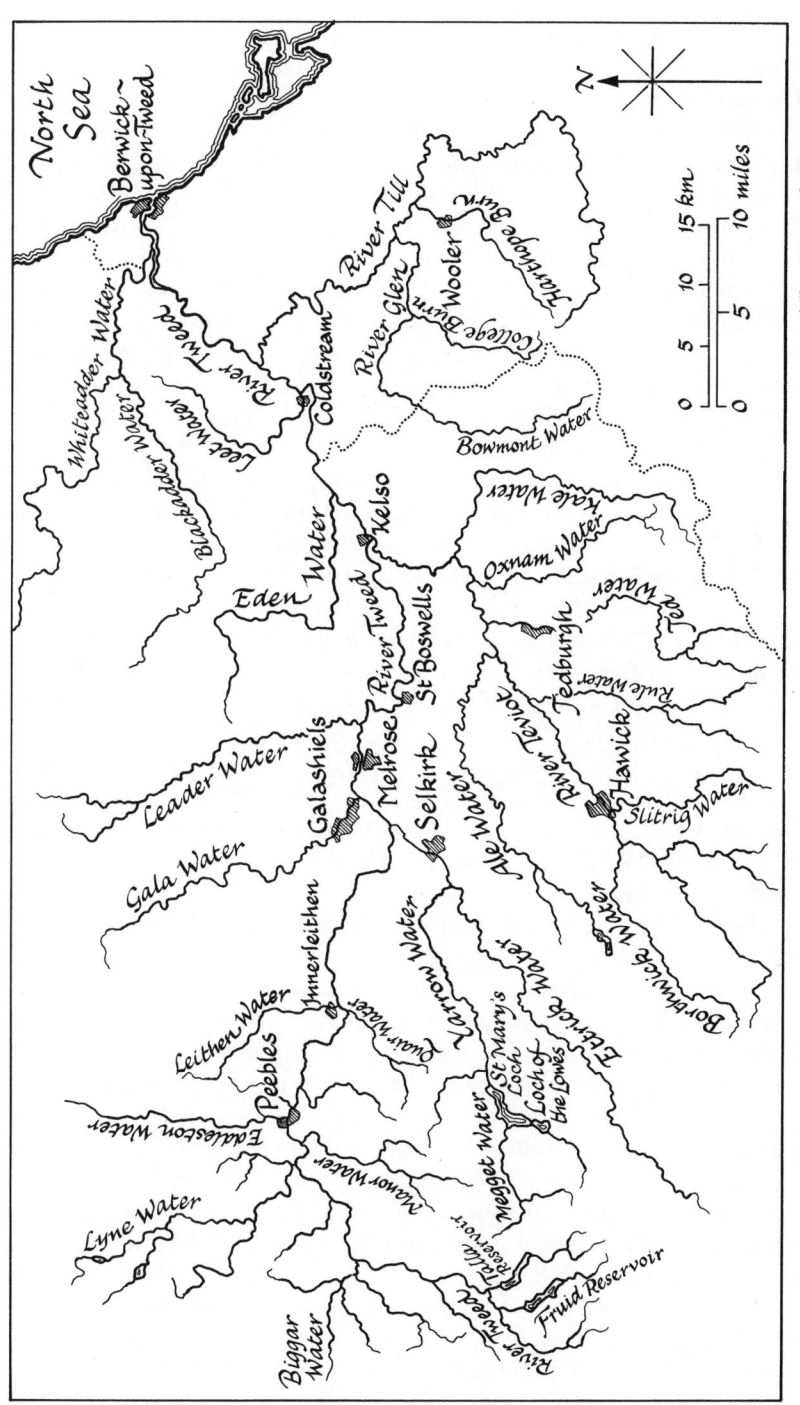

The Tweed River System

SALMON RIVERS OF SCOTLAND

It flows in an easterly direction through a pleasant moorland valley, haunted by whaups and peewits, past Tweedsmuir where it receives Fruid Water, the Menzion Burn and Talla Water. The waters of Talla were impounded at the beginning of the century and those of Fruid in 1967, and the two reservoirs supply water to Edinburgh. The country starts to mellow as Tweed passes Dawyck and Stobo, and more trees line the banks of the river. The next large tributaries to join Tweed are Lyne Water, flowing from Baddingsgill Reservoir near West Linton, Manor Water, which enters a short distance upstream of Neidpath Castle, one of the old Peel towers, and Eddleston Water, entering at Peebles. Downstream from Peebles the countryside changes to richer grazing and arable land with occasional softwood forests. At Innerleithen two more tributaries join Tweed, Leithen Water from the north and, from the south, Quair Water which passes the famous Traquair House, the oldest occupied dwelling in Scotland.

Tweed now passes a number of woollen mills at Innerleithen and Walkerburn producing a world-famous cloth named after itself. The surrounding hills now tend to close in on Tweed, and between Holylee, Ashiesteel, Caddonfoot and Yair there is some of the loveliest of the border country. In the dying months of the year the autumn colours of the trees bordering the river are incredibly beautiful and make an idyllic setting for the salmon angler fishing for the large autumn fish for which Tweed is renowned.

East of Galashiels the valley widens again and, with the water from Ettrick and Yarrow and Gala Water, the river becomes substantially larger. The surrounding land with its red soil tends to have a parkland appearance, particularly around Abbotsford, the home of Sir Walter Scott, and now his relatives. Tweed now flows more majestically and passes Melrose, Bemersyde, Dryburgh, St Boswells and Rutherford before reaching Kelso, picking up the waters of only one more tributary, Leader Water, on its way. Downstream from Galashiels, and after passing the Eildon Hills, the high ground becomes more distant and the river gradually assumes the appearance of a lowland water. Just before Kelso one passes Floors Castle, the seat of the Duke of Roxburgh, and almost opposite, on the south shore, the remains of Roxburgh Castle, well-known in Scottish history. At Kelso the River Teviot joins Tweed at the famous Junction Pool, which is probably the best salmon pool on the river, particularly in the spring when the fish tend to be held up at the cauld, a short distance upstream of the Teviot confluence. From Kelso to the sea, at Berwick-upon-Tweed, the river flows as a series of long, deep pools alternating with short stretches of more turbulent water. As Sir Thomas Dick Lauder says in his book *Scottish Rivers*. 'like a gentleman of large fortune, who has just received a great accession to it, the Tweed, having been joined by the Teviot, leaves Kelso with a magnitude and air of importance that it has nowhere hitherto assumed during its course, and which it will be found to maintain until it is ultimately swallowed up in that grave of all rivers – the sea.'

Four tributaries join Tweed downstream from Kelso, namely Eden Water,

THE TWEED DISTRICT

Leet Water, the River Till and, finally, Whiteadder Water, the latter coming from Whiteadder Reservoir. At Carham, Tweed forms the boundary between Scotland and England and from there on past Coldstream, Ladykirk and Norham the river has been the border defence to which the ruins of Wark and Norham Castles and a number of earthworks bear witness. Near Gainslaw House the border leaves the river and strikes north. The backup effects of the tide are felt as far upstream as the bridge at Norham and the tidal influence is increasingly felt downstream of this point.

Tweed is considered a Special Area in Scotland and instead of the salmon and sea trout fisheries being administered by a Salmon District Fishery Board, as in other parts of Scotland, they are managed by the River Tweed Commissioners. These consist of Proprietary Commissioners appointed by the Tweed Fisheries Acts of 1857 and 1859, who are salmon fishing proprietors, and Representative Commissioners appointed as representatives of the local authority pursuant to Section 5 of the Tweed Fisheries Act, 1969. As a result of local government re-organisation in 1973, the Proprietary Commissioners no longer have a majority in the Council, the balance now being 43 Representative and 38 Proprietary Commissioners. The Proprietary Commissioners comprise the Crown, fisheries companies, estates, trustees, syndicates, angling clubs and individuals who own either both or only one of the rights to fish for salmon and sea trout by net and rod on Tweed and its main tributaries, the Ettrick and Yarrow, Teviot, Till and Whiteadder.

There are 128 owners in these categories with a total of 204 separate fishings. The major owners are the Crown which has 3 net fishings and 21 rod fishings, and Berwick Salmon Fisheries Co. Ltd with 21 net fishings. Tweed is, therefore, divided into a number of beats each being owned by one of the commissioners. The names of these rod-fishing beats, starting upstream are: Stobo, Dreva, Drumelzier, Drumelzier Haugh, Dawyck Fishings, Lyne, Hay Lodge and Park, Peebles Burgh Water, Haystoun, Kailzie, Horsburgh Castle, Nether Horsburgh, Cardrona, Glenormiston, Traquair, Juniper Bank, Caberston, Pirn, Holylee, Elibank, Thornilee, Ashiesteel, Peel, Caddonlee, Part of Stream at Caddonfoot, Yair, Fairnilee and Rink, Sunderland (Tweed), Boleside, Pavilion (Upper, Middle, Lower), Drygrange (Tweedswood Fishings), Drygrange (Part), Gledswood, Old Melrose (Ravenswood), Bemersyde, Dryburgh, Maxton, Mertoun (Upper, Middle, Lower), Rutherford, Trows and Makerstoun (Upper, Lower), Floors (Upper, Lower), Junction, Hempsford and Maxwellheugh, Hendersyde and Sydenham (Eden), Sprouston, Hendersyde (Upper, Lower), Birgham Water, Birgham Dub, Carham, Wark North Upper, Wark North Lower, Wark Temple Pool, South Wark Farm (incl. Temple Pool), Lees, Learmouth Sands, Lennel (Upper, Middle, Lower), Cornhill, Tweed (Twizel Water), Policy Waters – Milne Graden, Ladykirk, Gliddyheuch, Tweedhill, Watham Dritness and Greenhill, Greenhill, Pedwell, Policy Waters – Paxton. The commercial net fishing stations are referred to later.

SALMON RIVERS OF SCOTLAND

Salmon enter Tweed in every month of the year, and the year's run has hardly ended in November before the first 'springers' of the next season appear. Practically the whole of Tweed is a spawning ground, with salmon being seen at spawning time on many fords and runs at the tail of pools. In addition, most of the tributaries of the Tweed, Ettrick, Teviot, Till, Whiteadder and Yarrow provide good spawning and nursery areas and, with rare exceptions such as Eden Water and Kale Water, there are very few which migratory fish cannot ascend to their upper reaches.

During the early part of the season, in February and March, salmon are seldom caught in any numbers much further upstream than Melrose, and the most productive beats at this time are those below the cauld at Kelso. Upstream of Galashiels and the Ettrick/Tweed confluence salmon fishing does not come into its own until much later in the year, and nowadays it is rarely worth fishing the reaches around Walkerburn and Peebles seriously until September at the earliest. This is not to say that no salmon ascend as far upstream until the autumn, but since the spring run started to decline in the mid-1960s few fish appear in the upper reaches until late in the year.

Over the last century there has been a marked cycle in the times of fish entering Tweed. This has been most apparent from the angling records of one of the large estates on the lower Tweed. Between 1863, when records were first available after the change in the time of the extended close season as a result of the 1859 Tweed Amendment Act, to about 1910, the autumn run was dominant. However, gradually the spring run took ascendance, and from the 1930s to the late 1960s the spring run was dominant. Once more the autumn run of fish is taking over and, although the situation has been confused as a result of the advent of UDN in 1967, there is now a greater percentage of autumn fish in the catches (Fig. 2). It is interesting to note that a salmon disease, with similar symptoms and behaviour as UDN, occurred on Tweed, as well as other Scottish rivers, from about 1879 to 1901. A bad outbreak of disease in salmon was also recorded on Tweed between 1924 and 1928, and one of the comments in the 1924 angling records for Birgham reads: 'Plenty of fish but disease very bad indeed, almost 90% of the fish touched by the middle of April'. 'Touched' will of course mean 'affected'.

In the last century the river was badly affected by pollution, particularly from the woollen mills and dye works between Innerleithen and Galashiels. However, as a result of the Salmon Fisheries (Scotland) Acts of 1862 and 1868, and latterly due to the efforts of the Tweed River Purification Board, Tweed is now relatively unaffected by polluting effluents. Unfortunately many of her tributaries have been tapped for water supply purposes. There are Talla and Fruid reservoirs in the upper reaches, Baddingsgill Reservoir at the top of the Lyne Water near West Linton and Whiteadder Reservoir on the upper part of the Whiteadder. A new reservoir is now scheduled in the Megget Valley and work is in progress here to build one of the largest dams in Scotland. The reservoir will flood the greater part of the Megget Valley and the salmon

THE TWEED DISTRICT

spawning and nursery grounds in that area. A second phase of the Megget scheme will involve St Mary's Loch from which a controlled flow will pass down the Yarrow. Afforestation and extensive land drainage have also had an impact on the river and many of the tributaries show the signs of erosion and sedimentation so characteristic of these forms of land use.

In 1909 there were 83 weirs on Tweed and its tributaries which were blamed for the delay of ascending fish and the holding back of pollutants during drought periods. Today there are only a few weirs left and, on the main river, these include caulds at Lees, Sprouston, Kelso, Rutherford and Gattonside. Since some of the weirs were 'blown' it has been said that the pattern of upstream movement of salmon has changed. Anglers and boatmen on some of the lower beats blame the loss of these weirs for their lower spring catches, saying that the 'springers' now no longer lie back in their waters but keep moving upstream until held up at the Kelso cauld.

A considerable amount of salmon fishing is available to the angler on Tweed, but much of it is expensive and difficult to acquire, being owned by long-established syndicates or reserved exclusively by estates for friends or business associates. However, lets can be obtained for varying periods of time through estate offices or sporting agents, and these are frequently advertised in the sporting press. Some local hotels own their own fishing while others can usually arrange fishing on neighbouring waters for their guests. Some hotels, such as the Tweed Valley Hotel at Walkerburn, run fishing courses. For the angler with more modest means, permits are available through local angling clubs and associations, and the largest of these is the Peebles-shire Salmon Fishing Association which has fishing, with the exception of certain private beats, from Wire Bridge Pool, a mile below Peebles, to Scrogbank below Walkerburn. Permits are available from Blackwood and Smith, 39 High Street, Peebles and Ian Fraser, Northgate, Peebles, who also lets fishing on certain small private beats. Fishing for salmon on Peebles Town Water is let by the day on a 'first come, first served' basis.

To attempt to list all the pools on the various beats of Tweed would be a lengthy business and readers are referred to the map after page 36 and to *Fisherman's Map of Salmon Pools on the River Tweed* produced by Maude Parker and published by Siftòn, Praed & Co. Ltd, of London. Those who are able to borrow or purchase a copy of John Younger's *River Angling for Salmon and Trout* published in 1860, and revised in 1864, should turn to the Descriptive List of all the *Salmon Rod Casts in the Tweed* which runs to 26 pages and lists 347 pools, beginning 3 miles above Peebles, and gives comments on each.

A description of the qualities and delights of every beat on Tweed could extend over two score or more pages. Suffice it to say that all have their charm. In early February there is a thrill to be had boat fishing on lower Tweed, whether on an open, spring-like day or in dark, forbidding weather with occasional showers of very wet snow. Sometimes the ice grue is so thick that one's tube fly or brown and gold devon never reach the water, but perch on the floating slush. Nevertheless this is a great time and one is always hopeful that the spring fish will be present in greater numbers than in recent years, and in 1978 this was the case. Perhaps the Junction Pool can be said to provide the best of the spring fishing, but other waters downstream also provide excellent sport. On Sprouston the Mill Pot, Winter Cast and Eden Waterfoot are good pools in the spring, and then downstream again there is the famous Birgham Dub and other pools such as the Three Stanes, Snipe, Wark Dub and, further down still, the Cauld Pool on the Lees. Upstream from Kelso, Upper and Lower Floors have excellent spring fishing in March and April and, at this time too, Rutherford and Mertoun come into their own. In recent years, due to low summer water levels and prolific weed growth, the summer fishing has been disappointing, although occasional summer fish and runs of grilse help sport when the water levels are right. In late summer Tweed salmon anglers wait longingly for the coming of October and November, as it is at this time that Tweed salmon fishing once more comes into its own. If water levels are low in October, and there is an early frost, then the lower beats fare well, and pools around Norham, such as Redwell, Holywell and Greenhill produce good fish. Further upstream, too, fish settle in under these conditions, and Lees and Wark get excellent sport. However, with a good rise in water fish surge upstream and the middle beats such as Dryburgh, Bemersyde and Gattonside start to pick up from the summer doldrums. The upper beats now also start to share in the sport as the autumn run steadily and predictably works its way upstream and, as the autumn colours develop in the trees and the yellow leaves start to drift down the pools, the splashing of autumn fish is to be seen all up and down Tweed. This is the time for big fish and the angler's hearbeat starts to quicken as he feels the steady draw on the line which could mean the start of a fight with a fish weighing 10–30 lb, or even more. Come November and the cold driving rains, with the beech leaves showering off the trees, the fish are settled around Peebles and pools such as Kailzie, Red Yett and the Dirt Pot produce heavy fish. Unfortunately by the time the fish have reached the upper waters they don't take the deep-sunk and heavily weighted tube flies so readily and some of the many anglers lining the banks between Peebles and Walkerburn regrettably resort to snatching, using lead core lines and weighted tube flies armed with large treble hooks. This practice is the only thing which mars an otherwise most enjoyable time of the salmon angling year on Tweed.

The salmon angling season is from 1 February–30 November and the only permitted lure before and after the netting season (15 February–14 September) is fly. Anglers fishing Tweed should be warned that being in possession of a gaff, before 1 May and after 15 September, even to land a rod-caught salmon, is a criminal offence.

The commercial salmon fishings, by fixed engine along the coast and by net and coble within estuary limits, are very extensive. They stretch down the Northumberland coast as far as Beal Point, the southern boundary of the Tweed, and up the coast to Cockburnspath. The river nettings extend upstream to Twizel Boathouse above the Till confluence. Working downstream from Twizel Boathouse to Berwick-upon-Tweed these net and coble fishings, both full-time and part-time, include: Twizel Boathouse, Damford, Milne Graden and Under Little Haugh, Bendibus, Canny, Pedwell, Westford and Scotch Bendibus, Holywell and Blunt, Greenhill, Watham, Wilford, Hornwell, Scotch New Water and Dritness, Start, Policy Waters, Paxton, Finchy Haugh and Streambank, Yardford, Gainslaw, Whiteadder (Canty), North Bells, South Bells, Low Bells, Heughshield, Broad, Ethermouth, Canny, Needle Eye and Cove Sands, Clayhole and Wean, English New Water, Toddles, Yarrow, Whitesands, Boatholes, Pool, Blakewell, Crows Batt, Gardo and Bailliffs Batt, Davies Batt, Tweedmouth Stell, Carr Rock and Elstell, Hallowstell and Colt, Shoreside (Crabwater) Outwaterstell, Meadow Haven, Sandstell.

There is an age-old ceremony at the Pedwell Fishery, Norham, of blessing the nets at the start of the season. A minister of the church conducts the service at the river-side. The service consists of a reading from the bible, the Lord's Prayer, a prayer for God's blessing on the nets, a blessing for the fisherman (the Pedwell Prayer), a prayer for seasonable weather and a hymn. The service concludes with these words:

'May the season which now begins be blessed with shoals for every boat'.

The Pedwell Prayer, which is believed to be of Cornish origin, is as follows—

> Good Lord, lead us,
> Good Lord, speed us.
> From all perils protect us,
> In the darkness direct us.
> Give us, good Lord,
> Finest nights to land our fish —
> Sound and big to fill our wish.
> Keep our nets from snag and break.
> For every man a goodly take,
> Give us, Good Lord.
>   Amen.

In recent years there has been illegal drift net fishing for salmon off the Berwickshire coast and this, together with the licensed Northumberland salmon drift net fishing by English fishermen, has been a constant worry for the River Tweed Commissioners. A patrol boat owned by the Commissioners has helped to control the illegal fishing and in 1978, with the aid of the fishery protection cruisers of the Department of Agriculture and Fisheries for Scotland (supported by Royal Navy vessels and helicopters), these poaching activities were substantially reduced. The Northumberland fishery continues to be a problem and it is to be hoped that in time this fishery will be phased out and so ensure a better escapement of salmon into Tweed, Scotland's second most important salmon river.

The Ettrick and Yarrow

The Waters of Ettrick and Yarrow run more or less parallel to one another through the hills of Ettrick Forest and join a short distance downstream of Philiphaugh, with Ettrick Water becoming the name of the main river as it flows through Selkirk to join Tweed near Sunderland Hall.

The Ettrick is the largest and southernmost of the two tributaries and rises high up in the hills, its source only a few miles to the north-east of Moffat. It receives its first major tributary, Tima Water, at Ramseycleuch not far from Ettrickhill, the birthplace of the poet James Hogg (the Ettrick Shepherd). A short distance downstream it is joined by another large stream, the Rankle Burn. This upper part of the Ettrick, as far downstream as Clinty Pool near Hyndhope, is all good spawning ground, with fish only reaching this area late in the year.

The Yarrow is a shorter river than the Ettrick and receives its water from the Loch of the Lowes and St Mary's Loch with the latter being fed by the Megget Water, a spawning tributary shortly to be impounded.

In the recent past, fishing in Ettrick for salmon has between the months of June and November, with the first salmon arriving in the river about June. In the lower reaches, dependent on water conditions, salmon could be taken from June onwards. In the upper reaches some salmon could be taken from June, but fish reaching this far quickly went stale and fishing was restricted to the autumn months. Recently, however, over the last three seasons, salmon have been penetrating into Ettrick and Yarrow in March and April and have been caught as far upstream as Philiphaugh, with the occasional fish being taken as far upstream as Ettrickbridge and Helmburn from May onwards, and at Newburgh and Tushielaw between June and July.

The Yarrow has not been seriously fished for salmon in recent years, but fishing effort increased in 1978 with encouraging results.

The general runs of salmon over the last three years in Ettrick and Yarrow appear to show an increased number of fish earlier in the year. The best fishing is in the first week of April and then, as water conditions allow, from September onwards. The early autumn runs consist of extremely small salmon and grilse in the 3-5 lb class, and an increased number of sea trout.

The main rod fisheries on the Ettrick are as follows: Potburn and Over Phawhope, Short Hotel, Brockhope and Overkirkhope, Nether Phawhope and Broadgairhill, Scabcleuch, Ettrick Hall, Midoz Hope and Glenkerry, Thirlstane and Ramseycleuch, Dundas Cottage, Ramseycleuch, Thirlstane and others, Flockfield and Gamescleuch, Cacrabank, Tushielaw, Hyndhope, Clinty Pool, Shaws Southern, Shaws Northern, Helmburn, Bowhill, Selkirk

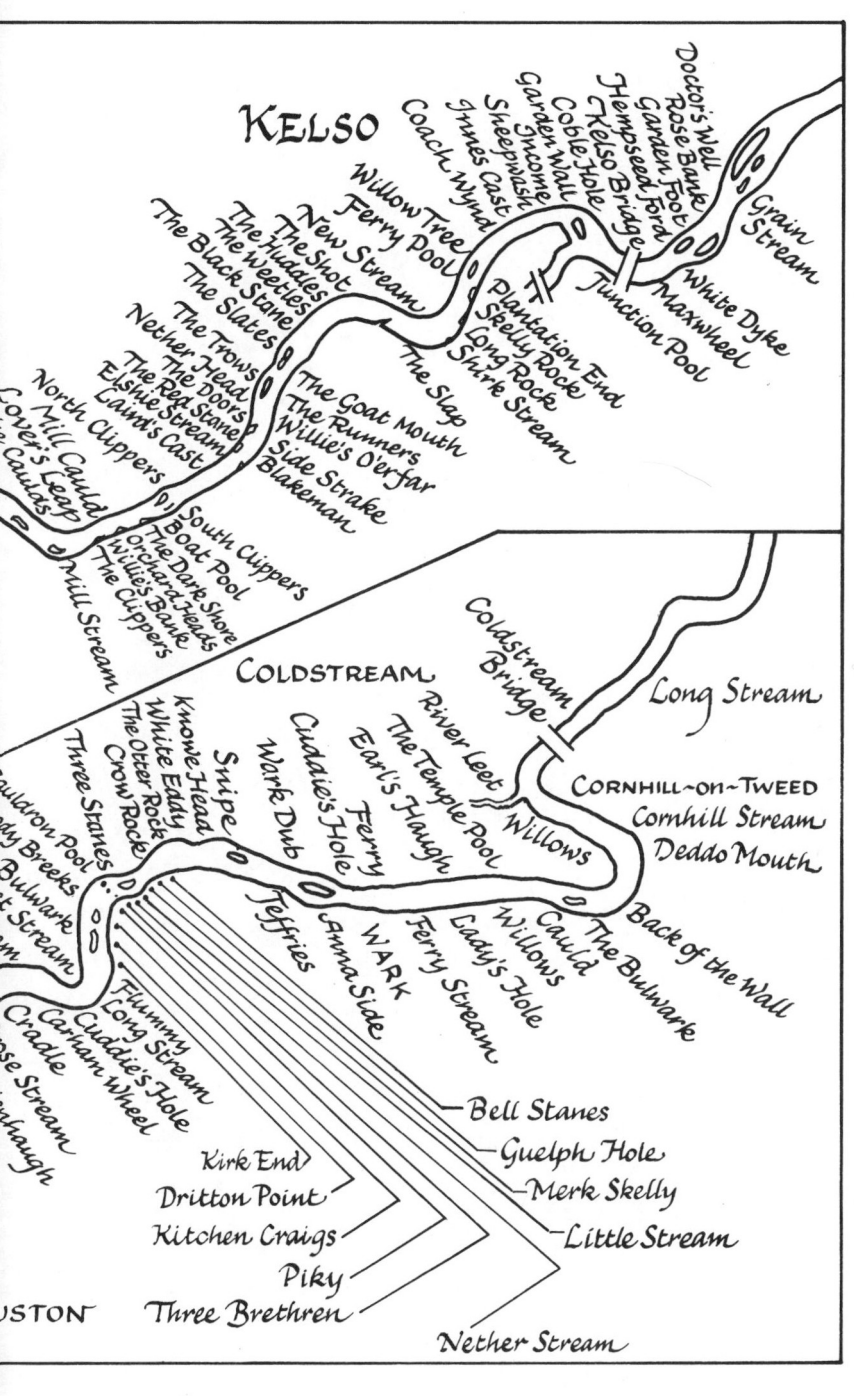

A hand-drawn map of fishing pools along the River Tweed between Melrose and Kelso.

MELROSE area (upper reach):
- Cauld Pool
- The General's Stream
- Boatshiel
- Old Bridge
- Foot Bridge
- Battery
- Eddy Pool
- Cowie's Hole
- Railway Bridge
- The Bullers
- Black Rock
- The Berry Bush
- Bridge Pool
- Paddock Head
- Drygrange Bridge
- The Boathouse Pool
- Monk's Pool
- Woodside
- Monksford
- Leaderfoot Bridge
- Ramp Haugh
- Cockburn's Pool
- The Pool
- Cromwiel
- The Corbie
- The Dish
- Haly Weil
- Foot Bridge
- Battery Stream
- Todholes
- Mungy Pool
- Harecraig
- Burnfoot Pool
- The Embankment Pool
- Birch Hough Pool
- Haugh Pool
- Gullet Str.
- Brockie's Hole
- Burnfoot
- Deanfoot
- Kirkback Pool
- Birkie Haugh Stream
- Gateheugh
- Long Stream
- Cauld Pool
- Mertoun Bridge
- Cauld Stream
- Upper Bridge Stream
- Backbraes Stream
- The Pot
- Corsehough Stream
- Corseheugh Stream
- Collarhaugh Stream
- Rutherford Ferry
- House Stream
- Between Br. The Dub
- Wow Bush
- House Pool
- Bridge Pool
- Foot Bridge
- Craig Pool
- The Webbs
- Lower Bloodies
- The Bloodies

ST BOSWELLS   **MAXTON**

Middle Bloodies

KELSO area:
- Page...
- Wiel Stream
- Birgham Dub
- Cowes Hole
- Edenwater Foot
- Cottage Stream
- Apron
- Little Davy
- Slap
- Sprouston Dub
- Prison Rock
- Scurry Pool
- Scurry Rock
- Bushie
- Butterwash Stream
- Mill Pot
- Winter Cast
- Bushes
- Redden
- Ferry
- Mill End

N (compass)

KELSO   **SPROU...**

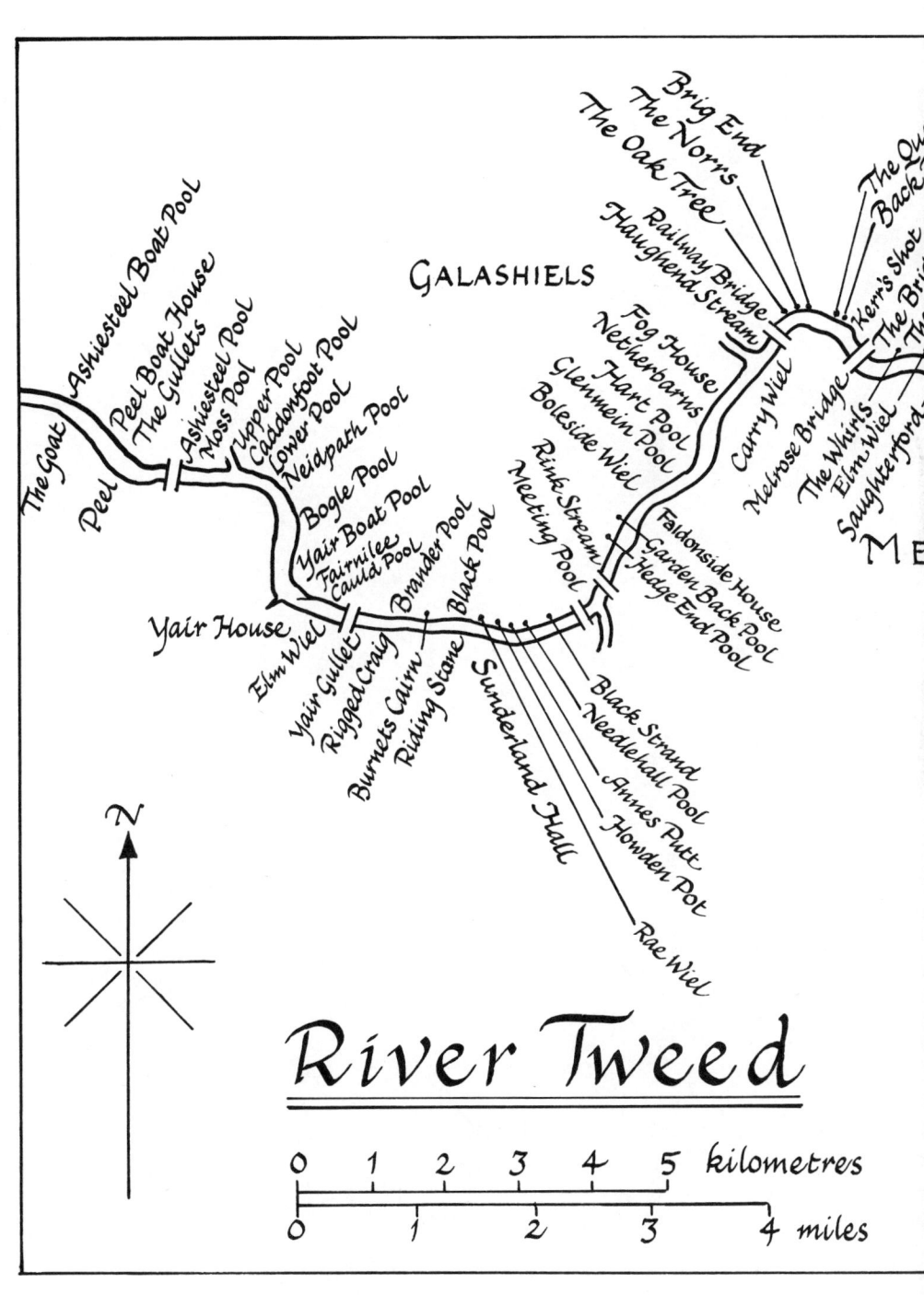

THE TWEED DISTRICT

Burgh, Sunderland, Sunderland Hall and Faldonside. The proprietor of eighteen of these fisheries is The Crown. Selkirk Burgh fishery is leased by the Selkirk Angling Association.

The main rod fisheries on the Yarrow are: Right bank – From St Mary's Loch to the confluence with the Ettrick; Left bank – St Mary's Loch to Buccleuch March, Harewood Glen (which is virtually unfishable) and Philiphaugh.

At one time there was a celebrated cauld in the town of Selkirk from where one could watch salmon ascending the long sloping face of the cauld. It was also a favourite place for poachers. The cauld has now been breached, and a favourite landmark destroyed.

The Teviot

The Teviot rises on the high ground between the two hills Black Burn Head and White Hope Edge, and by the time it reaches Teviothead, a few miles to the north-east, it has become a sizeable stream, having been joined by a number of small tributaries draining the surrounding high ground. Between Teviothead and Hawick, a distance of some 7 miles, the river is joined by a number of tributaries including Allan Water, Borthwick Water and, in the centre of Hawick, Slitrig Water. Downstream and to the north-east of Hawick the Teviot is joined over the next 9 miles by Trow Burn, Dean Burn and Rule Water and, near Ancrum, by the sizeable Ale Water. This latter tributary flows through Alemoor Loch and runs parallel with the Teviot, passing through Ashkirk, Hermiston and Lilliesleaf, before meeting it near Ancrum. By now the Teviot is a deep and generally slow-flowing river, meandering through rich agricultural land which turns the water very muddy during times of spate. Three more streams flow into the river before it joins the Tweed at Kelso, namely Jed Water, Oxnam Water and Kale Water, all coming in from the south.

There are two runs of fish up the Teviot, an early small run of spring fish in February, March and April which reaches the Monteviot area, near Ancrum, and a later autumn run of salmon and sea trout in October and November which penetrates into the headwaters. However, both runs are dependent on floods, and low water levels at either of these times of the year produce poor sport. A flood right at the end of the season sometimes brings up large, fresh fish, many of which will not spawn until early in the New Year.

A large part of the salmon fishing in the upper reaches of the Teviot, upstream of the Ale confluence, are in the hands of the Upper Teviotdale Fisheries Association and Hawick Angling Club and day permits are available from Stotharts Tackle Shop in Hawick. Fishing in the Monteviot area is owned by the Lothian Estates and details of fishing can be had on application to the Lothian Estates Office in Jedburgh. Other angling associations having salmon and sea trout fishing on the lower Teviot are the Jedforest and the Eckford

Associations, and day tickets for the latter can be obtained from the Gamekeeper's House in Eckford. A small stretch of the river near Sunlaws can be rented on a daily basis from Redpath's tackle shop in Kelso.

The Till

The Till rises from a number of small tributaries draining off the Northumberland hills such as Dunmoor Hill and Langlee Crags and flows north past the Devil's Causeway, Newtown, Chatton and Greendikes. Its main and most important tributary is the River Glen which is formed from the meeting of Bowmont Water and the College Burn near Westnewton. In its lower reaches below Etal, the Till is fairly slow flowing and has a bed of sand and large boulders. It is a treacherous river and should be treated with respect while wading. The river joins Tweed at Tillmouth close to Tillmouth Park Hotel. At one time there were a number of caulds on the Till but these have now all been breached. It is interesting to note that prior to the removal of the caulds coarse fish were very abundant in the river but they are much less so now that the caulds have gone.

There is a good spring run of sea trout in the Till and a number of salmon. The upper beats are now much better, since the destruction of the caulds, but the lower beats at Tillmouth and Etal are not so good. Above Wooler sea trout take very well from May on if there is a flood, and some salmon are also caught at Westnewton and other beats. Towards the end of the season, in September, all the hill streams hold sea trout which give the local anglers good sport. The spring sea trout average about 4 lb and the later ones are never less than 2 lb. The 'first return' fish are much heavier than those of the west coast of Scotland.

For some strange reason the Till sea trout take the angler's lure much better than the Tweed ones. A huge number of sea trout run Tweed, probably as many as there are salmon, but they are seldom caught, and then only by great perseverance. Most are caught during the autumn salmon season.

The Whiteadder

The Whiteadder Water rises up in the Lammermuir Hills but its upper waters have been impounded to form the Whiteadder Reservoir. Below the reservoir it flows rapidly through Abbey St Bathans and Chirnside to join Tweed in its tidal reaches a short distance upstream from Berwick-upon-Tweed. The Whiteadder has always been an excellent brown trout river and the numerous caulds prevented the ascent of salmon. However, some of the caulds have been removed, although the one at Chirnside is still something of a problem, and some salmon and sea trout do now ascend the river. But both the Whiteadder, and its main tributary the Blackadder, are still thought of primarily as brown trout waters.

6

THE FORTH-TEITH SYSTEM

The Forth-Teith river system has probably more large natural lochs and reservoirs on its course than any other river system in Scotland except the Tay. In the far north-west on the Teith branch of the system lochs Doine, Voil, and Lubnaig collect water draining off the Braes of Balquhidder and the hills of Strathyre Forest. This water reaches the Teith at Callander via the River Balvag and the torrential Leny Water. To the west of Callander lie Loch Katrine, Loch Achray, Glen Finglas Reservoir and Loch Venachar, which act as one large water supply system for Glasgow. This is an area of high rainfall and the water coming to these reservoirs drains off the steep neighbouring mountains such as Ben Venue and Ben Ledi. The Trossachs, which lie between Loch Katrine, Glen Finglas and Loch Achray, are a favourite tourist resort, and in addition the whole area has many historic and literary connections. There is a large Roman fort at Callander, while Rob Roy has many associations with Balquhidder and Brig o' Turk and, more recently, the radio and television character, Dr Finlay, is said to have had his residence in Callander.

On the Forth branch of this system there are, as with the Teith, large lochs in the upper reaches. Loch Chon and Loch Ard are virtually the head waters of the Forth, which flows out of Loch Ard a few miles west of Aberfoyle, with the Duchray Water joining it only a short way below the Loch Ard outfall.

The separate courses of the Forth and Teith eventually join up a short distance west of Stirling in a flat arable area known as The Carse, a good area for geese during the winter months. At the Forth-Teith confluence the larger River Teith loses its name to the Forth which, while the less significant river, both in size and salmon-producing capacity, gives its name to the remainder of the river which runs its meandering course east of Stirling, past Alloa and into the Firth at Grangemouth. It picks up the Allan Water and River Devon on its way.

The Forth

The Forth originates in the waters of lochs Chon and Ard in the Queen Elizabeth Forest Park. Salmon frequently reach Loch Ard in the spring and remain in the deep waters at the head of the loch until ready to spawn in the Water of Chon as far up as little Loch Dhu immediately downstream of Loch Chon. Loch Ard contains pike which are fortunately netted, thus reducing their toll on any seaward migrating smolts.

A short distance downstream from Loch Ard, and before Aberfoyle is reached, the Duchray Water joins the river on the south bank. The Duchray rises on the eastern slopes of Ben Lomond and flows through Glenn Dubh and Loch Ard Forest before joining up with the Forth. Salmon can ascend the Duchray Water for a distance of 4 miles, but further passage upstream is barred by an impassable fall. The lower reaches of the Duchray were an important spawning and nursery area, but in recent years spawning stocks have dwindled. It is believed, from preliminary investigations being made on this water, that the fish stocks in the upper reaches of the Duchray are sparse and unevenly distributed because of the natural water quality and particularly low pH values.

The next tributary of any size to join the Forth is the Kelty Water which flows in from the west about 6 miles south-east of Aberfoyle. This tributary is an insignificant stream, although sea trout may use it as a spawning area. The Forth continues its slow meandering course, being fed occasionally by small streams up which some sea trout go to spawn. The only sizeable tributary entering the river after the Kelty is the Goodie Water which drains out of the Lake of Menteith, the only 'lake' in Scotland. It is probably safe to say that practically all the salmon spawning areas lie upstream of the Kelty–Forth confluence, as below the Goodie Water confluence the Forth becomes very sluggish. Downstream from Stirling the Forth, now that it has received the substantial contribution of the Teith, and an additional flow from the Allan Water, assumes fairly majestic proportions but at the same time becomes a fairly industrial and polluted river and is not very attractive.

The salmon and sea trout fishing is very much better than many people realise. The sea trout fishing in particular has shown considerable improvement during the last few seasons especially during the months of August and September. The grilse run takes place in June and July but has been generally very poor in recent years. However, the run in 1977 was much improved and would have been much above average had it not been for 'illegal netting' off the east coast at the beginning of the run. There are stretches available for angling to the public upstream from Gartmore bridge and tickets for these waters can be obtained from the Glasgow Telephones and Civil Service Angling Association or the Station Buildings, Aberfoyle. Tickets for the $6\frac{1}{2}$ miles of river downstream from Gartmore bridge can be obtained from tackle shops in Glasgow, Kirkintilloch, Stirling and Falkirk. Fishing permits for the stretch of river within the vicinity of Stirling can be had from Messrs Crockhart and Son, 35 King Street, Stirling. Salmon fishing near Aberfoyle can be obtained by permit from Inverard Hotel, Aberfoyle.

Commercial netting is confined to areas of the Forth estuary only, the area being from high water mark west of Stirling to Crail on the East Neuk of Fife in the north-east coastal area to Dunbar on the south-east coastal limits. Netting is confined to net and coble, with stake and bag nets being operated in Shell Bay west of Elie in Fife. All netting rights are in private or Crown ownership. Many netting stations are not operative in that they are situated in areas where they are no longer considered to be a sound financial proposition.

Pollution is a continuing problem on the Forth and no real or lasting improvement can be expected until such time as there is a hardening of opinion in relation to pollution caused by heavy industrial establishments sited in the Forth area, particularly in the estuary. The pollution is, to a great extent, aggravated by reduced flows resulting from extensive water abstraction on the upper reaches of both the Forth and Teith. At times during the summer dissolved oxygen levels in the estuary drop almost to zero, resulting in the death of smolts and ascending adult fish.

The Teith

The Teith is by far the best salmon river in the Forth–Teith river complex, although its flow is unnaturally affected due to the demands on some of its upper waters for supply to Glasgow. Also, in dry years, the compensation flow from Loch Venachar is reduced to meet this city's demands and consequently there is a risk to the river environment. Fortunately lochs Doine, Voil and Lubnaig remain unaffected by any development and there are prolific spawning and nursery grounds upstream of Loch Doine in the mountainous area around Ardcarnaig and Inverlochlarig, the one-time home of Rob Roy. It is probably safe to say that the maintenance of salmon stocks depends on the continued access of fish to these grounds and to those immediately upstream of Loch Lubnaig in the lower River Balvag in the vicinity of Strathyre. The Monachyle Burn which enters the top end of Loch Voil was stocked with salmon fry and parr in 1974 and 1977. Results from the 1974 restocking appear to have been moderately successful. However, a new forestry development is about to commence along the side of this burn and as a result it is considered that the water will be reduced during the summer months and that it will, therefore, be out of the question to think in terms of its future use as a restocking area.

From Loch Lubnaig flows the Leny Water which follows a torrential course to join up with the Eas Gobhain, from Loch Venacher, at Callander to form the Teith. The first main tributary to join the Teith below Callander is the Keltie which flows in from the north. There is a small lochan on this burn which serves as a water supply for Callander. Salmon ascend the Keltie as far as the impressive Bracklinn Falls which are completely insurmountable and almost certainly impossible to open up. However, fish do spawn below them and so

THE FORTH–TEITH SYSTEM

the Keltie is a useful spawning and nursery tributary in its lower reaches. The caravan site situated near the road bridge over the Keltie is something of a hazard to immature migratory fish as children take a number of them when fishing with worm in the water adjacent to the site. Some form of education is obviously needed here.

Below Callander the Teith is an open river of long pools and swift runs passing through lovely country with a background of hills to the north. At Doune Castle another tributary enters the river from the north and this is the Ardoch Burn which flows out of Loch Mahaick, a small nature reserve lying on the Braes of Doune. This another good spawning tributary, particularly in the lower reaches, but it is not suitable for angling. This is the last major tributary to join the Teith which flows on past Blair Drummond Safari Park and meets the Forth at Drip.

The main beats on the Teith starting at Callander are as follows:

(a) Callander Town Water – this is administered by Stirling District Council and permits can be obtained through James Bayne, Main Street, Callander.

(b) Gart Estate, By Callander – this consists of about 2 miles of the north bank and is privately owned.

(c) Cambusmore Estate – this water is split into four beats and most of the fishing is on the north bank. The fishing is leased by James Bayne of Callander on a full seasonal basis to applicant members of the general public. A day permit can sometimes be obtained.

(d) Lanrick Castle – this is leased on a long let to an estate tenant.

(e) Moray Estates/Deanston Distillery – the Moray Estates have the north bank only. The water is leased to Doune Angling Club on Wednesdays and Saturdays, the remainder of the week the fishing is in the hands of the estate and is leased to certain general tenants.

The Deanston Distillery have the south bank on this stretch and fishing can be obtained by permit issued by the distillery but it is in the main confined to local Deanston residents.

(f) Blair Drummond Estate – both banks are owned by the estate and the fishing is strictly private. It is leased from Monday to Thursday inclusive to selected estate fishery tenants and the owners fish the river themselves on Friday and Saturday.

(g) Ochtertyre Estate – this beat is owned by Keir and Cawder Estates Co., Ltd. In general it is private but the estate does issue some permits.

(h) A short stretch of water (both banks) between Ochtertyre Estate and the Teith–Forth confluence is owned by Blair Drummond Estate. Eight rods are allowed to fish this stretch on a daily permit basis, the permits being obtainable from Messrs Crockhart, King Street, Stirling. The well-known Blue Bank Pool comes within this beat.

The Teith fishes particularly well during the early part of the season and it is true to say that the rod catch on the opening day (1 February) in each season is just as good as those recorded for the Tay and Tweed on their opening days and some large fish are caught.

The salmon enter the mid-reaches of the Teith very early, around mid-December, and this early run goes on until mid-February. The autumn run is during August and September. Grilse enter most mid-river beats about the middle of June although they are later at times, due to low water conditions. The sea trout run very early and they have been recorded on the 15 March but the time of entry is governed by water temperature.

The Teith is stocked fairly regularly with both salmon and sea trout.

Leny Water

The Leny is a good water for salmon and clean fish are taken from it very early in the season. It is interesting to consider the remarks of Calderwood with regard to the future importance of the Leny in relation to the abstraction of water from Loch Venachar to Glasgow: 'If, as I believe to be the case, the fishing value of Loch Venachar and the Venachar Water is for ever impaired by the lack of water from a former important source, it may still be possible to restore the Teith to its former value by increasing the water supply from Loch Lubnaig, and in so doing to improve also the fishing of the Leny and Loch Lubnaig.'

Calderwood suggested improvements to the Falls of Leny which involved easing the left of the two channels, which are separated by an island. He said that: 'It is probable that with easier ascent and an increased stock of fish brought about by the various means adopted in other parts of the district, and let us hope by reduction of both netting and pollution in the lower Forth, Loch Lubnaig would come to be a spring fishing loch of some repute.'

No work of any nature has been carried out to improve fish access over the falls but fish manage to get over them in their present state without a great deal of trouble if water levels and temperatures are suitable.

There is no doubt that the abstraction of water from Loch Venachar has impaired the value of the Teith and in 1976 the river did not receive its agreed compensation flow during the summer drought because of an emergency restriction on the flow in order to ensure the continuation of the water supply to Glasgow.

There are a number of owners on the Leny, including Leny House and the Forestry Commission, and all fishing is private. The fishing on Loch Lubnaig is owned by Keir and Cawder Estates Co., Ltd, the Forestry Commission and one farmer at the head of the loch. The fishing is let to the Forth Federation of Anglers. Permits to fish can be obtained from James Bayne in Callander. Tickets to fish on Loch Voil can be had from Sinclair's in Balquhidder.

THE FORTH–TEITH SYSTEM

The Allan

The Allan Water is, in its upper reaches, a small stream flowing through Strathallan and only assumes sizeable proportions after being joined by the River Knaik at Greenloaning. The Knaik is the major tributary and drains the range of hills to the south-east of Glen Artney. It is not a good salmon spawning stream and is more in the nature of a rocky trout stream flowing over large areas of bedrock and draining off rough hill pasture. By the lower Knaik, near Braco, there are many reminders of the Roman occupation, including a fort and a camp, and an old Roman road.

Below the confluence at Greenloaning the character of the river changes and to start with it becomes slower and more meandering, but as it approaches Dunblane it becomes steeper, faster and less meandering, and pools and runs alternate more frequently. Downstream from Dunblane, to its confluence with the Forth, it becomes quite torrential and a number of steep rapids occur. The Stirling to Perth railway follows the course of the river.

At the beginning of the century there were no fewer than 10 dam dykes on this river and, with a considerable population on the riverside, poaching was rife. However, most of these dykes have now been removed and only 2 remain. Many were used to supply water to paper mills but these have now all been closed. One woollen mill which closed recently was responsible for the various shades of blue and purple colouring the water in the Allan. It is hoped that the two remaining dykes will soon be removed so as to stop the 'sniggering' or 'snatching' which is carried out at these points when fish are running, towards the back end of the season.

The Forth District Fishery Board and the Allan Water Angling Improvement Association have done a great deal to improve this river which is a useful spawning stream and provides some salmon and sea trout angling in the autumn. Restocking with salmon and sea trout fry has been carried out in recent years and it would appear that the fishing tenants intend to carry out restocking on an annual basis. All fishing is by permit only and permits can be obtained from local tackle shops and hotels in the Stirling, Dunblane and Greenloaning area. The river is, unfortunately, overfished and some serious thought should be given to limiting the number of rods fishing on any one day.

The main run of salmon is in August and September. There are very few grilse in this tributary although at one time the Allan was a good grilse water. The main run of sea trout is between May and July.

The Devon

The Devon is now so fully developed for domestic and industrial purposes that

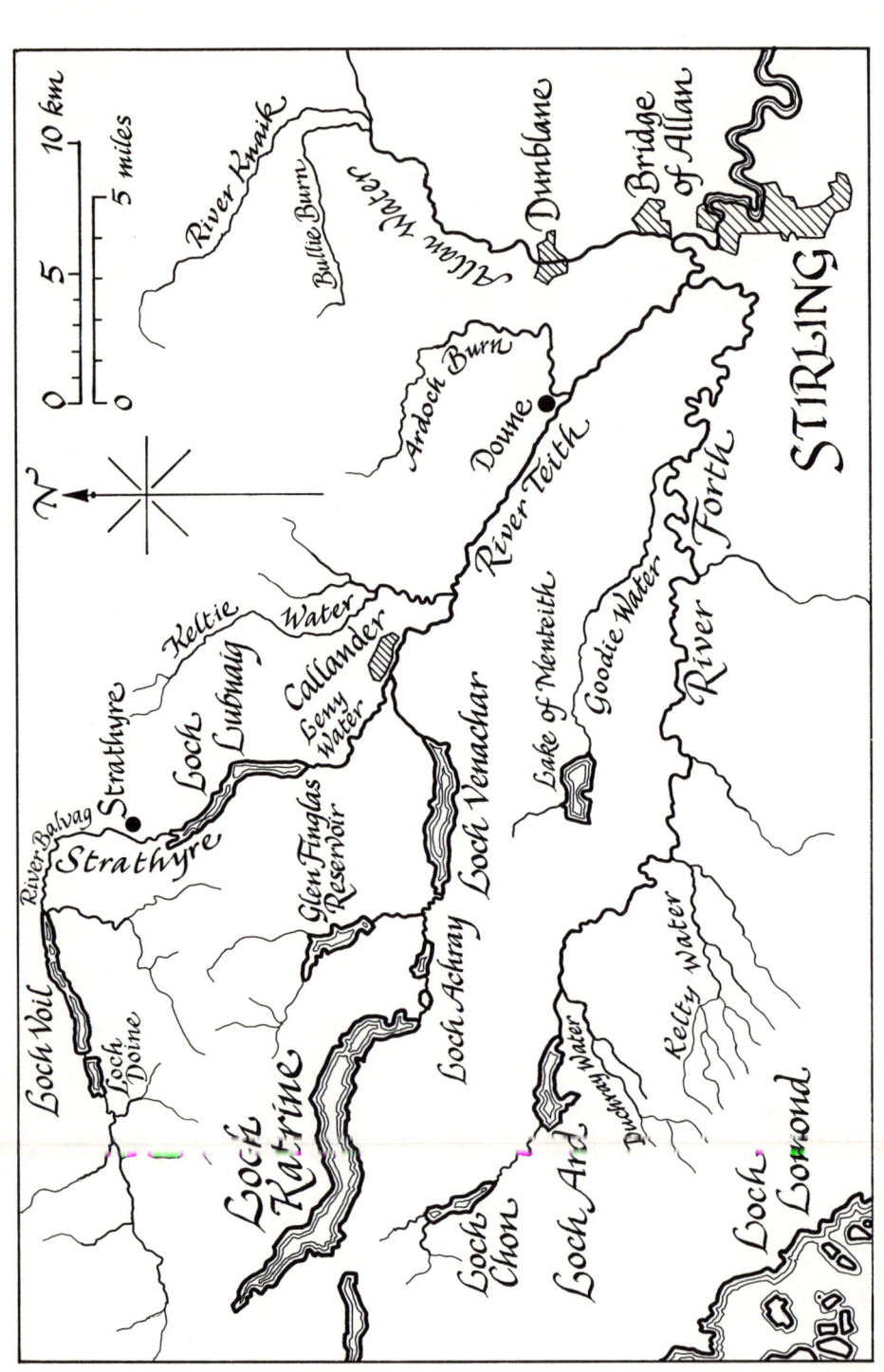

The Rivers Forth and Teith and their major tributaries

it cannot be fairly considered as a salmon river. Even at the turn of the century industry was starting to affect the lower reaches of the river where the warm cooling water from the distilleries was responsible for the death of many adult salmon. Also, abstraction in the head reaches was beginning to reduce the river's mean daily flow. Calderwood gave it scant mention in his book, even in 1909.

The first reservoir on the headwaters was the Glensherup which was formed in 1875, and this was followed by the Glenquey and Lower Glendevon in 1913 and 1918. Industries continued to develop along the Devon at Dollar, Tillicoultry, Alva, Tullibody and Cambus and with them came the construction of weirs and intakes for their needs. At present there are 6 weirs, and at least as many intakes, between the Crook of Devon and the river's confluence with the Forth at Cambus.

The Upper Glendevon Reservoir was built in 1948 and the Castlehill Reservoir, just downstream of Glendevon village was brought into service in 1979. The Devon can now be said to be a very developed system with the river's natural flow régime transformed into a regulated compensation flow, with the only non-restricted flows upstream from Dollar coming from the Glendey and Gairney burns.

Although there are excellent spawning grounds on the upper Devon, salmon and sea trout cannot reach them due to the insurmountable falls at Rumbling Bridge. The only spawning grounds available to them are in the neighbourhood of Dollarfield.

Salmon and sea trout tend to enter this river late in the season, probably because they are deterred by the warm water temperatures and poor water quality. Salmon and sea trout fishing on the lower Devon belongs to the Devon Angling Association and tickets can be obtained from tackle shops in Alloa and the neighbouring district.

7

THE TAY DISTRICT

The Tay river system is considered by many to be the finest salmon fishery in Scotland, although inhabitants of the Tweed area, Royal Deeside and Speyside might disagree. What cannot be denied is that the Tay drains the largest catchment area in Scotland frequented by migratory fish, covering an area of some 2,800 square miles. The landscape varies from wild high mountainous peaks, heatherclad mountain slopes and moorland to the north and west; beautiful narrow wooded valleys in the central area and one of the richest arable areas in the country to the east and south. For this reason anglers from all over the world have the widest possible choice of salmon fishing. They can select either the main river, one of the numerous lochs or one of the many tributaries such as the Dochart, Lochay, Lyon, Tummel, Garry, Tilt, Isla, Ericht, Almond and Earn, and many other smaller rivers and streams which constitute this vast river system. There are few days between the opening day of the season, 15 January, and the last day, 15 October, when fresh fish do not enter the Tay.

The source of the Tay is on the slopes of Ben Lui, a mountain 3,708 feet high, where several streams merge to form the River Cononish which flows east receiving streams draining Beinn Dubhchraig (3,204 feet) and burns coming down the hills around Tyndrum village. The river then turns south-east down Strath Fillan and becomes the River Fillan, winding its way through the gravelly river valley. Its course is subject to change as the gravel bed and banks of the river are continually being eroded. After passing Crianlarich it enters two small lochs, Loch Dochart and Loch Iubhair. The river now changes its name to the Dochart as it flows out of the latter loch and finds its way east and north-east down Glen Dochart, over the Falls of Dochart just above the village of Killin and enters Loch Tay. The River Lochay, having passed through Glen Lochay, also flows into Loch Tay at Killin. At Kenmore, at the east end of Loch Tay, the River Tay flows from the loch and continues majestically down Strath Tay past Taymouth Castle and along a delightful valley of arable land and fine old deciduous woods. Colonel Thornton had this to say of the area in his account of *A Sporting Tour through the Northern Parts of England and Great Part of the Highlands of Scotland* (1896): 'There certainly never was a more interesting assemblage of all the beauties of Alpine scenery, and the most finely-cultivated grazing farms. . . . The features are so various, so noble, and so majestic, that they surpass the art of the painter.' About a mile

THE TAY DISTRICT

downstream of the loch the River Lyon joins the Tay on the left bank at the Appin of Dull. After the confluence, the river passes the village of Aberfeldy and flows on past many fine mansion houses to its junction with the Tummel 15 miles downstream of Loch Tay. The Tummel joins the Tay on its left bank at Logierait and with its entry the size of the Tay is almost doubled. As it continues down the valley through the township of Dunkeld and Birnam it makes a fine contrast with its sparkling waters standing out magnificently against the green fields and wood-studded slopes. In its 31-mile descent from the Tummel junction to Perth, the Tay is again increased in size as the Braan joins it on the right bank at Birnam, the Isla joins it on the left bank just below Meikleour and the Almond joins it on its right bank a short distance upstream of Perth. It is a short distance below this confluence with the Almond, at a point known as The Woody Islands, opposite Scone Palace that the furthest upstream influence of the tide is recorded. Here a simple backing-up of fresh water occurs and the water is entirely fresh. The river then flows on through the fair city of Perth passing the harbour on its right bank, and from this point onwards is virtually in its tidal reaches. The Earn joins the Tay on the right bank at Jamesfield some 7 miles downstream from Perth. The Tay then flows out into the Firth and to the open sea, 31 miles below Perth and approximately 117 miles from its source on the slopes of Ben Lui. The Tay District Salmon Fisheries Board limits are Fife Ness in the south and Red Head on the Angus coast in the north.

In the nineteenth century the Tay was extremely heavily netted with many fishing stations on the coast, in the estuary and up river. It was estimated that there were some 70 different stations worked in the spring and about 200 during good summer fishing seasons. However, over the years many of these fisheries ceased to work (for mainly economic reasons) and in the river rod fishing became more profitable than netting. The Tay Salmon Fisheries Company Ltd, and a few smaller operators, now work the few stations which remain. In 1978 The Tay Salmon Fisheries Company Ltd owned or leased net and rod fishing in the Tay district with an annual value of £50,000 out of a total valuation of £75,741. With the conservation of the salmon stocks as its policy, the Tay Company has rationalised the fishing effort and abandoned marginally economic fisheries to concentrate on the better fisheries. Prior to 1938 coastal net fishings of the Tay district were fished to a limited extent by the Tay Company, but are not now exercised. It is understood that these fisheries were not very profitable and that the greater escapement was expected to benefit the Tay river fisheries. The Tay Company have also drastically reduced river netting and little netting is now carried out around or above Perth.

The present position is that no fixed engines are fished on the Tay district coastline except for an occasional fly net at Carnoustie and Arbroath. There are approximately 17 sweep net stations in use at times below Perth and 3 stations above Perth, namely the Bertha and Cleekim stations near the mouth of the

Almond and one at Stanley. It is estimated that the net fisheries of the Tay produce an average of 40,000 fish per year.

For well over a century it has been the policy of the Tay District Salmon Fisheries Board to improve the access of salmon to spawning tributaries. Over the years difficult obstacles have been made passable and many useful easements have been made at great expense. The Board has been helped financially on many occasions by The Tay Salmon Fisheries Company Ltd, and many fish ladders and other remedial works have been carried out on difficult falls, gorges and mill dykes to allow fish to ascend more easily to their spawning grounds. The Tummel, Tilt, Ericht and Almond are some of the tributaries where these works were carried out. It is, perhaps, rather ironical that after all these improvements were carried out the river system should be extensively developed for hydro-electric power. In the 1930s the Grampian Electric Supply Company harnessed Loch Rannoch and Loch Ericht to produce hydro-electric power and the associated Rannoch and Tummel Bridge power stations came into operation in 1930 and 1933 respectively. At this stage the waters passed into the Tummel below the power stations. Fish ladders were installed to allow fish up to spawn in the tributaries above Loch Rannoch. There was, however, a high impassable fall on the River Ericht flowing from Loch Ericht into Loch Rannoch but no steps were taken to allow fish to enter this part of the river system. This first part of the development affected the River Tummel to some extent, by the flooding of spawning and nursery grounds and by creating obstacles to check the free ascent and descent of migratory fish. Between 1937 and 1942 the Grampian scheme was extended to divert the upper reaches of the Garry into Loch Garry and then by tunnel into Loch Ericht. No compensation water or fish pass provisions were made in respect of this scheme, with the result that the river and its tributaries ceased to be available as spawning grounds above the point of diversion and for some distance downstream of the intercepting weirs. In addition the headwaters of the Spey and water from Loch an t-Seilich were also diverted to Loch Ericht.

With the advent of the Hydro-electric Development Act in 1943 the Grampian Electric Supply Company was incorporated into the North of Scotland Hydro-electric Board and the way was cleared for extensive hydro-electric developments throughout Scotland. On the Tay river system the Tummel-Garry scheme was further developed. To appreciate these developments one should refer to the map on page 51 which will make the following description much clearer. Starting at the head of the Tummel system the Gaur Power Station utilises the water impounded behind the dam at the outlet of Loch Eigheach. This reservoir collects the water from Loch Laidon and Loch Ba on Rannoch Moor, close to the source of the Tummel, and the River Ba, in the Black Mount region. Fish can still ascend to Loch Eigheach by the Gaur fish pass, one of the longest fish passes in Scotland with 70 pools, but few fish are seen in the area. Downstream from the Gaur Power Station the River Gaur flows into Loch Rannoch, which also receives water (via Rannoch Power

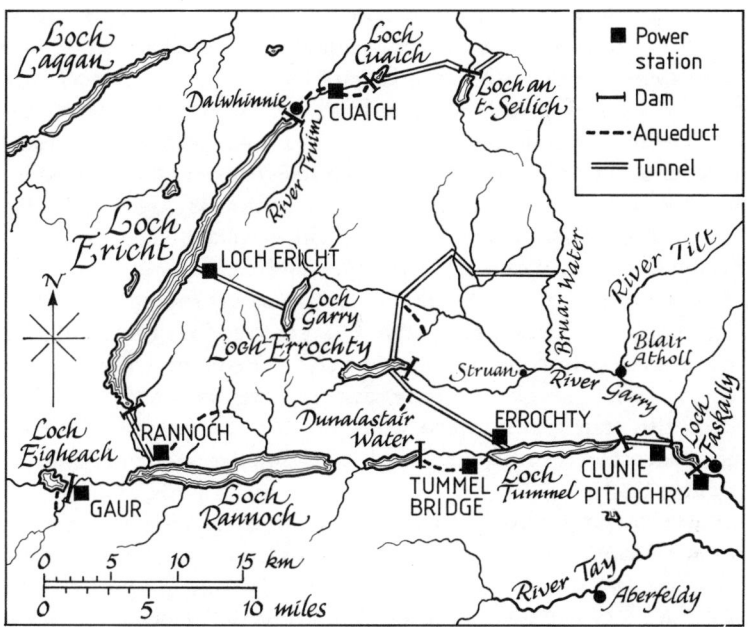

The Rivers Tummel and Garry and the Tummel–Garry Hydro-electric Scheme

Station) from Loch Ericht which in its turn has collected the waters of the upper Garry from Loch Garry and water from Loch an t-Seilich and Loch Cuaich in Glen Truim. Loch Rannoch, with its large catchment area, is the main storage reservoir in the region. It feeds into a small reservoir at Dunalastair, from which the water is led to the Tummel Bridge Power Station at the head of Loch Tummel. At Dunalastair Dam and at the weir at Kinloch Rannoch fish passes have been provided. The other three power stations on the Tummel, Errochty, Clunie and Pitlochry, were constructed as part of the post-war Tummel-Garry scheme. The Errochty station is fed from Loch Errochty, a new loch built across the River Errochty. Water is brought to the loch from the Garry and one of its major tributaries, the Bruar, by a system of tunnels. Compensation water from the Errochty Dam operates a small power station on the River Errochty near Trinafour. From Loch Errochty water is piped to the power station near Dalcroy on the shore of Loch Tummel.

The effect of this extended scheme on the River Garry is that the river is now almost completely dry during the summer months and a fish barrier, or heck, has been placed across the Garry at Struan to prevent fish ascending above this point in times of flood and becoming stranded. The only spawning and nursery areas left for Garry fish are in the lower Errochty, under reduced flow, the Tilt and the lower Garry between Struan and Loch Faskally. About $1\frac{1}{2}$ miles downstream from the original outlet of Loch Tummel is the Clunie Dam which raised the level of the loch by about 15 feet. A fish pass has been built there, with 43 pools. From the dam a tunnel conveys water to Clunie Power Station on the shore of Loch Faskally, just below the junction of the River Tummel and River Garry. The dam at Pitlochry, which gave rise to Loch Faskally, and its integral power station were provided in the interests of the lower reaches of the river, and are intended to even out, as far as possible, any irregularities in the flow of the water caused by the varying discharges of the stations upstream. There is a fish pass at Pitlochry Dam which is now a major tourist attraction and visitors can watch the salmon ascending the pass through windows in an underground chamber. The fish pass is roughly 270 yards long and has 35 pools. Three of these pools are larger than the others and have been provided to serve as resting places for the fish. The salmon are counted by an electronic recorder which not only distinguishes between ascending and descending fish, but also between small grilse and large salmon. Inside the Pitlochry Dam there is a hatchery with accommodation for over one million salmon eggs.

The other major hydro-electric scheme on the Tay river system is the Breadalbane scheme which involves harnessing the waters running into the River Dochart, Loch Tay and Loch Earn. In a catchment area of 200 square miles there are 7 power stations and 6 dams. The first scheme was the Lawers scheme which collected water from the mountainous area around Ben Lawers to the north of Loch Tay. Aqueducts gather in water from this area to Lochan na Lairige where it is stored behind a large buttress dam and is passed to Finlarig Power Station on the north shore at the western end of Loch Tay. The Killin section of the Breadalbane scheme has 3 dams and 3 power stations. A dam at Lubreoch in lovely Glen Lyon raised the level of Loch Lyon by 70 feet to provide the main reservoir. Water from hill streams above Glen Dochart and Glen Lochay supplements the natural catchment of the loch, and is conveyed to Loch Lyon by tunnels across Glen Lochay. All the water from Loch Lyon passes through the Lubreoch Power Station and discharges continuously into the River Lyon. A trap was provided near the power station tailrace, where the salmon were trapped and stripped by the staff of the Tay District Salmon Fisheries Board. The eggs were taken to the hatchery at Pitlochry Dam and the eyed ova or resulting fry were distributed in the various tributaries. Three miles downstream at Stronuich a small reservoir or headpond has been created by a small dam. In the dam there are a turbine, through which compensation water is released into the river downstream, and a Borland fish pass which allows salmon to pass up and downstream. Stronuich also receives water discharged from the Cashlie Power Station situated on the north shore of the reservoir. The water is passed from the Stronuich headpond to the main power station in the section, in Glen Lochay. The Falls of Lochay just upstream of the power station, previously a barrier to salmon, have been by-passed by a Borland fish pass. This pass and the provision of pool-type fish ladders at two other falls higher up the river have opened up the whole of the River Lochay in an attempt

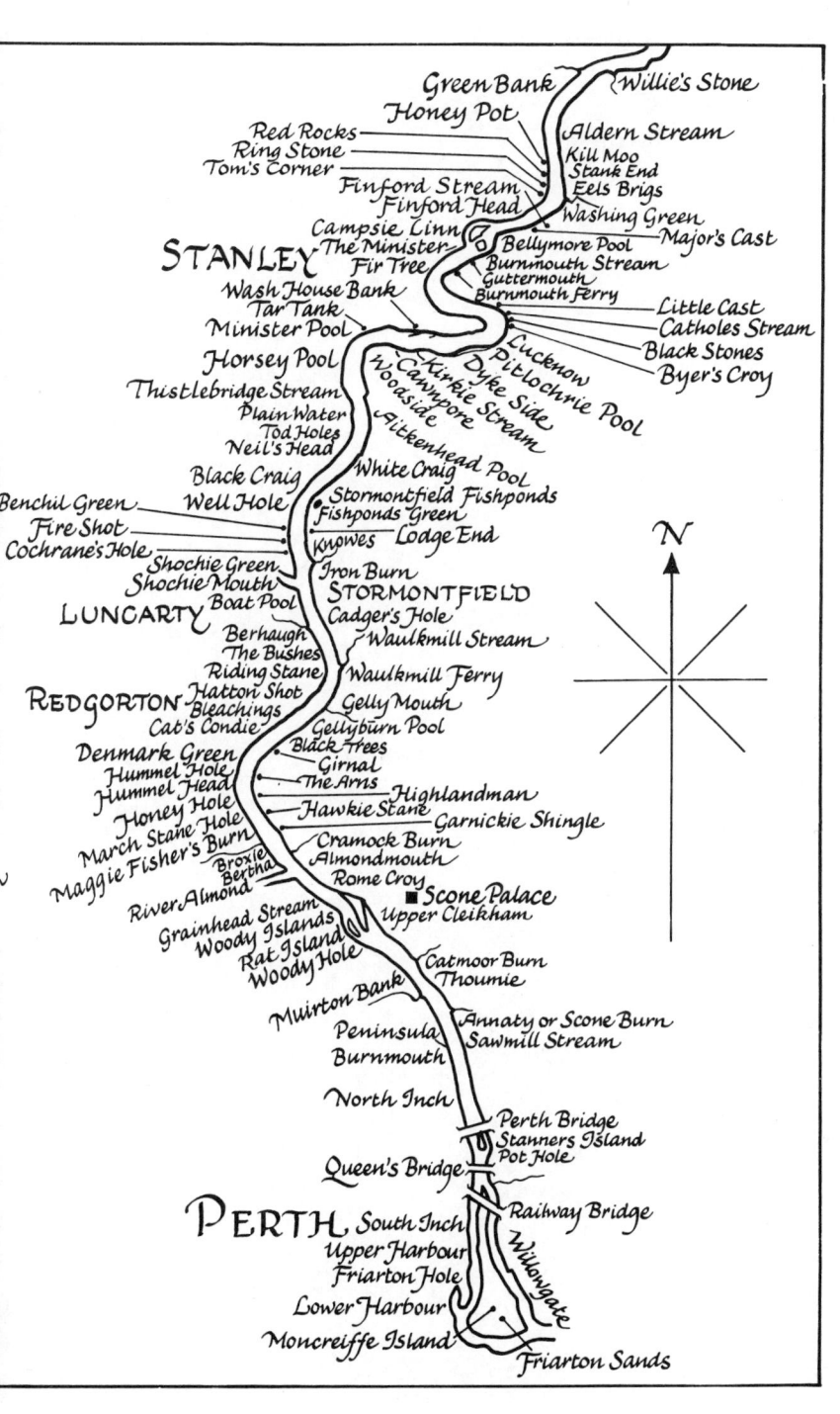

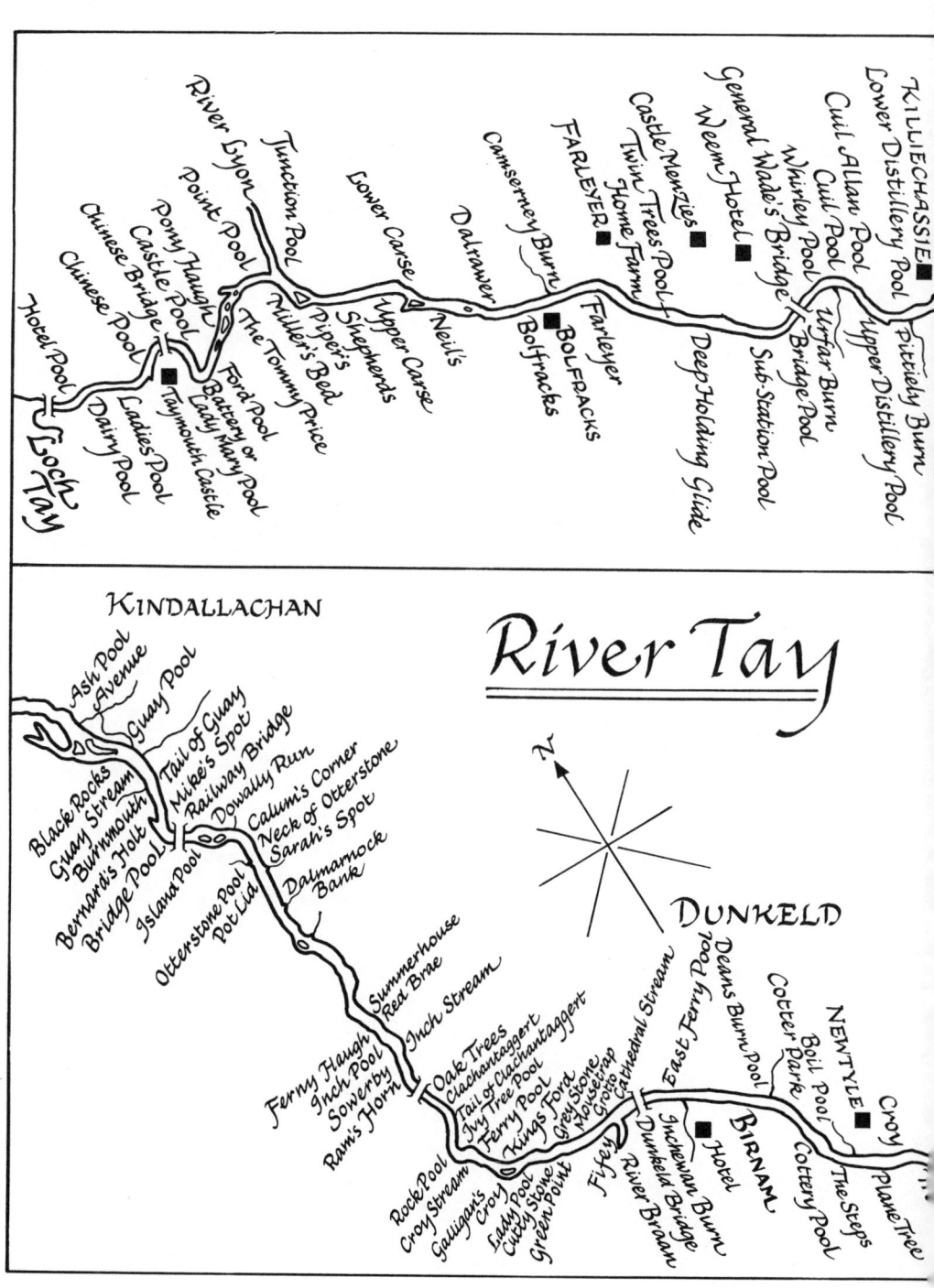

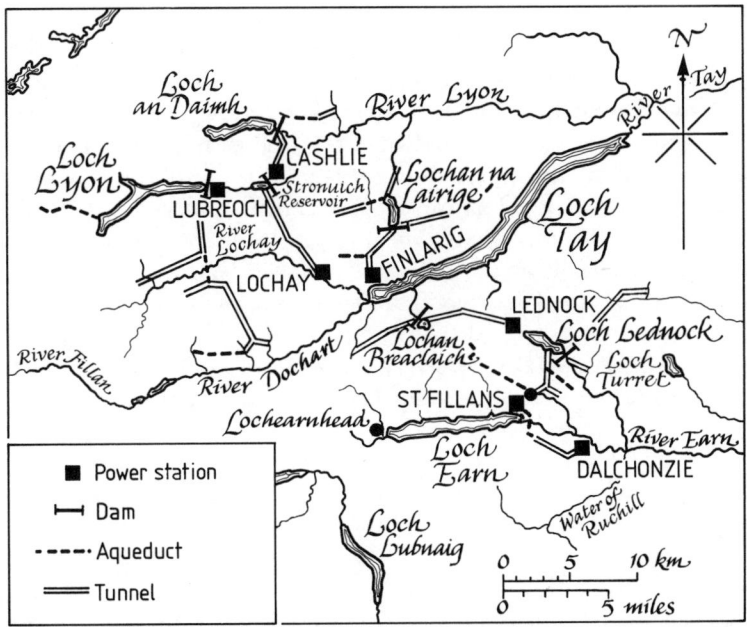

The upper tributaries of the River Tay and River Earn and the Breadalbane Hydro-electric Scheme

to compensate for the flooded spawning and nursery grounds in other areas.

The third section of the Breadalbane scheme is St Fillans, which has 3 power stations and 2 dams. Water from Lochan Breaclaich, in the mountainous area to the south of Loch Tay, is taken by tunnel to Lednock Power Station at the head of Loch Lednock which also collects water from several adjacent catchment areas including the headwaters of the River Almond. Water from Loch Lednock is passed to St Fillans Power Station close to the foot of Loch Earn. Water from Loch Earn is utilised in a further development. A small weir with a fish ladder is situated in St Fillans village just below the outlet of the loch. This weir regulates the flow released down the River Earn and diverts into a tunnel water for the Dalchonzie Power Station which is close to the River Earn about half way between St Fillans and Comrie. A very full description of all the schemes promoted by the North of Scotland Hydro-electric Board is given in a glossy booklet entitled *Power from the Glens* published by the Board in 1976.

The overall effect on fisheries of the considerable hydro-electric developments in the Tay river system will not be known for many years to come, and the loss of salmon stocks may prove incapable of assessment. However, the loss of extensive spawning and nursery areas as a result of flooding or drying out of the headwaters of the Tummel, Garry and Lyon, all of which were famed for their spring runs of salmon, can only be viewed with concern by fishery managers and anglers alike. The Tummel and Lyon were frequented by a heavy class of spring fish and the Garry by smaller springers. The compensation flows from the various schemes allow easier access to the higher reaches for the later runs of salmon and grilse, and a large number of fish are able to reach the reduced spawning facilities in these rivers. Overcrowding of the spawning fords may, however, be to the detriment of the earlier runs of fish which normally spawn first. In all probability this may be one of the reasons for the recent steady decline in the numbers of spring fish ascending the Tay, in particular the heavier individuals. The Tay was always famed for its large fish of 40 lb or more and it would indeed be a tragedy if these monsters disappeared. Recent analysis of the weight of Tay fish shows that the present average weight of salmon caught is 12.6 lb compared with 15 lb previously.

The salmon disease, UDN, was very prevalent in the Tay system in the late 1960s, but in recent years it has not been so much in evidence.

The Tay

This fine angling river is one of the longest and widest in the country and flows through a rich arable valley, whose slopes are adorned with mixed deciduous and coniferous woodlands. From the foot of Loch Tay to Perth there are a wealth of large, deep pools, many of which are best fished from a boat as they are too wide to cover properly from the bank. However, since the invention of the fixed spool reel, bank fishing is more commonly practised than it used to be. Harling is a very popular method of fishing on these big pools, as they can be covered very thoroughly from bank to bank by this means. Two anglers sit facing the stern of the boat using either two or three rods. Once the boat has been launched at the head of the pool the lines are paid out and the boat is propelled from one bank to the other with the bow angled upstream. The boat is allowed to drop a yard or two downstream with each traverse of the river. When a fish is hooked the other lines are taken in and, in most cases, the boat lands to net the fish. In the 'old days' one or two ghillies rowed the boat, but nowadays outboard motors are generally used, these proving more efficient, especially in strong currents. The lures used include Kynoch Killers, minnows and spoons, but fly is sometimes used. Boats are also used for ordinary methods of fishing, to cover lies near the centre of the river more effectively. Single bank owners often come to an agreement whereby pools are fished by each owner on alternate days.

It would be almost impossible to comment on every beat because all beats can produce good catches when the season and conditions are advantageous. Among the best spring fishings are Islamouth, Stanley, Redgorton and Scone. The weir at Stanley was breached in three places in the early 1970s on the instructions of the District Fisheries Board, when Stanley mill changed from water to electric power. The gaps in the weir now allow spring fish to spread

THE TAY DISTRICT

out over the river system more quickly, as the weir tended to hold fish back when water temperatures were low. The rod beats above Stanley appear to have benefited in the spring from this easier access, but recent mild winters may be a contributing factor.

The tendency throughout the whole river is for the spring run to be less numerous and the summer and autumn runs to be improving. Indeed it is estimated that almost 75% of the total annual catch is now taken in the last three months of the season. A conservative estimate of the Tay rod catch is in the region of 12,000 fish with Islamouth accounting for about 1,000 and other main beats for 500 each in a season. The rod results on other beats are not so well known but the annual value in the valuation roll gives an indication of average catch. There are probably twenty lesser beats with an annual catch of around 150 fish, twenty with a catch of around 70 and many others with catches of 50 and under. The Tay also has a reasonable run of sea trout, but over the last few years their numbers have shown a marked decline.

Although many of the fish entering the Tay pass upstream into the tributaries to spawn, there is a considerable amount of spawning in the main river and there are many good spawning fords and nursery areas which, due to the compensation water released from the reservoirs, are well covered with water at all times.

'Spring' fish enter the Tay from November onwards and are distributed over the whole river system by the opening day of the fishing season. This means that there is an opportunity of catching fish on all beats right from the start. Of the many beats on the Tay the majority are let through the estate factors or sporting agents, including Malloch (Field Sports) Ltd of Perth.

The main Angling Associations on the Tay and tributaries, apart from the Pitlochry Association, are the Perth and District Angling Association, the Strathmore Angling Association and the Blairgowrie Angling Association. The Perth and District Association (confined to members only, with a membership of 500 approximately) leases waters on the River Earn near Bridge of Earn and also leases during the summer months, from mid-May to the end of July, waters on the Tay at Waulkmill. These consist of the Redgorton and Lower Scone beats, with two particularly well-known pools, the Fish Ponds and Waulkmill. The Association have both banks of this stretch of the river over this period. It also owns a short stretch of water near Ballinluig. The Strathmore Angling Association leases a large amount of the River Isla. This is a strong association with a membership of 200–300 and it runs its own hatchery, which is almost entirely used for rearing trout, at Glamis. The Blairgowrie Angling Association leases waters on the Ericht, which are showing improved catches of salmon annually as the Ericht is now producing a much larger number of migratory fish.

The city of Perth owns waters from the North Inch downstream to the boundary of the burgh of Perth. Approximately 2,000 permits are issued per annum and a limited number of day permits are issued daily to visitors visiting the city. Members of the Perth and District Angling Association can also fish this water if they are residents of Perth. Permit holders can fish this water throughout the season from 1 January – 15 October. This stretch is all tidal, but good catches of salmon and sea trout are caught annually, and the autumn has undoubtedly been best in recent years. Tickets are available from the Perth and Kinross District Council offices at 1 High Street, Perth. There are three hotels on the lower Tay that have their own water and residents can obtain fishing through the hotels. These are Ballathie House Hotel above Stanley and Birnam Hotel and Dunkeld House Hotel at Dunkeld.

It would be difficult to name the best pools on the lower Tay as, being a deep, fast-flowing river, many pools merge in higher water conditions. When harling one normally fishes through one pool into the next as there is, on many stretches, no dead water in between the pools.

At the present time Islamouth and Meikleour (south bank) are probably the best beats throughout the year, fishing well not only in the spring but also in the summer and autumn months. The Long Head pool and Castle Rock pool are famed on the Islamouth beat. On the Cargill/Ballathie beat the Pot Shot and Cradle pools deserve mention.

The Alderns and Major's Cast pools on Taymount and Stobhall beats also have a high reputation, with the Little Head pool on Upper Stanley sharing a similar standing. Probably the most famous pool on the Tay is the renowned Pitlochrie pool on the Lower Stanley beat.

Naturally the above-named pools are only a few of the many excellent ones found on the Tay. Other pools can be equally productive when the water is flowing at the height that best suits them. A map of the pools on the Tay, drawn by Maude Parker in 1931, is still available, while a more recent one was published in 1977. Unfortunately, however, to go into more detail concerning these pools would require a complete book on the Tay, as they are so numerous.

One should not finish an account of the Tay without mentioning the early and significant research work on salmon carried out on this river. The earliest work was that carried out at Stormontfield, near Scone Palace. Rearing ponds for young salmon were erected there, close to the banks of the Tay, in 1853 to start some of the first artificial salmon propagation experiments. The resulting work, which included the results of marking young salmon, conclusively showed that salmon parr are the young of salmon and not a separate species. This work is admirably summarised in a little volume written by William Brown in 1862 entitled *The Natural History of the Salmon as Ascertained by the Recent Experiments in the Artificial Spawning and Hatching of the Ova and Rearing of the Fry at Stormontfield on the Tay.*

Further pioneering work was done in the first decade of this century by H. W. Johnston, who demonstrated that the scales of salmon could be used to determine the age and growth of the fish. It seems a little unfair that other scale exponents such as Hutton, in England and Wales, and Dahl, in Norway, should receive all the credit for this discovery.

Another Tay fisheries expert was P.D. Malloch whose book the *Life History and Habits of the Salmon, Sea Trout and other Freshwater Fish*, published in 1910, is still a classic. It is interesting to note that he was one of the first managing directors of The Tay Salmon Fisheries Company Ltd, and that his son, the late 'Willie' Malloch, was also manager of this company and a much respected fishery expert.

Loch Tay

In the words of Sir John Murray, who carried out the extensive *Bathymetrical Survey of the Fresh Water Lochs of Scotland*, 'Loch Tay is one of the largest of the Scottish fresh water lochs, unsurpassed in the beauty of its surroundings, and well-known to anglers on account of its salmon fishings, which are among the best in Scotland.' Loch Tay is over $14\frac{1}{2}$ miles long and has a mean breadth of $\frac{3}{4}$ mile. It is a deep loch, with a maximum depth of 508 feet and an average depth of almost 200 feet.

There are several hotels on the shores of the loch which cater for anglers who return each year to troll for the heavy class of spring salmon. The opening day of the season is always celebrated at Kenmore when the fishers are piped down to the loch and their boat 'blessed' with the national 'water of life' before setting out on what is often a very cold and blustery day. However, the opening day is rarely fishless unless the weather conditions are exceptionally bad.

It is usual to catch fish on spinning lures on this deep loch, but occasionally fish can sometimes be caught on the fly. The annual catch used to be around 500 salmon, but in those days about 20 boats or more fished it constantly for most of the season, with ghillies who knew the loch intimately. Nowadays fewer boats fish it with fewer experienced ghillies, and the annual catch now rarely exceeds 300. There is no doubt that with the aid of outboard motors larger areas of the loch are now fished and explored, but intimate knowledge of such a large expanse of water is hard to replace.

The Kenmore, Killin, Ardeonaig and Clachaig hotels are amongst the ones most popular with anglers fishing the loch.

The Dochart

The Dochart is a late river as, although fish enter Loch Tay from November onwards, they are held back at the Falls of Dochart at Killin by low water temperatures in the spring. Once the temperature is high enough the fish move quickly up the Dochart, through the lochs and up into the Fillan and Cononish. At one time quite a strong run of heavy fish reached the Cononish by May or June, depending on water temperatures. This run has now dwindled away and most fish now frequenting the headwaters are summer and autumn fish.

The Dochart is an attractive river with deep pools and shallow, gravelly stretches. Angling catches are not easily assessed but a fair number of fish are caught in the Dochart and its upper tributaries. Its main tributary, the Fillan, has a fairly flashy nature and there is considerable movement of gravel in much of its course, with the accompanying erosion of the banks.

The Lochay

The Lochay flows into the head of Loch Tay not far from the point where the Dochart enters. The Lochay is about 15 miles long and has good spawning and nursery areas in its headwaters. For many years these were inaccessible to salmon because of impassable falls, 70 feet high, a mile or so from the mouth. As was described on page 52, the river was developed for hydro-electric power and the falls were made passable with the aid of a Borland fish pass and pool passes were built on two other falls higher upstream. Up to that time the only section of the river that was fishable was from the falls to the mouth. Now, however, there is angling potential on most of the river's length. Counts of salmon ascending the Borland pass on the Lochay over a 17-year period are as follows:

Table 1
Counts of salmon and grilse at the Borland fish pass on the Lochay, 1963-1979

Year	Count	Year	Count	Year	Count
1963	145	1969	168	1975	115
1964	157	1970	312	1976	No count
1965	277	1971	475	1977	No count
1966	113	1972	145	1978	No count
1967	276	1973	351	1979	No count
1968	217	1974	231		

The Lyon

The River Lyon, from Loch Lyon to its junction with the Tay some 2 miles below Loch Tay, is approximately 30 miles long and flows through one of the loveliest glens in Tayside. The first 6 miles above the junction have the best of the spring fishing as there is a gorge at this point which checks the ascent of

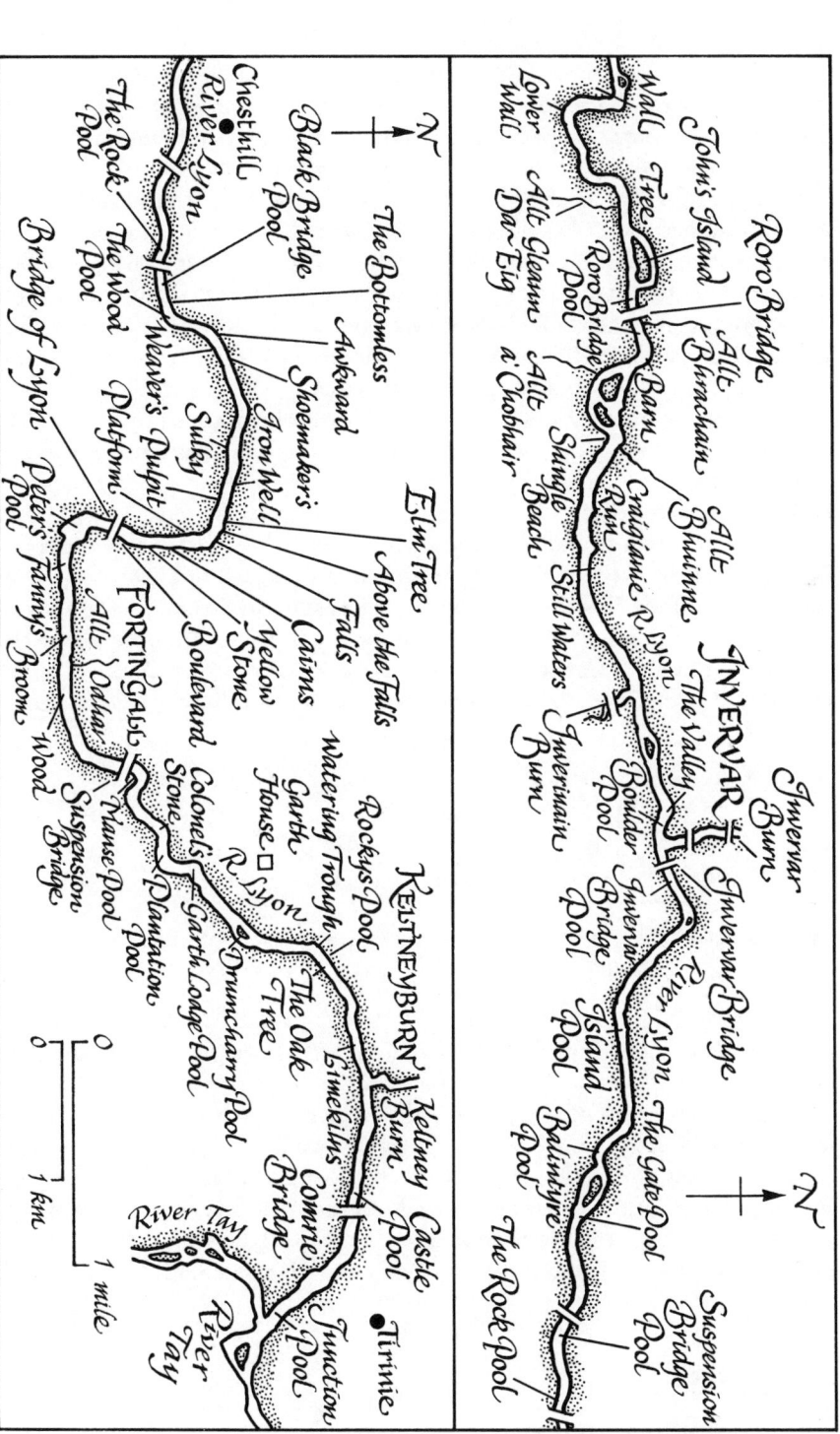

Salmon Pools on the River Lyon from Roro Bridge to the Tay

fish until the water temperature reaches about 45°F. In some years, when there is heavy snow on the surrounding mountains, it is not until early April, or later, that they pass this point. Many anglers stay at local hotels at Kenmore and Fortingall to enjoy this early fishing for a heavy class of salmon which, unfortunately, is not as abundant as it was. Above the bottom beat the river flows through a thickly-wooded gorge, above which there is a sluggish stretch which extends upstream to within a mile or two of Balgie Bridge. Above Balgie Bridge the river valley is most picturesque and has many fine holding pools, gorges and waterfalls. It is in this stretch that probably the best fishing on this river can be had from May onwards. At one time this stretch yielded excellent catches but this is not now the case.

The main spawning grounds on the Lyon occur below Loch Lyon and in the many tributaries running into it. However, as has been mentioned earlier, the Lyon has been harnessed for hydro-electric purposes and most of its headwaters have been diverted to the Lochay, leaving only a compensation flow and freshet provisions. As no fish pass was incorporated in Lubreoch Dam at the foot of Loch Lyon, fish are unable to pass through this loch and on to their old spawning grounds. There is, however, a fish pass in the Stronuich Dam 3 miles downstream of Lubreoch so that fish can ascend as far as Lubreoch where they can be caught in a trap for stripping by staff of the Tay District Salmon Fisheries Board. The fish counts at this pass are as follows:

Table 2
Counts of salmon and grilse at Stronuich Dam, 1963–1979

Year	Count	Year	Count	Year	Count
1963	216	1969	43*	1975	138
1964	250	1970	103	1976	146
1965	154	1971	254	1977	139
1966	162	1972	356	1978	438
1967	185	1973	340	1979	334
1968	153	1974	362		

Although the counts for the periods 1971–1974 and 1978–1979 show some improvement, these figures can only be a fraction of the numbers passing this point when the river had an entirely natural flow. In schemes of this sort not only are large areas of spawning and nursery ground lost but also the movements of fish can be affected. For example, a change in the water temperature régime could occur due to the diversion of flows from the upper and higher part of the catchment which might affect the ascent of returning adults. A higher spring water temperature could well draw the fish up the river earlier in the year and would naturally affect angling catches as could a higher than average river flow.

* counter working only part of season.

THE TAY DISTRICT

The Garry

The Garry from its source north of Loch Garry to its junction with the Tummel at the head of Loch Faskally is about 22 miles long. The river used to be an excellent salmon water, and in the early 1900s had a promising future. Two difficult falls near Struan, which impeded the free ascent of fish into the headwaters, were eased at this time by the Tay District Salmon Fisheries Board with the permission of the Duke of Atholl. This allowed fish to utilise potential spawning areas above and below Loch Garry and in the Errochty and the Bruar, below the falls of Bruar. The Garry was frequented by good runs of early fish, normally smaller than the average Tay springer, as well as by runs of grilse and summer fish. The latter frequently carried sea lice, which proved they wasted no time in ascending the Tay.

With the impoundment of Loch Garry and the diversion of the headwaters of the Garry to Loch Ericht in the 1930s fish were unable to reach these upper spawning areas and, as there was no provision in the scheme for compensation water, the reduced flow made the fish more vulnerable. In the 1950s the spawning area was further reduced when the North of Scotland Hydro-electric Board tapped all the left bank tributaries of the Garry down as far as the Bruar and led them back by aqueduct to a point not far below Dalnaspidal and then by tunnel to Loch Errochty. The diversion causes this section of the Garry to virtually dry out during the summer months and the dry river course is an eyesore to all passing travellers be they anglers or not. A weir has been built across the Garry at Struan to prevent fish reaching this area during high flows.

The main spawning areas in the Errochty, the Bruar and the Garry, between Struan and Blair Atholl, still produce a reasonable stock of fish, but these are mainly summer fish few of which ascend the river before May.

The main fishing in the Garry is now almost entirely confined to the section from Struan to the junction with the Tummel, at the head of Loch Faskally. The best fishing is in the deep gorge at Killicrankie and just above. Most of this angling is owned by Atholl Estates and application for fishing lets should be made to the Estates Office in Blair Atholl.

The Braan

The River Quaich rises in the hills to the south of Kenmore and flows eastwards down Glen Quaich to Loch Freuchie. The River Braan flows out of Loch Freuchie passing Amulree to join the Tay near Dunkeld. The Braan flows through open moorland in its upper reaches, entering coniferous woodland before joining the Tay. The Braan is roughly 12 miles long with its main tributaries, the Cochill, Tombane and Ballinloan burns, joining on the left bank.

Unfortunately salmon can only ascend one mile up the Braan from the Tay before coming to the impassable falls at Hermitage, which is a National Trust for Scotland property and of scenic beauty. A short distance upstream of Hermitage there is a second impassable fall at Rumbling Bridge.

Salmon frequent the Braan below Hermitage, near the village of Inver, and may be seen making repeated unsuccessful attempts to clear the falls in the autumn and consequently have to spawn in the river downstream.

The Tay District Salmon Fisheries Board may in the future obtain spawning stock from this area and have already planted eyed ova in the tributaries above Rumbling Bridge.

The Tummel

The Tummel from its source in the mountains of Black Mount deer forest above Loch Ba to its junction with the Tay at Logierait is approximately 58 miles long.

In the latter part of the last century most of the fishing was confined to the section of river between the Falls of Tummel and Ballinluig, as the falls in those days were almost impassable. Baskets were set on the falls in the old days to catch fish which fell back in their attempts to ascend, but these were removed in 1868. In the early part of this century private proprietors and the Tay District Salmon Fisheries Board made several attempts, ending in success, to ease these falls. This allowed fish to spread over a much larger part of the catchment and fish were readily caught upstream of the falls particularly in the stretch between Loch Rannoch and Loch Tummel. Over the years the upper Tummel system gradually became a productive area for migratory fish and the angling beats improved considerably with those in the Faskally district being the best.

However, with the extensions to the Grampian Electric Supply Company's works in the 1940s and 1950s promoted by the North of Scotland Hydro-electric Board there were inevitable changes to the river régime as described at the beginning of the chapter. These developments have resulted in extensive flooding of spawning and nursery grounds and the elimination of a number of angling beats by the reservoirs. The remaining part of the river is subject to varying flows due to power station generation or changing compensation flow provisions.

There is little serious salmon angling in Loch Faskally and the Tummel between Clunie Power Station and Clunie Dam, and yet before hydro-electric development this area, which was a delightful stretch of river, produced good salmon catches.

The fish counts at the Clunie Dam fish pass are as follows:

THE TAY DISTRICT

Table 3
Counts of salmon and grilse at Clunie Dam, 1953–1979

1953	268	1962	158	1971	77
1954	424	1963	167	1972	151
1955	142	1964	228	1973	184
1956	118	1965	168	1974	141
1957	95	1966	77	1975	224
1958	77	1967	96	1976	95
1959	124	1968	86	1977	272
1960	113	1969	77	1978	221
1961	122	1970	52	1979	137

These are catastrophically low figures for what was an important salmon producing area, particularly when at one time it was thought to have had a spawning stock of some 5,000 fish. Nowadays only a handful of fish ascend the Gaur Pass and the only untouched spawning areas on the system are grossly underpopulated. Probably the best spawning areas utilised by the present stock are Kynachan and Kinardochy burns at the head of Loch Tummel. The Tay District Salmon Fisheries Board is stocking these streams each year in the hope of strengthening the dwindling stock in the Tummel. There is practically no angling above Loch Tummel and only a limited amount between Clunie Dam and Pitlochry. It is also rare for anyone to catch a salmon in Loch Faskally.

The counts of fish at Pitlochry Pass are considerably higher than those at Clunie which points to the fact that the majority of the fish passing upstream of Faskally must be destined for the lower Garry and Tilt, although the proportion of fish caught is very small.

Table 4
Counts of salmon and grilse at Pitlochry Dam, 1951–1979

1951	5,630	1961	3,741	1971	6,186
1952	5,790	1962	3,998	1972	7,771
1953	5,368	1963	4,353	1973	11,977
1954	5,357	1964	4,522	1974	8,250
1955	4,182	1965	4,558	1975	6,710
1956	3,555	1966	4,879	1976	5,564
1957	4,339	1967	6,148	1977	5,453
1958	3,513	1968	4,365	1978	9,024
1959	3,074	1969	5,361	1979	8,490
1960	3,936	1970	5,253		

The Port na-Craig stretch of the Tummel immediately below Pitlochry Dam is owned by Clunie More Estate and the North of Scotland Hydro-electric Board. The former leases its fishing to the Pine Trees Hotel in Pitlochry, while the latter lets the fishing to the Pitlochry Angling Club. There are certain

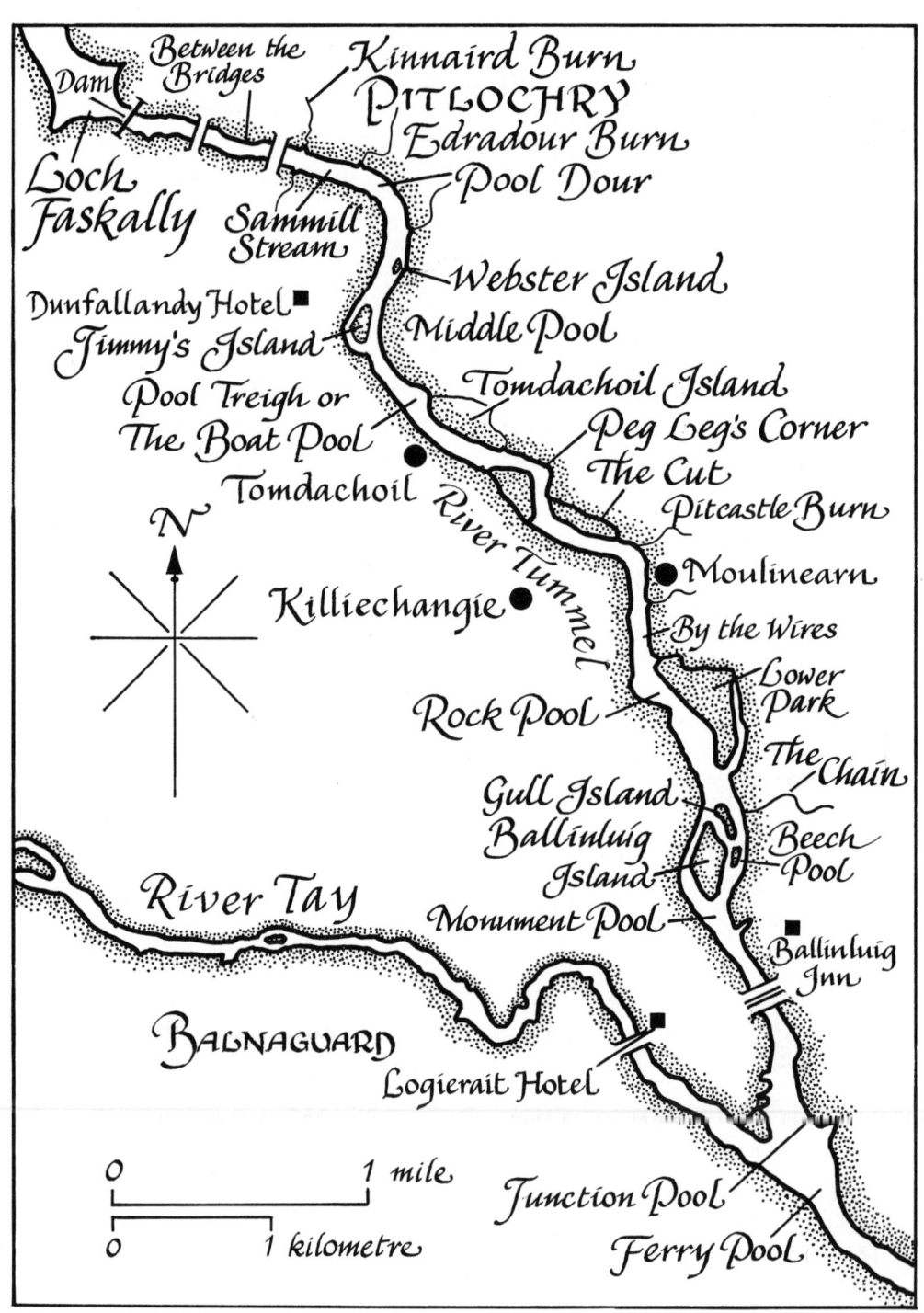

Salmon Pools on the River Tummel

arrangements between the two proprietors over the days on which each lessee fishes. Fishing on the lower Tummel is in the hands of a number of proprietors.

Considerable research on the effects of hydro-electric installations on the movements of salmon in the Tummel Valley has been carried out by the staff of the Freshwater Fisheries Laboratory at Faskally. Various investigations have been carried out over the years including work on the effects on young fish of passage through the Francis turbines at Clunie Power Station. The results revealed that the mortality caused by the turbines was about 25% under normal operating conditions.

The Tilt

The Tilt is a remote river rising in the mountains of south-west Aberdeenshire in the Forest of Atholl and only a track goes some of the way up Glen Tilt. In the lower part of its course it passes close to Blair Castle the seat of the Duke of Atholl, chief of the Clan Murray.

The River Tilt and its tributaries constitute an important large spawning and nursery area. In its upper reaches the Tilt has a sizeable tributary in the Tarf Water, while nearer Blair Atholl it receives Fender Burn which drains off Carn Liath (3,193 feet). The production of this spawning area has undoubtedly been mainly responsible for maintaining the good stock of fish passing upstream of Pitlochry.

Fish do not appear in the Tilt until late in the season and it is, therefore, not advisable that any angler takes an early let. However, towards the end of the season fishing can be reasonable and lets can be obtained from the Atholl Estates.

The Isla

This long river rises in the mountains west of the South Esk catchment in the Caenlochan National Nature Reserve. Its course is fairly swift at first and the river cascades over some most spectacular falls on its way, but as it reaches the rich farmland of Strathmore between Blairgowrie and Coupar Angus it meanders slowly to the Tay. It joins the Tay just below Kinclaven Bridge at the top of the famous Islamouth beat. In its lower reaches the Isla is joined by the Ericht between Meigle and Coupar Angus and by the Dean Water near the Bridge of Crathies. In this area the river is very canal-like and rather uninteresting and it is very difficult to identify individual pools and places where salmon are likely to 'take'. However, the river has always had a fairly good run of autumn fish. Unfortunately two impassable falls, about 2 miles apart, prevent fish reaching the headwaters. The lower fall is 50 feet high and is at the Slug of Auchrannie and the upper, 70 feet high, at the Reekie Linn near the Bridge of Craigisla. If there had been only one obstacle preventing access it is likely that the Tay District Salmon Fisheries Board would have attempted to ease it, but the cost of easing two falls of these heights is prohibitive. The main spawning areas are in the vicinity of Brigton and the Bridge of Ruthven.

On the upper reaches of the Isla system there are two storage reservoirs used for domestic supply to Dundee. These are the Backwater and Loch of Lintrathen. Salmon are prevented from reaching these waters by a series of falls.

Most of the angling on the Isla is let to the Strathmore Angling Association and a fair number of fish are taken, mainly on bait and spinner.

The Ericht

The Ericht begins where the two main tributaries, the Ardle and Black Water (the lower reaches of the Shee), meet about 5 miles upstream of Blairgowrie. The Ardle and Shee drain a large area to the north and west of Blairgowrie; the Shee rising just south of Deeside, and the Ardle in the mountains to the north and east of Pitlochry and Blair Atholl. Both these tributaries have a good spawning and feeding potential, with the Ardle being the better of the two. For many years these areas had practically no salmon because of a number of difficult obstacles on the Ericht at and above Blairgowrie, including a series of difficult falls in the Craighall Gorge. The Tay District Salmon Fisheries Board, realising the excellent potential of the river system, secured the co-operation of local fishing proprietors and proceeded to ease these barriers and open up the spawning and nursery grounds above to the salmon. In 1936 they installed fish ladders on two of the worst weirs, one at Blairgowrie and one at Oak Bank, a mile upstream. Also eyed ova, fry and adult fish were placed above these obstacles from the early 1930s to 1950. However, a really bad natural obstacle (Craighall Gorge) above Blairgowrie prevented the completion of this work, and except at extreme high flows most fish were unable to pass through the gorge. The Tay District Salmon Fisheries Board, in conjunction with the North of Scotland Hydro-electric Board, eventually mounted a further attempt to ease the gorge and improve the other ladders. In 1960, at a cost of £8,000, Craighall Gorge was eased by rock blasting and for the first time fish were able to utilise the wealth of spawning and nursery areas in the Ardle and, to a lesser extent, the Shee to the full. The Ericht itself has fewer spawning areas except just above the junction with the Isla. The river system now maintains a useful stock of some 5,000 adult fish which spawn throughout the catchment. These fish are mainly summer and autumn fish, but a few spring fish are now appearing. However, poaching has proved to be a problem in the Blairgowrie area and heavier fines are needed to curtail this activity.

Angling in the summer and autumn can be quite successful on the Ericht and its tributaries. The Blairgowrie Angling Association leases waters, and permits are available at Crockhart's tackle shop in Blairgowrie.

The Almond

To the south of a line between Loch Tay and Aberfeldy run three glens. From north to south they are Glen Cochill, Glen Quaich and Glen Almond, and of the rivers flowing through these lovely glens only the Almond holds salmon. The headwaters of the Almond are tapped at Dalriech and diverted to Lednock Reservoir and from there to Loch Earn. Below Dalriech the Almond flows through the Sma' Glen, a well-known tourist spot, which has something for the historians of many eras, as there are cairns, stone circles, pictish forts, a Roman fort and signal station and one of General Wade's military roads. Below the Sma' Glen the valley widens out and lacks the grandeur of the mountains.

There are several mill weirs on the river, particularly in the lower reaches, and many of these have been eased for ascending fish. At Buchanty, situated well upstream, there is an impressive fall, known as Buchanty Spout, which always attracts visitors when fish are ascending. In recent years the North of Scotland Hydro-electric Board first eased the falls and then the Tay District Salmon Fisheries Board placed gabions some distance below them in order to raise the water level and so make the leap at the falls less formidable. A fish pass was also put in the weir at Dalriech to allow fish to reach spawning grounds at the top of the glen, but few fish have ever used it and the pass is now is disrepair. One of the main weirs to give problems on the river is Lows Weir situated a short distance downstream of Almondbank. It was built to divert water for industrial purposes into Perth lade, or mill race, and at low flows the water left in the river below the weir can be negligible. At one time the weir was almost insurmountable and although fish attempted to swim up it, few were successful except at certain flows. It was, and to some extent still is, a renowned haven for poachers, as fish can be easily gaffed out as they struggle on their long ascent of the sloping weir. Although the weir has now fallen into a state of disrepair allowing fish to ascend more easily, it could still be vastly improved for the benefit of the late running fish 'heavy in spawn'.

Although a large stock of fish now ascends the Almond they do not as a rule enter the river until late in the season. There is a certain amount of angling on the river but not until late in the year when the fish are generally 'stale'.

The Freshwater Fisheries Laboratory of the Department of Agriculture and Fisheries for Scotland, has a salmon-rearing station on the banks of the river near Almondbank. Most interesting research work is being carried out at this station where young fish of known parentage are being reared and released in the river. The return of some of the young fish as adults to the lade supplying water to the station is already providing interesting results, and of course additional stock for the Tay system.

The Earn

The Earn is the southernmost of the rivers in the Tay System, although many would have it that it is not strictly a tributary of the Tay. However, it does enter the Tay in its estuary about 7 miles downstream of Perth and should be considered a tributary, and of course it also comes under the jurisdiction of the Tay District Salmon Fisheries Board. The river originates in Loch Earn, a large loch receiving its water from numerous tributaries draining off the hills to the north and south and also the Ogle flowing down Glen Ogle at the western end of the loch and which it enters at Lochearnhead.

Mention has already been made of the hydro-electric developments on the Earn (page 53) and one of the first major tributaries to join the Earn is the Lednock which is impounded in its upper reaches as part of the Breadalbane Hydro-electric scheme and has a compensation flow below the dam. An interesting feature of the Lednock Dam is the allowance made in the design for possible earthquake shocks because of its proximity to Comrie, a centre of minor earth tremors.

Another tributary to join the Earn at Comrie is the Water of Ruchill which flows north through Glen Artney passing the sites of a Roman fort and camp shortly before entering the main river. A few miles downstream, just before Crieff, Turret Burn joins the Earn, and this stream has also been impounded as part of the Loch Turret Water Supply scheme and is now on a compensation flow. The next major tributary on the Earn is the Machany Water which comes in from the south a short distance below Kinkell Bridge. This is a good spawning stream for migratory fish but their upstream passage is blocked at the Falls of Ness. Unfortunately many of the Earn tributaries have been tapped for either hydro-electric or water supply schemes and another affected tributary is the Water of May whose upper tributaries have been diverted to Glenfarg Reservoir. The May is a good spawning tributary but since abstraction started it is said to have deteriorated. The last tributary to join the Earn in its tidal reaches is the River Farg.

As a result of the impoundment and abstraction of water, the flow in the Earn is restricted. However, the provision of compensation flows, together with water generated from Dalchonzie Power Station just west of Comrie, ensures that the river never experiences the drought conditions which occurred before these developments. A further water abstraction scheme is proposed to operate in the vicinity of Freeland Farm, 5 miles from the confluence with the

THE TAY DISTRICT

Tay estuary. This scheme will normally abstract a total of 15 million gallons per day from the river which will be pumped to Glenfarg Reservoir. The present compensation flow of 60.5 mgd existing at Freeland will remain.

The Earn is an attractive river flowing through relatively low-lying land. In its upper and middle reaches it consists of series of fast gravelly and stony runs and long gravelly pools, while in its lower reaches it tends to become more sluggish as it meanders through rich farmland in the wide lower valley from Forteviot to Ferryfield. The volume of tidal movement in the estuary is great and produces a stemback of the freshwater flow in the river which is felt as far upstream as the railway viaduct at Forgandenny.

Although some salmon enter the Earn in the spring the main run of fish occurs at the back-end of the year, in September and October. There is also a run of grilse from July and a run of big sea trout from late June. The main spawning takes place between mid-November and mid-December, and occurs in the river upstream of tidal limits and in a number of the tributary streams.

There are about 40 riparian owners of salmon fishing on the river and 6 angling clubs or associations – Auchterarder, Comrie, Crieff, Dunning, Perth and District, Thistle. Some years ago the River Earn Angling Improvement Association was established to conserve the River Earn and its tributaries for the pursuit of angling.

There are 6 main net fisheries on the lower Earn and, named from the furthest upstream, they are: Freeland, Gravel Bank, Carey, Cordon, Earnmouth and Ferryfield. Carey and Earnmouth fishings are worked by The Tay Salmon Fisheries Company Ltd.

The Eden

The Eden rises near Burnside, 3 miles south-west of Strathmiglo, to the west of the Howe of Fife and flows east and north-east, entering the long, wide estuary near Guardbridge. It is a fairly slow moving river, having little fall, and is rich in nutrients due to the high fertility of the farmland through which it flows. It has many nice runs and pools and is pleasantly wooded along some of its length. From Cupar to Prestonhall there are long flowing flats with the occasional pool, then from Prestonhall to Kemback the river consists of fast, broken water with only small pools. Downstream from Kemback to Nydie Mill the river has excellent runs and pools, and this is probably the best angling stretch on the river. A large part of the river from Nydie Mill to Bruckly is tidal and is a good beat for sea trout and finnock. Downstream from Bruckly to Eden Mouth the river is tidal, with Eden Mouth being literally at the mouth of the estuary.

A large weir just below Springfield has recently been breached thus allowing salmon to ascend to spawning grounds as far up as Dunshelt. Salmon and sea trout spawn mainly in the Eden but there are a number of good spawning tributaries including the Ceres Burn, the Ladyburn and the Fernie Burn. A large fall on the Ceres Burn about a mile upstream of its confluence with the Eden restricts the ascent of salmon beyond this point.

The Eden has had a number of pollution problems in the past, and particularly in the estuary (due to a paper mill and a laundry), but this has been cleared up. The last of the main sources of pollution are around the Springfield area, but the local authorities are going ahead with the construction of a new sewage plant, which will take the sewage effluent from Springfield and a nearby hospital and also the waste from a piggery and an abattoir.

The time of the runs of salmon and sea trout have remained fairly constant over the years, although the season is from 15 February–15 November: the salmon fishing is at its best between October and November, and sea trout from August to October. The runs are improving, especially sea trout, probably as a result of pollution control.

UDN did occur a few years ago but there is no sign of it at present.

The Eden Angling Association, which has been in existence for over 70 years, rents most of the fishing on the Eden. Some of their leases are from the Crown, and some are from riparian owners. Commercial fishing rights are in the hands of the owners who operate regularly at Kincaple and below.

There are no restrictions as to membership and daily permits are available to the public. This is probably some of the cheapest salmon and sea trout fishing in Scotland and a season membership ticket costs only £2.

8

THE NORTH ESK AND SOUTH ESK

The North Esk

The North Esk is formed from two streams flowing from the Grampian Mountains, the Waters of Mark and Lee. It is the Lee that flows through Loch Lee, a water which is renowned for its char and which has been impounded to serve as a bulk water supply to South Kincardine and Stonehaven. Below the junction of the Mark and the Lee at Invermark, the river becomes the North Esk. A short distance downstream, at Tarfside, the Water of Tarf comes in from the north. This stream and the Mark are two of the river's main spawning tributaries in Glen Esk.

For 15 miles, from Loch Lee almost to The Loups of The Burn, a series of falls a mile upstream from Edzell, the river flows over a bed of clean gravel in the magnificent open country of Glen Esk. This is a beautiful and unspoilt glen which, in August, is brilliant with the purple heather of the grouse moors and the rich orange of the rowan berries. It is an area, as one might expect, renowned for its heather honey. Much of this part of the river is fished by the Earl of Dalhousie (Invermark) and the Lord Ramsay (Millden).

About $1\frac{1}{2}$ miles upstream of The Burn, a large eighteenth century house belonging to the London House of Overseas Graduates Trust, the river flows through a deep gorge which, in its upper reaches, is incredibly peaceful and almost silent in its remoteness. It is no wonder that the large rocks which protrude from the black depths of the river in this deep precipitous gorge are called the Rocks of Solitude. A little way downstream, as it passes The Burn, the river becomes faster and more turbulent as it cascades down The Loups of The Burn. The extensive woods hereabouts were planted by Lord Adam Gordon. In 1950 the Loups were eased for ascending fish by blasting and a fish pass was installed. Fish are now able to pass on upstream when they arrive early in the spring. The fishing on the left bank of this section of the river is owned by the London House for Overseas Graduates Trust and is available to university staff and students visiting The Burn. It is a difficult section of river to fish and most fish are caught spinning, although some fish are taken on worm and shrimp. However, there are some good pools including the Pot, Coffin, Jack London's Run, Kitbog, Major and Holly Tree.

The river flows out of the gorge downstream from The Burn and runs in a series of long gravelly and stony pools through rich farmland all the way to the sea. Between the water known as The Lower Burn and the junction of the West Water come the beats of Gannochy, Arnhall, Dalladies and Edzell. The West Water joins the North Esk on the right bank at Stracathro and the confluence forms the important Junction Pool. The West Water is a most important tributary and holds a large stock of fish. It is a good spawning stream below the Falls of Saughs throughout Glen Lethnot and it also provides good angling. There are falls, or loups, too on the lower reaches of the West Water and these are surmountable to salmon, having been blasted and improved in 1947, and as much spawning occurs above the loups as below. However, both salmon and sea trout still tend to congregate below the falls during drought conditions and it is hoped to instal a fish pass in the near future. There are a number of beats on this water including Reidhall, Dunlappie, Lundie, Nathro and Hunthill.

A little below the West Water confluence a smaller stream, Cruick Water, enters on the right bank. Below the Stracathro fishings come the beats of Inglismaldie, Pert, and Balmakewan before the next important tributary enters, on the left bank, a short distance downstream of North Water Bridge. This is the Luther Water, a long tributary which drains a rich agricultural area known as the Howe of Mearns, and is an important spawning and nursery stream. Between the junctions of the Cruick and the Luther there is the well-known Boat Pool which always holds a good stock of fish. The angling on the Luther is owned by the Crown and part is let to the Laurencekirk Angling Club and includes lands of Thornton Estate, Wakefield, Pitgarvie, Luther Mains, Balmakewan, Drumnagair and Caldhame. The Luther fishes best in the autumn. Tickets can be obtained from Scott's Craft Shop in Auchenblae.

Below Balmakewan come Gallery, Hatton and Kirktonhill, Canterland and Craigo. Calderwood, in his book *The Salmon Rivers and Lochs of Scotland*, refers to Craigo Dyke and states (in 1909): 'I have no hesitation in saying that the dyke in its present form is much against the interests of the river. . . .' Fortunately the powers of conservation prevailed and an improved pass in Craigo Dyke was completed in 1949. Joseph Johnston & Son Ltd, the commercial salmon netsmen in Montrose, used to operate a net and coble fishery a short distance downstream of the dyke but this has been gradually phased out and the dyke has slowly disintegrated. Whether this has had the desired effect of improving the angling in the river or not is a matter for others to decide.

From the Marykirk railway viaduct, upstream of the A937 Laurencekirk road, to Denmouth of Morphie (2 miles downstream) on the left bank and from the viaduct to Gallery Burn (500 yards downstream) on the right bank, are the Canterland Fishings of Joseph Johnston & Son Ltd. This is some of the little public salmon fishing available on the North Esk. Up to four permits are issued on any one day. Tickets can be obtained from the office of Joseph Johnston in Montrose.

Joseph Johnston own both banks of the river from Morphie Dyke (just west of Mill of Morphie) to the sea. The company operates a net and coble fishery on this stretch but it is also a good angling beat, particularly in the early spring and autumn, with some excellent holding pools such as the Pondage and the Batts. A new fish pass was put in Morphie Dyke in 1950, but the upper proprietors, through their North Esk Improvement Association, are still continuing to find ways of improving this pass further.

Joseph Johnston issue some tickets to fish for salmon and sea trout on this lower beat and the finnock fishing is particularly good below the A92 Montrose to Aberdeen road bridge all the way to the sea.

The North Esk fishes best for salmon in the spring and autumn and most beats, certainly up as far as The Burn, catch fish in the early spring. The grilse tend to move quickly through the lower beats and few are caught in that part of the river. In recent years the commercial river catches of grilse have increased considerably and this has been well documented by Mr W.M. Shearer of the Freshwater Fisheries Laboratory, Pitlochry. The figures he gave in an article in *Salmon Net* in 1971 reveal this trend very well.

Table 5
Average percentage composition of the North Esk river catch for five-year periods, 1925–1974

Period	Percentage	
	Salmon	Grilse
1925–29	90	10
1930–34	90	10
1935–39	89	11
1940–44*	79	21
1945–49	78	22
1950–54	67	33
1955–59	74	26
1960–64	56	44
1965–69	60	40
1970–74	43	57

The North Esk District Fishery Board has carried out a number of improvements to the river over the years. Some of these have already been mentioned and include easing the loups at The Burn and West Water, installing modern fish passes on the dykes of Craigo and Morphie, demolishing disused dams, clearing up pollution and extensive planting of ova and fry. Much of the work on The Loups of The Burn was carried out with advice from the late William Malloch and actively supervised by the late Graham Smart and the late John de B. Stansfeld, the latter gentlemen being at that time the directors of the firm of Joseph Johnston. The increased catches of salmon and grilse resulting from

* Four years only, no record for 1943.

the improvements have been described by Graham Smart in an article in the first issue of *Salmon Net* in 1965.

Further ways of improving the river are always under consideration and at present an improvement to the mouth of the Luther Water is in progress, where at low water a rock shelf hinders the access of fish. The generosity of proprietors is to be applauded and half the cost of the improvement will be met by the Johnston Bequest.

The North Esk has not been without its share of man-made activities threatening to affect the stocks; these have included water abstraction from Loch Lee, pollution from a sewage works outfall and damage to redds and nursery areas from the laying of gas pipelines. However, there is no doubt that the greatest damage to salmon stocks in the North Esk, as elsewhere, lies in the illegal drift net fishing prevailing off the Scottish east coast where boats, ostensibly fishing for white fish, mackerel or dogfish, are setting drift nets designed to take salmon. Many of these boats, on being apprehended by the overworked staff of the District Fishery Boards, are endeavouring to ram the Boards' boats and imperil the lives of the bailiffs. Fortunately, the guardians of the North Esk have always been eminent men in the field of salmon fisheries and research. The river not only has its statutory District Fishery Board, to look after its interests, but also some of the staff of the Freshwater Fisheries Laboratory at Pitlochry, to monitor its adult and juvenile stocks of salmon and sea trout. Much of this work is carried out at a trapping site at Kinnaber, near Morphie Dyke, where a proportion of the smolt run is tagged. An automatic fish counter has been installed both here and at Logie. The results of this work are published annually in the report *Fisheries of Scotland* of the Department of Agriculture and Fisheries of Scotland.

The South Esk

The South Esk rises over 3,000 feet up in wild mountainous country on Cairn Bannoch in the Grampian Mountains. It is joined a short distance downstream from Glendoll Lodge by the equally large White Water, which rises in the Caenlochan National Nature Reserve, on the east and south sides of Tolmount (3,143 feet). In late October and November salmon can be seen spawning in this area, and a bird's eye-view of them can be had from the Bailey Bridge over the White Water at the foot of The Scorrie (below the Edinburgh Academy Field Centre at Blair House).

After its initial rush down the upper valley the river meanders more slowly along Glen Clova, past the Ogilvy Arms Hotel which owns the salmon fishing in the immediate vicinity. Only two streams of any consequence enter the river before it reaches Cortachy Castle, and these are Rottal Burn and the Burn of Glenmoye, the former being a spawning area for salmon and sea trout. Below

Gulla Bridge the river falls steeply with long bouldery runs and short rocky pools, although one or two pools such as the Elly and Crossbog are bigger. The latter, particularly, is a good holding pool. A short distance downstream from Cortachy, where the river passes through attractive woodlands, the Prosen Water comes in on the right bank and helps to make the South Esk a river of respectable size. The Prosen Water itself is an attractive stream with salmon ascending Glen Prosen and providing some angling.

Below the Prosen confluence the river is boulder-strewn and runs between steep wooded banks. A short distance above Shielhill Bridge the Quharity Burn enters the river on the right bank. This is a reasonably good spawning stream for sea trout and a limited number of grilse. Downstream of Shielhill Bridge the river continues to flow between steep wooded banks, followed by a gorge-like area upstream of Inshewan, which was traversed in 1975 by two British Gas Corporation pipelines. Below Inshewan the river has an uneventful journey to Brechin, being joined by the Noran Water about mid-way between Tannadice and Brechin. This stream flows out of Glenogil Reservoir down Glen Ogil and over the Falls of Drumly Harry which bar the upstream ascent of salmon and sea trout. Between Tannadice and Brechin the banks of the South Esk are tree-lined and the river tends to have a uniform flow over a gravel bed.

Just below Brechin the river receives its first serious pollution in the form of sewage effluent from Brechin sewage works. This source of pollution has been a serious problem for many years. In 1909 Calderwood referred to the Brechin sewage works and wrote '. . . for several years it has been quite inadequate; the land has become sewage sick, and the effluent to the river – which enters a large and rather still pool* – is most impure. The whole place advertises its position for a considerable radius by the objectionable odour, and no self-respecting fish would remain in the water immediately below. In low water conditions a horrible scum floats on the surface of the pool referred to, and the side of the river near the outfall is loaded with sewage fungus. Certain proposals for the improvement are now under consideration.'

Sixty-six years later the Chairman of the South Esk District Salmon Fishery Board states in his Annual Report for the year ended 31 July 1975: 'The Sewage Works Convener told your Board's representatives that he still had doubts on the perfect function of the works (i.e. the new extension works opened in early 1975 and costing around £200,000) and it is regretted that he was found right. By mid-summer 1975 the sewage condition at Brechin was little better than in previous years. The Craig Pool is no more than an open septic tank. . .' Such is progress.

Below Brechin the river flows slowly from Kinnaird to Bridge of Dun. The Kinnaird weir at the top of this stretch has a satisfactory pass to allow the easy ascent of fish. There were several other weirs on the river, but the only three remaining are those at Cortachy, Craigeassie and Aldbar, and all are easily

* Craig Pool.

surmountable by fish. The Kinnaird beat, belonging to the Earl of Southesk, is the best on the river and yields good catches, particularly in the spring. However, salmon penetrate well upstream during the spring, and fish with sea lice still on them can be caught at the upper end of the Kirriemuir Angling Association water at Gella Bridge in March and April, and even as far upstream as Clova.

A short distance downstream from Bridge of Dun the river flows into the Montrose Basin, a large area of water which floods and ebbs with the tide and leaves a vast expanse of mud at low tide. The river flows out of the Basin under the Aberdeen to Dundee road and railway bridges, and makes its way into the harbour estuary. A deeper channel has been dredged here to allow for a greater volume of shipping, as Montrose has become a supply depot for the North Sea oil industry.

The commercial fisheries are operated by Joseph Johnston & Sons, who have net and coble fisheries in the Basin and stake nets on the north shore of the estuary; and the Tay Salmon Fisheries Company Ltd, who have a net and coble fishery at two stations on the south bank of the estuary at Ferryden.

The salmon conservation work of the South Esk District Salmon Fishery Board involves the river and sea life of the salmon. In 1976 illegal drift netting for salmon off the Scottish east coast became a serious problem and an arrest was made by the Board's officers and police of a boat drift netting within the Board's coastal boundaries. On the river the Board is concerned with pollution and the stocking of suitable headwaters with fry. The problem concerning the latter is the surprising shortage of suitable spawning grounds in what would appear to be likely areas. For example, the Rottal Burn in Glen Clova has suffered a loss of gravel as a result of the straightening and dredging of the river channel to assist agricultural drainage. The remaining gravel in this burn, as in many other places in the area, is compacted and unsuitable for spawning fish. Attempts have been made to improve the situation by inserting small groynes across the burn to hold back any moving gravel. Each autumn the Superintendent to the District Board catches and strips a number of spawning fish and rears their eggs in the Clova Hatchery which can hold a quarter of a million eggs. The resulting fry are planted out in suitable streams, some of which have had their populations of brown trout and eels removed to prevent predation on the fry.

Salmon fishing on the South Esk is available to the angler on the waters of the Kirriemuir Angling Association and Ogilvy Arms Hotel. The fishing on the former can be very good at all times of the year although it does require a reasonable level of water as there are few good holding pools during periods of low water. The fishing on the Clova stretch tends to be less rewarding and worming tends to be the angling method most commonly used. Tickets for the Kirriemuir Angling Association can be obtained from the Post Office at Dykehead or J. Norrie, Kirriemuir, at £2 per day. Fishing permits can also be had from the Justinhaugh Hotel for the Justinhaugh stretch of the river, which is near Tannadice, and a limited number from Forfar Angling Club for their waters at Whitewell, adjoining Justinhaugh. The House of Dun Hotel also has available for its guests a pleasant mile-long stretch of river immediately upstream from the Bridge of Dun. A few tickets are also available from the Sports Shop in Brechin for the River Street stretch in Brechin. Holidaymakers in Montrose can get fishing permits from Montrose Angling Club for their waters downstream from the Bridge of Dun. Fishing on other stretches of the river can be obtained at times through the usual sporting agents.

The Bervie

The Bervie Water rises in the hills to the north of Drumtochty Forest and flows south east past Glenbervie and skirts to the east of the Howe of the Mearns and enters the sea at Bervie Bay close to Inverbervie.

This attractive little river is more of a sea trout water than a salmon river. The sea trout run in June and July while salmon do not enter until late August, and the peak of the run is not reached until October. There is a record of a very large salmon of 50 lb caught at the mouth of the Bervie by Provost Burnett just before the Second World War, so there is a likelihood of large fish being taken even in this small river.

The fishing on the lower mile of the river is owned by Kincardine and Deeside District Council and administered by Inverbervie Angling Association, who sell tickets to residents and visitors. The Laurencekirk and District Angling Association have the fishing in the vicinity of Glenbervie. The best of the salmon fishing is private and is centred around Arbuthnott.

9

THE ABERDEENSHIRE DEE

The Aberdeenshire Dee is known throughout the world as one of the finest salmon rivers in Scotland. It is set in the picturesque scenery of Royal Deeside which is at its best when the purple heather covers the surrounding hillsides in late summer. It has a large catchment area with many short tributary streams running into it along its entire length. The Dee is unique in that it rises on a stony plateau on the summit of Scotland's wildest mountain range, the Cairngorms, and comes welling out of a spring known as the Wells of Dee and tumbles over the rocks of a wild corrie to plunge as a small stream into the defile of the Lairig Ghru, the highest and remotest hill pass in Scotland.

The Lairig Burn and the Gharbh Choire Burn meet at the foot of Cairn Toul (4,241 feet) to form the River Dee which flows down Glen Dee between Cairn Toul and Ben MacDui (4,296 feet) and then through the eastern range of the Cairngorm Nature Reserve. Its course lies past the Forest of Mar and the Chest of Dee, where it turns due east and is joined by the Geldie Burn near the White Bridge (well-known to hill walkers); 3 miles further downstream it reaches the Linn of Dee. The Linn is a series of small falls in a very narrow rocky gorge and, although they are not by any means insurmountable, they are liable to hold fish up temporarily until the water temperature is favourable. The falls in the Linn are, in fact, the only obstacle to migratory fish on the whole of the River Dee, and from this point to the sea the fish have a completely free passage. Fish have been known to reach the Linn as early as April. However, the time they reach this point depends on the severity of the winter, the water temperature and the river flow. A good pool near the Linn is the Rock Pool. Between the Linn and Braemar, a distance of 8 miles, a number of tributaries join the Dee and these include the Lui Water and Quoich Water from the north and the Ey Burn and Clunie Water from the south, the latter entering the Dee at Braemar. Both the Lui and Quoich have falls in their lower reaches and in the case of the Quoich they are known as Linn of Quoich or Punch Bowl. A fish pass was built on the falls on the Lui but it was never a great success and had to be demolished. The Freshwater Fisheries Laboratory at Pitlochry had salmon fry traps on two tributaries of the Lui at one time, and obtained some useful results on the survival rates from the egg to the fry stage of salmon eggs planted out at the 'green' stage (i.e. newly fertilised).

Downstream from Braemar the Dee flows through a pleasantly wooded valley and the stretch between Braemar and Crathie is probably the loveliest part of Deeside. A short distance below Braemar there is Invercauld House on the left bank, in a very attractive setting, then there is the old Invercauld Bridge and Bridge of Dee, but the finest sight of all is Balmoral Castle, on the right hand bend of the river just upstream of Crathie, where the Royal family spend their summer holidays and where Her Majesty the Queen Mother, a keen salmon angler, has always loved to fish.

There are two tributaries which join the Dee near Crathie, both on the right bank. The first is the Gelder Burn, which comes in above Crathie, and the other is the Girnock Burn, which enters a few miles downstream. The Girnock is of particular interest, as the Freshwater Fisheries Laboratory has a series of traps on the stream and its small tributaries to monitor the movements of juvenile and adult salmon. This is in order to relate the size of the adult run in any year to the subsequent production of smolts from the egg production of that run.

Just before the river reaches Ballater two large tributaries join the Dee, the River Gairn from the north and the Muick (pronounced Mick) from the south. The Gairn is a large tributary with excellent spawning grounds and the fish press well up into the side tributaries in the autumn. The Muick flows out of Loch Muick and though the river is a spawning tributary for salmon and some sea trout, the falls at the Linn of Muick are rather difficult to negotiate.

The section of the river dealt with so far has some famous angling beats along its course among which are Invercauld, Balmoral, Abergeldie and Birkhall. Between Ballater and Aboyne the Dee flows quietly but swiftly through many fine pools all of which afford good angling both with fly and, early in the year, spinner. Probably the most famous 'cast' is the Douchels near Ballater. The main beats in this stretch are Cambus o' May, Glen Tanar and Birse Castle. Both Aboyne and Dinnet are favourite haunts of ardent anglers who fill the many hotels in these two towns, and Ballater, much earlier in the year than any holidaymakers would dare to venture forth to enjoy the scenery for which Deeside is famous. Three tributaries join the river in this stretch, the Water of Tanar and the Burn of Birse enter from the south and Tarland Burn, which flows through Aboyne and joins the left bank of the river. Water from lochs Davan and Kinord flows into the river near Dinnet, but the stream flowing from these lochs is of no value for spawning.

The river between Ballater and Banchory is splendid angling water with many famous beats and among these are Carlogie, Ballogie, Dess, Woodend, Inchmarle, Blackhall and Cairnton, the latter being by far the most famous. There are some fine salmon 'casts' on these beats including Bridge, Greenbanks, Clay, Calm and Mill pools.

Two streams join the Dee just before Banchory and both tend to be predominantly sea trout spawning tributaries, although some salmon and grilse do ascend them. They are the Burn of Cattie which comes in on the right bank and the Burn of Canny which joins the Dee at Invercannie where water is abstracted for Aberdeen. Some big sea trout enter the Canny in the autumn.

Opposite Banchory the Water of Feugh joins the Dee. This is one of the largest tributaries and has two sizeable tributaries of its own, the Water of Aven and the Water of Dye. Although salmon and grilse run up these waters for spawning the Feugh is a particularly good sea trout stream. The Falls of Feugh, a short distance upstream of the river's confluence with the Dee, are a famous tourist attraction, and thousands of visitors to Deeside visit this picturesque cascade of water to watch the salmon and sea trout fighting their way through the turbulent waters. Some attempts have been made to ease the falls for ascending fish but they still tend to delay the ascent of fish in the early part of the year when water temperatures are low. Downstream from Banchory the last spawning tributary of any consequence, the Sheeoch Burn, enters the river on the right bank, at Kirkton of Durris. In 1975 its spawning beds were badly affected by the North Sea gas pipeline construction work.

The final 20 miles of river from Banchory to Aberdeen, where the river discharges into the sea beside the harbour, has some excellent pools. There are many good beats in this section and among the best known are Crathes, Park and Drum on the left bank and Durris, Tilbouries and Altries on the right. These beats have an excellent reputation, particularly during the early months of the year when the spring fish pause in the face of the snow bree coming downstream from the high mountain tops. The last 7 miles of this stretch is not such good angling water as the higher part, but its serenity, as it wends its way through what is by now a far more populated area, is still graced by tree-lined banks and parkland right up to the point where it enters Aberdeen.

There is good spawning throughout the main river from above the Linn of Dee almost to Aberdeen. As has been mentioned there are many excellent tributaries joining the river throughout its length. In the upper part of the river system the best are the Lui, Quoich and Ey and it is chiefly salmon that spawn in this area. Between Braemar and Ballater the Gairn, Girnock and Muick are good spawning streams but the Gairn is the best of the three as it has a number of good tributaries such as Morven Burn and Glenfenzie Burn (known locally as 'Fingie' Burn). It is mainly salmon that use these waters although a few sea trout also use them. Downstream from Ballater the tributaries are used chiefly by grilse and sea trout, although the Tarland Burn and Water of Tanar are exceptions and tend to be predominantly salmon spawning areas.

The Dee District Salmon Fishery Board run a hatchery at Dinnet with a capacity for about one million eggs. The upkeep for this is paid for by the Aberdeen Harbour Board. In most years about half the eggs are planted out at the eyed stage and half as unfed fry, mainly into the tributaries where it is felt that the stock of naturally produced young fish is low. Prior to the present hatchery at Dinnet there was one at Drum, but this was closed in 1914.

The Dee is famous throughout the world as an angling river. The river opens to salmon angling on 1 February and by this time a large stock of fish, many of which have entered the river in December and January, has accumulated in the river. Catches of 20 or more fish per beat on the opening day are not uncommon. In recent years, due to mild winters, the spring fish have been distributed over a much longer section of river on the opening day. It is the common belief that there have been fewer spring fish in the Dee in the last ten years, but in 1977 many beats had a much better spring season than they had had for some years, even though the winter was much more severe than many recent ones. Summer and autumn fishing is spread over the whole length of the river and from late April onwards beats downstream of Braemar can have excellent catches. The famous autumn run of the old days, however, shows no sign of returning and the Dee closes on 30 September. The average weight of salmon is in the region of 9 lb, but a few heavy fish up to and over 30 lb can be caught throughout the year. The Dee does not seem to have the large runs of grilse which some of the neighbouring rivers have had in recent years. Sea trout stocks seem to be increasing again after being decimated in the early years of the UDN epidemic.

In the opening months of the season spinning is the method of fishing most commonly adopted. The river at this time is normally high and water temperature is low, with the result that fish are lying deep. In hard frosty weather it is not unusual to lose a few days because of floating ice, commonly known as 'grue', which makes even spinning impossible. After the winter snows have melted, many anglers turn to greased line fishing which, in the clear water common on the Dee, is not only very effective but is also a real art to fish properly. There is a gentleman's agreement that fly only should be used after 15 April but nowadays this agreement is not strictly adhered to. However, some proprietors owning beats such as Cairnton, Invercauld and Park are extremely strict about this rule.

The rod catch on the Dee declined rapidly from 1964 to 1971 and did not show a marked recovery until 1978 when the numbers of fish taken approached the level of the 1963 catch.

Table 6

Rod catches on the Dee, 1963–1978 (the figures are approximate)

Year	Catch	Year	Catch	Year	Catch
1963	13,008	1969	5,843	1975	7,215
1964	10,666	1970	5,245	1976	6,214
1965	9,263	1971	5,144	1977	7,805
1966	9,509	1972	7,712	1978	11,123
1967	7,995	1973	5,592		
1968	6,744	1974	4,988		

The record fish of 52 lb, an autumn fish, was taken from the Park Beat in October 1917. Several fish of over 40 lb have been taken in the spring since the 1950s and these include one of 47 lb, 43 lb and 42 lb.

The Dee has been one of the rivers that has suffered badly from UDN. It was first seen on 12 February, 1968. Outbreaks of the disease have occurred both early in the season and throughout the year and consequently during periods of very low and very high water temperatures. The rivers north of the Dee have few bad outbreaks in the early months of the year and seem to get their worst outbreaks in May and June and then again in the early autumn. In 1969 it was thought that a considerable proportion of the spawning stock was lost. The years 1970 and 1971 were also very bad and from April 1972 to February 1973, 9,700 diseased fish were buried. From the records of disease in 1977 it would seem that the disease is at last on the wane.

Probably the most important single factor in making this river into such a successful salmon fishery was the foundation of the Dee Salmon Fishing Improvement Association. This was formed by the Marquis of Huntly in 1872 with the aim of improving the rod fishing on the Dee by renting net fishings below Banchory and removing the nets. At that time there were some 16 net stations between Banchory and Bridge of Dee. There was also netting in the tidal waters at the Pot and Ford stations and the harbour, and also along the coast with fixed engines. The Association was almost wound-up in 1887 due to lack of finance, but at a general meeting of proprietors that year a method was adopted to finance the Association whereby proprietors were rated according to the rental or annual value of their fishings. Since that time the voluntary assessment on members of the Association has varied from as high as 12% to as low as 1% in 1961. Over the years the Association has succeeded in achieving its object of stabilising netting on the Dee. The Pot and Ford stations ceased netting in 1968 and the river stations up as far as Banchory were closed many years ago. The harbour nets and coastal nets are all that now remain. The Association continue to exercise their vigilance on all matters concerning the river. Along with the Dee District Salmon Fishery Board they have kept a careful watch on proposed water abstraction schemes and both organisations have helped to promote works to aid the ascent of fish where barriers were hindering their upstream movement.

The river and some of its tributaries contribute to the Grampian Region's water supply for Aberdeen and the rural area. This means that at times of low water flow a substantial amount of the dry weather flow is abstracted from the river. The main abstraction takes place at Invercannie on the Cairnton beat above Banchory, where approximately 15 mgd is taken into supply daily. In low water conditions, beats below this abstraction point are affected by the loss of this part of the river flow.

The Aberdeen Harbour Board, who owns the harbour and the netting station in the harbour area of the river and some of the coastal nets in Aberdeen Bay, supports the Dee District Salmon Fishery Board, the Dee Salmon Fishing Improvement Association, the Association of Scottish District Salmon Fishery Boards and the Atlantic Salmon Research Trust in every way possible. Not only has the Board agreed to a 48 hour weekly close time but it has also helped to finance other vital conservation policies such as the running of the hatchery. In this river, as in many others, the owners of net fisheries play a large part in helping to improve the fishings and play an important integral part in fishery management. It is unfortunate that many members of the angling fraternity, who so often blame the legal netsmen for any reverse a river system may suffer, do not take the trouble to find out what an important part these people play in safeguarding stocks of fish in our rivers.

There is little pollution in the River Dee and any pollution which does exist, such as the sewage effluent near Victoria Bridge in Aberdeen, is likely to be controlled in the near future. The work of the North-East River Purification Board covers the monitoring of water quality of the rivers within its area and any unsatisfactory results are quickly investigated.

Much of the salmon fishing on the River Dee is private but some estates let their fishings at certain times of the year and notice of lets can be obtained from sporting agents, from daily newspapers such as *The Scotsman* or *Glasgow Herald* or from sporting journals such as the *Field* or *Scottish Field*. A number of hotels along Deeside have arrangements with estates for hotel guests to fish and these include the Invercauld Arms Hotel in Braemar and the Banchory Lodge Hotel in Banchory. Permits can also be obtained from Mar Lodge in Braemar and the Glentanar Estate Office in Aboyne. There are also a number of angling clubs and associations around Aberdeen which sell tickets for sea trout fishing on the tidal waters.

A delightful little book on the life of a salmon journeying up the River Dee was written by W. Murdoch many years ago and is well worth reading if it can be found. It is called *More Light on the Salmon* – (What a Dee Salmon Sees, Hears and Does on its Journey from the Grey North Sea to the Mountain Pool in the Cairngorms). It was published by *The Fishing News* in Aberdeen.

There are two maps depicting the pools on the Dee, one by Maude Parker, produced in 1931, and one published recently by the Waverley Press (Aberdeen) Ltd.

The Cowie

The Cowie Water is a small salmon river to the south of the Dee and lying in the Dee District. It rises in the Well of Monluth close to the headwaters of the Sheeoch Burn, a tributary of the Dee, and flows east through Fetteresso Forest to enter the North Sea at Stonehaven. The Cowie is joined by two major tributaries from the north, namely the Cowton Burn and Burn of Monboys. Another small river which also discharges into Stonehaven Bay, but a little to the south, is the Carron Water.

The Cowie is mainly a sea trout river, with fish coming in from June onwards. Salmon enter much later and, as on the Bervie, the autumn months are best for salmon fishing. There are some excellent holding pools on the river and in times of high water fishing can be very good.

Sweep nets are operated in the mouth of the river at Bridge of Cowie.

At one time the Carron Water was inaccessible to migratory fish due to the presence of an insurmountable weir which was built across the river in Stonehaven. However, large floods in 1977 breached the weir and on being rebuilt a fish pass was incorporated. It is reported that both salmon and sea trout have since ascended the river.

The fishing on part of the Cowie is in the hands of the Stonehaven and District Angling Association from whom day tickets can be obtained.

River Dee

Invercauld Water — Inver Burn, Clachanan, Cairnaquheen, Weaver, Upper Boat Pool, Geordie Mitchell, Clerach, Laundry Pool, Polmonier, Crathie Burn, Skolpach, BALMORAL CASTLE, Balmoral Bridge, Manse Pool, Suspension Bridge, Gelder Burn, Polslake

Lower Invercauld Water — Jock Robertson, Clachanturn, Fir Park, CRATHIE, Telegraph, Cradle, Little Ann, Ann-Foul, Red Brae, Pol Mahalmicle, Dalradaie, Big Broch Roy, Little Broch Roy, Geddie Burn, Foot Bridge, Corbie's Haugh, Coynach, Polslake, Craigens, John Brown, Duchalls, Bog's Well, Girnock Burn, Jock's Cast, Little Shenval, Shenval, Polhollick or Boat Pool, Newton, Balgairn, Streams of Gairn, Foot Bridge, Little Polveir, Polveir, Red Brae, Ministers Pool, River...

Balmoral Water

Abergeldie Water — Larch Tree, Boat Pool, Birkhall Water, Glebe Water

Ballogie Water — Sands, Midhole, Slip, Rail End, Big Flat, Potarch Bridge, Burn of Ang..., Upper Inchbare, Lower Inchbare, Strath, Priest's Hole, Corner, Kelpie, Bulwark, Hackle

N

kilometres 0 1 2 3 4 5
miles 0 1 2 3

10

THE DON

The Don rises in the Grampian Mountains above Cock Bridge which lies at the foot of the infamous Lecht Road which runs between Cock Bridge and Tomintoul and is usually the first road to become blocked by the early winter snows. The upper half of the river's course, from Cock Bridge to Alford, is carved out through steep and often well-wooded hills and has the appearance of a Highland river. In this section, running through Strathdon, it is joined by a number of tributaries draining off the Ladder Hills including Ernan Water, Water of Nochty and Water of Buchat. A few miles below Alford the country changes to a gentler and flatter landscape, and by the time Inverurie is reached the river winds through meadow land with earthy banks. At Kintore, and for several miles further on, the Don is rather like an English lowland river; the margins of the river are weedy and sedge-clad islands occur here and there. At times old river channels are passed, where bends and loops of the river have been cut off as oxbows. Within a few miles of the river mouth, below Dyce, the banks again become steeper, and the river passes through beech woods, while rocky and bouldery runs alternate with pools. Before the old Brig o' Balgownie is reached, near Old Aberdeen, the river becomes much contracted, deep and still and some of the pools between the Brig o' Balgownie and the Bridge of Don are up to thirty feet deep. A short distance below the Bridge of Don the river breaks through banks of sand and enters the sea.

There are about a dozen dykes along the course of the river but most of them have a gently sloping downstream face and are no obstacle to fish. However, one dyke, known as Whyte's Dyke, at the top of the tidal reach and just above Devil's Rock Pool, is a hindrance to fish. The dyke diverts water to two lades, the one on the north bank takes water to Kettock's Mill, while the one on the south is no longer used. It has two narrow fish passes built into it and, due to their narrow width, it is very easy for poachers to put in cage traps during the hours of darkness and many fish are caught in this way. A short distance upstream from Whyte's Dyke the 450-year-old Cruives have been recently breached, with the central part of the structure being removed with the help of the army. This has made a vast improvement to the ascent of fish.

Because of the severe depletion of fish stocks in the river over the past few years as a result of industrial pollution, it has been difficult to ascertain the pattern of runs. Roughly speaking, there is generally an early run from December to April and a late run from September to the end of October. Since

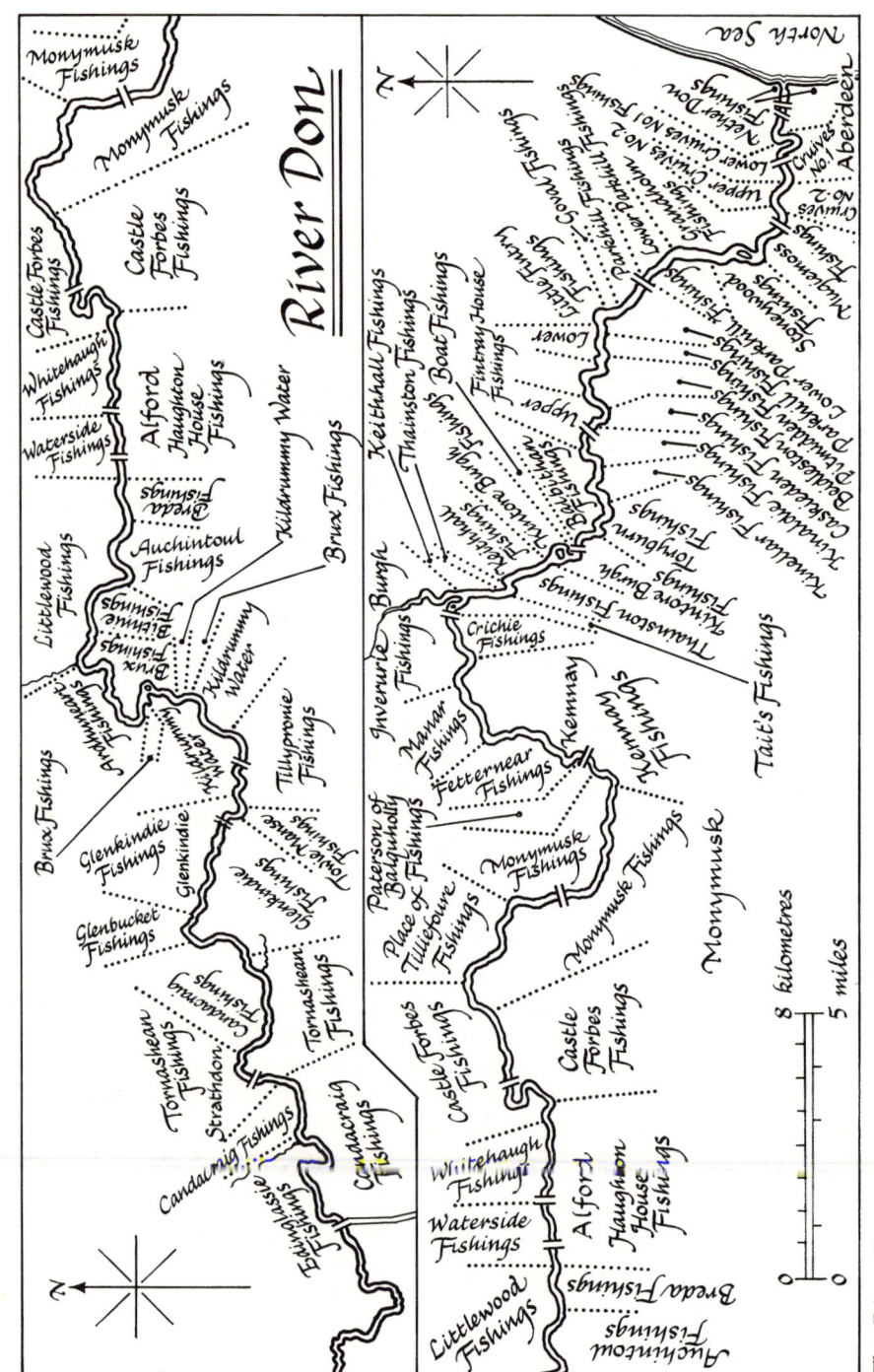

The River Don

1977, as a direct result of the reduction in pollution and the prevailing high river flows, fish have entered the river in considerable numbers from the beginning of the year and runs have been continuous, occurring whenever the river rose following rain.

In recent years the main source of pollution has been from paper mills in the vicinity of Stoneywood. Other forms of pollution fouled the river less than ten years ago, but these have been either diverted into a trunk sewer discharging into the sea, or accepted by the Persley sewage works. Due to the combined efforts of the Don District Salmon Fishery Board, the North-East River Purification Board, the Scottish River Purification Advisory Committee and, more recently, the polluters themselves, the pollution from pulp effluent is becoming less.

There is considerable poaching activity on the Don and the Superintendent to the Don District Salmon Fishery Board and his bailiffs have to be constantly on the alert. Poachers have used sniggers, various types of nets, cyanide and cages wedged in the fish passes of the dykes and weirs in the lower reaches of the river. Seals, too, have been a problem and a number of seals have been seen in the estuarial waters and lower reaches of the river in the last two or three years and one was recorded as far upstream as Fintray, eight miles from the estuary. Attempts to remove them have, for the most part, been unsuccessful.

UDN is no longer a major problem in the Don and, according to reports, no more than 5% of the salmon in the river are affected.

The Don District Salmon Fishery Board operates a hatchery at Mill of Newe, Strathdon, with a capacity of approximately a million eggs. Adult fish are caught and impounded by Fishery Board staff during October and the hatchery is usually stocked with about 750,000 eggs. Fry are introduced into five burns in the headwaters of the river during the period from late April to the end of May.

The rod fishings in the river comprise 63 separate beats ranging in rateable value from £800 in the lower reaches to £10 for several small beats in the upper reaches. Among the larger beats are: Castle Forbes and Monymusk, Kemnay, Balbithan Island (owned by Gordon District Council), Manar at Inverurie, Don and Ury (owned by Gordon District Council), Kintore (owned by the Crown Estate), Fintray, Parkhill at Dyce (owned by Aberdeen and District Angling Association), Waterton at Newhills, Persley and Grandholm. All these beats, and many others, have excellent fishing pools.

A number of proprietors of salmon fishings on the Don make fishing available to the public either on a day ticket basis or simply by giving permission to individuals who approach them. Some hotels with their own beats also issue day tickets and members of the Aberdeen and District Angling Association are entitled to fish on beats at Inverurie, Kemnay and Kintore owned by the Association. Starting at the top end of the river the following fishings are available on a day or weekly rental: Edinglassie and Candacraig (through the Colquhonnie Hotel, Strathdon); Kildrummy Water (Glenkindie

Arms Hotel, Glenkindie); Kildrummy Water; Haughton House Fishings (Haughton Arms Hotel, Alford and Forbes Arms Hotel, Bridge of Alford – residents only); Castle Forbes Fishings (Secretary, Forbes Estate Management Co., Alford); Monymusk Fishings (Grant Arms Hotel, Monymusk); Kemnay Fishings (Kemnay House, Kemnay); Manar Fishings (tickets from E.J. Duncan, 4 West High Street, Inverurie); Inverurie Fishings (Inverurie Angling Association, tickets from E.J. Duncan); Kintore Burgh Fishings (tickets from Kintore Arms Hotel or Post Office, Kintore); Upper and Lower Fintray Fishings to Upper Parkhill (Aberdeen and District Angling Association – tickets from J. Somers & Son, Thistle Street, Aberdeen), and Grandholm Fishing (J.D. Paton, Grandholm, Persley, Aberdeen).

It should be remembered that the Don is also an excellent brown trout river and some superb brown trout can be caught throughout the length of the river. They come well to the dry fly.

There are 3 major commercial netting firms, one of which, the Aberdeen Salmon Company Limited, represents 9 individual proprietors. Fishing is carried out along the coast with stake and bag nets.

11

THE YTHAN AND UGIE

Ythan

The catchment of this north-east coast river lies in between the Ugie catchment to the north, the Don catchment to the south and the Deveron catchment to the west. It drains an undulating area of marginal arable land and richer farmland in this part of Aberdeenshire. Its sources are the Wells of Ythan and a series of springs situated around 800 feet, to the east of Huntly. It flows fairly quickly in a north-easterly direction down the glen to Auchterless before turning sharply south-east as it continues its passage through an undulating wood-studded stretch past the village of Fyvie, then in an easterly direction as it winds and twists its way through a steep valley past the ruins of Gight Castle. It flows into a flatter area near the village of Methlick before passing Haddo House, on the right bank, surrounded by richly wooded countryside. Turning once again in a more south-easterly direction the river flows past the town of Ellon and, a short distance downstream at Kirkton of Logie Buchan, enters a long estuary some 4 miles in length. It then flows over a sandy bar at Newburgh and discharges its waters into the North Sea some 15 miles north of Aberdeen.

This small river winds and twists its way through this lush rolling arable countryside for a distance of approximately 40 miles, picking up many feeder tributaries from the hilly ground on either bank. The most important of these are the Little Water, rising to the north of the Ythan on the Hill of Corsegight and entering the Ythan on its left bank upstream from Methlick and the Ebrie Burn, draining the catchment to the north of the Ythan and joining the river on its left bank some distance upstream of Ellon.

The Ythan is a useful angling river; its best months for angling are July – October, but the earliest salmon are taken in March and from that month to the end of the season many anglers enjoy good sport. The river seems to fish best in the autumn and the month of October accounts for a large number of fish killed in the present era. Salmon average around 12 lb and the few grilse which are caught around 4 lb. The Ythan is probably best known by many anglers for its sea trout fishing. This starts in May in the estuary and many trout are caught not only in the main river and tributaries but also in the large expanse of estuary above Newburgh, where many boats can be seen daily fishing this stretch of water in the summer months. The sea trout average 2 lb in weight, though many finnock and larger sea trout, up to 10 lb, are caught annually. Finnock provide excellent sport in the upper reaches during the early part of the season, February – April. In recent years, however, sea trout stocks have shown a definite decline, as in other areas of Scotland. This could have been caused by damage to stocks as a result of the disease known as UDN or, as some people believe, damage caused by the dumping of industrial waste on their feeding grounds at sea. It is to be hoped that this decline is only temporary as this sporting species provides good angling. The trend at the present time is for runs of salmon to tend to get later, which is common to most rivers in Scotland. However, 1978 has shown definite signs of a better spring run on some east coast rivers, but this is not noticeable yet on the Ythan. The autumn run still appears to be the strongest in this river.

There are three strong angling associations on the Ythan, namely the Fyvie, Newburgh and Aberdeen Angling Associations, the latter having a large annual membership. Other sections of the river are also open to the public on a daily or weekly permit basis. Many summer visitors to the area can enjoy good angling at reasonable cost. Angling tenants normally stay at either the Udny Arms Hotel, Newburgh or Ythan Arms Hotel, Methlick.

There are many useful angling pools on the river, amongst the best are the Machar pools. All the pools on the river are natural and, probably because of the stability of the banks, few if any man-made pools are to be found.

The river and its many tributaries have an adequate supply of spawning and feeding areas. Probably the best tributaries with these facilities are the Little Water and Ebrie and Fordoun burns, all of which can accommodate a large population of spawning fish. Sea trout also populate the smaller burns flowing into the main river, of which there are a considerable number. The Ythan and its feeder burns have rich feeding areas owing to the nature of ground which this catchment drains. Weed growth in the river is now becoming a problem, especially in dry seasons such as 1976 when large banks of weed were to be found downstream of the village of Methlick. There is little doubt that the lime and artificial fertilisers which run off the arable land bordering the river tend to encourage this growth.

The main owners of the Ythan include The Crown, Esslemont Estate, Ellon Castle, Kinharrachie Estate, Haddo House Estate, Schivas Estate and Udny Estate. Many of these estates make part of their waters available to the public on a permit basis or let angling associations have access to their fishings.

The Ythan is mainly a spring-fed river and, having no loch of any significance on its catchment, is essentially a spate river. It rises and falls particularly quickly as most of its catchment is well drained.

Netting is an important part of the Ythan fishing. Sweep net stations are operated in the estuary and bag net and stake nets are fished on the adjoining coast line of the Ythan District. These have always been important net fisheries and are mentioned by both Grimble and Calderwood.

A great deal of work is done on the ecology and birds of Ythan estuary by

Aberdeen University staff at their field station at Newburgh, and a visit to this station is well worthwhile.

The Ugie

The Ugie rises in the north-east corner of Aberdeenshire and drains a mixture of peat bog land, marginal arable and rich arable land. It is a picturesque little river running through a countryside studded with farms and woodlands, with the rich green foliage of the trees, pastures and arable cropped fields revealing many changes of colour throughout the seasons of the year and contrasting with the clear rippling waters of the Ugie.

The Ugie has two main branches the North Ugie Water and South Ugie Water. The former rises in the upland area around the townships and villages of New Pitsligo, Craigmaud and Ladysford. Its many feeder tributaries drain the peatland and hilly arable land of this upper catchment area before joining together and flowing south-east through the township of Strichen to the confluence with the South Ugie near Torterston village.

The South Ugie rises in the countryside just west of the township of Maud. Its many feeders join together near the town and the river flows east towards its confluence with the North Ugie. This branch of the river drains mainly arable land and the consequently well drained countryside causes the river to rise and fall more quickly than its neighbour. It is on the headwaters of the South Ugie that the Fedderate Reservoir, which supplies Fraserburgh's water, lies. The South Ugie is mainly slow flowing with little fall between Maud and the junction with the North Ugie, and consequently during the recent dry summers weed growth has proved a problem. In places this growth has covered the entire width of the river causing havoc to anglers trying to fish.

From the confluence of these two branches to the sea, the Ugie follows a very winding sluggish course in an easterly direction to discharge its waters into the sea at Peterhead.

The Ugie is a useful little river for angling and has a modest salmon and grilse run and a strong run of sea trout. The season begins in June and runs on into October with the best months being July – September. The first fish are normally killed in June. The largest and most significant fishing on the Ugie is Pitfour fishing whose average annual catch in recent years has been 70 salmon, 85 grilse, 800 sea trout and 750 finnock. Sea trout average $1\frac{1}{2} - 2$ lb, but larger fish are caught occasionally. The best pools on the river are Flats, Scotts Pool, Pot Sunken, Meadows and Cruives Pot. The latter is the only man-made pool amongst these.

There is a strong angling association on the river, called the Ugie Angling Association, which has an approximate annual membership of 300 anglers. Day and weekly permits are also available for holiday makers staying in the neighbourhood. There are good spawning and feeding areas for salmon and sea trout in the many small tributaries, sections of the main river and its two branches. Amongst the best tributaries are the Cairngall Burn rising at Lenabo, Gonar Burn at New Pitsligo and Water of Fedderate at Maud. The river is essentially a spate river with no lochs of any significance on its catchment. There are, however, the Fedderate Reservoir and two smaller man-made lakes at Brucklay and Pitfour on its catchment.

Due to intensive agricultural drainage the river now rises and falls more quickly than it used to; this has resulted in a narrowing of the bed and a tendency for the river to flood more easily as a result. Weed growth is also a serious problem especially in dry summers and there is little doubt this is strengthened by the fertiliser washed off the arable land bordering the river. Many pools are so badly affected by this growth that fishing is impossible when it is at its worst.

Netting is exercised in the estuary by sweep net and on the coast by stake and bag net. Illegal netting off-shore has also escalated in recent years and there is little doubt this has had a very marked influence on the stock of fish entering the river.

UDN has been prevalent in the river since the late 1960s and, although outbreaks are now not so numerous, there is little doubt that this disease had an effect on sea trout stocks in the early 1970s. However, as in most other east coast rivers, the run of sea trout is once again improving.

In recent years with the oil and gas finds in the North Sea, the river has been traversed by no less than 4 gas pipelines from St Fergus, with a likelihood of more to follow in the future. As far as one can see, the effect of these pipeline crossings on the river has only been minimal and the disturbance only temporary.

Water is abstracted from the river Ugie, both for the Fraserburgh supply (from the Fedderate Reservoir on its headwaters) and for the Peterhead supply (by means of pump abstraction from the river just above Balmoor Bridge). Incorporated in this scheme is not only a low barrage and fish pass, but also a method of pump recirculation which brings the tide back to serve the fish pass in times of low water flow.

There have been no abnormally high floods in recent years and thus no damage due to flooding. No improvements to pools or banks have been undertaken lately.

No hatchery is sited on the river, but restocking with fry is carried out periodically when stocks in certain burns show a decline.

12

THE DEVERON

The Deveron rises in the hill of west Aberdeenshire in the remote area known as the Cabrach, and flows north before being joined on its left bank by the Black Water. It then swings in a north-easterly then easterly direction as it flows on its 17 mile journey down Strathglass to the town of Huntly. This first part of its journey is through a countryside of fields and woodlands and the river consists of fast gravelly runs, rocky cascades and deep pools. As it passes the town of Huntly it is joined on its right bank by the River Bogie, a long and useful tributary carrying the waters draining off the hills of Strath Bogie. The next section, some 22 miles in length, is to the town of Turriff and the river flows through chiefly arable land. Not far below the confluence with the Bogie another major tributary, the Isla, enters on the left bank. This is a long tributary which flows through the town of Keith and drains the surrounding hills. At Turriff the Idoch Water flows in on the right bank. The last section from Turriff to Banff is over a distance of about 11 miles and is in an area of mellow countryside of fields and woodlands and the river is more slow moving with long deep pools and gravelly fords. The only significant tributary in this stretch is the King Edward Burn. The river flows into the sea at Banff over an ever-moving bar of gravel whose presence frequently alters the river channel.

The Deveron has a very high reputation as an angling river and has a long season extending from 11 February to 31 October. It not only has runs of spring, summer and autumn salmon but also a good run of grilse and a very good run of sea trout. The Deveron is essentially a spate river, having no lochs of any significance on its system, and it is largely dependent on rainfall to bring fish into the river after the winter snows on the hills have melted.

The river has only one significant barrier to hold fish back for any length of time and this is the dyke on the Coniecleugh beat some distance below Huntly. It is only likely to hold fish up for any length of time when water temperatures are low.

The beats on the Deveron, starting from the furthest upstream, are as follows: Cabrach Lodge, Glenfiddich Lodge, Lesmurdie, Beldorney, Edinglassie, Invermarkie, Huntly Angling Association, Huntly Lodge, Castle Hotel, Corniehaugh, Avochie, Woodside and Inverisla, Coniecleugh, Rothiemay Castle, Upper Mayen, Mayen House, Redhill, Garronhaugh, Glennie, Turtory, Ardmeallie, Church Water, Boat of Turtory, Marnach Lodge, Euchrie, Inverkeithny, Netherdale Upper, Church Water, Netherdale Lower, Drach

Law, Laithers, Ardmiddle, Carnousie, Muiresk, Turriff Angling Association, Forglen, Mountblairy, Dunlugas, Scatterty, Eden, Inverichnie, Montcoffer, The Wrack, Banff and MacDuff Angling Association.

Probably the best spring beats are Corniehaugh and Coniecleugh, mainly because many fish enter the river before the season opens. The tendency is for the early fish to run through the lower beats but the dyke at Coniecleugh holds them up if the water temperature is low. Other beats with a good reputation are Glennie, Laithers, Forglen, Mountblairy, Dunlugas, Scatterty, Inverichnie, Montcoffer and The Wrack.

The trend in recent years is for the runs to get later in the season, with summer and autumn runs predominating. However, if there is plenty of water in the spring there is usually a good run of fish. Salmon average 9–10 lb, grilse 6 lb and sea trout just under 3 lb. The average annual rod catch over the last ten years has been just over 2,000 salmon and grilse and just under 2,000 sea trout. Two very large salmon have been taken from the Deveron, one of 61 lb caught by Mrs Morrison in 1924 and one of 56 lb taken by Col H.E. Scott in 1920.

The Bogie is a very useful sea trout tributary and a few salmon are also taken. However, the Isla is not very productive for the rods and only a few fish are caught each year.

Night fishing for sea trout is a very popular sport and is practised over a wide area of the river system although, on the main river above Huntly, not so many sea trout are caught. It is the bottom beats just above Banff which are famed for their sea trout and though fish of up to 15 lb can be taken, fish of 6–10 lb are fairly common. Salmon of over 40 lb used to be taken nearly every year but in recent years the largest reported was one of 36 lb.

The Deveron system has a wealth of excellent spawning and nursery areas both in the main river and in some of the tributaries. Spring fish spawn high up the river, and the Cabrach area and Black Water produce a redd count of 1,000 each year. The River Bogie, and the Forgue, the Idoch Water and King Edward Burn accommodate a large proportion of the sea trout spawning population. The Isla, however, is disappointing as a spawning tributary, mainly because of difficult access in one or two places around the town of Keith, and also because the spawning gravel is inclined to be hard to work as it is compacted in many areas. The District Fishery Board, however, are making efforts to ease the bad access and improve the Isla generally as a spawning tributary.

No hatchery is operated on the Deveron and there has been no artificial stocking.

UDN first appeared in the river in 1967 and was extremely bad that autumn. Although there have been bad outbreaks from time to time since then, it now seems to be abating, and over the last two or three years has lessened considerably.

Several large spates have occurred in recent years, the worst being in July

1958, September 1965, March 1968 and August 1970. These caused a certain amount of bank erosion with consequent movement of gravel, but the general character of the river remained unchanged. Weed growth, particularly water buttercup, is proving to be very troublesome in dry summers. The large increase in the use of artificial fertilisers on neighbouring farmland is probably part of the cause. In some areas weed cutting on the shallower fords is necessary to allow free access to ascending fish.

Water is abstracted from the river at Turriff as part of the Grampian Regional Council's water supply scheme. Water is pumped from the river through gravel bed intakes. Although few river systems can afford to lose any water during drought conditions, this scheme is infinitely preferable to a scheme previously proposed which involved impounding the headwaters in the Cabrach area, and to which objection was raised in the 1960s by the Deveron District Salmon Fishery Board. The Cabrach scheme would have meant the loss of a significant amount of spawning and nursery ground with the formation of a reservoir, and the dam would have prevented free access for migratory fish. The flow in the river could have been curtailed for long periods, thereby affecting angling over the entire length of the river. The present scheme has not affected the spawning areas, and the main river down to Turriff remains unaffected.

The main angling associations on the river system are at Huntly, Turriff and Banff and visitors and locals alike can enjoy excellent salmon and sea trout fishing under the control of these associations. A number of hotel waters are also available to visitors. The sea trout fishing is very popular and many good catches can be had on these waters.

No sweep netting takes place at the mouth of the river but there are fixed engines along the coast and on either side of the river mouth. These constitute an important netting industry. The right to net salmon at the mouth of the Deveron was purchased from the Duke of Fife in 1907 by the riparian owners.

13

THE SPEY

The Spey has the second largest catchment in Scotland, much of which consists of the Grampian, Cairngorm, Monadhliath and Badenoch mountain ranges. These provide, nearly all year round, a plentiful supply of clear, cold water as the winter's accumulation of snow melts slowly in the warmth of the spring and summer days. Many of the corries high up on the steep mountain slopes are packed with snow at the end of winter, as a result of many days and nights of drifting, and it is not unusual to see the snow still lying on the ridges and in the deep gullies well on into June and July.

These snow-clad mountains now provide Speyside with a new industry as it has become one of the largest ski resorts in Scotland. During the winter and spring months many hundreds of people enjoy this sport on the commodity which, when melted, will provide almost as many anglers with hours of pleasure, fishing on the rivers in the valleys below, as it flows on its way into the sea many miles away. Due to its large, high-altitude catchment and the ample snow reservoir stored on it the Spey rarely runs lower than medium height except during frosty spells in the spring. Any droughts normally occur in the period late July to September. For this reason fish are able to 'run' unheeded into the river throughout the year. There are no natural barriers to impede their passage as they ascend to the spawning fords and no man-made obstacles to check their ascent, except in the headwaters of the Spey and two of its tributaries, the Tromie and the Truim. As a result of an unhindered passage there is an even distribution of fish throughout the entire catchment and the fish can move at will.

The Spey rises in the southern part of the Monadhliath mountain range on the slopes of the Corrieyairack Forest and close to its source is little Loch Spey. From Loch Spey the river runs quietly down the strath for a distance of some 14 miles until it reaches Spey Dam where water is diverted westwards to Loch Laggan as part of the supply to the British Aluminium Company power scheme. The dam was built in 1942 and has a pool fish pass incorporated. From this point the Spey flows on through a sluggish gravelly area abounding with pike before quickening again in an area of deeper rocky pools intermingled with gravelly stretches.

Just upstream of the village of Newtonmore the Spey is swollen in size as the Truim, the first major right bank tributary, joins it. The Spey in these upper reaches has been referred to by J.R.P. Sclater as 'The River of Content' in his semi-religious booklet of that name published in 1913, and in which he says of it: 'It is in a land of far distances that the river runs towards the sea. Its springs are in the everlasting hills. Its early course is through a vacant, wine-red moor, and the winds that blow over it are austere and pure indeed. Grey buttresses of rock stand sentinel as it passes the lower levels, where the birch, the alder, the hazel and the rowan join together to give grace and beauty to its banks.'

The Spey continues its journey now in a north-easterly direction, being joined at Newtonmore by a left bank tributary, the River Calder, and at Kingussie by the Allt Mor. The Spey assumes a sluggish role as it meanders through the wide marshy flood-plain to Loch Insh, an area abounding in wildfowl and pike-infested pools. The River Tromie joins the Spey just upstream of Loch Insh, coming in on the right bank. As part of the Tummel hydro-electric scheme some water is diverted from this tributary to Loch Cuaich, the take-off point being when it has been dammed at the mouth of Loch An t-Seilich in its upper reaches near Gaick Lodge. Loch Insh is a large shallow loch with a good number of pike and trout. At one time char were common also and local inhabitants used to pitchfork them out of the river to which they migrated at spawning time.

After leaving Loch Insh the river flows fast, with gravelly stretches alternating with long pools. Just below Loch Insh the attractive River Feshie enters on the right bank. On nearing Aviemore, the Spey is joined by the River Druie whose tributaries start their torrential courses on the northern slopes of Cairn Gorm (4,084 feet) before entering Loch Morlich and the area of Rothiemurchus Forest. Deep, slow-moving pools are now more frequent in the stretch of the Spey between Aviemore and Grantown-on-Spey and the river increases in size after two more sizeable tributaries join it. The first of these is the River Nethy, coming in on the right bank, and the second, and by far more important, is the River Dulnain which runs a circuitous course, rising behind Lynchat and Kincraig and flowing north eastwards through Carrbridge to enter the Spey at Dulnain Bridge. The last major tributary to join the Spey does so some distance downstream of Grantown-on-Spey. This is the River Avon (pronounced A'n) which enters the right bank near Ballindalloch Castle. The source of this tributary, Loch Avon, lies many miles to the south at the foot of Beinn Mheadhoin in the Cairngorms and is only a matter of a few miles from the upper reaches of the River Gairn, (a tributary of the Dee which enters that river at Ballater). The Avon is, along with the Dulnain, one of the most important spawning tributaries on the Spey system and is certainly the longest. A few smaller tributaries enter the Spey downstream of Ballindalloch including the River Fiddich and the Burns of Aberlour and Rothes.

The Spey, from Grantown-on-Spey to the sea, has a succession of excellent holding pools and runs which have made it famous as a salmon river, and it is this section of the river which, along with the River Avon, provides the best angling. It is not difficult for anglers to find a beat to suit their own agility. Much of the water requires deep wading, but for those getting on in years or with some infirmity which prevents wading there are many pools fishable by boat or from the bank. Some pools are heavily wooded or have high banks and for this reason the famous 'Spey Cast' was introduced, whereby a long line can be put out without the fly passing behind the angler and therefore cast without the trees and banks impeding the smooth flow of the line.

The most well-known beats from Grantown-on-Spey to the sea are Castle Grant, Tulchan, Ballindalloch, Pitcroy, Knockando, Laggan, Carron, Wester Elchies, Aberlour, Easter Elchies, Arndilly, Rothes, Aikenway, Delfur, Orton and Gordon Castle.

Sea trout abound in the Spey during the summer months and an angler who runs into bright low water conditions during his holiday can rest during the day and look forward to late evening fishing with a chance of a salmon and almost a surety of some sea trout. Many fine baskets of these game fish are landed on the Spey and Avon each year. It would be quite impossible to pin-point any particular pool or beat as the best on the river. Obviously different water temperatures and height of the river will suit some beats better than others and conditions vary considerably over the season. By the end of the year most beats will have returned a useful contribution to the river's annual catch which will be a five figure number.

A special mention must be made of one or two of the tributaries, especially the Avon and its two main tributaries Conglass Water and the River Livet. The Avon river system is some 50 miles long, flowing into the Spey near Ballindalloch. It has no obstructions to fish ascent and fish run up it from March onwards. The annual salmon catch is in the region of 700. It has a wealth of good spawning and feeding areas from Loch Avon to its mouth, and the Conglass and Livet accommodate many fish. The Conglass has little angling and is mainly used by sea trout but the Livet provides good angling for both salmon and sea trout and has a good spawning stock of both. The Tromie is some 15 miles in length and is an important spawning tributary and many fish pass through the dam and on into the headwaters above. Fish tend to enter the Tromie from May onwards and there is some angling for salmon but not for sea trout which rarely enter this tributary. The fish counts at the pass at Tromie Dam in recent years are as follows:

Table 7
Fish counts at Tromie Dam, 1965–1973

1965	470	1968	223	1971	485
1966	386	1969	427	1972	571
1967	401	1970	418	1973	230

The Truim has its headwaters tapped and led into Loch Ericht as part of the Tummel hydro-electric scheme. However, salmon ascend right to the top of its headwaters, where excellent spawning facilities are to be found. There is a little angling in its lower reaches and, if water conditions are suitable, fish ascend this tributary from April onwards. No sea trout run this river.

There is some angling in the upper Spey above Spey Dam and there are good spawning grounds in this area. Salmon ascend the fish pass in the dam quite readily, but there is no counter to record the numbers. The Calder is mainly a sea trout tributary and is the only tributary in this upper section of the river system which is frequented by sea trout. The Feshie is a very good angling water and salmon ascend it from March onwards. Falls a little way above the junction with the Spey hold fish back until the water temperature is right. This stream like all the other tributaries mentioned so far is a good nursery area. The Nethy has a limited amount of angling late in the season when fish start to ascend to spawn. The Dulnain has a certain amount of angling for salmon and, to a lesser extent, sea trout late in the season. Fish ascend the Dulnain as far as Dunachton Estate, on its headwaters. The Druie and Fiddich are useful spawning and nursery rivers but have no angling potential. The Aberlour has impassable falls about half a mile above its confluence with the Spey, so there is only limited spawning and no angling.

A very large amount of the Spey and its tributaries is fished by angling associations and these include the Badenoch Angling Association, which has the fishing on the left bank of the Spey from Spey Dam to below Kingussie and 2 miles of the right bank below Ruthven Bridge at Kingussie; the Abernethy Angling Association; the Strathspey Angling Improvement Association, which has extensive fishing on the Seafield Estates extending from below Nethy Bridge to a little downstream of Grantown-on-Spey and also fishing on part of the Dulnain; the Strath Avon; the Glenlivet; the Aberlour; the Rothes; the Fochabers; the Mortlach; the Speymouth; the Kingston; and the Garmouth and Lossiemouth. In 1975 the number of permits issued by these associations was over 10,000. By far the largest angling association is the Strathspey which issued 4,823. This association is based on the Grantown-on-Spey area. Permits to fish these association waters can be obtained in the nearest towns to the fishings, such as Newtonmore, Kingussie, Aviemore, Boat of Garten, Grantown-on-Spey, Aberlour and Rothes. In many cases the local hotels have arrangements to fish these waters as well as some of the private waters. Lets on some of the private stretches can be obtained through the usual sporting agents.

A large number of beats changed hands between 1930 and 1955, but in recent years the only beat that has changed ownership is Tulchan below Grantown-on-Spey, which has been sold twice. Among the main beats which have stayed in their present owners' hands for many years are Ballindalloch and Castle Grant. A map of the pools on the Spey by Maude Parker is available from many tackle shops.

Netting is an integral part of the Spey fishing, and sweep netting in the estuary is owned and operated by the Crown Estate Commissioners. On the east, or Portgordon, side of Spey Bay stake nets are also owned and operated by the Crown Estate Commissioners, but further to the east bag nets are worked by two proprietors. On the west side of Spey Bay stake nets are owned by the

Crown Estate Commissioners but let by them. There are no bag net fisheries on the west side. The Spey District boundaries are Benthills, Lossiemouth to the west and Cowhythe Head beyond Portsoy to the east.

The Spey District Salmon Fishery Board work tremendously hard to improve the stock of fish in the river and to try and offset the damage being done by illegal drift and hang nets set off the coast. In order to increase the stock of fish in the river system the Board has built a large hatchery on the Knockando Burn near Knockando. The hatchery has a capacity for $4\frac{1}{2}$ million eggs and is worked on the trough system. It was built during an epidemic of UDN, and this particular site was chosen as there is a dam placed across the burn a short distance upstream of its confluence with the Spey. The dam diverts water to a distillery and effectively prevents the ascent of fish, thus keeping the water supply to the hatchery free of the disease. The fry from the hatchery are planted each year in all the major tributaries, apart from the Burn of Aberlour, and in many of the minor streams as well. Eggs for the hatchery are taken from adults which have been netted in many of these tributaries. Those fish which are ripe when caught are stripped immediately, while those not quite ready for stripping are transported to specially designed holding pens on the Advie Burn where they are held until ripe. About 1,000 female fish are caught for this purpose each year. The design of the holding pens is worth a special mention as it is extremely ingenious. A loop occurs on the burn which is practically U-shaped. A channel was dug across the loop, sluiced at both ends and the channel partitioned off into a number of pens. Any spate water goes down the main channel and only sufficient water to maintain the stock of fish held in the pens is allowed through the channel. When fish are needed to be caught for stripping, water can be reduced accordingly. The damage to fish held is therefore reduced to an absolute minimum.

UDN first occurred on the Spey in September 1967, and a rapid spread of the disease, with a heavy mortality, followed. After this first initial outbreak the mortality rate declined and, although an occasional marked fish is seen, few deaths occur.

Pollution problems have been greatly reduced since the advent of the river purification boards and any problems that occur are quickly dealt with by the North-East River Purification Board in whose area the Spey system falls. Many distilleries have co-operated fully in treating their 'pot ale' which, being highly polluting, was a serious problem at one time when discharged to the river. Pike frequent the upper system of the Spey and the District Fishery Board staff used to net these in Loch Insh, Spey Dam and the canal-like stretches of the river around Loch Insh.

The trend in the runs of fish in the Spey has been towards a marked increase in grilse and summer salmon and even a slight swing to autumn. The spring run, however, is difficult to assess as not only have the winters been milder, allowing the fish to become distributed more widely, but also the lack of kelts in the lower reaches as a result of UDN has seemed to create the tendency for

River Spey

N

Streamy Churchyard
Burn of Tulchan **Water**
Upper Tulchan
Bridge Pool
Lower Tulchan
Dummy
Bridge
Bog
Spearnick
Straan
Lodge Stream
Drain
Dunbar
Tulchan
Stream of Dalvey
George
Boat
Slopanrowan
Dhu
Rock
Gled
Bulbain
Old Woman
Dolly
Stone
Boundary
Tail of Stream
Castle Grant Water
Top of Stream
Dellifure Burn
Dellifure Pool
Polcrain
Dunbar
Polwick
Tulchan
GRANTOWN
Slop Thomas
Clach-na-Strone
No. 2 Burn
Slop Aindrea
No. 1 Burn
Bridge Pool
Polan Cearan
Big Stream
Upper Slates
Polnagour
Bridge Pool
Lower Slates
Long Pool
Craigroy
Castle Grant Water
Garropool
Macleod's Pool
Association Water
Slop Gachrach
Congash Burn
Uiskano

early fish to move more rapidly upstream. But this is only speculation.

The average weight of Spey salmon is 10–12 lb, but some larger ones are caught and a few of 30–40 lb are taken each year.

14

THE LOSSIE, FINDHORN AND NAIRN

The Lossie

This east coast river flows into the Moray Firth between the Spey to the east and the Findhorn to the west. It rises on the moorland south of Dallas on the north side of Carn Kitty and flows in a northerly direction through a mixture of moorland, wooded countryside and marginal arable land down through the villages of Dallas and Kellas. It then flows through better arable farm land as it approaches and passes the town of Elgin before entering the sea at Lossiemouth.

The Lossie is a much smaller river than its neighbours and, flowing for the main part through arable land and loam banks, it is at times liable to change its course as banks erode. It is not a rocky river and has for the most part a gravelly, muddy bed. There is a high waterfall on its upper headwaters which sea trout negotiate, but few salmon pass this point. It is a spate river with no loch of any significance on its headwaters. The Elgin Angling Association fish the lower half of the Lossie from its mouth to some distance upstream of the town. Kellas Estate fish the centre section and day tickets are available. The top section is fished by Dallas Angling Association.

There is a useful summer run of salmon, grilse and sea trout. In the bottom reaches the best angling months are June – September. In the upper section sea trout can be caught from July onwards, but salmon and grilse are later in arriving. Water height is a crucial factor in determining when Dallas Association get their first salmon. The month of September is normally the best in this upper area and the average catch is 10–15 salmon and grilse and 50–100 sea trout, 1½–3 lb in weight. The bottom sections naturally kill many more fish.

Most of the pools on the Lossie are small but deep although there are also some nice runs. Trees and scrub offer good bank cover on most stretches of the river.

There are good sections of spawning and feeding areas, especially on the headwaters of the main river. The Auchness Burn, which joins the Lossie above Dallas, can also accommodate some spawning fish, but there is a fall approximately 1 mile up this burn, beyond which fish cannot ascend.

Sweep nets are operated on the mouth of the river and bag and stake net stations are worked on the coast on either side of the mouth.

The Findhorn

The River Findhorn is formed from two major streams running from the Monadhliath, or grey, mountains. These are the River Eskin, a peaty stream, and the Abhainn Cro Chlach (called the Cro for short), which is a clear stream rising on the north side of the mountain range behind Newtonmore. The Findhorn, from the meeting of the tributaries to Tomatin 15 miles downstream, flows over a gravelly and rocky bed, through wild mountainous moorland country of juniper and heather frequented by red deer, wild goats and grouse. This part of the river and all the major tributaries entering it, including the Eskin, Cro, Mazeran, Elrick, Kyllachy and Funlack, is the major spawning area.

Following the river from Tomatin one passes what was once Shenachie village, now a few ruined cottages and near here is a large pool, the Pollochaig, which is the main holding pool in the upper reaches. There is no road along this stretch of the river other than a path for about 5 miles to Drynachan Lodge. Still following the river one reaches the stone bridge of Dulsie 8 miles north-east of the lodge. At this point starts the rocky wooded gorge for which the Findhorn is renowned. The gorge continues for at least 20 miles until it reaches the famous Sluie Pool to the east of Forres. Two bridges cross the river between Dulsie Bridge and Sluie Pool, these are Logie Bridge on the Nairn to Grantown road and Daltulich Bridge near Randolph's Leap, almost 8 miles from Forres.

The tree-clad slopes of this gorge, which is in places 200 feet high, constrict the width of the river so much that at certain points a fit man (such as Randolph) could leap over. The river drops rapidly through the gorge from one deep pool to another with runs and falls in between. It is a natural and beautiful place and known only to a few who have reason to be along the riverside, but it can be dangerous for the unwary angler who doesn't appreciate how quickly the river can rise after heavy rain.

At Logie Estates, near Doune of Relugas, the little River Divie enters the river on the right bank. The Divie flows through moorland country and is joined by the Dorback Burn near Ballenreich. The Dorback is, like the Divie, a moorland river and flows out of Lochindorb in which stands an island holding Lochindorb Castle — the one-time stronghold of the Wolf of Badenoch. The Divie and Dorback are important spawning tributaries but spawning fish can only enter the Dorback, or reach the upper reaches of the Divie, under flood conditions. Nearly the whole of the gorge area of the Findhorn is unsuitable for spawning which only occurs in very small areas where fish may find some gravel.

Below the Sluie Pool the river widens out but still flows between wild and attractive scenery as far as the A96 Aberdeen to Inverness road bridge. From here to the mouth of the river at Findhorn Bay the countryside is flat and the river widens out into thin gravelly and shallow pools and fords. Some late-running fish spawn in this section. One fairly large tributary enters the Findhorn in Findhorn Bay, near Broom of Moy village. This is the Muckle Burn which, at one time, was considered the best sea trout water running into the Moray Firth, but since the end of the last war the water abstraction associated with extensive farming in this area has reduced the runs of sea trout drastically.

As an angling river the Findhorn depends greatly on hard winters in the mountains, with heavy snows and full gullies creating a slow release of clean water throughout the spring and into May. After this time the fishing depends on July and August floods to let some stock into the middle and upper reaches. Given that, one can be assured that in the early spring, February – April, rod fishing up as far as the Sluie Pool will be good. When the river temperature rises enough the fish will pass through the gorge, generally in early May, and all beats up to and including the lower Tomatin area will yield fish. Later in the season all beats will produce fish. The autumn fishing is generally excellent except in the Tomatin area where the fish are heavy in spawn, with spawning starting in early October.

The average weight of spring salmon is about 10 lb, although fish of 20 lb or more are fairly common. The runs of grilse have been exceptionally good in the past 10 seasons and the runs of summer salmon have also been good, but the nets take more than their fair share during periods of low river flow. Although the rod season was 11 February–30 September, since 1978 an extension of the fishing season has been granted taking it up to 6 October. The net season is 11 February–26 August.

Two netting companies operate on the Findhorn and along the neighbouring coast; these are the Findhorn Salmon Fisheries Ltd, which fishes by net and coble within the river, and the Moray Firth Salmon Fisheries Company Limited that fishes with a limited number of bag and fly nets along the coast. The river nets, if given the right flow conditions, can more or less, so it is said, 'clean the river out'. The fords in these lower reaches of the river are so shallow at times of low flow that only the smaller grilse and sea trout can negotiate them in safety during the weekly close season.

Below Broom of Moy, near the main Aberdeen road bridge, the netting company owns the fishing to the sea except for two pools. These two pools are owned by trustees of an estate and administered by the Forres Angling Association. Only persons resident within the Forres and Rafford area (and visitors staying within the area) can obtain permits to fish. The fishing can be very good and there are times when these two pools are about the only places on the whole river that are well-stocked with fish in the summer and autumn months. The permit charges are very moderate but there are no daily tickets. The association water extends to about a mile upstream of the Aberdeen road bridge and it has all the net fisheries water after 26 August. The Findhorn and Kinloss villages have permission to fish for sea trout within Findhorn Bay.

Above the Association water are the private fishings of all the estates. Most

THE LOSSIE, FINDHORN AND NAIRN

of these beats are let on a weekly basis by the estates. It is found that most of the lets are renewed every season to the same rods. From time to time certain estates advertise the lets of vacant weeks in the *Field* and other sporting papers. However, there is some public fishing in the upper reaches at Tomatin and the Freeburn Inn issues salmon fishing permits, but as there are a limited number preference is given to hotel guests.

The first beat above the Association water belongs to the Moray Estates Development Company which owns both banks as far as lower Dounduff, and the left bank up to Daltulich Bridge. Logie Estate has the other bank to the bridge. Dunphail Estate marches with Logie on the right bank and extends almost to Logie Farm cottage. From here Glenferness Estate takes over this single bank fishing up to Dulsie Bridge. On the left bank Coulmony Estate has from Daltulich Bridge up to the white streens (small streams running off a steep hillside) near Glenferness House. Thereafter Lethen Estate has the single bank to Dulsie Bridge and then both banks for over 2 miles until it reaches the march with Cawdor Estates. Cawdor Estates have both banks of the river as far as the Pollochaig Pool which it shares with Moy Estate. Moy Estate has about 2 miles of both banks, and the left bank (except for a small section which is owned by Tomatin House) as far as the main road. The right bank is the property of Corrybrough Estates up to the old main road at Tomatin. From the road bridge to 3 miles upstream the right bank is fished by Clune Estate and the left bank by Kyllachy. Then, continuing on the left bank, is Glenkyllachy with about 3 miles of water, followed by Glenmazeran for about 2 miles after which Coignafearn has the remaining fishings. Marching with Clune Estate on the right bank is Dalmigavie Estates for about 4 miles and again Coignafearn, which has the whole of the upper section.

The main threat to salmon stocks on the Findhorn has been from forestry, and the large plough scars on the hillsides near Tomatin bear witness to the damage caused by increased and more rapid run-off of water and increased peat silt entering the river and small burns.

Artificial propagation has always been carried out on the Findhorn, initially on a limited scale by Findhorn Salmon Fisheries Ltd but in recent years by the Findhorn District Salmon Fishery Board, and the average stocking was increased to 500,000 fed fry annually. The fry are usually released into burns where fish have no access or if, as often happens, low water prevents fish ascending to spawn in such streams as the Mazeran then all streams in that area receive their quota of fed fry in late May.

The Nairn

This east coast river is sandwiched between the south catchment of the River Ness and north catchment of the River Findhorn. It is smaller in size than its two neighbours, but is a reasonably long river approximately 30 miles in length. It rises in the north-east corner of the Monadhliath mountain range near the village of Aberarder. Many short burns form its headwaters and as they gather together the river begins its journey down Strathnairn in a north easterly direction past the estates of Brin, Flichity and Farr before being joined by a left bank tributary carrying the overflow waters from Loch Duntelchaig, which is harnessed for Inverness town water supply. Thence on down the strath under the main A9 Perth – Inverness road and under the viaduct carrying the main Inverness – London railway lines, past the battlefield of Culloden Moor before wending its way through a flatter landscape as it passes Kilravock and Cawdor castles before finally discharging its waters into the sea in the Moray Firth at the town of Nairn.

The headwaters of the Nairn are in a rather desolate area and there is considerable evidence of land erosion. The river in these upper reaches is heavily silted. Further downstream the Nairn flows through deep rocky pools lined with alders and other good bank cover, which affords excellent shade for these little holding pools. As the Nairn levels out and passes into the coastal plain, it flows through rich arable land. In this stretch a lot of gravel is to be found in the river bed and in the early 1970s a large amount of gravel was extracted from the river bed in this area for use at the Ardersier oil-rig construction site. Due to these workings, the course of the river was considerably widened in some places and will be liable to change for many years.

The Nairn is a useful angling river with the season opening on 11 February. The first fish are normally taken in March or April, but in 1978 fish were taken on the opening day, and March and early April were more productive than usual. Although in recent years there has been a dramatic decline in the salmon catches. The Nairn Angling Association have 8 miles of double bank fishing from the Whitebridge to the sea and in 1977 obtained a further mile of single bank fishing above the bridge. There are many good pools in their water, probably the best being the Gauge pool and Blairnafade. This Association limit the type of fishing allowed according to the height of the water and for this purpose have a multicoloured gauge which shows red, white or blue. When the gauge shows white any lure can be used; when blue, spinning and fly fishing are permitted; and when red shows, fly only is permitted. Fishing above Daviot is later than in the lower section, but there are many useful beats in this section with Inverarnie, Farr, Flichity and Brin probably the best.

July is probably the best angling month on the river, but much depends on the height of water.

Sea trout stocks, like the salmon stocks, seem to have dwindled in recent years, but the Nairn can have good runs of this species and it is hoped that this decline is only temporary. The extensive poaching which occurs on this river must have had some effect on the stocks.

The main spawning and feeding areas are to be found in the headwaters, probably the best of all being the River Brin which has a wealth of good gravel and a fairly constant water level in low flows. The smaller tributaries and main river in the Aberarder vicinity are also good, and the Farr Burn is also a useful spawning area. Spawning areas in the stretch around Kildrummie have not settled down since the gravel was taken from the river and are at present too unstable to be of any real significance. The bottom 2-mile section of the Cawdor Burn between its junction with the Nairn and the falls at Cawdor Castle is also able to accommodate a spawning stock.

The Nairn Fishery Board have recently planted up to 60,000 fry in some years, but there is concern that smolts can find their way into the lade serving Cantray Mill Trout Farm, which at present is not protected by a smolt screen at the upstream end. As this lade is sited on the side of the river where the flow is less rapid, it is probable that some smolts do choose this course as they move downstream. There is also no adequate grid at the downstream end of the lade to prevent adult salmon ascending. It is planned that both ends of this lade will, therefore, be protected by screens for better conservation of the migratory fish stock of this river.

In the early part of this century a number of weirs existed on the river, none of which had fish passes installed on them, and they tended to check the free passage of fish on their upstream migration. The only one which exists today in an undilapidated state is the one at Cantray. This is still required to enable the lade at Cantray Mill to serve the trout farm. A fish pass has been installed in the weir approximately 100 feet wide. The weir is constructed of gabion baskets and boulders.

There is a certain amount of gravel movement in the river probably due to forestry and hill drainage and road building on the Nairn catchment. Since the gravel abstraction from the bed of the river in the early 70s there is also an increased movement of gravel from this point downstream. The sand quarry near Daviot is also believed to have an effect on the suspended solid load in the river. Certainly the A9 road improvements in this area had a temporary effect on the river, with heavy suspended solid loads occurring at high flows.

There are no sweep nets on the mouth of the Nairn river but bag nets and stake nets are operated on the Moray Firth coast to the east and west of the river mouth.

15

THE NESS DISTRICT

The Ness District extends from the small streams flowing into Loch Quoich and which rise in the mountains only a few miles from the west coast near Loch Nevis and Loch Hourn, to the mouth of the River Ness at Inverness. The coastal limits extend to a point 7 miles from Cromarty on the Black Isle to the north and Whiteness Head near Ardersier to the south.

At one time there was intensive netting carried out in the river as high up as the Dochfour weir. This weir forms the barrier at the end of Loch Ness to raise the water level and to serve the Caledonian Canal which runs parallel to the river but which is some distance away. The netting at this point has been phased out over the years and no netting now takes place in the river or at its mouth. Fishing by net and coble does, however, take place within the estuary limits and about 10 different proprietors have netting rights in the outer estuary. There are also fixed engines on the coast.

The large system of lochs rarely allows the river water temperature to drop below 40° – 42°F and it is often 5° higher than that in the Garry or the Moriston. In low water conditions fish are often attracted to the Caledonian Canal entrances and they have been known to use the canal system between the Inverness Firth and Loch Ness and Loch Ness and Loch Oich under these conditions. They can also go the 'wrong way' to or from the Lochy system. A few years ago smolts were released from the Invergarry Hatchery and were caught 14 days later in the canal at Laggan on the Lochy system.

UDN appeared in the Ness system in the late 1960s and, although no severe outbreaks have been reported recently, it is still apparent in most years.

The Ness District has three major hydro-electric schemes in its area, these are the Garry, the Moriston and the pump-storage scheme at Foyers on Loch Ness. As part of the compensation for damage to fisheries, the North of Scotland Hydro-electric Board built the Invergarry Salmon Hatchery with a capacity for well in excess of 5 million eggs. The hatchery has now been handed over to the Ness District Salmon Fishery Board. This Board also regularly set nets for the pike which occur in lochs Meiklie, Dundreggan and Oich.

THE NESS DISTRICT

The Ness

This short river, only 6 miles in length, flows out of Loch Ness over the Dochfour weir. It falls roughly 50 feet from the Loch to its mouth, and is therefore mainly fairly fast flowing water. It has no major obstructions, except for the weir, to impede the passage of fish.

The Ness system is similar to the Awe system as it was in the past, in respect of the seasonal distribution of its fish. The Orchy above Loch Awe fished best in the spring due to the fish passing rapidly up the River Awe and Loch Awe before resting. Similarly, on the Ness system it is the upper rivers, the Garry, Oich and Moriston, which receive the spring fish which seldom rest in the Ness. Although the season opens on 15 January and Inverness town water is fished hard from then on, only an occasional fish is taken in the early months. The Ness fishes best from mid-July to the closing day (15 October) and by this time there is a heavy resident stock over the whole 6-mile stretch. The pools are mainly large and smooth with fast runs. In the old days experts advocated groyning these pools in order to check the run of spring fish, so that they could be caught more easily but it is doubtful if this would have had the desired effect. A lot of the angling in the Ness is done from a boat in the larger pools above the Islands. Fly fishing and spinning are allowed but prawning is generally frowned upon. The average catches are about 1,200 per annum.

The main beats are Dochfour, Lower Dochfour (now Laggan), Ness Castle, Ness-side, (all double bank fishing), Holm, and the rest of the water fished by the Inverness Angling Club. Laggan, Ness Castle and Ness-side have all changed hands recently.

The Ness has a wealth of spawning grounds, which is unusual for such a short river close to the sea. It has recently been described as one big spawning bed. There are no significant streams running into the Ness and all spawning takes place in the main river. It also has excellent feeding areas. The steady flow, clean water and excellent gravelly bed all help to make this a productive river. Ness fish are above average weight, with salmon of around 12 lb and grilse 6 lb. Some much heavier fish can be taken. The early fish passing through the Ness are of a heavy spring class and average 15 lb. Sea trout also run the Ness and spawn in it. Good fishing can be had for these fish both at the mouth and in the river.

Tickets to fish the town water can be obtained from any local tackle shop.

Loch Ness

This loch is $24\frac{1}{2}$ miles long and about 1 mile wide. It is over 750 feet deep, the deepest point being situated south of Urquhart Castle, and has average depth in the region of 400 feet. It is a very popular loch for angling, fished entirely by boat, and trolling minnows or other spinning lures is the most effective method.

The best spring fishing is normally found in the western end near Fort Augustus or Invermoriston, and at Foyers. Large spring fish are often caught, with some of 30 lb or over being taken in recent years. In the summer and autumn the better fishing is normally spread over a larger area of the Loch, with Foyers, Urquhart Bay, Dores Bay and Lochend being favourite haunts of the anglers. A few fish are also caught at the top end of the loch in the summer and these are probably late Oich fish.

Many of the grilse and summer fish spawn in the Endrick at Drumnadrochit and this river can produce a few late fish when water conditions are suitable. There is good spawning above and below Loch Meiklie. Another north bank tributary, the Coiltie, at Lewiston, has good spawning and produces fish for anglers. However, falls a mile upstream prevent fish ascending further. On the south bank the burns and rivers are too steep to provide good spawning, but fish do spawn in the lower sections of the Tarff, Foyers and Farigaig.

Sea trout enter the loch from May onwards. The runs, however, have shown a marked decline in recent years. The sea trout spawn in the same rivers as the salmon and also in some of the smaller burns flowing into the loch.

An average catch for the loch is in the region of 500 fish per annum, with recent years (except 1976) producing even more. It is said that in recent years one boat killed 59 fish in one season. All boats fishing Loch Ness have to be licensed and numbered and application for a licence should be made to The Secretary, Loch Ness Proprietors Association, Lochside, 2 Ness Place, Inverness. Many of the hotels bordering Loch Ness have licensed boats which are made available to guests.

In 1896 the British Aluminium Company brought into commission at Foyers the first large aluminium smelting plant in Great Britain. This plant was in continuous operation for 70 years and ceased production in 1967. Shortly after the North of Scotland Hydro-electric Board assumed control at Foyers in 1967, they promoted a new scheme involving pump storage, similar to the Awe-Cruachan scheme. The high level reservoir is Loch Mhor, formed under the original development by enlarging and joining Loch Garth and Loch Farraline. When the power station at Foyers is generating, water flows from Loch Mhor through 2 miles of tunnels to the power station and discharges into Loch Ness. Anglers fishing the River Ness complain that the fluctuating water levels in the river, as a result of this scheme, affect their angling success, and are most concerned.

River Oich

This river is some 6 miles long and connects Loch Oich with Loch Ness. It has some nice pools and fast stretches of water. It fishes throughout the spring, from 15 January onwards, and also has a summer run of grilse and salmon.

There are 3 owners, the top end proprietor owning both banks and the other 2 being single bank proprietors.

Catches have shown an improvement in recent years.

There are excellent spawning and feeding areas throughout the 6-mile length which can accommodate and produce a useful stock of salmon.

Loch Oich

This is a long narrow loch some 4 miles long and a quarter of a mile wide. It is much shallower than Loch Ness, with much of it being 50 feet deep, although some of the deepest areas are up to 150 feet in depth.

Angling is mainly by trolling, as on Loch Ness, and early and late fish can be taken. The heaviest ever recorded weighed $44\frac{1}{2}$ lb.

There is a large pike population frequenting the loch and these are dealt with by the Ness District Salmon Fishery Board staff.

The Garry

The tributaries of the River Garry rise in the mountains to the west of Loch Quoich and from this loch the Garry flows east into Loch Poulary, just downstream of Quoich power station. From there it flows into Loch Garry and then on another 4 miles before entering Loch Oich.

The Garry used to be famous for spring salmon, with heavy spring fish averaging 18 lb and many over 25 lb. An average year produced a catch of over 400. There were falls below Loch Garry which held fish back until the water temperature rose above 48° and which were only passable in low water conditions. There were 20 pools of renown in the 4-mile stretch, with the little Crooked Pool having a fine reputation.

Once the fish ascended the falls they pushed on through Loch Garry (where fish were rarely taken) into the upper Garry and Loch Quoich. The upper Garry had a good reputation in the old days and was praised by Geoffrey Braithwaite in his book *Fine Feathers and Fish*, in which he refers in particular to the Kingie Pool and the Stickles. This part of the river produced about 70 salmon a year.

The main spawning areas were in this section of the river system and there were a few in the Gairowan and River Quoich, but by far the best spawning tributary was the Kingie which flows into the upper Garry, 3 miles below Loch Quoich. This tributary accommodated a large proportion of the Garry fish on excellent spawning grounds.

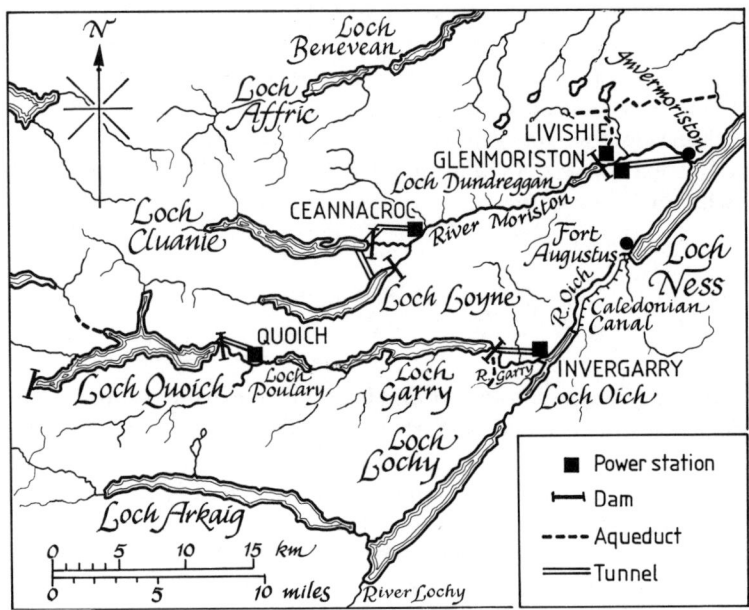

The Rivers Garry and Moriston and the Garry–Moriston Hydro-electric Scheme

The Garry river system was harnessed for hydro-electric power by the North of Scotland Hydro-electric Board in the early 1950s. At the western end of Loch Quoich, which is the main storage reservoir, 2 small cut-off dams prevent the water spilling over the watershed to the west coast. West of these dams water from 6 small streams, flowing into Loch Hourn, is led by an aqueduct eastwards into the reservoir. At the eastern end of the loch the largest rockfill dam in the country was built. From Loch Quoich a tunnel carries water to Quoich Power Station on the Garry. There is no fish pass in Quoich Dam and fish are prevented from reaching the power station by a heck or fish screen built across the river a short distance downstream of the power station. Fish are trapped at the heck in the autumn and held by the Ness District Salmon Fishery Board until they are ready for stripping. The end of Loch Garry has also been raised by a dam at its outlet, built across the gorge where the River Garry has formed a deep channel. In this dam a Borland-type fish pass enables salmon to pass up and down the river. From the dam a tunnel carries water to Invergarry Power Station near the mouth of the river at Loch Oich. Only the upper part of this station is visible from the main road. The river below Garry Dam receives a compensation flow from the loch and during the winter months this flow is reduced and is not increased to summer level until 1 April. As a result of this, fish remain in the lower part of the river until then. This means that the lower beat fishes well from 15 January–1 April, when fish start to move up the river. From then on the rest of the Garry can be fished. Fish normally ascend the falls at the Borland pass and enter the loch from May onwards.

The lower Garry is privately owned and an average season produces about 250 big spring fish and some grilse. Lets for this section of the river and Loch Oich can be had from the Rod and Gun Shop in Fort William. The upper Garry is owned by the North of Scotland Hydro-electric Board and is let to the Tomdoun Hotel and Garry Goulach Holiday Centre. About 50 fish are killed on this beat each year.

The spawning and nursery areas have been vastly reduced as salmon no longer have access to the tributaries running into Loch Quoich or to the first 3 miles of the upper Garry and the Kingie. The only natural spawning area remaining is in the main river, the streams running into it and Loch Garry below the heck. Compensation for the loss of the spawning area consisted of provision of trapping facilities at the heck, holding tanks for adult fish close by and a large hatchery at Invergarry to house the eggs taken from the fish trapped at the heck. In a normal year about a million eggs are taken from the fish caught at the heck, but in 1976 only 250,000 were obtained. The resulting fry are planted out at the 'unfed' stage by the Ness District Salmon Fishery Board staff, and the areas usually planted are those debarred to salmon, namely the upper Garry and the Kingie. Although the North of Scotland Hydro-electric Board have done everything possible to help preserve the Garry, nothing can replace the spawning and feeding areas which were lost to the river system.

The fish counts at the Borland pass in the Garry Dam since 1965 are as follows:

Table 8
Fish counts at Garry Dam, 1965–1979.

1965	377	1970	192	1975	564
1966	371	1971	269	1976	331
1967	320	1972	230	1977	290
1968	166	1973	280	1978	426
1969	226	1974	258	1979	259

The Moriston

The Moriston rises in the mountains above Loch Cluanie and flows in an easterly direction on its 25-mile descent to Loch Ness at Invermoriston. Glen Moriston is a very beautiful wooded glen and the drive from Shiel Bridge to Invermoriston is most spectacular. Halfway down Glen Moriston there is a stretch of the river which is very sluggish but apart from that, the river is fast flowing and during the last part of its descent to the loch there is a very rugged rocky stretch with a falls which, for many years, debarred the passage of salmon. It was not until a bypass was placed on the left bank at these falls in the late 1800s that fish were able to ascend the river. This bypass was extremely costly and an estimated figure of £2,000 is given, which was a lot of money in those days. At a later date an even better pass, with a much shallower gradient, was placed on the right bank. From this time on the Moriston began to produce a good run of fish and angling began to improve.

When the North of Scotland Hydro-electric Board harnessed the Moriston, Loch Loyne and Loch Cluanie were dammed. Water is passed from Loch Loyne into Loch Cluanie and from there water is passed by tunnel to Ceannacroc Power Station. No fish pass was installed in either Cluanie or Loyne dams but a fish heck and small impoundment was placed just upstream of Ceannacroc Power Station to prevent fish ascending. A dam was also placed across the river 10 miles further downstream to form Loch Dundreggan, a headpond from which water is passed to the Invermoriston Power Station. The power station is on the left bank of the river 300 yards above the outflow to Loch Ness. A Borland-type fish pass is incorporated in Dundreggan Dam.

The effect of this scheme on the fisheries has been the loss of large spawning and nursery areas above the Ceannacroc fish heck, in all the tributaries running into Loch Cluanie and in the main river down to the heck. There is a trap in the fish heck and fish are caught here from mid-September onwards and kept before being stripped in the same manner as at Loch Poulary on the Garry. However, as the Ceannacroc trap is above the power station tailrace, in dry seasons fish tend to be diverted by the flow of water from the power station and will not come forward to the trap. In an average season only 50 fish are trapped at this point. The ova are hatched at Invergarry Hatchery and planted out as unfed fry in the Moriston and the tributaries between Ceannacroc and Cluanie Dam. The largest tributary above the heck is the River Loyne, but as this river is dammed one mile upstream of its confluence with the Moriston and no compensation flow arrangements were provided, its value as a nursery area is limited.

As part of the scheme the gradient of the falls at Invermoriston was improved and there is now no obstruction to impede the fish ascending this section of the river. The old bypasses no longer play any part in access to the river. The Borland pass at Dundreggan Dam is operated manually and fish are counted as they ascend. The annual fish counts at this point are as follows:

Table 9

Fish Counts at Dundreggan Dam, 1965–1979

Year	Count	Year	Count	Year	Count
1965	349	1970	418	1975	572
1966	347	1971	485	1976	377
1967	346	1972	571	1977	376
1968	222	1973	230	1978	393
1969	427	1974	485	1979	278

Natural spawning takes place above and below Dundreggan Dam. The stock of juvenile fish above the dam is very good but below the dam it is most disappointing. This could be accounted for by the wide range of flows and rapid fluctuations in this section of the river.

It is to be regretted that the fish heck was not placed immediately below the Ceannacroc Power Station tailrace, in the way that the heck on the Garry has been sited below the Quoich Power Station, as this could well have led to more fish being taken in the trap. Adult salmon caught in the trap average about 12 lb.

In the old days Moriston fish were very long and thin in shape and were nicknamed 'Campbells'. A few years ago, as a result of a shortage of cock fish on the Moriston, the Moriston hens were crossed with Garry cocks and an improvement seems to have resulted from this experiment.

Angling is mainly confined to the lowest section of the river and the section above Dundreggan. The North of Scotland Hydro-electric Board, who own the section between Dundreggan Dam and the lowest beat banned angling on their water in order to conserve what, at that time, was considered to be a poor stock of fish. There is some controversy over whether or not this ban should now be lifted. The lowest beat provides the best angling on the river, as fish are held in this area until 1 May when the winter compensation flow is raised to summer level and fish can then run the river freely. It is a sluggish piece of water and spinning produces the majority of the catch which amounts to some 250 fish a year. Fishing opens on 15 January and fish are normally caught on the opening day. The catch consists mainly of spring fish with a few grilse and summer fish later in the season. This beat is owned by Glenmoriston Estates to whom application for permits should be made. The section between Ceannacroc and Dundreggan has a reasonable angling potential from June onwards. It is owned by the North of Scotland Hydro-electric Board and although some sections are very sluggish, there are some excellent pools, the best being the Bobbin above the loch and the Alder just below the heck.

16

THE BEAULY DISTRICT

The Beauly river system lies in the main river valley of the Aird District at the head of which is Glen Affric. The river, as it runs along its course from Loch Affric and then Loch Benevean, changes its name twice. It starts off as the River Affric below Loch Benevean and then, a short distance upstream of Fasnakyle Power Station, it becomes the River Glass at the confluence with the Tomich Burn. It retains this name after being joined by the River Cannich but later, after entry of the River Farrar, becomes the River Beauly for the final part of its course to the Beauly Firth and the sea.

This river system, like so many other east coast systems, has been very fully developed for power by the North of Scotland Hydro-electric Board. Apparently there was good reason for harnessing the waters of Strathglass as, since the earliest times, the people of Strathglass lived in fear of floods. Four times in the nineteenth century the whole valley was devastated by flood water and the flood of 1892 swept away every bridge except two between Loch Affric and the Beauly Firth.

Salmon ascend the Beauly, Glass and lower Affric but their further ascent is barred by the Badger's Fall and a series of falls in the fearsome gorge below Loch Benevean.

The Glass

The River Glass starts where the River Affric and Tomich Burn join. The latter is a good spawning tributary and salmon can ascend it for a distance of 3 miles until the Plodda Falls prevent their further ascent. The next major tributary to join the Glass is the Cannich. The Cannich rises in a glen almost parallel to the River Affric and just to the north of it and it has a very similar catchment to the Affric having two lochs, Loch Lungard and Loch Mullardoch, on its headwaters and a steep gradient to its junction with the River Glass. The water resources of this river system were scheduled for development on two occasions, once in 1929 and once in 1941, but each time the schemes were rejected. However, they were finally developed by the North of Scotland Hydro-electric Board after the passing of the Hydro-electric Development (Scotland) Act in 1943. Loch Mullardoch was impounded 12 miles upstream

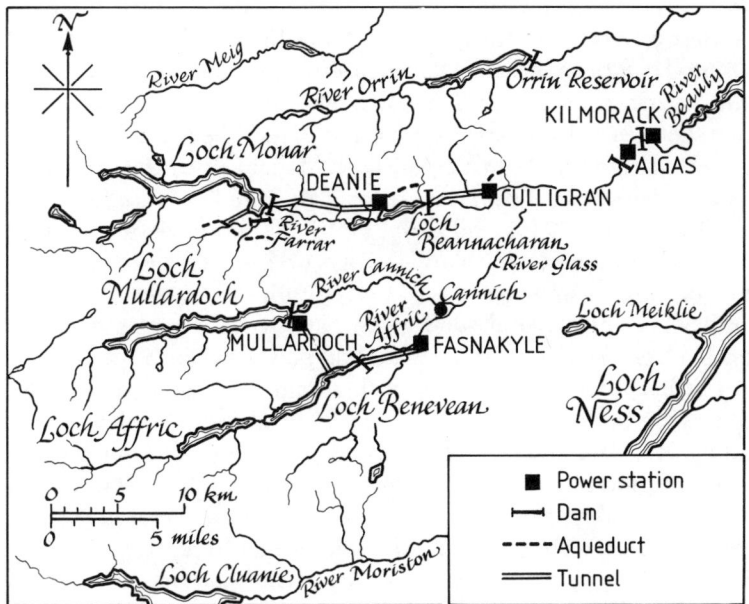

The Rivers Beauly and Glass and the Glen Affric, Strathfarrar and Aigas–Kilmorack Hydro-electric Scheme

from the village of Cannich with a dam 116 feet high, and as a result of the raising of the water level in this loch the waters of Lungard and Mullardoch now merge. From Loch Mullardoch a tunnel carries water to Loch Benevean. Benevean Dam is in a gorge about a mile and a half below the original outlet of Loch Benevean. Water passes from the loch by tunnel to Fasnakyle Power Station. No provision for fish passes was required as both these dams were in sections of their respective rivers already debarred to salmon by impassable falls. Most of the Glass is owned by the Lovat Estates. The salmon fishing can be very good but the river level tends to fluctuate as a result of generation at Fasnakyle Power Station. Above the power station the fishing is of little value. Lovat Estate have seven beats on the Glass and the Struy Estate has one, which includes the Junction Pool. Some fishing on the Glass can be obtained through the Glen Affric Hotel, although hotel guests have first choice. The main run of salmon starts in late July and early August but the season continues until mid-October. It is very productive in August, September and October.

The Farrar

The Farrar rises in the mountains of the Monar Forest, many of which are over

SALMON RIVERS OF SCOTLAND

3,000 feet high, and flows into Loch Monar. Below the loch the river runs down a most attractive strath into Loch Mhuillin and, a mile further downstream, into Loch Beannacharan. Downstream from these lochs the river has a turbulent course over two sets of falls, one at Deanie Lodge and one at Culligran, before levelling out as it joins the Glass. The Farrar has an excellent tributary on its right bank, just below Loch Monar, called the Misgeach Burn and this and a large part of the Farrar below this point have excellent spawning grounds. In the late 1950s and early 1960s the North of Scotland Hydro-electric Board developed Strathfarrar. This entailed raising the level of Loch Monar by placing an arch-type dam 113 feet high at its outlet. This increased the length of Loch Monar to about 8 miles. No fish pass was placed on the dam. Water is led from Monar to an underground power station at Deanie near the west end of Loch Beannacharan. A further dam was placed across the River Farrar below the outlet of Loch Beannacharan which raised the level of the loch by about 8 feet. A Borland fish pass is installed on this dam. From here water is passed to Culligran Power Station below the Culligran Falls. There are smolt screens on the intake to prevent damage to descending smolts. At one time there were electric screens installed at Deanie and Culligran tailraces, but these caused more damage to ascending adults than the turbine blades. Also included in this scheme is an aqueduct which diverts right bank tributaries below Loch Monar back into the loch.

The Misgeach Burn and the Farrar above and below Loch Beannacharan down to Culligran Power Station have an agreed compensation flow, and there are still very valuable spawning areas in the less turbulent sections of the river. The section of the Farrar from Culligran to its junction with the Glass is subject to a wide variation of flow due to generation at the power station. The upper reaches of the Farrar are owned by Lovat Estates and the lower by Struy Estate and Culligran Estate. The former do not exercise their angling rights in the Farrar to any great extent but tend to use the area entirely as a breeding and nursery ground which they plant each year with fry and smolts. The Struy Estate and Culligran Estate fishings, however, have a useful potential and a reasonable number of salmon and grilse are caught on this part of the river in most seasons.

The Borland fish pass at Beannacharan Dam is operated manually and a visual count of the fish is made by the staff of the North of Scotland Hydro-electric Board and the counts since 1965 are as follows:

Table 10

Counts of salmon and grilse at Beannacharan Dam, 1965–1979

Year	Count	Year	Count	Year	Count
1965	203	1970	92	1975	213
1966	146	1971	250	1976	150
1967	264	1972	470	1977	176
1968	124	1973	124	1978	326
1969	200	1974	339	1979	123

THE BEAULY DISTRICT

In order to check the downstream passage of smolts, to ensure that they were using the pass and not passing through the smolt screens and into the turbines, the North of Scotland Hydro-electric Board installed a trap in Beannacharan fish pass in 1971 and 1972. In these two years they caught and released downstream 7,075 and 6,051 smolts respectively.

The Beauly

The Beauly has been developed for hydro power by the North of Scotland Hydro-electric Board as part of the Strathfarrar scheme. Two dams have been built across the gorges at Aigas and Kilmorack. The Aigas Dam is the furthest upstream and is 58 feet high; it creates a ponding effect back almost to the old ferry at Aigas Island and a certain amount of angling water and spawning ground is flooded. The Kilmorack Dam is further downstream at the end of the gorge. It is also 58 feet high and causes a ponding effect to Aigas Dam. The famous rock at the foot of the Aigas Gorge known as the Lord and Lady Lovat Rock has been preserved and sticks out of the water below Aigas Dam. This dam has drowned out a number of famous pools including the Red Rock, Mare's, Mill and Stone. There was little spawning ground in this area as the river was too rocky and turbulent but there is some spawning ground in the small burns which flow into the section between the dams. There are Borland fish passes in both dams, with the entrance to the passes being in the centre of the dams and the turbines discharging on either side. The passes are worked manually and a visual count of the fish passing upstream is made by the staff of the North of Scotland Hydro-electric Board. The Kilmorack pass works extremely well for ascending fish but at times the fish are slow to use the Aigas pass, and it is sometimes necessary to alter the flow below Aigas Dam and simulate flood conditions artificially during appropriate climatic conditions in order to stimulate fish to ascend. However, they are inclined to stay between the two dams for considerable periods at certain times of the year and under certain conditions.

Table 11

Counts of salmon and grilse at Kilmorack and Aigas fish passes, 1965–1979

	Kilmorack	Aigas		Kilmorack	Aigas
1965	8,900	8,641	1973	7,890	7,362
1966	8,670	8,390	1974	7,842	7,150
1967	13,956	12,749	1975	5,601	5,393
1968	4,903	4,300	1976	4,937	4,331
1969	7,248	6,983	1977	5,653	4,912
1970	5,194	4,769	1978	10,617	9,280
1971	10,621	8,954	1979	9,926	9,502
1972	5,356	5,315			

It can be seen from these figures that the differences are not very great and that the majority of fish ascending Kilmorack do pass on upstream beyond Aigas. What the figures do not reveal is the time lag between the two dams. In years when kelts congregate at the upstream face of Kilmorack Dam the drum gates are used to spill the fish over: this seems to be more satisfactory than allowing them to use the Borland pass which they seem loath to enter.

Below the Kilmorack Dam the excellent salmon fishing owned entirely by Lovat Estates begins and from the dam to the sea many fine salmon pools occur, and there is little rocky water. The big long pools are easy to wade and some fish well from a boat. There are three main beats, the Falls, Home and Dounie. The Falls beat has 8 named pools of which probably the Ferry and the Cruives are the most well-known, the former being a very large pool. Fish do not ascend the Cruives until the water temperature is above 42°F. The Home beat has 13 named pools of which Silver and the Groams are held in high repute. Many of these pools occur in most pleasant surroundings of arable farmland and deciduous woodland. Because of the width of the river a lot of wading is necessary, but the even, gravelly bed makes wading safe and easy. The Dounie beat extends almost to the A9 road bridge and has 10 named pools, the Willow, Fly and Minister's being the best, but the Long Reach, a very long pool, is one of the other good pools where many fish are taken. All these beats are four-rod beats with ample fishing for this number of rods. The Falls probably fishes best in the early part of the year and then fishes consistently well for the rest of the season. The Home is slower to start but is probably the best beat over the rest of the year. The Dounie is excellent for sea trout early in the season and is sometimes let to a syndicate of local people until 1 June. It then fishes well for salmon and grilse for the remainder of the season.

There are 2 other beats on the Beauly between the Farrar junction and Aigas Dam and these are the Aigas and Eskadale beats, both of which afford good sport once the fish ascend the dams. There are 7 other beats let on a day ticket basis. These include, on the river, the Caravan Park beat, the Wester Lovat beat and the Tidal beat. In the estuary there is a beat on each bank both of which extend as far down the firth as Bunchrew. Spinning is only allowed on the estuary beats. Finally there is beat between the dams. Information concerning lets on any of these beats can be obtained from the Lovat Estates office in Beauly.

The number of people fishing these beats each year are said to be considerably in excess of 1,000 and good catches are obtained. In 1975 the record catch for one beat was 48 fish in one day and catches of up to 12 fish for one rod in a day are not unusual.

In 1966 a very large flood considerably altered pools in the section of river below Kilmorack Dam and major bank repairs were required to stabilise the eroded banks. Gabion weirs were used to retrain the river in certain places and these have proved to be a considerable asset.

The Beauly and its main tributaries below the Farrar junction have excellent

THE BEAULY DISTRICT

spawning and nursery areas. Sea trout spawn mainly below Kilmorack and only a few ascend the fish passes. The Belladrum Burn and the Bruiach Burn, which flow into the Beauly below Beaufort Castle, are good nursery streams. Loch Bruicheach, out of which this stream flows, is part of the Inverness water supply scheme and compensation flows for this stream form part of the provisions of the scheme. One other good spawning tributary is the Teachmuick Burn.

As there is no district fishery board on the Beauly the Lovat Estates make themselves responsible for the upkeep and improvement of this river. As far back as the 1800s Lord Lovat bought up all the netting rights in the Beauly Firth, and others further east came into the hands of the Moray Firth Salmon Fisheries Company. There is no doubt that this played a large part in turning this river into a major salmon fishery. At the same time two hatcheries, which still exist, were set up to produce fry for the river system. They have a combined capacity of one and a half million fry. One of the hatcheries which is supplied with spring water tends to bring the fry on rather quickly in a cold year, as the temperature of the spring water is much higher than that of the stream water which supplies the other hatchery. The Lovat Estates also run a separate smolt-rearing station capable of producing over 500,000 smolts each year. Fry and smolts are liberated in the Glass, Farrar and Beauly, as well as many of the tributaries, each year.

The Lovat Estates do not exercise any of their netting rights in the estuary. They do, however, run a sweep net fishery below the stone weir upstream of Beaufort Castle. This normally only operates during the height of the grilse run.

The Beauly in recent years has become largely a summer and autumn river as the spring run has shown a marked decline. A few fish are caught in March and April then the summer run builds up through May, June and July. There is a slight decline in August before the autumn run appears and continues until the end of the season on 15 October.

Pollution in this river system has been kept well under control with excellent co-operation from the local authorities and the Highland River Purification Board.

UDN appeared in the river system in 1969 but there was no serious outbreak. Most years some marked fish are observed but numbers of these have become fewer in recent years.

17

THE CONON DISTRICT

The River Conon is the largest river in Ross-shire and flows into the head of the Cromarty Firth near Dingwall. It is fed by four large tributaries, the Black Water, Bran, Meig and Orrin – rising in the deer forests of Inchbae, Strathvaich, Strathgarve, Kinlochluichart, Fannich, Strathconon, Cabaan and Corriehallie. These are romantic names which spell out the colour of the hills and moors clad in heather, bracken, bog myrtle and deer grass. It is from such country that the turbulent rocky burns and streams of clear water, stained with peat in flood, flow rapidly downstream gradually maturing into swift-moving rivers with deep pools alternating with torrential runs. As the arable farmland of the lower Conon valley is reached they join the river after which the valley is named, and during the last few miles of its course the Conon meanders more sedately through arable farm and parkland before sweeping into the estuary and out to sea.

In the last twenty years there have been major changes in these central Ross-shire valleys as, with the advent of hydro-electric development, the North of Scotland Hydro-electric Board has very fully exploited the potential of the area for hydro power. The waters of the Conon and its tributaries are now held back by 9 dams, channelled through miles of pipeline and aqueducts and pass through 6 power stations with much of the water collected in the reservoirs actually passing through 3 power stations before reaching the sea. Some of the tributaries, such as the Black Water and the lower Orrin, are only a shadow of their former selves and it is only during periods of heavy rainfall that, for a short but delightful spell, these rivers assume some of their former grandeur. Even the Conon, which graciously accepts more than its former quota of water due to the diversion of waters from the reservoirs in the upper reaches of its tributaries, behaves in a chameleon-like way, with its water levels changing unpredictably due to power generation rather than to moods of the weather.

The largest tributary of the Conon is the Bran which flows from Loch a' Chroisg west of Achnasheen. It increases in size at Achnasheen where it receives an appreciable flow of water from Abhainn a' Chomair running out of Loch Gowan. Its course then lies east down Strathbran flowing rapidly over excellent potential spawning beds and nursery areas. The surrounding land is rather bleak and exposed and consists chiefly of unimproved sheep grazing as far as Caiseachan. Here the Bran deepens and meanders sluggishly past

THE CONON DISTRICT

Achanalt and Strathbran Lodge until reaching Loch Achanalt and Loch a' Chuilinn, the home of large trout, pike and perch. The outlet from Loch a' Chuilinn is dammed by a barrage to hold up waters for release downstream to Achanalt Power Station. The river is diverted through the power station at an intake weir and, when the station is not 'on load', the water passes down an attractive salmon ladder in the form of a pool overfall pass built into the side of the falls which used to cascade over a quarter of a mile down to Grudie Bridge. Just before the Bran flows into Loch Luichart it receives water from Loch Fannich via both the Grudie Bridge Power Station and the River Grudie, and this additional flow produces a very attractive series of rapids which are a great tourist attraction.

Loch Luichart is one of the largest lochs in Easter Ross, although not the size of Loch Fannich. Its area was increased after the construction of Luichart Dam in 1954. It is a very deep loch and holds some large trout, char, perch and pike. A pike of 32 lb was netted during pike clearance operations conducted by the North of Scotland Hydro-electric Board between 1955 and 1963.

Water leaves Loch Luichart either through Luichart Power Station, when it is discharged into the Conon about a mile downstream of the dam, or through the dam itself via a Borland fish pass and a compensation turbine. The river below the dam now assumes the name of the Conon, and the Conon Falls a very short distance below the dam have now been opened up for ascending salmon by incorporating a series of salmon ladders which have been attractively landscaped into the rocky area to give a most pleasing ornamental effect.

Half a mile below Luichart Power Station the Meig joins the Conon at Sir William's Pool. The Meig might be considered the main tributary, although not the largest, as it flows through Strathconon, a valley named after the main river rather than itself. The Meig rises in the remote area of Glencarron Forest and flows through Glen Fhoidhaig before reaching lovely Corriefeol and Loch Beannachran (known locally as Loch Scardroy). Downstream from here the river flows through a beautiful wide valley of rich farmland with steep hills on either side. Near Milltown are the remains of Strathconon House, the old residence of the late Captain Combe, which was destroyed by fire many years ago. Fortunately the unrivalled collection of stags' heads were rescued and may still be seen in the village hall in Strathconon. Below Bridgend the Meig is impounded to form a diversion reservoir and much of the water is passed through the hills to Loch Luichart. There is a fish pass in Meig Dam and a compensation flow from the dam ensures the ascent of salmon. A short distance below the dam there was, until 1976, a fish trap operated jointly by the North of Scotland Hydro-electric Board and the Department of Agriculture and Fisheries for Scotland. Here the salmon smolts descending the Meig were tagged and the returning adult salmon counted and examined for tags. Below the old trap site are the spectacular Black Falls situated in a steep and narrow ravine. Flowing out of the ravine the Meig passes Little Scatwell and quarter of a mile below the farm gently joins the Conon.

Below the Meig confluence the Conon runs past Scatwell House and the village of Scatwell and flows into Loch Achonachie, a reservoir formed by Torr Achilty Dam. A little over halfway down the right shore of the loch, water from Orrin Reservoir enters through a small power station. The Conon assumes more majestic proportions below Torr Achilty Dam as a result of a larger compensation flow and generation flows from the Torr Achilty Power Station. The Black Water is the next tributary to join the Conon about a mile and a half below Torr Achilty Dam at the Junction Pool a little to the east of Contin, a name meaning the 'meeting of the waters'.

The upper reaches of the Black Water are almost entirely flooded out by Glascarnoch Reservoir and, as relatively little spawning area remains upstream of the reservoir, no fish pass has been incorporated into Glascarnoch Dam. The compensation flow for the Black Water comes not from Glascarnoch Reservoir but from Loch Vaich. The flow is sufficient to maintain a healthy stock of young salmon which are planted out as fry from the local salmon hatchery at Contin by the Conon District Salmon Fishery Board. It is only after heavy rain that the river runs full and it depends mainly on the burns running off the western slopes of Ben Wyvis to give it a respectable appearance and to attract tourists to the falls a short distance west of Garve on the Ullapool road. East of Garve the river runs into Loch Garve and, shortly afterwards into little Loch na Croic. Both waters hold trout and large pike. At the head of Loch na Croic is a barrier and trap which prevents the upstream movement of salmon. The fish remain in the loch during the summer and are trapped as they attempt to move upstream in the autumn. They are held in part of the loch which has been netted off until they are ready for stripping. The eggs are held in the Contin salmon hatchery and the resulting fry are released in the upper reaches of the Black Water. The Bran, which had never been a salmon river due to the Conon Falls barring the ascent of fish, has also been stocked for many years in an endeavour to establish a spawning run. Downstream from Loch na Croic the Black Water becomes a more fishable river and below the Falls of Rogie the river forms a series of deep rocky holding pools, and flows between steep-sided banks as far as Achilty. At Achilty the valley widens out into flat farmland and the last 2 miles of the river tend to be less interesting, and its confluence with the Conon resembles an uninspiring backwater.

The last tributary to join the Conon is the Orrin which flows in from the right bank at the Kettle Pool near Brahan Castle. The river rises in a remote glen bounded by the mountain ranges of Strathconon and Strathfarrar. Below Loch na Caoidhe and Am Fiar the river enters a wide valley of wild deer forest and flows past the remote Corriehallie Lodge. Gone are the days when the menfolk at a funeral carried the coffin across the river which they waded on stilts. It is years since this remote glen had any inhabitants.

East of Cabaan the river runs into Orrin reservoir, the waters of which are diverted to Loch Achonachie. Below Orrin Dam the river flows at a compensation level supplied from the Borland Pass and compensation turbine. About 4 miles downstream from the dam are the Orrin Falls in the grounds of Sir John Stirling of Fairburn. These have a vertical fall of 12 feet and are reputed to be the highest falls salmon can surmount in one 'leap'. Certainly they are very spectacular and the wooden bridge over the river at the falls is an excellent vantage point to watch the attempts of the fish as they congregate below them in June and July. Downstream from the falls the river is uninteresting and it gives the impression of a uniform channel at Orrin Bridge, near Urray.

As in other Scottish river systems, there have been changes in the salmon stocks, both in size and seasonal distribution. The Conon river system, opening on 26 January, used to have an early run of spring fish which usually reached the Coul beat above Moy Bridge by late March and ascended the Black Water as far as Rogie Falls by mid-April. Spring fish were taken from late January to May, with progressively more fish being caught on the Coul and Moy beats and on the lower Black Water. The spring fish were followed by early summer fish in late May and early June, a few weeks before the grilse run started in earnest in early July and continued until mid-August. Many anglers felt that the season, closing at the end of September, was too long as many fish were in an advanced spawning condition at this time. However, since about 1968 there have been marked changes in the time of ascent of fish and, as in many other rivers, the spring run has almost completely disappeared. There is no evidence that this is in any way a result of hydro-electric developments and, with the many other factors affecting salmon stocks such as the high seas

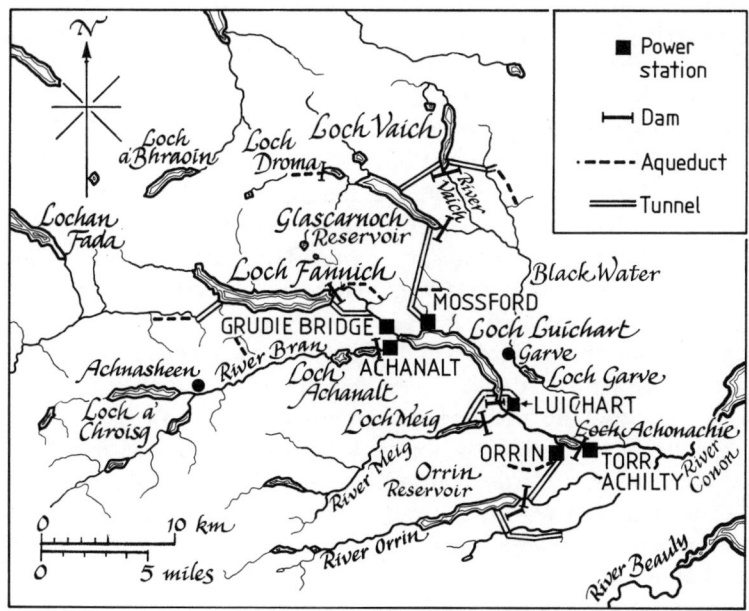

The Rivers Conon, Black Water, Meig and Bran and the Conon Basin Hydro-electric Scheme

salmon fisheries and UDN, it would be unwise to try and attribute changes in either the size of the runs or the time of their ascent to alterations to the natural régime of this river system. There can be no doubt, however, that angling in the upper reaches has been affected by delay in access and the more restricted flows, as on the Black Water and Orrin. Whatever has caused the loss of spring fish, there is no doubt that the Conon is the poorer for their absence and, to those who knew it before the advent of UDN and when spring fish were abundant, it is a very sad state of affairs.

The Conon

The estuary of the Conon is netted by the Moray Firth Salmon Fisheries Company and at one time their operations started in February and finished in August. However, with the loss of the spring run and with the rise in fishermen's wages, netting is now only carried out with the help of students for three or four weeks during the height of the grilse run. The first real holding pool for salmon is the Bridge Pool and, before the construction of the new road bridge, a good cast was just below the old bridge on the right bank. It was fished chiefly in the spring by spinning and was not fished much with fly.

The early spring fishing on the Lower Brahan beat lies upstream of Conon Bridge as far as the old cruive dykes and is owned by the North of Scotland Hydro-electric Board. The cruives have not been operated for many years and are passable to fish at all times, being in a poor state of repair. The Slaggan is the first pool above Conon Bridge and was always a likely spot for a fish or two and, in former times, was the scene of some record catches with double figures to a rod in one day. Under normal flows it fishes well up in the neck of the pool as far down as the end of the old wall on the right bank, with fish lying nearer the right bank than the left. During high flows, when Torr Achilty Power Station is generating, there is more current and the pool can be fished out to its full length of almost 100 yards. Occasionally the last cast near the big trees on the right bank will produce a fish. Above the Slaggan the river runs either side of a large island of about 50 acres. The right channel has one or two good casts, such as the Brander, but the left channel is the larger and more popular, with the Little Junction and the Top Box producing the most fish. The former usually yields the first fish of the season. The Greenbank, just upstream of the cruives, is a good pool a little later in the spring. This lower beat fished best at the start of the season when there was a spring run and, although a few large summer fish are caught after the end of May, few grilse stop in this beat for any length of time.

Upstream from the cruive dykes are the Middle and Upper Brahan fishings which extend upstream to Moy Bridge, on the left bank and to the Kettle Pool on the right bank. Both banks are owned by the North of Scotland Hydro-

THE CONON DISTRICT

electric Board. The favourite pools lie in the parkland of Brahan Estate with most of the fish coming from the Rushing Pool, the Ferry Stream and the Kettle. Upstream from the Kettle is the Upper Brahan beat, the left bank being owned by the North of Scotland Hydro-electric Board and the right bank by Fairburn Estate. The Plock and the Major, a short distance below Moy Bridge, produce the most fish from this beat.

Immediately above Moy Bridge lies a deep, wide pool some 200 yards long, known as the Boat Pool, with the neck being referred to as the Junction Pool. It is here that the Black Water joins the Conon as it sweeps round the corner close to the Moy–Contin road. The Junction Pool and the top of the Boat fish best close to the left bank, but lower down the Boat fish lie closer to the right bank. Some large fish have been taken from this stretch and one of 26 lb was taken in the mid-60s.

The Moy beat and the next beat, the Coul, which extends up to Torr Achilty Dam, come into their own by mid-April. The Coul beat in particular produces a reasonable number of spring fish from mid-April, the productive pools at this time of the year being the Deer Fence, New and Clachuil. Later in the year, when the grilse arrive, the Deer Fence stream and the Junction Pool come into their own. The Coul beat is a delightful stretch to fish with wide open pools and clear banks giving good access and easy casting. The fishings on the left bank of the Coul and Moy beats are owned by the North of Scotland Hydro-electric Board, while those on the right belong to a syndicate.

Torr Achilty Dam at the top of the Coul Water is the first barrier the salmon have to negotiate. Frequent operation of the Borland Pass ensures there is little delay and all fish passing upstream are counted; 25 years of counts reveal wide fluctuations in numbers of fish ascending. In 1961 only 743 salmon and grilse ascended, a surprisingly low number to which it is hard to attribute any cause. Certainly not to the Greenland fishery which was only in its infancy at this time. As was the case on other rivers where counts were made at dams, such as the Tummel, the years 1971 to 1974 produced high figures, but these were due to good runs of grilse.

Table 12
Counts of salmon and grilse at Torr Achilty Dam 1955–1979

Year	Count	Year	Count	Year	Count
1955	3,019	1964	2,388	1973	3,496
1956	2,283	1965	2,883	1974	3,395
1957	3,217	1966	2,436	1975	1,362
1958	1,557	1967	4,933	1976	1,813
1959	2,027	1968	2,404	1977	868
1960	1,793	1969	2,485	1978	3,115
1961	743	1970	2,277	1979	1,737
1962	1,277	1971	5,173		
1963	1,644	1972	6,224		

The salmon fishing above Torr Achilty Dam is most disappointing considering the numbers of fish that pass upstream. In Loch Achonachie an occasional fish is taken in the tailrace of Orrin Power Station. Above the loch the fishing is owned by the North of Scotland Hydro-electric Board and is divided into two beats: Luichart Power Station to Poil a' Chroisg (left bank); Scatwell to the head of the loch (both banks). Scatwell Estate has the fishing from Scatwell to Luichart Power Station on the right bank. The lower beat, which includes the old submerged Falls Pool at the head of the loch, is the better of the two, but it does require Luichart Power Station to be on load to produce sufficient water movement to fish a fly or lure effectively. The upper beat has two good pools, Sir William's and Poil a' Chroisg, the latter being the better of the two with the fish lying into the left bank. The fluctuations in water levels are a problem in this stretch of the river and probably unsettle the fish. The same situation occurs, of course, below Torr Achilty Dam, but the fluctuations are not so rapid and, providing he times his fishing to coincide with a rise in water level, the angler can capitalise on the situation. Quite often the fish take as the water level is rising and then, after a short unsettled period, they start to take at the higher flows. The same situation occurs as the water levels drop.

Many salmon spawn below Luichart Power Station immediately upstream from Sir William's Pool. During the 1957 spawning season fish were found to be stranded when the power station went off load. As a result of this a small gabion weir was installed downstream from the spawning area to maintain the water level over the redds when the power station stops generating.

Fishing on the Conon stops below Luichart Power Station. Salmon can now negotiate the Conon Falls and during the period 1957 to 1965 the fish were counted through a trap constructed on the falls which was operated by personnel employed by the Department of Agriculture and Fisheries for Scotland and the North of Scotland Hydro-electric Board as part of a salmon research scheme. For reasons of policy no salmon were allowed into the Bran in earlier years but in 1960 the first salmon entered Loch Luichart and ascended the Bran.

The Bran

Although salmon first ascended the Bran in 1960, only two fish have been caught in this river. The first fish, a grilse, was taken at Caiseachan on 15 September 1960, and the auspicious occasion was duly recorded by Major Sir Reginald MacDonald-Buchanan of Scatwell Estate, on whose water the fish was taken, by having the fish mounted. The second fish was taken in Loch Luichart on 29 September. After 1960 it was 6 years before any more salmon were allowed to enter Loch Luichart as a result of the management policy of the Conon District Fishery Board. Since 1966 fish have been allowed to ascend in some years and not in others, but no sport fishery has been established. It is unlikely that one will develop as, due to their late arrival in late August and early September, the fish would be coming into spawning condition.

However, it is gratifying to see salmon using this river for, as long ago as 1837, Stoddart states in his *Angling Reminiscences* (page 105) that 'the falls a short way below Loch Luichart are a great obstacle to the progress of salmon which, were they removed, might proceed inland above thirty miles and over a succession of spawning beds of a first rate quality.'

The Orrin

The situation for salmon on the Orrin in recent years has become one of utter tragedy. At one time salmon ascended the Orrin as far as the falls and congregated in the large round pool into which flowed water from the lade which was used to power the hydro-electric plant for Fairburn Estate. A sweep netting station at the pool took its toll, but those fish escaping the net ascended the falls and passed on into Cabaan Forest.

With the advent of the hydro-electric scheme in the Conon Basin, ancillary operations by the Orrin damaged the river environment. A sand washing plant about a mile below the dam site dirtied the water and river bed gravel extraction widened the mouth of the Orrin so that there was no concentrated flow of water entering the Conon. After impoundment of Orrin Reservoir in 1959 no salmon were allowed to ascend the dam, although a four-channel steel-lined Borland fish pass was incorporated into the dam at great expense. Netting continued at the falls, but on a reduced scale, and those fish ascending the falls were only able to spawn in the stretch of river between there and the dam. From the early 1960s the Conon District Salmon Fishery Board has been trapping salmon above the falls, which have been eased by reducing their height by installing a wall across the tail of the pool. The salmon are held in the old lade until they are ready for stripping in the autumn. A number are still allowed to spawn in the river as far as the dam and this area is also planted with unfed fry each year. With the advent of UDN the position became pitiful, with large numbers of the fish impounded in the lade dying before they were ready to strip, and the graves of fish in the surrounding woodland tell their own story of the ravages of this incurable disease.

The Black Water

The fishings on the Black Water are owned by the North of Scotland Hydro-electric Board and are divided as follows: Junction Pool to Achilty Bridge;

Achilty Bridge to Rogie Falls, and Rogie Falls to the foot of Loch na Croic.

The lowest beat, from the Junction Pool to Achilty Bridge is leased by the Craigdarroch Chalet Complex in Contin. There is a lot of dead water on this beat, but if the river has more than its compensation flow it can fish quite well, with the Bridge Pool and the Martins producing the most fish.

The middle beat is the beat *par excellence* on the Black Water. This has always been a good stretch and, in the past, always produced a good head of spring fish, particularly in the Preserves, the Long Pool and the Hut. It is now mainly a grilse river and though the Falls Pool, the Pulpit, the Hut and the Preserves are the most popular, the Long, Square, Fat and Field produce their fair share of fish. Although some fish negotiate Rogie Falls, the majority ascend the fish pass built into the left bank by the North of Scotland Hydro-electric Board.

The upper beat is leased to the Loch Achonachie Angling Club and does not fish well until July during periods of high water. A lot of fish lie in the deep pool by the large island at the mouth of the Rogie Burn and do not take readily. However, there are 2 or 3 reasonable pools between the island and the foot of Loch na Croic which hold fish during high water and also an occasional large trout.

Angling records on the Black Water are available for the period 1943 to 1979 and reveal a number of broad trends. Unfortunately no information on fishing effort is available so that the value of comparisons between years or decades is limited. However, the low figures for the period 1974–1978 are probably a reflection of the low flows prevailing in these drought years.

Table 13

Rod catches of salmon and grilse on the Black Water, 1943–1979

Year	Catch	Year	Catch	Year	Catch
1943	158	1956	389	1969	157
1944	147	1957	274	1970	246
1945	188	1958	326	1971	126
1946	122	1959	166	1972	157
1947	102	1960	279	1973	131
1948	96	1961	284	1974	44
1949	179	1962	229	1975	60
1950	182	1963	187	1976	85
1951	242	1964	268	1977	69
1952	239	1965	331	1978	91
1953	246	1966	261	1979	113
1954	369	1967	323		
1955	279	1968	201		

The Meig

The flow down the Meig from Meig Dam to its confluence with the Conon is now reduced to a compensation level, the summer flow being about three times larger than that in winter. Only when water spills over the dam, an infrequent occurrence, is the flow appreciably increased. The result of such low flows tends to be the formation of an area of slack water at the Meig confluence and this is most marked during times of high flow from Luichart Power Station. However, fish homing to the Meig find the right route and pass upstream to the dam, although some fish may initially be drawn up to the power station during the higher flows. There is no angling below the dam and little spawning, although a few fish spawn in the gravelly area just upstream from the wooden bridge on the farm road to Scatwell. Before the fish trap was dismantled all fish passing upstream were checked through the trap and then allowed on to ascend the pass and enter the reservoir. The numbers of salmon and grilse passing upstream through the trap are given below and reveal the expected annual fluctuations. It is interesting to note that from 1957 to 1975 the poorest runs of fish occurred every seventh year, starting in 1961 and again in 1968 and 1975.

Table 14

Numbers of salmon and grilse entering Meig trap 1957–1976, and passing through Meig Dam 1977–1979

Year	Number	Year	Number	Year	Number
1957	613	1965	829	1973	240
1958	256	1966	546	1974	585
1959	246	1967	835	1975	49
1960	220	1968	160	1976	262
1961	149	1969	266	1977	134
1962	231	1970	294	1978	1,326
1963	375	1971	572	1979	912
1964	479	1972	345		

In the pre-hydro days the annual rod catch on the Meig over a seventy year period was 45, with annual catches ranging from 1 to 139. There are 38 named pools on the river and these include Colin's, Smith, Manse, Captain's, Peter's, Taylor's, Yellow Stone, Giant Rock, Heron, Tinker and Hades. Fish appeared in the Meig from late July. There was considerable fishing by Strathconon Estate in those days, and the casting platforms remaining on some of the pools still bear witness to a life long past. During this halcyon period the largest salmon caught was one of $29\frac{1}{2}$ lb and was taken by Lt Col Combe, the eldest son of Captain Combe, on 23 September 1923 from the Bob-a-Ruschach Pool. A cast of it can be seen in the Strathconon village hall. In recent years only two or three local rods fished this river and only three or four fish are caught each year.

SALMON RIVERS OF SCOTLAND

However, the numbers passing upstream are still suffficient to maintain a viable stock and the main spawning areas are the outfall from Loch Scardroy, below Corriefeol and in wind-swept Gleann Meinich which is now afforested.

18

THE ALNESS, ALLT GRAAD AND BALNAGOWN

The Alness

This Ross-shire river rises in the mountains of Kildermorie deer forest to the north-west of the Cromarty Firth and flows south-east, joining the Cromarty Firth near the town of Alness. The total length of this river from source to mouth is some 20 miles. It is mainly spring-fed and swollen by surface water. In its upper reaches it flows down a kindly strath with an abundance of fine gravel and deep pools before descending a rough rocky fall. From this fall it flows through a section of boulder-strewn water with the odd deep section, into a larger gorge with deep rocky pools and, after passing Kildermorie Lodge, enters Loch Morie 10 miles from its source. Loch Morie is a deep loch and is renowned for its char and ferox trout. The loch was impounded by a small dam in 1978 in order to provide artificial freshets. After flowing out of Loch Morie the Alness begins its 10-mile descent to the Cromarty Firth, quietly at first and then faster as it enters a wooded ravine past Ardross Castle and under the road bridge that carries the road over to Struie, and thence through the village of Alness and into the Firth. A lot of its beauty is lost to the public eye as its course is through a very steep valley which is largely out of sight of main roads.

The Alness has one main tributary, the Black Water, which flows down Strath Rusdale and is almost as long as the upper Alness. It joins the main river on its left bank 3 miles below Loch Morie. There are many attractive angling pools, runs and deep pots and amongst the most famous are the Douglas, the Raven Rock, Iron Bridge, Inchlumpie and Ferry. The fishing is mainly owned by Novar, Ardross Castle and Teaninich. The Alness Angling Association fishes a large part of this river. Catches are in the region of 200 salmon and a similar number of sea trout. Netting takes place at the mouth of the river and the nets are drawn on to a large gravel beach at the mouth or on to specially constructed cairns nearby. This is a useful fishery, especially during the grilse run.

The Alness has an abundance of spawning gravel both below Loch Morie and above and there are excellent nursery areas. The river tends to hold a good stock of summer fish and, before UDN appeared, was also famed for its sea trout.

The Alness District Salmon Fishery Board has stocked the river recently with 100,000 salmon fry and a smaller number of sea trout fry. The river has been badly affected since 1967 by UDN and bad outbreaks of this disease have occurred, particularly during the month of July. In the early 1970s a Denil fish pass was erected in the weir near Alness where water is diverted to Dalmore Distillery. This has improved the free ascent of fish especially during times of low water flow, when the area below the weir used to be badly poached. Large areas of the Alness catchment have recently been afforested and the drainage needed for this development has caused some increase in gravel movement in the river system.

The Allt Graad

The Allt Graad is a small river which rises in the mountains to the north-west of the Cromarty Firth and flows south-east through the village of Evanton into the Cromarty Firth. The upper reaches drain the deer forests of Wyvis and Kildermorie and flow into Loch Glass. From Loch Glass the river flows quietly down Glen Glass before entering the Black Rock Gorge. This is a narrow ravine with many falls which are completely inaccessible to migratory fish. After passing through the gorge the river flattens out and flows for a further 2 miles before entering the Cromarty Firth. There is little angling on this river and many of the pools were destroyed by severe floods and revetment works designed to prevent floods. The few pools can be poached easily.

There are few spawning areas and only limited feeding areas between the Firth and the Black Rock Gorge. At present there is only a small stock of salmon and sea trout and if the river is to produce a good stock of migratory fish then the feeding areas above the Gorge will have to be utilised. The commercial netting is owned by Novar Estate and the sweep nets are drawn either on to the gravel beach at the mouth of the river or on to banks in the Firth.

The Balnagown

The Balnagown rises to the west of the Cromarty Firth on the slopes of Beinn Tharsuinn and flows east to enter the Firth near the village of Kildary. The river flows quietly down Strath Rory through the undulating moorland where it is crossed by the road to Bonar Bridge via Struie. Further downstream it passes the farmlands of Scotsburn, and at this point enters a gorge passing Balnagown Castle whose electricity supply was once produced by the harnessed waters of the river. After leaving the gorge the river flattens out before entering the Firth in the grounds of Tarbat House

THE ALNESS, ALLT GRAAD AND BALNAGOWN

The falls beside Balnagown Castle have been impassable for a considerable time and it is between this point and the Firth that the migratory fish stock is established. There are only a few angling pools and limited spawning and feeding areas in this section of the river. The stock is limited to a late salmon run but there is a reasonable sea trout run earlier in the year. If the extensive feeding areas above the falls were utilised and the falls improved to allow the free ascent of fish this river could support a reasonable stock of salmon and sea trout. There is no netting on this river at present.

19

THE KYLE OF SUTHERLAND

The Kyle of Sutherland forms the estuary of all rivers in this group. Its general direction is east-west and it begins at the confluence of the rivers Cassley and Oykel. It flows east until it merges with the Dornoch Firth. From the confluence of the Oykel and Cassley to the district's statutory limit, the Kyle and Firth stretch for some 27 miles.

The Oykel enters the Kyle from the west and the Cassley from the north-west. The upper part is flat and tidal, flowing between loam banks of meadow land with numerous sand banks and islands to break up its monotony. These are frequented by many species of gulls, waders and wildfowl. After its slow meandering passage for 7 miles it is joined by the River Shin from the north and just below this point it passes Carbisdale Castle, built by one of the Duchesses of Sutherland, which is reputed to have 366 windows. It was in the hills behind this castle that the legendary Scottish figure, Montrose, was defeated in his last battle. At the narrows below the castle the only rail link with the north crosses the Kyle. A short distance below the railway bridge the Kyle widens out into a large bay and then narrows again as it passes through the village of Bonar Bridge where the main A9 trunk road crosses it. It is opposite Bonar Bridge that the Carron joins the Kyle from the west. This is 11 miles from the confluence of the Oykel and Cassley. The Kyle widens out again below Bonar Bridge and remains wide until it merges with the Dornoch Firth. The Evelix flows into the Kyle from the north, 10 miles east of Bonar Bridge.

The Kyle is the county boundary between Ross and Cromarty and Sutherland. The netting stations for all the Kyle of Sutherland rivers are all sited on the Kyle and no netting takes place in the rivers. These stations, owned by Benmore Estates, are chiefly situated at Bonar Bridge. West of this point netting used to take place, but the riparian owners of the river fishings pay Benmore Estates an annual amount not to exercise these rights. At the present time the nets do not operate at Bonar Bridge before 15 April. Other proprietors have netting rights to the east of Bonar Bridge but few are exercised. There is, however, a fairly intensive netting effort east of Tain on the Ross-shire side.

Angling, mainly for sea trout, is leased by the Bonar Bridge Angling Association and, prior to the disease UDN, large numbers were taken each year both east and west of Bonar Bridge. The Angling Association are stocking some of the small burns of the Kyle with sea trout fry annually, and the stock seems to be increasing once again. The section of the Kyle west of Bonar Bridge serves a useful purpose and is able to hold numbers of salmon above the netting zone during drought periods, when they are unable to enter the rivers because of low water flow. At the same time, apart from the main rivers which flow into it, there are several streams which can accommodate a few pairs of salmon and sea trout during spawning time.

The Carron

The Carron rises in the mountains to the south-west of the Kyle of Sutherland in Gleann Beag and Gleann Mor. It is mainly spring-fed and swollen by surface water from the mountains of the Freevater Deer Forest. In the winter the many burns that feed it tumble erratically down the hillsides, the water as clear as crystal, coming from the snow-clad mountains and corries above. In the summer the water is stained with peat and makes a contrast with the purple heather and deer grass on its banks. The river flows north-east through the narrow glens of Beag and Mor before entering a rugged gorge graced by clumps of silver birch. It cascades majestically over the Falls of Glencalvie and passes the lodges of Glencalvie and Amat. After this point it flattens out and, apart from numerous little gorges and cascades, it meanders its way through the crofting areas of Strath Carron and past the lodges of Gruinards and Braelangwell, where it negotiates a deeper gorge with the famous angling pool named Moral. Below Moral lie Gledfield House and the Gledfield Falls below which the river flows quietly past Invercharron House and enters the Kyle. The last section of the river is tidal up to the Boat Pool.

There are many attractive angling pools, runs and little pots, some of which have platforms, ladders and catwalks to enable the fisherman to gain easier access to the better places. Amongst the best pools are the Bridge, Washerwoman, Moral, Keeper's, Park, Glencalvie and Falls, all of which have their own character, solitude and beauty.

The Carron has 3 main tributaries, the Alladale River, the Water of Glencalvie and the Black Water. The Alladale River rises amidst the crags and moorlands of Alladale Deer Forest and flows down Glen Alladale past the lodge and joins the Carron on the left bank some distance above Glencalvie Falls. The Water of Glencalvie rises in the mountains of the deer forests of Diebidale and Glencalvie and joins the Carron on the right bank about half a mile below the Falls. The Black Water rises in the mountains of the Freevater Deer Forest. It flows down Strath Cuileannach past Croick Manse and the old church which still has on its windows the names of the inhabitants of the Glen who took refuge there during the time of the evictions. The river joins the Carron on its left bank just below Amat Lodge.

There are three sets of falls on the Carron, namely at Glencalvie, Moral and

Gledfield. In addition to these, there are falls on the Water of Glencalvie and the Black Water. Although the Gledfield and Moral Falls tend to hold fish back at low water temperatures, they are easily accessible once a water temperature of 50°F is reached. The Glencalvie Falls are, however, a very formidable obstacle and few fish are able to ascend them in most seasons. Whether or not they should be eased has been a very controversial matter for many years.

The Carron and its tributaries below Glencalvie Falls are well stocked with salmon and the Black Water is a useful sea trout river. The tendency in recent years is for heavier runs of grilse and summer salmon and fewer spring fish, with both grilse and salmon showing a tendency towards a heavier average weight.

The main spawning and feeding areas are in the Carron below the confluence with the Water of Glencalvie, the lower part of the Water of Glencalvie and the Black Water. The quality of spawning gravel is good. As a result of the waters in Gleann Beag, Glean Mor and the Alladale having few spawning fish the river's total natural smolt production is affected.

The fishing is owned by proprietors of Glencalvie, Amat, Braelangwell, Gruinards, Dounie, Cambusmore, Gledfield and Invercharron. The latter six enjoying the early spring fishing and the former four having the best summer fishing. There is no salmon fishing on the Alladale, but the Water of Glencalvie can yield a few salmon late in the season and the Black Water below Croick Falls can be good for sea trout and the occasional salmon. Angling is by fly only, by proprietors' agreement, and rod catches are in the region of 700 per year.

The Kyle of Sutherland District Salmon Fishery Board re-stock the Carron annually with unfed fry and in recent years around 200,000 fry have been planted each year. A small pilot hatchery was started in 1975 on one of the left bank burns of the Carron. If this proves successful a larger hatchery could follow.

The Croick Falls on the Black Water were eased in 1964 in order to allow the sea trout and salmon over this obstacle more easily. There have also been some river improvements in the form of holding pools on the lower beats.

In the late 1950s the headwaters of the Carron were diverted by tunnel from Gleann Beag, about $1\frac{1}{2}$ miles up river from Deanich Lodge, to Loch Vaich in the Conon Basin as part of the Conon Basin hydro-electric scheme. This section of the river is now subject to compensation flows.

Since the last war there has been extensive hill drainage in the catchment area of the Black Water and to a lesser degree on other parts of the Carron catchment. There has also been afforestation on the lower Carron catchment, particularly along the left bank. These developments are thought to have increased the movement of gravel in the river system, and, along with the hydro-electric development in Gleann Beag, cause the Carron to rise and fall more quickly, and shorten the duration of high water flow.

The Einig

This river is a major tributary of the River Oykel. It rises in the mountains to the south and west of the head of the Kyle of Sutherland. It is named the Einig from the confluence of its two major tributaries, the Corriemulzie (known locally as the Mulzie) and the Rappach Water, near Duag Bridge. The river runs north-east down Glen Einig and after a mile enters a steep wooded gorge with numerous falls whose beauty is lost to most folk, due to the inaccessible nature of the gorge. The river descends steeply through this gorge over a distance of 3 miles before levelling out a few hundred yards above its confluence with the Oykel, half a mile below Oykel Bridge Hotel. At the bottom end of the gorge, a mile above the Oykel junction, there is a large fall and beautiful angling pool called the Einig Pool. The Pool has sheer sides with rocky ledges. There are many lies for salmon but some have been filled in with gravel in recent years.

The Mulzie rises in the mountains of the Freevater Deer Forest to the south. It runs from Loch a' Choire Mhoir and flows gently north through Strath Mulzie, which is frequented by herds of red deer, and enters a gorge below Corriemulzie Lodge. Here it descends steeply over falls for a distance of 2 miles to its junction with the Einig. The Mulzie has one main tributary, Abhuinn Dubhach (known locally as the Letters Burn), which is barred to migratory fish due to inaccessible falls at its mouth. This burn enters the Mulzie on the right bank one mile below Corriemulzie Lodge.

The Rappach Water rises in the mountains to the west and is fed by streams draining the deer forests of Rappach and Rhidorroch. It is similar in character to the Mulzie and enters a gorge half a mile above its confluence with the Mulzie. It has one main tributary, the Poiblidh Burn which runs out of Loch an Daimh. The Junction Pool is the pool furthest upstream on the Rappach where serious angling takes place.

There are many falls on the Einig system, all of which are accessible provided the water height and water temperature are suitable. The Einig and its tributaries have a good stock of salmon but few sea trout. The main spawning and feeding areas are high up the Mulzie and the Rappach Water and little spawning takes place in the Einig. Angling is by fly only. The lower Einig, up to the first main falls three-quarters of a mile above the junction with the Oykel, is fished by the Oykel proprietors and catches are included with those for the Oykel. The rest of the river is owned by the proprietor of Corriemulzie Estate. Fishing is best from May onwards. The catch is in the region of 80 fish a year. Part of the Einig gorge is so inaccessible that fishing is difficult, but several falls were eased in 1964 to enable fish to ascend to the headwaters more easily. The Letters Burn, which is impassable to fish due to falls, has recently been planted with fry. The trout and eels were first poisoned to ensure a better survival of fry.

The river is not affected by hydro-electric schemes but there have been extensive afforestation and drainage schemes on the catchment in recent years.

The Oykel

The Oykel, which was the Eccialbakki of the Norse sagas, rises on the south side of Ben More Assynt to the north-west of the head of the Kyle of Sutherland. It is mainly fed by surface water which tumbles down the steep slopes of Ben More and Carn na Convaroan. The river flows quietly down the glen past Benmore Lodge and is momentarily checked as it enters Loch Ailsh, a loch of about 2 square miles in extent. From this loch it continues down Glen Oykel negotiating small gorges on its way. It is fed by two hill lochs during this part of its course, Loch Craggie and Loch na Claise Moire. Further downstream it enters a large gorge before reaching Oykel Bridge Hotel. It cascades steeply and majestically through this gorge for about a mile until it meets the Einig. After this, apart from negotiating one small gorge, it meanders down a further 6 miles passing Langwell Lodge on its journey through gravelly areas with loam banks and croft lands. In olden days the many fords in this area were the only access points between Sutherland and Ross-shire, until the river joins the Kyle below Inveroykel Lodge. Many years ago during times of high flow the inhabitants used to cross these fords on stilts. There are many beautiful fishing pools, runs and sparkling pots which afford hours of pleasure to the ardent angler, and McConnochie (1924) lists 79 named pools amongst which the most famous are the Inveroykel, Blue, Brae, Langwell, Rock, Long, Sgealbag, Junction and George. All these pools have their own attraction and abound with salmon at various times of year.

The trend in recent years is for the spring run of salmon to be smaller and the summer runs much greater. The main spawning areas are over almost the entire length of the river, apart from the gorges, and in some of the burns. Angling is by fly only. The fishings are owned by the lower Oykel proprietors and Benmore Estates. The annual catch, including that for the lower Einig, is in the region of 1,000. Loch Ailsh and the river also provide good bags of sea trout.

The Oykel is considered to be fully stocked and fry have recently been planted in inaccessible side streams after first poisoning the brown trout and eels. There is no hatchery on the Oykel but there is a holding pen on one of the burns for keeping brood fish for stripping. Over recent years groynes have been erected in order to improve pools.

There have been extensive afforestation and agricultural drainage schemes on the Oykel catchment which has increased the movement of gravel in the river system.

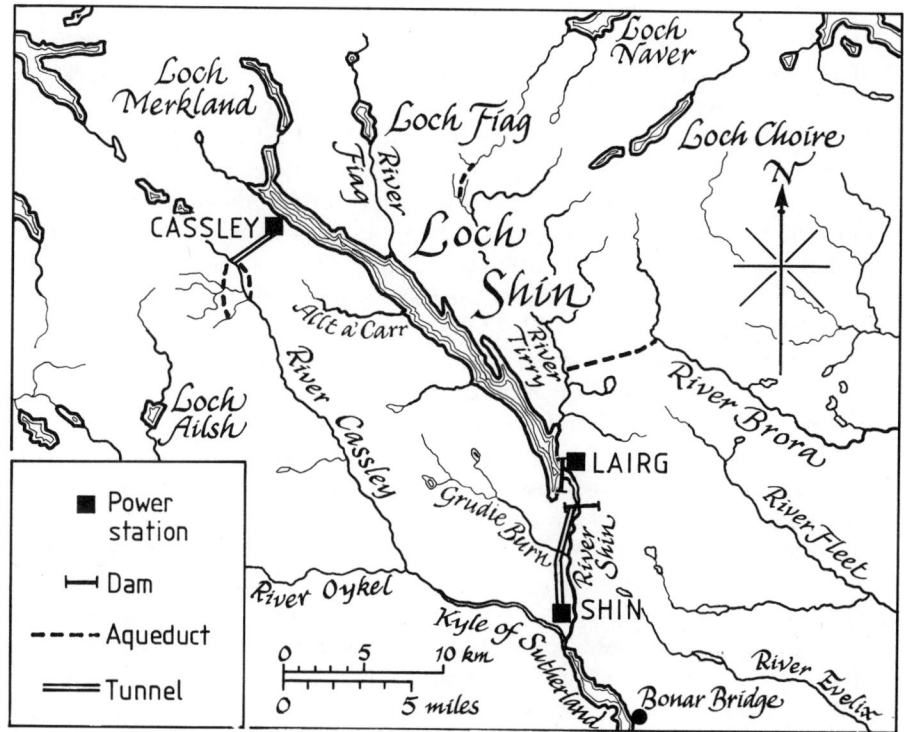

The Rivers Oykel, Cassley and Shin

The Cassley

This river rises to the north-west of the Kyle of Sutherland on the north side of Ben More Assynt. The main tributary is Garbh Allt which passes through a chain of small lochs known as the Gorm Lochs and emerges as the Cassley. This river then flows down Glen Cassley past Duchally Lodge and over the Glen Muic Falls. Below the falls it levels out again and continues to meander through the glen, zig-zagging through meadow land and passing an old Pictish broch. After passing Glencassley Castle and Glen Rossal it enters a large gorge 16 miles downstream from the Gorm Lochs. Here its momentum quickens as it flashes through the narrow gorge and cascades over a spectacular series of waterfalls in the middle of which stands a lone pine growing on solid rock in the middle of the river. This tree was mentioned in a number of books written in the 1880s and it still defiantly withstands the pressure of water that engulfs its bole several times a year. There is an old cemetery on the river bank near the tree and below it the river begins to slow up and quietly descend the last mile to the junction with the Kyle, overlooked by the mansion house of Rosehall Estate.

There are many excellent fishing pools between the confluence with the Oykel and Glen Muic, amongst which the most famous are Crag, Scalpick Mohr (Upper Platform), Round, Cemetery, Falls, Rossal, Castle, Long, Washing and Junction. All of these have a different character. The Long Pool is over a mile in length and at times of low water can be fished like a loch. Once fish reach it, it holds a good stock of fish for the rest of the season. The Cassley has only one main tributary, the Muic Burn, which flows down Glen Muic and joins the Cassley on the right bank a few hundred yards below the Muic Falls. This is a short tributary with inaccessible falls 2 miles up from the confluence with the Cassley. All the falls on the Cassley are easily accessible at certain water heights, but the lower falls hold fish back when water temperatures are low; the main falls in this series hold fish back until the water temperature is 52°F. The fish are, therefore, held back in the bottom mile of the river until mid or late April in most years.

The lower series of falls are worthy of special mention because the importance of water temperature to ascending fish is clearly shown here. There are 3 falls and 3 pools in this section of the river. The uppermost falls of this series are the most formidable, consisting of a wide rock barrier which stretches from side to side at the head of the falls pool. In low and medium water heights water is confined to the right and left banks, the centre rock formation being dry. The right-hand channel is a cascade of water tumbling down the rock face and is rarely accessible to fish, although a number can be seen attempting it. The left-hand channel is wider and broken by a turbulent pool half way up, it is here that fish can ascend freely by jumping into the pot and then out of the pot and up the remaining fall. No fish ascend this fall until the water temperature is 52°F or over.

From the tail of the Falls Pool to the Crow's Nest Pool below the river flows through a series of turbulent steep runs before splitting round a rock buttress and descending another formidable fall into the Crow's Nest. The left-bank channel has a long shoot of water cascading into the pool below and fish require a six foot jump and then a heavy swim through a narrow channel where the velocity is very high. They seldom attempt this channel until the water is low and then never when the water temperature is below 48°F. The right bank channel has a series of small pools connected by small falls with a sheet of water flowing over a shelving rock. It is this channel that fish ascend freely in medium heights of water, but they will not ascend until the water temperature is 48°F.

The tail of the Crow's Nest Pool is known as the Cemetery Pool and from the tail of the Cemetery to the Round Pool below there is a wide fast rush of water leading to a fall on the right bank. This also is a fairly formidable fall. However, it has no clearly defined jump and fish normally swim up it. The velocity is extremely high and they will not ascend from the Round Pool until the temperature is 45°. The fishing records of Rosehall Estate clearly demonstrate this. Often the Round Pool kills the first fish of the season in January,

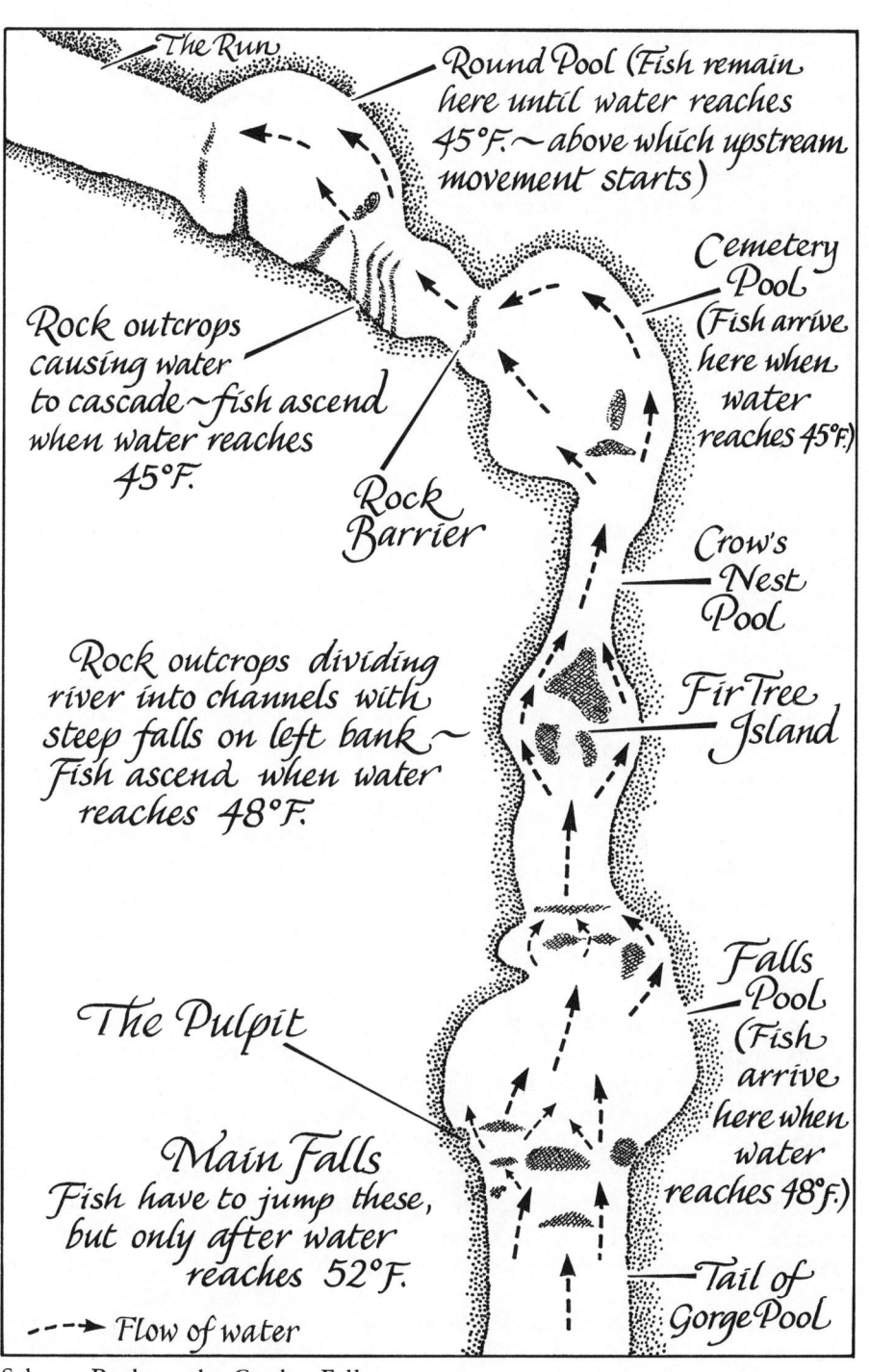

Salmon Pools at the Cassley Falls

SALMON RIVERS OF SCOTLAND

while the earliest a fish was killed in the Cemetery was 4 March and the earliest in the Falls was 30 March.* Taking an extract from the Rosehall Estate fishing records for 3 consecutive years before and after the harnessing of the river for hydro-electric power this point is clearly demonstrated.

――――――――――――――――― Table 15 ―――――――――――――――――

Rod catches showing the days when the first fish were taken in the Round, Cemetery and Falls pools. The figures in brackets indicate the number of fish caught downstream prior to these dates

	Round		Cemetery		Falls	
1956	15/2	(0)	9/4	(32)	23/5	(281)
1957	29/1	(0)	14/3	(21)	17/4	(125)
1958	3/3	(5)	14/4	(52)	3/5	(133)
1970	24/1	(0)	4/5	(93)	6/5	(100)
1971	4/2	(4)	5/4	(67)	14/4	(81)
1972	11/1	(0)	23/3	(25)	17/4	(125)

As can be seen from the table there are early runs of spring fish in the Cassley, but the trend has been for the April and May runs to have decreased and the summer runs to have increased considerably. The average weight of both salmon and grilse has increased by $1\frac{1}{2}$ lb since 1960.

The main spawning and feeding areas are above and below the Muic Falls and in the Gorm Loch area. The Glen Muic burn also accommodates many sea trout and salmon. There is an abundance of spawning gravel in this river and the feeding is good. Angling, by proprietors' agreement, is by fly only. The best beats are owned by proprietors of Glencassley, Glen Rossal, Invercassley Cottage and Rosehall fishings. The spring fishing is confined to the latter and the summer fishing is enjoyed by all. The annual catch is in the region of 900. Few sea trout are caught compared with the number in the river. There is no angling in the Muic Burn. The river is stocked annually by the Kyle of Sutherland District Salmon Fishery Board and in recent years approximately 200,000 unfed fry have been planted annually. There is no hatchery on the river.

Some falls at Duchally were eased in 1966, as rocks had rolled into the gutter above the falls making free ascent of fish difficult. Improvements to pools on the Rosehall water have also been carried out in the last 15 years, by use of gabions to form groynes, and 5 new pools have been made. The headwaters of the Cassley were diverted by tunnel into Loch Shin in 1959, as part of the Shin hydro-electric scheme. A diversion dam with Borland fish pass incorporated in it was built immediately below the tunnel entrance, about a mile below the lowest Gorm loch and two miles above Duchally Lodge. At the same time, burns for a distance of one mile on the north and two miles on the

* As shown in Table 15, the first fish of the season was caught in the Round Pool in 4 out of 6 years.

south side of the river were led back by aqueducts to above the dam.

The river below this point is now subjected to a compensation flow, with an annual block grant of water being available for freshets. Since these developments fewer salmon and grilse have spawned above the dam and more have spawned in the middle length of the river.

In recent years widespread hill drainage has been carried out on the south bank between Rosehall and Duchally and at the same time there has been afforestation on both banks of the lower catchment. This has led to an increase in the amount of unstable gravel in the river.

At times the river can rise very rapidly and anglers are advised to keep an ever-watchful eye on the water level in wet weather.

The Shin

The Shin is a short river whose tributaries rise in the mountainous area to the north-west of the Kyle of Sutherland. The main tributary rises in two lochs, Lochan a Bhealaich and Loch Ulbhach Choire, which lie between Carn Dearg and Carn an Tionail. The resulting Allt Beithe joins two other streams to form Allt nan Albannach which, after a short distance, flows into Loch Merkland. The waters of Merkland feed into Loch a Ghriama which feeds Loch Shin via a short length of stream called Garbh Uidh. Loch Shin is a large, narrow loch 17 miles long and a mile wide in places. It receives a considerable flow of water from the Fiag, fed from Loch Fiag, and the Tirry. The Shin flows out of Loch Shin and meanders quietly down the glen for 2 miles, passing Achany Lodge. It then enters a narrow gorge, tumbling over many falls of varying sizes including the Shin Falls. These Falls are a beauty spot visited by hundreds of tourists who watch the salmon leaping this formidable barrier on the journey to their spawning grounds. Below the gorge the river flattens out for a mile before entering the Kyle. There are many good angling pools on this short stretch of water, amongst the most famous are the Home, Little Falls, Piper, Fir Dam, Rocky Cast, Angus, Cromarty, Culag, Falls, Long, Lady Herbert, Meadow and Ladies. They all have their own attraction to the ardent angler who can revel in their solitude and extreme beauty.

The entire régime of the Shin was altered in 1959 when a hydro-electric scheme harnessed Loch Shin. The main loch was dammed just west of Lairg, and raised by 30 feet. A diversion dam was built a mile downstream of the main dam, flooding out half a mile of the river. Borland fish passes were incorporated in both dams. A tunnel was driven from the diversion dam, on the right bank parallel to the Shin, to a power station situated at Inveran four miles away. The tailrace from the Inveran Power Station enters the Shin on the right bank a quarter of a mile above the confluence with the Kyle. This tunnel carries the water from the diversion dam, picking up water from the Grudie

Burn on the way. Screens were placed across the tailrace below the power station to prevent the entrance of fish. The Shin is placed on compensation flow and is supplemented by freshets from a block grant of water for use at the discretion of the Kyle of Sutherland District Salmon Fishery Board.

There is a good stock of salmon in the Shin, but few sea trout. Runs of fish have altered since hydro-electric development and there are now fewer spring fish than there used to be but large runs of grilse and summer fish. Very few adult salmon now frequent the tributaries. In spite of the fish passes few salmon now enter Loch Shin and nearly all natural spawning now takes place in a very confined area below the diversion dam. The Kyle of Sutherland District Salmon Fishery Board attempted to utilise the old feeding areas of the river and the burns flowing into Loch Shin by planting upwards of a million unfed salmon fry each year. Poor smolt returns from these plantings have caused these numbers to be reduced to 250,000 fry. In order to provide alternative feeding grounds, the Board poisoned the brown trout in the upper reaches of the Grudie Burn, which are inaccessible to salmon owing to falls in the lower reaches, and now plant out 250,000 fry annually. At the same time a smolt trap was built above the point at which this burn is diverted into the pipeline to Inveran Power Station, and smolts are trapped there and transported to the Shin. There is no hatchery on the Shin, but holding pens for holding brood fish for stripping are sited in the diversion dam.

Angling is by fly only. Sir John Egerton and Lairg Lodge own the fishings and although the former has the best of the spring fishing both proprietors enjoy good sport in the summer. The annual catch is in the region of 750 fish. Afforestation on both banks of the Shin and its tributaries may have added substantial loads of gravel to the river bed. The river throughout most of its run through the gorge can only be fished from the right bank and therefore requires to be fished left-handed. Generally, however, a short line, fished square or at right angles to the river, is all that is required. A longish rod is best, as the fly can then be held comfortably to work in the stream.

The Evelix

The Evelix rises in the mountains to the north of the Kyle of Sutherland and flows east before turning sharply south-west and entering the Kyle on the north bank not far from where the Kyle joins the Dornoch Firth. There are two lochs at the head of the river, Loch Laro and Loch an Lagain, neither of them large. Immediately before it joins the Kyle the Evelix flows into Loch Evelix and thence by fish pass to the Kyle.

Loch Evelix was modified by Mr Carnegie who resided at Skibo Castle, just above Loch Evelix. Fish can ascend by the fish ladder from the Kyle in very low flows and they normally remain in this freshwater loch until conditions in the

THE KYLE OF SUTHERLAND

river are favourable, enabling them to continue on their journey to the spawning grounds. There are formidable falls on this river and no major tributaries, the river itself being a small one. Spawning and feeding areas are mainly between Loch Evelix and Loch an Lagain. The river is well stocked with salmon and sea trout, but there is no main spring run, the main runs being June – September. Loch Evelix is an excellent fishing loch.

The main owners of the fishing are Skibo, Ospisdale, Evelix Farm and Birichen Estate. The catch is in the region of 100 salmon a year.

20

THE BRORA AND FLEET

The Brora

The Brora is considered to be one of the best salmon rivers in Sutherland. Its upper reaches are inclined to be flashy but the lower part of the river, benefiting from the cushioning effect of Loch Brora, runs off more slowly.

The Brora rises in the hills of east Sutherland and wends a rocky course down Strath Brora through the deer forests of Dalnessie and Ben Armine past the shooting lodges of Dalreavoch and Scibercross, a distance of some 15 miles, before being joined on the left bank by the Black Water. Balnacoil Lodge stands overlooking the junction of these two rivers and a new bridge which replaces the old ford over the Black Water immediately above the confluence. This carries the Brora to Rogart road up Strath Brora. From this point the river, now increased in size, meanders slowly through a succession of runs and deep pools many of which were created by Gordonbush Estate, and flows through fairly flat rough grassland into Loch Brora. At the head of the loch is a pronounced sand bar which has grown in size in recent years, possibly as a result of hill drainage. Loch Brora is $3\frac{1}{2}$ miles long and half a mile wide at its widest point and has 3 main basins connected by the Killin and Carrol narrows. It has an average depth of about 22 feet and a maximum depth of 93 feet. The loch is overlooked on the north bank by Gordonbush Lodge with its grouse moors and deer forests lying beneath Col-bheinn. On the south shore is Uppat House with Ben Horn towering behind it.

The final 3-mile descent from the loch to the estuary is through rough pasture and arable land. The river is boulder strewn and has long deep pools alternating with fast rapids. Just before passing through Brora the river passes the only coal mine in Sutherland, which is situated above a deep cutting about half a mile long over which pass the road and rail bridges. The mine has only recently been closed. Below these bridges the Brora flows out to sea over a sandy bar.

The Black Water is the only main tributary of the Brora and is in fact larger than the Brora and drains an appreciable part of the Brora's 165 square mile catchment. It rises in the mountains of Borrobol, Ben Armine and Kildonan deer forests and really begins where the Skinsdale, Seilga and Coirefrois burns join. Below this point the Black Water flows through a narrow, rocky gorge, with deep pots and pools, for a distance of 3 miles before cascading over the Balnacoil Falls and thence to the confluence with the Brora a quarter of a mile below.

The Brora has a large stock of salmon, grilse and sea trout, with salmon entering the river during most months of the year. Angling catches on the whole river system are in the region of 800 salmon annually. In the spring the lower Brora used to be the best beat, with fish being caught on the fly from the opening day (1 February). However, in mild winters fish can be caught on the opening day, and throughout February, above the loch. The bar across the top end of the loch can check the passage of fish when the upper Brora is low and during periods of low water temperature and in the long drought in 1976 fish were held back in the loch for a considerable time. However once March and April come in, the entire river system, up to the Balnacoil Falls, is usually populated with salmon and, by May, when the water temperatures are higher, the whole Black Water is populated. The Brora also has a marked autumn run of heavier fish which tends to stay below the loch, and this is probably the reason that this river is the only east coast river in this area which does not close on 30 September but remains open until 15 October. The loch provides good sport with salmon and sea trout and also brown trout and char, and the local angling association fish this loch extensively. Also boats are available for letting on a daily basis from Gordonbush Estate Office.

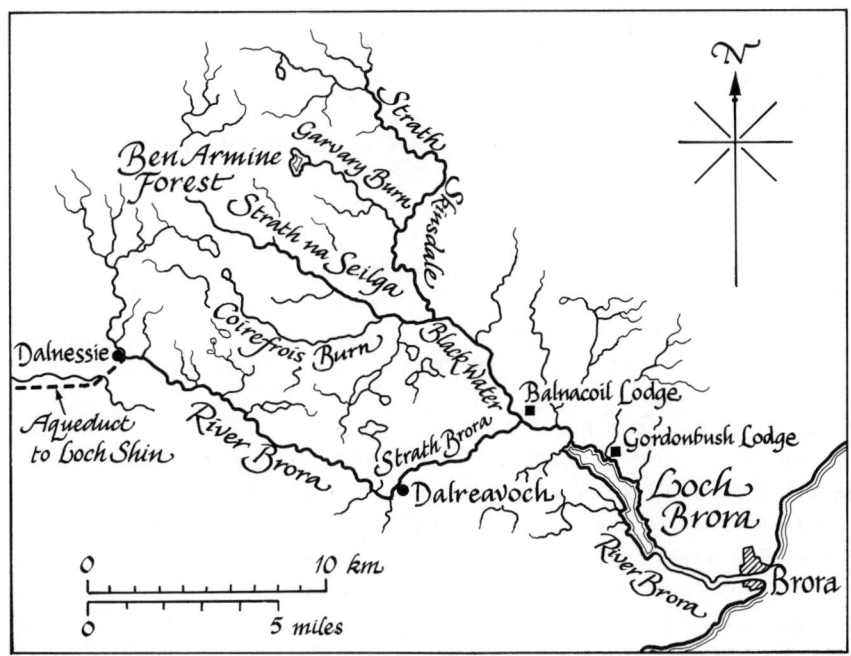

The River Brora

The angling rights are shared by Sutherland Estates, Gordonbush and Dalnessie. Gordonbush is the largest single owner with rights on the lower Brora, the upper Brora and the Black Water. The lower Brora has some 20 main pools, the most famous being the Magazine, Pot, Benzie, Madman, Rallan and Ford. Above the loch the most famed in high water early in the year is Pheadair, a pool some 200 yards in length on the lower reaches of the Black Water. Spectacular catches are frequently made on this pool. On the Brora itself the Flat, Snag, McDonald and Chemist are among the best pools, although there are many others which can be very productive.

There are extensive spawning grounds and feeding areas in the upper and lower Brora and Black Water. On the Black Water, the Skinsdale and Coirefrois burns are excellent spawning areas, while on the Brora some spawning occurs in a number of streams including the Ascoile Burn as far as the falls. In the lower Brora some late-run fish spawn at the top of the tide, often on unsuitable river bed, including a ford used by local traffic.

Netting rights are owned jointly by Sutherland Estates and Gordonbush, but regular netting ceased before 1920. In recent years netting at the river mouth has only been exercised intermittently, mainly when conditions prevented fish entering the river and there was a build-up of fish in the estuary. At one time Loch Brora was netted each year but there has been no netting in recent years.

Although there is a hatchery owned jointly by Sutherland Estates and Gordonbush sited on Gordonbush Estate, at Old Town on the north bank of the loch, it has not been operated for many years, nor has there been any salmon restocking programme. However, within the last 20 years Norwegian sea trout fry, from the Loch More Estate hatchery on the River Laxford, have been planted out in the Brora and Black Water by Sutherland Estates and Gordonbush, with noticeably good results.

The Brora has its upper reaches tapped by the Shin hydro-electric scheme and water is diverted at Dalnessie through an aqueduct and via the River Tirry into Loch Shin. This has had a marked effect on spate flows down the Brora and, although artificial freshets can be provided, the ascent of fish into this area is likely to have been impeded. Prior to this scheme a large proportion of the sea trout population of the Brora, and some salmon, used this area for spawning.

Forestry and agricultural drainage has been fairly significant. In the early fifties a considerable area of land was drained under the Hill Farm Improvement Scheme; 150 miles of ditches were cut on the Black Water catchment area and some more on the upper Brora above Dalreavoch. Miss Lindsay Laird, who wrote a report on this river for the Atlantic Salmon Research Trust, refers to this drainage scheme and points out that, although the drains are rapidly silting up, they had the initial effect of causing the river to rise and fall faster than previously. There is a current programme of forestry development in the Black Water-Skinsdale region and the drains for this run down the side of the hill, so that rapid fluctuations in river level are likely to continue and there may be a great deal more silt reaching the river.

The Fleet

The Fleet is a small river rising to the east of the village of Lairg and flowing east down Strath Fleet parallel to the road from Lairg to Golspie. The river rises in rolling moorland terrain, with most of its catchment area below 1,000 feet, and drains the grouse moors of Tressady, Rovie and Morvich estates. There are several lochs on its watershed, but none of them of real significance. From its source near the village of Lairg the Fleet flows quietly down the Strath and 3 sizeable streams flow into it from the north. The first, Allt na Luibe, is overlooked near its confluence by Blarich and Tressady lodges, while the second, the Torbreck, joins the Fleet near Dalmore. The third stream, Garbh Allt, joins the river near the village of Rogart. The section of river between Blarich and Rogart flows fast, but not steeply, over a rugged rocky course before flattening out below Rogart into an almost canal-like waterway as it meanders through loam loops into Loch Fleet. The loch is overlooked by the Mound Rock to the north and Cambusmore Lodge to the south. The alderwoods at the Mound are a National Nature Reserve, while part of Loch Fleet is a reserve of the Scottish Wildlife Trust.

At this point, on the right bank of Loch Fleet, a small river known as the Torboll or Charnaig flows into the loch from the west. The Torboll rises in the hills around Loch Cracail Mor south-east of Lairg. It flows south, then east, down the strath through Loch Buidhe and then down Strath Charnaig or Carnach into Loch Fleet. This is at first a gentle meandering stream which increases in size as it gathers water from several burns, and then flows fairly quickly and steeply out of Loch Buidhe over various falls and cascades into Loch Fleet below.

There is a causeway separating upper Loch Fleet from the main loch and the sea. This carries the A9 road from Bonar Bridge to Wick and used to carry the Mound–Dornoch railway, which is no longer used. There is a sluice in the connecting channel through the causeway, to prevent fish entering the river system during low water conditions, and large numbers of salmon can often be seen congregating on the seaward side of the sluice in summer. When the water flow from an up-river spate is sufficiently strong the gates are opened automatically by the water pressure.

There is also a very elaborate fish pass system to ease the access of fish into the Torboll River and it is in fact one of the oldest fish passes in Scotland.

Both the Fleet and the Torboll have an appreciable amount of spawning and feeding areas and carry a moderate stock of salmon, grilse and sea trout during June–September. Access, however, is not clearly defined in upper Loch Fleet, hence the sluice, and in dry seasons fish are held back for long periods below the causeway. This provides a great temptation for poachers and poaching incidents are common below the sluice.

The angling rights on the Fleet are shared by Tressady, Blarich, Rovie and Morvich, with the latter two probably having the best fishing in the section above Loch Fleet. Fish are normally taken during conditions of high water or when there is a wind ruffling the surface of the pools during low water conditions. Cambusmore owns the fishing on the Torboll. Annual catches on both rivers are in the region of 100 salmon and grilse and a substantial number of sea trout. Netting rights are shared by Cambusmore and the Sutherland Estates, but are rarely exercised. UDN has been seen in the river system but has never reached epidemic proportions.

21

THE HELMSDALE

To many Scottish salmon anglers the word 'Helmsdale' immediately conjures up an image of spring salmon fishing in a wild and remote moorland country of turbulent streams and rocky pools. It is just this and, as W. L. Calderwood says in *The Salmon Rivers and Lochs of Scotland*, 'for ideal conditions of salmon angling with the fly there is no river in Scotland which surpasses the Helmsdale, and very few which may be compared with it.' Although this remark was made nearly three-quarters of a century ago it still holds today. This is particularly so with respect to the quality of the spring fishing which, while now almost non-existent in many rivers previously renowned for their spring salmon, still maintains a very high yield at this time of year. It is almost certainly due to the proprietors being able to draw upon reserves of water stored behind sluices erected at the foot of Loch Badanloch and Loch an Ruathair (known locally as Achentoul Loch) in the upper reaches of the river.

The Helmsdale is formed from two sets of feeder streams and lochs up in the Forests of Badanloch and Achentoul. In the Badanloch Forest the uppermost of five lochs is Loch Rimsdale, into the top end of which flows the Rimsdale Burn. Water from Loch Truderscaig flows into Rimsdale Loch from the south-west. Immediately downstream of Loch Rimsdale is Loch nan Clar which abuts on to the top end of Loch Badanloch which also receives water from little Loch an Alltain Fhearna. Below Loch Badanloch the Badanloch Water passes Badanloch Lodge and widens out to form Loch Achnamoine. Downstream of Loch Achnamoine the river joins the other major tributary, flowing down from the north through Kinbrace, in Strath Beg. This tributary also receives water from a number of lochs, three in this instance. They are Loch an Ruathair, a little south of Forsinard Hotel, Loch Druim a' Chliabhain, which is to the west of Forsinard, and wee Loch Arichlinie, fed with water from Loch Druim a' Chliabhain via Allt Airigh-dhamh which then flows into the main tributary at Kinbrace.

From Strath Beg the Helmsdale (or Ullie as it is called on some maps) flows south-east in a series of long flats and rocky pools, through a picturesque land of heather-clad moors and woods of birch and rowan to enter the sea at Helmsdale. On its seaward course it collects water from a number of burns. The uppermost, entering from the west, is Abhaina na Frithe, known locally as the River Free of Frithe (or the Free), which runs past a Pictish tower and enters the main river near Borrobol Lodge. Just before entering the main river the Free receives a tributary from Loch Ascaig. The next major tributary is the Suisgill Burn flowing in from the north, this too is not far from a Pictish tower. These towers and brochs are a feature not only of the Strath of Kildonan, where there are at least seven of them, but also of north Sutherland as a whole and are evidence of a much earlier occupation by man. The Kildonan Burn, renowned for its gold, enters the Helmsdale from the north and a short distance downstream the Craggie comes in from the south. At Kildonan are the Kildonan Falls which are said to determine the upper limit of spring fishing, although fish have been caught further upstream in March and it is thought that they ascend even earlier than this in a mild winter. There is an old railway station at Kildonan which, 'in the good old days,' was used by visiting anglers brought from the south by the Highland Railway. This area was the scene of the Sutherland gold diggings in the 1860s and 80s and from which £6,000 worth of gold was obtained. The next burns of any consequence below the Craggie are the Kilphedir, coming in from the north a short distance downstream of Torrish (after which the Yellow Torrish fly was named), and the Caen, which also comes in from the north near the Marrel Pool.

There are six proprietors of the Helmsdale, from source to mouth they are: Achentoul, Badanloch, Borrobol, Suisgill, Kildonan and Torrish. The river is divided into twelve beats, six above Kildonan Falls and six below, and they are numbered one to six above and one to six below. They are also numbered from the bottom of the river up, so that 'number one above' is the beat immediately above Kildonan Falls and 'number one below' is from the Marrel Pool upstream to the head of Salscraggie. Each proprietor has two beats, one above the falls and one below. The two beats can be fished either by two rods on one beat or one rod on each beat. The beats are fished in rotation by each proprietor, so that if 'number one above' is fished then 'number one below' is also fished on the same day by the same proprietor, and he fishes the two next beats the following day. The changeover of beats is at 8.00 p.m., so that if a proprietor wishes to fish after 8.00 p.m. on any day he starts on the beat he is due to have on the following day. Rods change within their beats at any time of day. During the winter and spring months two rods are usually on each of the six lower beats, the upper beats being ignored at that time of year. However, later on in the year, particularly in June and July, rods are frequently influenced by the tide in the time they change over within the day and this results in some hair-raising journeys over the intervening stretches of road as anglers rush from one beat to the next.

The division of the upper and lower beats is as follows: *One below* — From the Marrel to the head of Salscraggie, including the upper and lower Caen, the Sand, the Alder and the Stall; *Two below* — Salscraggie to the tail of the Wood Pool; there are six pools including Kilphedir. It was in the Upper Torrish Pool that a salmon of 45 lb was caught by a Mr John Rutherford of Kildonan House. He played it for three hours in the course of which it ran upstream three miles; *Three below* — The Wood Pool to the tail of Baddywood; *Four below* —

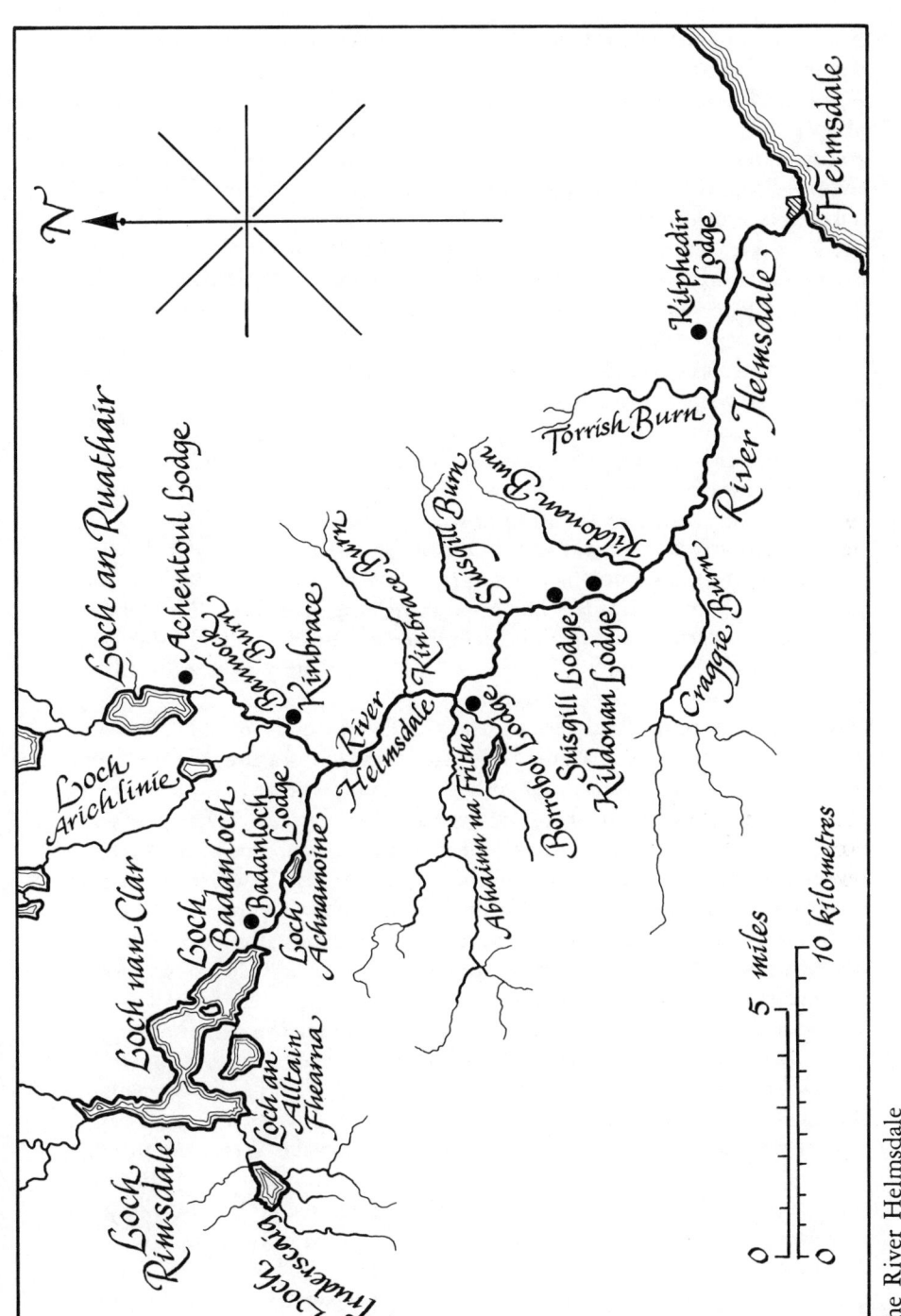

The River Helmsdale

Baddywood to Kilearnan Bridge. There are some sluggish pools on this beat which are best fished in high water with an upstream breeze; *Five below* — Kilearnan Bridge to head of Whinney Pool and includes the Foam, Duible and Short pools; *Six below* — From the head of Whinney Pool to Kildonan Bridge and includes such pools as the Manse, Little Rock, Flat, Fall and Porters; *One above* — From Kildonan Bridge to Suisgill Lodge water gauge. This beat and number five below are the best two beats for sea trout; *Two above* — From Suisgill Lodge water gauge to the foot of the island above Surfaceman's House; *Three above* — From the island to Kinbrace Railway Bridge. This is a long beat which has 11 pools, of which the pool into which flows the Free at Red Braes, opposite Borrobol Lodge, deserves special mention. *Four above* — From the Bridge to the junction of the Bannoch Burn (Badanloch Water); *Five above* — From the Junction to Loch Achnamoine; *Six above* — Loch Achnamoine.

The stretch of river between Loch Achnamoine and Loch Badanloch – the Private Water – is part of Badanloch Estate. Local anglers and visitors may obtain permits from the Fisheries Manager at Kinbrace to fish the beat from the Old Road Bridge to the head of the Flat Pool below the Marrel.

The entire river is subject to the rule of fly only at all times of the year.

The commercial salmon fisheries in the Helmsdale district consist of one or more bag nets off Helmsdale and a sweep netting station within Helmsdale harbour. The commercial fisheries are owned by the Helmsdale River Board. Their open season is from 11 February–26 August, but netting normally only takes place from 1 June–15 August.

The management of the Helmsdale is under the direction of Commander Rickards who carries out a number of conservation measures for the salmon stocks. Each autumn about 200 to 250 salmon are netted on number three above and stripped when ripe. The eggs are then hatched in the hatchery of Kincardine Fisheries Ltd in Ardgay near Bonar Bridge. The resulting fry are released as unfed fry into streams on the Helmsdale system which are inaccessible to salmon but prolific in natural food. River improvements are also undertaken and these have included installing gabions along unstable banks bordering some of the pools in number three above and the construction of holding pools in number five above.

The sluices at Badanloch and Achentoul play a very important role and are very valuable assets to the river as they enable the river flow to be controlled, and consequently optimum flows prevail for long periods. Normally the sluices at Achentoul are set at a fixed height which guarantees a good regular flow but when a short, fast, artificial spate is required it is released from this loch and can get down the river in about 14 hours. Badanloch is drawn on particularly in the summer as it has the greater water holding capacity. However, the water takes about 24 hours to get down the river as it is slowed down by Loch Achnamoine. The controlled flow – the best fishing height of the river – can be maintained, even in a drought summer, from early April until mid-August by careful regulation of the outflows from the two dams.

22

THE BERRIEDALE, LANGWELL, DUNBEATH AND WICK

Berriedale Water and Langwell Water are best considered together as they share a common estuary, their junction being sited about 300 yards upstream from the sea. These rivers rise in the mountains of the Berriedale and Langwell deer forests in the south-east of Caithness on the Duke of Portland's Estate and between them they drain an area of some 70 square miles. The Berriedale, the northernmost of the two, is by far the longest and is almost 20 miles in length, about double the length of the Langwell. After receiving the waters of the Langwell, the Berriedale flows into the sea at the small village of Berriedale. Sweep netting is exercised in the estuary and bag nets are operated along the coast.

The Berriedale

This river has a run of early fish with the first fish of the season being caught in March. The earliest fish ever recorded was one of $19\frac{1}{2}$ lb taken on 24 February 1924. The best months for angling are July, August and September, but the time can vary greatly depending on when spates occur. In recent years the trend has been for the main run to start later in the season. Salmon average about 6 lb and grilse about 4 lb. There is a reasonable run of sea trout in July but few of these are caught and any that are taken only average about $1\frac{3}{4}$ lb. The annual average rod catch is 76 salmon and grilse and 10 sea trout.

The pools on the river are all natural and no attempt has been made to create new ones. The best pools are The Falls and Lord Galway's. The river has good spawning and nursery areas which are mainly confined to the main river, the best area being upstream from Corrichoich.

The estate does not run a hatchery of its own but plants out 20,000 salmon fry and 5,000 sea trout fry each year.

There are three beats on the river one of which is fished by estate employees and members of the community who perform a public service, and the membership is limited to 24. The other two beats are let through the Portland Arms Hotel, Lybster where tenants normally stay.

SALMON RIVERS OF SCOTLAND

The Langwell

This river is very much smaller than its neighbour. The section of river immediately above the junction with the Berriedale flows through a narrow gorge which is extremely dangerous. The best angling period is mid-July – September and the earliest fish is usually taken after the first big spate in mid-July. The runs of fish have tended to appear later recently. There is very little evidence of sea trout running this river in spite of the fact that 5,000 sea trout fry have been planted annually over the last 8 years. Only one has been recorded in 1975, and it was only a small fish.

There are reasonable spawning grounds in the main river upstream of Alltnabea and, as on the Berriedale, 20,000 salmon fry and 5,000 sea trout fry are planted out each year.

The best pools are the Parapet, Turnol, Lady's Tent and the Putting Stone. No angling associations or tenants have fished this river in recent years, but a stretch of the lower river has been available to the estate angling club since 1978.

Due to lack of water over the past few seasons and to underfishing the catches in recent years have been negligible. Another reason for this is the fact that the gorge above the confluence with the Berriedale is too dangerous to fish. In the years 1972–1976 only 3 fish each year were recorded, but in 1959 9 were taken.

Both these rivers have suffered from sporadic outbreaks of UDN but these have never reached epidemic proportions.

The Dunbeath

This north-east coast river lies to the north of the Berriedale and Langwell rivers. It rises in the deer forest of Dunbeath Estate and flows in a south-easterly direction to discharge its waters into the sea beside Dunbeath Harbour. Just before it enters the sea it passes under the main A9 road.

Dunbeath Water does not drain a large catchment and has no loch of any significance on its catchment. It is essentially a spate river flowing for most of its length over a gravel and stone strewn course through a typical Caithness moorland countryside. It has a small falls below which there is an area of birch wood, but apart from that stretch it flows through open heath land allowing unhindered casting. The fishable section of the river is about 6 miles in length and overall the river extends for approximately 12 miles.

The river opens on 11 February and occasionally a fish is landed on the opening day. March and particularly April used to be quite good when fish were able to run freely, but in low water conditions fish cannot enter the river. The spring run has now declined and, although a few are still caught in April, the main runs are definitely later than they used to be. The best angling months, water conditions permitting, are June–September when in most years a good run of grilse and summer salmon frequent this pleasant little river.

Angling can be very good under the right conditions, anglers requiring only a medium-sized rod to cover the water adequately. Small flies of most patterns do well and Hairy Mary, Stoat's Tail and patterns with a touch of red seem to be most favoured. Amongst the best angling pools are the Falls, Rock, Bridge and Ladies pools. Salmon average 9–10 lbs and grilse 5–6 lbs. The biggest recorded was a 42 lb fish killed by Macdonald the head keeper of the estate in the 1920s.

There are two man-made pools constructed of concrete and steel, which were made about 9 years ago. These are named the Bothy pools after an old whisky-smuggling bothy sited near by. They are placed just below the Falls pool about 4 miles upstream from the mouth. Between 1930 and 1950 catches of 15–20 fish to four rods was a good day, but in recent years a catch of 6–8 fish to two–three rods is more usual.

There is one main tributary flowing into the Dunbeath named the Burn of Houstry which enters about a mile from the mouth. Salmon very often run this tributary when it is running high and the Dunbeath is low, but fall back again when the position is reversed.

The Dunbeath has excellent spawning and feeding areas, mainly above the falls and in minor burns flowing into the river. The Burn of Houstry also accommodates a few spawning fish. There is no hatchery on the river, but it is stocked annually with around 10,000 salmon fry. Sea trout fry were also put in the river 3 years ago and a few more sea trout were caught in 1977.

Sweep nets are operated in the bay at the mouth of the river, and there is little doubt that, in dry weather conditions, these nets can account for a large number of fish.

The fishing on the river is not let to the public.

The Wick

The Wick rises in the north-eastern part of the County of Caithness. The upper river system comprises the Burn of Acharole, the Kensary and Camster burns and the latter two join to become the Strath Burn. All three streams rise in the hills to the south of Watten village and flow in a northerly direction until the Acharole and the Strath Burn join approximately a mile south of Watten village. The river continues to flow north for a short distance before turning almost due east as it is joined by the water flowing out of Loch Watten. This is a reasonably large loch being some 3 miles long and about a mile wide. It lies almost due west of where the Wick River turns east on the last stage of its journey of approximately 9 miles to the sea, which it enters in the town of Wick. The river for a large part of its length is slow-flowing and almost canal-like in some stretches, but is split up by faster flowing runs.

The Wick Angling Association has leased the angling rights on the river from Memfrigg Estate on a 10-year lease. They also lease the netting rights in the estuary and bay but do not exercise them. However, there are some bag net stations to the north of the river near Ackergill.

The earliest fish normally enter the river in April and the first fish of the season is generally caught during that month which is, along with July, August and September, one of the best months for fishing. There is no substantial run of fish in May. However, as in many other rivers, the runs are tending to get later. Salmon average about 12 lb and grilse 6–7 lb. A few sea trout are caught in the lower reaches of the river and estuary, usually during low water conditions, and average 1–1½ lb. The average salmon rod catch is 200–230 in good years and 100–150 in poor years.

There are good spawning and nursery areas high up the river system with the Acharole, Camster and Kensary burns providing accommodation for a good many pairs. In the main river the best spawning areas are between Watten and Bilbster. A hatchery is run by the Wick Angling Association and at present it has a holding capacity for 150,000 eggs but there is room for expansion. The Association has restocked the river each year for the last 30 years with 130,000–150,000 salmon fry and it has plans to rear to the parr stage.

The best pools on the river include Black's, Pot, Little Pot, Katie Gow's, Faroul, Wash, Shepherd's, Willow, McPhail's, Bridge, Hughes, Jasper's, Willie's Dyke and Durrand's.

The Wick Angling Association is an active club with 130 adult members, 150 junior and secondary school members and caters for 100–160 annual visitors. Day and weekly tickets can be obtained locally. There are no private beats on the river. In the days before UDN a catch of 12 fish per day was not unusual, but in recent years 4 fish on one day is considered good.

Pollution has troubled the river system over the past number of years. However, improvements have been made recently and with the help of local authorities initially and now the Highland River Purification Board steps have been taken to alleviate the problem. The angling association has also helped in many ways and the strength of both salmon and sea trout runs should improve immensely in coming seasons.

UDN has been present in the river system since the late 1960s but has never reached epidemic proportions.

23

THE THURSO

This river has the reputation, along with the Naver, of being the best salmon river in the North. Although some fish are taken in January and February, it fishes best from March to the end of the season in October, during which time excellent catches can be had when conditions are favourable.

The Thurso rises on the northern slopes of the Knockfin Heights and the area drained by Runsdale Water among the deer forests of Glutt and Dalnawillan. It passes Glutt Lodge and Dalnawillan Lodge as it meanders northwards down the glen on its way to Loch More. By the time the river reaches the loch it has increased in size as a result of many small tributaries flowing into it during its downstream course. Loch More covers an area of some 500 acres, its holding capacity having been improved by the erection of a V-shaped barrage. Work began on this barrage in 1907 and it is thought to have taken approximately one year to build, the works being favoured by an exceptionally dry period. One leg forms a slipway for spilling spate water and the other leg has a long gradual pooled fish pass running parallel to it, baffled by large stones placed at intervals. Sluiced apertures are incorporated in the barrage to allow fish to enter the loch at different water levels. The purpose of the dam was primarily to release artificial freshets, if required, for angling and fishery management purposes. However, through experience it has been found that the stored water is best used by prolonging and supplementing natural spates. The release of stale water freshets during dry weather conditions is of no benefit to either angling or movement of fish.

After flowing out of Loch More the river tends to run north-east until it is joined on its right bank by the Little River. This major tributary rises on the northern slopes of Coire na Beinne and has 3 small lochs, namely Ruard, Stemster and Rangag, on its headwaters and drains an appreciable acreage before its junction with the Thurso. From this confluence, the Thurso flows north through the flat Caithness terrain with fast stretches of river alternating with more sluggish areas. Some 24 miles downstream from the loch the river flows into the sea at Thurso.

The sole owners of the angling and sweep netting on the Thurso are Thurso Fisheries Ltd. From Loch More to the sea the river is divided into 14 beats – 13 numbered and one private. They are numbered from the river mouth upstream – 1–4 being from Thurso Bay to Halkirk, 5–9 from Halkirk to the junction with the Little River and 10–13 and the private beat between the Little River junction and Loch More. Beat 12 includes Loch Beg, which lies just downstream of Loch More.

Beat 1 is reserved for the Thurso Angling Association and visitors are allowed to join the rota.

Beats 2–13 are fished by guests staying at the Ulbster Arms Hotel, Halkirk or at the Lochdhu Hotel. Two rods are allowed per beat and the beats rotate downstream by two beats each day. Anglers, therefore, fish even numbers one week and uneven the next. To cover each beat of the river they must fish for two consecutive weeks. Fishing is by fly only.

The private beat is fished by guests of the owners.

Loch More can be fished by any beat.

Each beat has 8–10 named pools, all of which can be productive.

Before Loch More was raised in 1907 its area was only 170 acres and had an average depth of 7 feet. It had a very high reputation for salmon fishing and was fished by up to six boats a day. At this time there were only seven beats on the river and a large proportion of the catch came from the loch. After it was raised the area extended to over 500 acres and the average depth increased accordingly. The river and Loch Beg now kill the majority of fish. However, in a dry season when the loch has been drawn down it can still be productive and bank fishing is now preferred to boat fishing in these conditions.

The Thurso above Loch More, the Little River and the tributaries flowing into the loch all flow through peaty terrain, but their beds consist of large stretches of good spawning gravel and ideal nursery areas. Between Loch More and the sea the river bed consists largely of red sandstone and Caithness slabs. There are several deep canal-like stretches along the river, particularly on beats 3, 6, 7 and 12. These are long deep stretches which are invaluable for conservation of stocks in hot, dry weather conditions. Fish under these conditions fall back into these areas. Even angling benefits, as fish can be caught on these stretches in low water, providing there is a good wind to ruffle the surface of the water.

Thurso Fisheries Ltd manage a salmon hatchery capable of holding $1\frac{1}{2}$ million eggs, and eggs from surplus native fish are hatched here and used to restock the fishery. Surplus fry are sold to clients in Denmark, France, Spain and other parts of the United Kingdom, including the Thames. One consignment of eggs was sent to the Falkland Islands with a view to establishing runs of salmon in this distant area of the southern hemisphere.

Apart from restocking underpopulated burns, the owners also stock a small loch every other year and also the river above the Falls of Glutt, about 13 miles above Loch More. This area is electro-fished from time to time to remove predatory trout and eels and then stocked in alternate years. The small loch mentioned is the Grassy Loch situated on a tributary on the Sleach catchment of Loch More. The loch was specially prepared for fry planting and not only were the predators poisoned but the loch was also dredged and sluiced so as to enable it to be almost completely dried out when required. Up to 50,000 fry

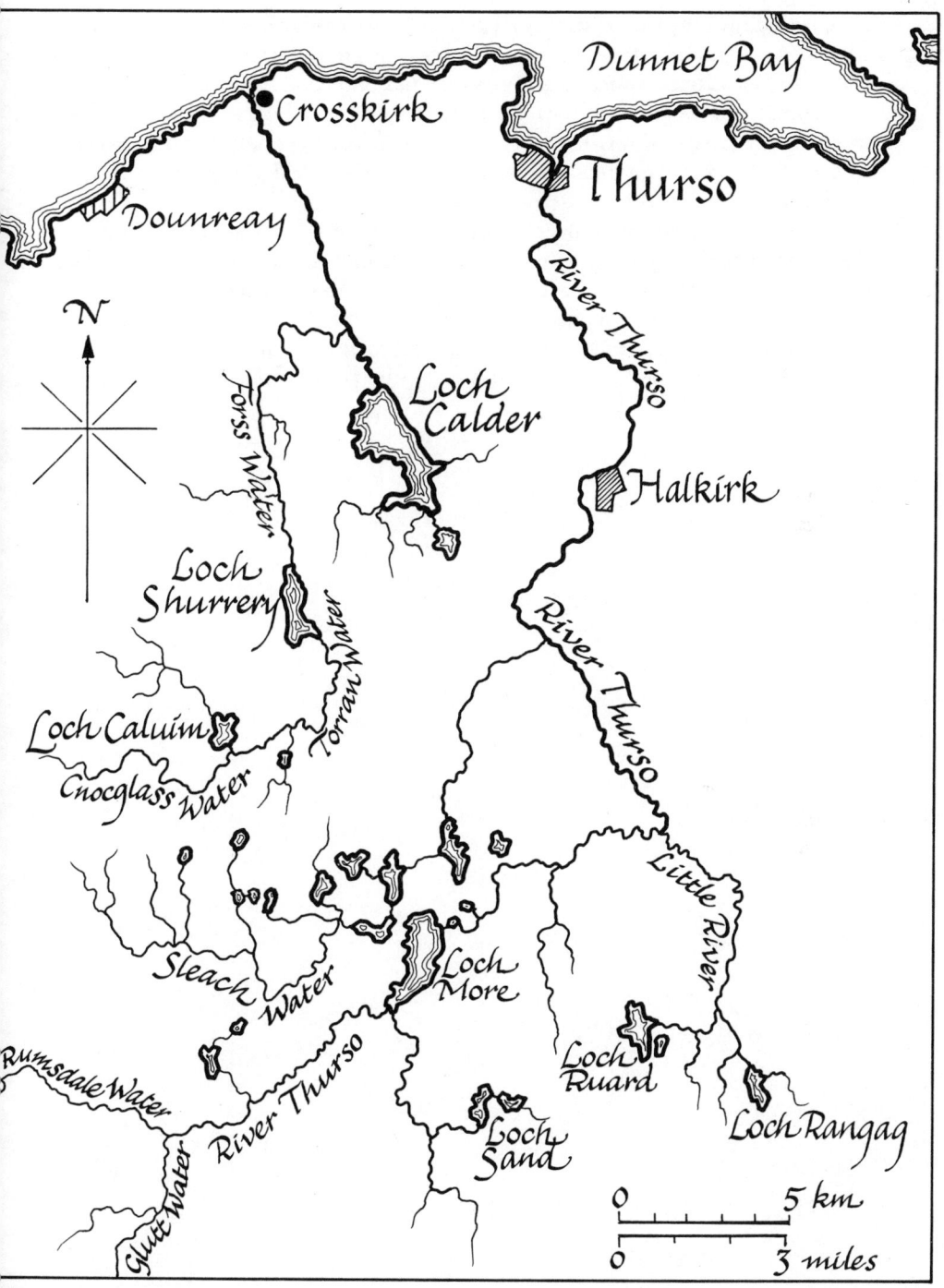

The River Thurso

are released into the waters of this loch every other year and in April and May, when the smolts are starting their downstream migration, the sluice is opened. The scheme has been a success and the loch has produced one-year-old smolts of six inches in length and two-year-old smolts nine inches long, sizeable smolts indeed. This is a big step forward from the rearing ponds at Braal on the Thurso, which have not been used since they sprang a leak during the Second World War.

The sweep nets on the estuary are owned by Thurso Fisheries Ltd. They do not commence fishing until 1 June. There are a number of bag net stations in the Thurso district from Holborn Head to Men of Mey and these are operated by a number of owners including the Crown.

Regarding disease, it is most interesting to note that UDN has never actually been confirmed on the Thurso, although an occasional suspected case has been reported.

24

THE FORSS, HALLADALE, STRATHY, NAVER AND BORGIE

The Forss

The Forss rises in the hills on the Sutherland-Caithness border and flows north to discharge its waters into the sea on the north coast about 6 miles west of Thurso. Its source is Loch Torr na Caerdaich which is the central loch of a series of three. The river flowing out of this loch is known as the Cnocglass or Torran Water. It wends its way down Glen Urban through the deer forest of Dorrery in a north-easterly direction, collecting the water flowing out of Loch Caluim on its left bank, and then following a rather twisty course before turning north and flowing into Loch Shurrery. This loch is about a mile long and fairly narrow and from its mouth the Forss Water begins. The first significant tributary below Loch Shurrery is the Allt Forsiescye which comes in on the left bank. The next tributary, which comes in on the right bank just before the Forss passes under Westfield Bridge, is a small one which flows out of Loch Calder. From Westfield Bridge to the sea the river flows north down Lythmore Strath. After it passes under the Bridge of Forss it goes over a rough fall, which gives its Norse name (Forss) to the river, close to Forss House. The final mile of its course to the sea at Crosskirk Bay is remarkably sluggish and fishes best in a good wind.

The Forss opens on 11 February, a full month later than its neighbours the Halladale and Thurso. It has a run of spring fish which is normally held back in the lower section of the river below the falls until the water temperature rises to about 48°F, either in late April or early May depending on the severity of the past winter. There is also a fairly good grilse run as well as an autumn run.

Fish used to ascend unhindered to the headwaters of the river to occupy the excellent spawning facilities in the Cnocglass above Loch Shurrery where there is accommodation for a large population of spawners.

However, since 1955–56 Loch Shurrery has been dammed under the Caithness County Council (Loch Shurrery) Water Order, 1955, in order to provide water for the Dounreay Atomic Energy Station. A compensation flow of 2.5 mgd is discharged daily into the river from the dam, and provisions allow for a 365 million gallon per annum block grant for the provision of freshets. This allowance is held in the reservoir to be released, at times agreed between the Council and the Fishery Board, as freshets of not more than 10 mgd. As the Forss is mainly a spate river the impounding of Loch Shurrery reduces the size and duration of the spates and the fish pass in the dam impedes the free ascent of salmon. In recent years the numbers of fish seen above the dam has shown a marked decline and the numbers spawning in the Cnocglass are very much reduced. Several factors may have helped to cause this decline amongst which UDN, coastal netting and the damming of Loch Shurrery are likely to have played a significant part.

The Forss is a useful angling river with the Forss House beat probably being the best, having almost the sole share of the early fishing. Other owners are Broubster and Shurrery with two beats, and above the loch, on the Cnocglass, Dorrery Lodge and Dorrery Farm. The beats above the falls can expect reasonable angling after the end of April. The Forss House beat kills fish regularly on the opening day, 11 February, and March–May are good months. In this section below the falls there are sixteen named pools most of which are slow-flowing pools and fish extremely well if there is an upstream wind. The best of these are the Falls, Rock, Long, Hut, Sea, the Two Stone Walls and Graham's. Above the falls the Bridge and Pilkington's are the best.

Major Radcliffe, who bought Forss House in 1919, and whose family sold it in 1972, was a very keen angler and made many improvements to the lower pools shortly after he purchased the property. He also built and ran a hatchery for many years but this is no longer in existence.

The Forss House beat used to average 150–200 fish a year most of which were caught in the spring, but in more recent years the records show a marked increase in summer and autumn catches. The average weight of salmon is 9 lb and grilse 6 lb, the latter being a pound heavier on average than 20 years ago. The largest salmon caught weighed 42 lb and was killed in the Corner Pool by the keeper, D. Coupar, on August 14 1954. This fish is by far the largest taken from the river although fish in the 20 lb range are caught occasionally.

During Major Radcliffe's ownership of Forss House only the sweep netting station in the estuary was operated by him and not the coastal netting. However, the new owner of Forss House has increased the netting in recent years.

There is no significant sea trout run in the Forss, although a few are caught most years.

UDN was first seen in 1969 and after one very bad season outbreaks have been few and far between. However, some fish are seen with the disease during most seasons.

It is unfortunate that the District Fishery Board ceased to function for some years. However, attempts were made in 1973 and 1976 to reconstitute the Board and the latest attempt in 1979 was successful and a Board is once again in existence.

THE FORSS, HALLADALE, STRATHY, NAVER AND BORGIE

Halladale

The Halladale rises in Achentoul Forest and flows close to the road (A897) from Forsinard down almost to the sea, where it enters the sandy Melvich Bay at Bighouse. The upper part of the river from Forsinard to the graveyard at Trantlemore is owned by Forsinard Estate, while the lower section from Trantlemore to the sea is owned by Liberton Proprietors Ltd, who also have the commercial bag and sweep net fishery at the mouth.

The upper part of the river runs fast over rocky terrain and the pools are short and bouldery with a few good ones situated in a small section of river of gorge-like character. Two major tributaries contribute to the flow of the river in this area and they are the Forsinain Burn, which flows out of Loch Sletill, and the River Dyke which enters the river from the west above Trantlemore. Below Trantlemore the river receives water from the Smigel Burn and from two smaller streams running out of Loch na Seilge and Loch Akran. In this lower section the river is more sluggish with long, wide pools.

The Halladale tends to be a spring fish river, although few spring fish have been taken over the last 5 years because of low flows. Unlike its neighbours, the Naver and Helmsdale, it has no large lochs to rely on for a regular supply of water during dry weather. Furthermore, the coastal netting has probably affected this river more than its neighbours.

A number of river improvements are planned. These include erection of gabion weirs in the upper reaches to provide more holding pools, and consequently more fishable water, and a generous restocking programme.

The largest salmon known to have been caught on rod and line in this river is one of $30\frac{1}{2}$ lb, a cast of which can be seen in the Forsinard Hotel.

The fishing is let through the estate factors.

The Strathy

This little north coast river's catchment is sandwiched between that of the Naver to the west and that of the Halladale to the east.

Its source is in the mountains surrounding Loch Strathy, a small loch on its headwater. After flowing out of the loch the Strathy flows almost due north on its journey of approximately 14 miles to the sea. It flows for the main part of its course through moorland. It is joined by a sizeable tributary, the Uair, on its right bank a few miles below the loch. At this point the Strathy flows through a wooded section. Further down the strath the river passes Bowside Lodge, the residence of previous owners of the river, which now belongs to the Department of Agriculture and Fisheries for Scotland, as does the river. Opposite Bowside Lodge there is another wooded area on the left bank and after this it is only a short distance before the river flows through Strathy village and discharges its waters into the sea in Strathy Bay just east of Strathy point.

The Strathy is essentially a spate river, which during high water conditions in the summer months carries a dark peat stained colour. For the most part it is a very shingly river with few holding pools. There is, however, an almost canal-like stretch some 6 miles up-river from the sea deep enough to hold fish for long periods in low water conditions.

In the late 1930s a lot of work was done on the river both to improve the pools and increase the stock of fish. Both salmon and sea trout fry were planted annually in reasonable numbers and although salmon and grilse stocks benefited there was practically no result from the stocking of sea trout. At the same time as this stocking, 14 pools were formed, mainly with the use of gabion baskets and concrete weirs. However, due to the gravelly consistency of the bed and unsuitable banks, these weirs were nearly all undermined and over the next decade were almost completely destroyed.

Angling is limited to a short period over the summer months from late June to the end of September, when it closes. Most of the fish caught are grilse and about 20–30 are caught per season. These average around 7 lb, but the biggest recorded was $16\frac{1}{2}$ lb and was caught in the 1920s. The best pools are the Rock, Manns and Forestry pools and the canal-like stretch called the Dye pools can be good in high water. In one day 8 fish to three rods is the best catch recorded.

Spawning and feeding areas are to be found over almost the entire length of the river, and also in the Uair. This tributary does not, however, hold many fish.

The Strathy has no proper estuary and the river discharges its water into the sea over a sandy beach. At times of drought conditions the flow of the river is very small and on occasions the sandy beach absorbs almost the entire flow of the river. It is therefore highly probable that this accounts for the poor stock of fish in the river system, because not only does this prevent fish ascending but, even worse, it would prevent descending smolts having a free passage to the sea during their migration. If these conditions coincided with migration the smolts would be held back in the lower reaches of the river and would be decimated by predators.

Netting takes place at Strathy Point to the west of the river mouth and is carried out mainly with bag nets, but on occasions sweep nets are used.

The fishing on the river is let to tenants by the Department of Agriculture and Fisheries for Scotland.

Naver

The Naver competes with the Helmsdale in being one of the best salmon rivers in northern Scotland and, like the latter, has the reputation of being a good spring fish river. Although perhaps 'spring' is a misnomer, as any angler standing thigh-deep in ice-cold water and being buffeted by a blustery snow-laden wind in mid-January will agree, however many salmon he is pulling out of this delectable river.

The Naver flows from the 6 mile-long loch of that name, which is fed by Loch Meadie via the River Mudale. Immediately downstream from Loch Naver the Mallart River enters the Naver from the south bringing with it the waters of Loch a' Bhealaich and Loch Choire lying in the Choire Forest at the foot of Ben Klibreck. The Naver, now well-supplied with water, receives no more major tributaries during its 18-mile-long course to the sea, which it enters at the lovely Torrisdale Bay near Bettyhill.

From the loch to the road bridge at Syre the river is open and moorland in character with a bed at first composed of boulders and rocks and later of coarse gravel. Below the road bridge and Dalvina Lodge the river has a charming sylvan appearance and pools which would capture the hearts of the most insensitive of anglers. The Syre Pool is one of the best-known pools on the river and holds many more fish than any of the others. Below Rhifail the river meanders slowly through unstable sandy and gravelly banks. However, a little below Skelpick, the river assumes some of its former character before it flows into the estuary at Torrisdale Bay.

The river is divided into 6 beats with a further stretch called the Private Water and another referred to as the Club Water. Beat 1 is from the foot of Loch Naver to Ceann-na-coille; Beat 2 is from Ceann-na-coille Burn to the lower end of Dalvina Pool; Beat 3 is from the lower end of Dalvina Pool to Skail Burn; Beat 4 is from Skail Burn to the lower end of Steep Brae Pool; Beat 5 is from Steep Brae Stream to lower end of Parapet Pool; Beat 6 is from the lower end of Parapet Pool to Apagill Burn opposite the old cruives; Private Water (belonging to Skelpick Lodge) is from the old cruives to Achnabourin Burn; Club Water is from Achnabourin Burn to Naver Bridge and the estuary.

Beats 1 to 6 are fished in daily succession from Beat 1 down, so that over the week each angler has fished all 6 beats. On the Club Water a limited number of permits are issued to visitors on application to the Fishery Manager. The beats are let through agents and the Fishery Manager. Fishing is by fly only throughout the year.

Loch Naver fishes best in March and April, but later in the season sport with salmon is slow, although it is fished throughout the season by anglers staying at Altnaharra Hotel at the top end of the loch. The river is good throughout the season, but it is particularly renowned for its early fishing in February and March. The Club Water and estuary fish well for sea trout in March, April and May.

The fishing on the Mudale and Loch Meadie is available from Altnaharra Fishings. Salmon are often in Mudale from March onwards. It is a deep canal-like water with several good holding pools. It fishes best in spate conditions or when a strong upstream wind is blowing. The Mallart River is available for fishing through Altnaharra Fishings from May to July (fly only).

There are two falls on the Mallart, a short distance upstream from its confluence with the Naver, so few fish ascend this river before April. However, it is usually good for fishing during June if water conditions are right. The Mallart is very peaty and fish tend to become very dark in a matter of days.

The commercial fishery is operated by one sweep net and usually only works from 1 June – 31 July. It is operated at one of the two stations at the mouth of the river. Due to the clarity of the water, lying over pure white sand, the netting operations are most spectacular and attract many spectators who have a good view, from the low cliffs, of the salmon coming into the river and being encircled by the net. There are no bag net stations in the vicinity of the Naver.

A very nice custom of the Naver Fishery Board is one of giving a salmon each season to every pensioner in Bettyhill and also to every house in Strathnaver and, as there are in the region of 40 houses in the Strath, this is a most generous practice. In addition to this gift, any ratepayer in Bettyhill may purchase a salmon at the bargain price of £1.

The Naver Fishery Board has as its Fishery Officer Commander Rickards, who also manages the fishings on the Helmsdale. The conservation of salmon is very much the concern of this Board and 250–300 salmon are caught each autumn and, when ripe, are stripped of their eggs which are hatched in the hatchery of Kincardine Fisheries Ltd in Ardgay. The fry are planted out in the headwaters of the Naver to ensure a good return of salmon in the future and to maintain the high reputation of this lovely river.

The Borgie

The Borgie rises in the mountains to the south of Loch Coulside and flows north through this loch and into Loch Loyal lying between Ben Loyal and Beinn Stumanadh. Lochs Craggie and Slaim are practically extensions of Loch Loyal and from them the Borgie flows down Strath Borgie and through the Forestry Commission plantation. From the falls there is a 5-mile stretch of river before the sea is reached at Torrisdale Bay, about a mile west of the mouth of the Naver.

During 1959 and early 1960 the proprietor of the Borgie erected a low dam, about $3\frac{1}{2}$ feet high, at the foot of Loch Slaim. The dam was provided with 3 sluice gates which enables the flow of the river downstream to be changed when required. The dam raised Loch Slaim by about 3 feet and Lochs Craggie and Loyal by about 2 feet and first came into operation in the spring of 1960. Normally the sluices are closed at about the New Year, in order to fill up the lochs in the early spring. They are then opened as required and used to supplement the flow of the river during May, which is considered the best spring month for fishing. June is not considered one of the better fishing periods and the sluices are usually closed again throughout this month to store

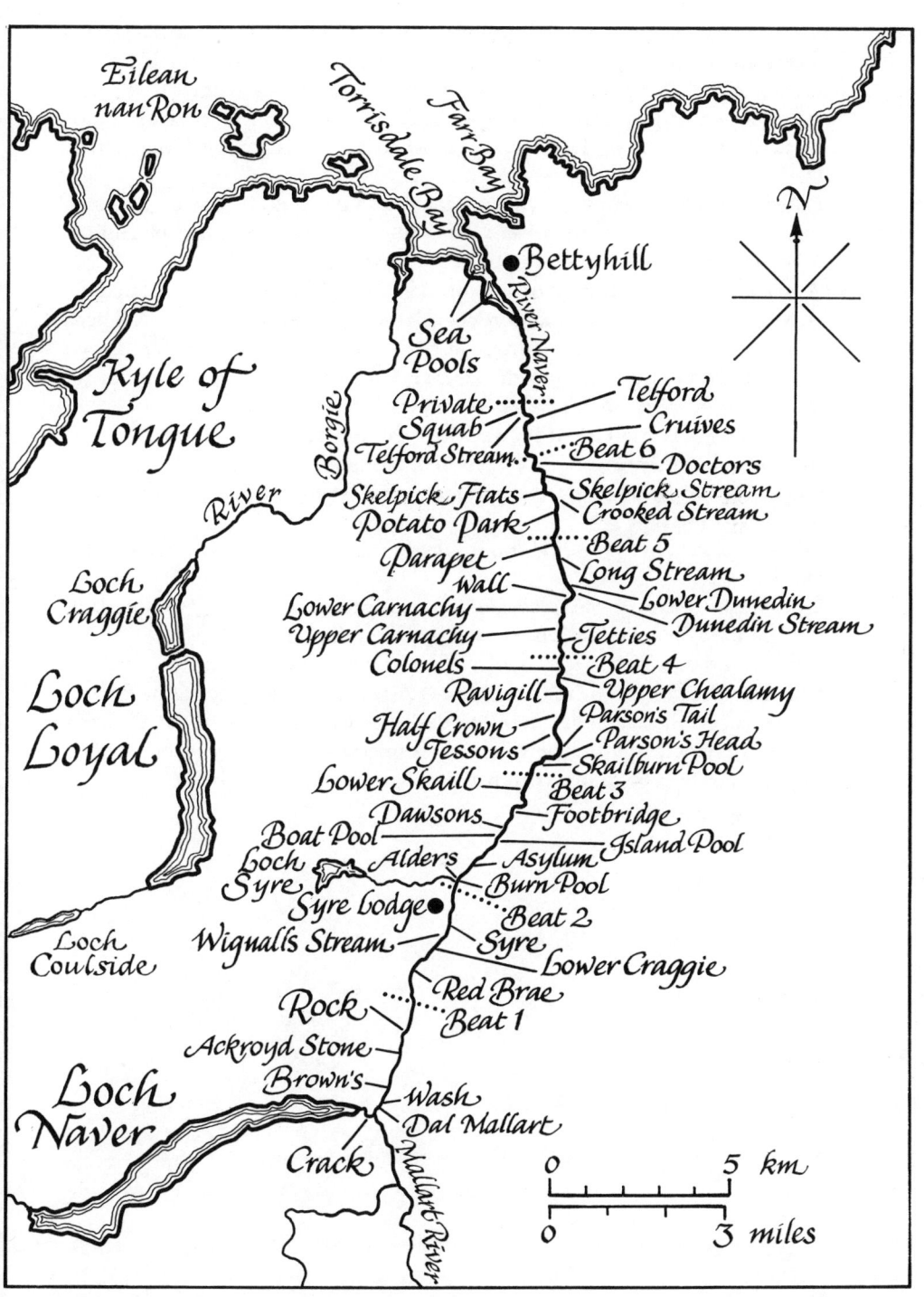

Salmon Pools on the River Naver

more water for use in July and August when the grilse run is heaviest.

There are 3 main beats below the falls and one above, plus 2 small private stretches. About 9 rods can be accommodated when fishing is at its peak. The number of named pools and casts is about 50, most of which are man-made, some at the beginning of the century and others more recently with the help of university students.

In recent years the runs of fish have tended to be later and the numbers of grilse in the catches have increased. The present average rod catch of salmon and grilse is about 260 with the best year having a total of 535.

A large spate on the Borgie on 31 July 1956 caused a great deal of damage, mostly to the weirs, and it took more than 10 years to reinstate the river. There is a shortage of good spawning areas on the river and the best areas are above lochs Coulside and Loyal, below the Falls and in a burn which joins the Borgie below the falls. Feeding areas are, however, more plentiful.

A hatchery was built in 1948 and this has the capacity to hold 500,000 salmon ova. In the spring about 200,000 of the resulting fry are planted out at the unfed stage throughout the whole river system. No sea trout fry are hatched or planted.

UDN appeared in the Borgie about 10 years ago but at present there is little or no disease.

Gravel movement in the river is not a great problem, although a drag line had to be used in 1958 to remove some accumulations.

There is no netting at the mouth of the river at present and the nearest netting is at the mouth of the River Naver. An eel trap was built on the Borgie in 1963 to catch the silver eels on their seaward migration. It is sited approximately half way up the river and is operated from July to November each year. Its average annual catch is in the region of 250 lb.

25

THE KYLE OF DURNESS AND CAPE WRATH

The Hope

The tributaries of the Hope rise in the mountainous area of the Merkland, Altnaharra and Reay deer forests and drain the steep slopes of Ben Hee, Meallan Liath and Saval Beg, all of which are over 2,000 feet high. There are three main tributaries which join at a point just below Gobernuisgach Lodge, one of the lodges of the Reay Forest Estate. The streams are the Allt a' Chraois, Allt na Bad and the Glen Golly River. Below their junction the Strathmore River begins and flows north down Strath More for some miles under the shadow of Ben Hope on its right bank before entering Loch Hope, a narrow loch 6 miles in length. Out of this loch flows the River Hope, a short interesting river flowing fairly quietly on its $1\frac{1}{4}$-mile descent into the sea on the east side of Loch Eriboll. The Hope is exclusively owned by the proprietor of Hope Lodge and is a useful late river. Like most of its neighbours to the west of it, only an occasional fish runs early and the main runs start in June. Mid-July to the end of August is considered the best period, although fish run into the river even after the season is closed. The trend recently is for the salmon run to get later and the former grilse run has virtually disappeared.

The $1\frac{1}{4}$-mile length of river includes a tidal stretch. There are some 6 recognised pools most of which were formed by croys and walls constructed many years ago. It is considered to be a two-rod beat and fishing is by fly only. Maintenance of the croys is required from time to time. There is no hatchery on the river and no regular restocking apart from occasional stocking of the headwaters by the proprietors of the Strathmore River.

The Hope salmon average about 8 lb, and sea trout on the loch up to 12 lb with one of 18 lb being taken a number of years ago.

There has been no serious outbreak of UDN and even isolated records are scarce.

Loch Hope is a useful sea trout and salmon fishery and is fished by 6 or more boats mainly in July, August and September. Catches of both salmon and sea trout remain fairly constant. Fishing on the loch is arranged through the Tongue Hotel.

The Strathmore River can provide useful fishing in times of spate. There are a number of natural and man-made pools throughout its length which can afford good sport when the river is in order.

The spawning and nursery areas lie mainly above the loch, and throughout Strath More and Glen Golly there is an abundance of both of these essential commodities. Several years ago attempts were made by the upper proprietors to establish sea trout in Allt a' Chraois to improve Loch an t-Seilg at the head of this burn. A difficult falls was eased to allow better access on Allt a' Chraois and sea trout fry were planted in this burn. Salmon and sea trout fry have also been planted in Glen Golly.

The Dionard

The Dionard is a longish river which flows north and whose source is in the mountainous country to the north-east of Loch Stack and in the Reay Forest. It drains the eastern slopes of Meall Horn and the northern slopes of Meall an Lochain Sgeireach before entering Loch Dionard underneath the eastern face of Foinaven. From Loch Dionard the river gradually increases in size with the entry of a number of tributaries along its 10-mile course. The river flows close to the Rhiconich–Durness road for the last few miles before flowing into the Kyle of Durness and the sea at Balnakeil Bay.

The Dionard, although yielding an occasional early fish, has its main runs of fish in June–August. Large numbers of salmon, grilse and sea trout ascend during this period. It is probably more renowned for sea trout than for salmon and grilse, although there is a substantial run of the latter two. The lower part of the river is flatter than the rest and has some useful pools where good sea trout and salmon catches can be made. Higher up, the river becomes more rugged and pools are smaller with many rocky pots and runs. Good baskets can also be taken in this section, but the tendency is for fish to pass through this section and into the loch more quickly during spate conditions.

The loch itself has a very high reputation as a sea trout fishery and many people consider it to be as good as, if not better than, Loch Stack for size and numbers of sea trout and salmon. But it has the disadvantage of being both inaccessible and, as it nestles among high mountains, not always suiting the wind to make it fishable. The easiest access is up the side of the river, but this is a long walk which has only recently been overcome with the use of a snowcat. Access from the Reay Forest and Gobernuisgach is a long mountainous walk of around 4 hours. Anglers from this quarter normally stay the night in a bothy and ponies are used to carry provisions and the catch. The ownership of the Loch is shared by Gaulin Estate, Reay Forest Estate and Gobernuisgach. The river is shared by Gaulin Estate and the Department of Agriculture and Fisheries for Scotland, the former having the largest share.

The annual catch of the river, loch and Kyle of Durness amounts to over 100 salmon and grilse and a larger number of sea trout of a good size. The Kyle of

Durness contributes a reasonable share of the sea trout catch as, although it is tidal, anglers can still readily catch these fish.

UDN has appeared from time to time in recent years, but never in epidemic proportions.

The Durness Hotel has access to some of the fishings on the Dionard and is a very popular resort for anglers.

The Kinloch

This short little north coast river rises on the east slopes of Meallan Liath and the west slopes of Ben Loyal. Many of its feeder burns cascade down the mountain sides into Loch an Dherue a small loch on its headwaters, which momentarily checks their rapid descent. The Kinloch River flows out of this loch quietly at first then more rapidly as more burns swell its size and it enters a more rugged gorgy course, cascading over several falls and smaller rapids as it flows down the strath in the shadow of Ben Loyal and Ben Hope. It flows in a north-easterly direction past Kinloch Lodge, the residence of past and present owners, before discharging its waters in the sea at the head of the Kyle of Tongue. For many years few salmon could ascend this river because of two very formidable falls. In 1890, however, the then owner of the river blasted these falls and made stone dams across the tails of the falls pool, in order to increase the depth of water in the pool and thereby lessen the height fish had to jump in order to ascend the river. In 1947 these stone dams were replaced by concrete dams. Due to these improvements salmon can now enter the river and ascend freely to the spawning areas above.

The spawning and feeding areas are to be found in the section 2 miles above the mouth up to Loch an Dherue and in one or two of the side tributaries. These areas can provide an adequate stock of salmon for the size of river involved. No hatchery is run on the river, but eyed ova are planted out from time to time in Vibert boxes in understocked areas of the headwaters.

The main angling months are June–September with late July and August usually the best. However, fish have been caught in March, and early May can be good provided there is plenty of water.

The annual average rod catch varies between 40 and 60 with an average weight of 7–9 lb. The best day ever recorded was 21 fish, all caught on fly and 10 of these were caught by beginners.

There are several man-made pools on the river, some of which were constructed in 1890. These consisted of a stone-made dam at the tail with no defined gap. More recently between 1940 and 1960 others were constructed by means of gabion weirs and concrete dams and groynes. Amongst the best angling pools are the Little Falls and Junction Pool, but many other pools can also provide good sport.

An occasional sea trout runs the river, but being a very rocky river it is not really favoured by this species. Tenants normally stay in either Tongue or Ben Loyal Hotels.

Colonel D. Moncrieff who owned the river between 1937 and 1957 was responsible for many of the improvements to pools and was indeed one of the pioneers of the art of improving rivers with groynes, many of which he sited sloping slightly upstream in order to avoid bank erosion below the dams. The present owner is one of his sons.

As this little river is almost entirely a spate river, heavy floods sometimes cause damage to the man-made pools and these require attention when this occurs.

The Polla

The Polla rises in the mountainous countryside between the catchment areas of the Dionard to the west and the Hope to the east. It drains an area of rocky heath and rough grassland frequented by herds of red deer and a few sheep.

It has on its headwaters a small loch called Loch Staonsaid out of which the Polla flows on the start of its journey of approximately $5\frac{1}{2}$ miles down Strath Beag before it discharges its waters into the sea at the head of Loch Eriboll.

The Polla's course is at first fairly rocky and rugged with two formidable falls some distance below the loch, which debar access to migratory fish above this point. From here to the sea the river has some nice natural pools most of which are rocky. Although the Polla opens on 12 January it is essentially a summer river, dependent on water conditions as to when fish are able to enter the river. It is entirely a spate river rising and falling very quickly after heavy rainfall. July–September are the main months for angling and runs of sea trout and grilse enter the river when water conditions are suitable over this period. Grilse average 5–6 lb and sea trout $1\frac{1}{2}$ lb, but there are also finnock to provide good sport.

Recently runs of both grilse and sea trout have declined badly and, in spite of an annual restocking with 6,000 salmon fry and 4,000 sea trout fry, angling catches show a steady decline. The river does, however, fish well when it is dropping and during the right conditions anglers can still have good sport.

The spawning and feeding areas of the Polla are limited because of the inaccessible falls 3 miles up the river system. There is no doubt that if fish were able to ascend to its upper reaches and utilise the spawning and feeding areas available the stock of the Polla would be greatly improved.

Angling is kept in the hands of the proprietor.

The Grudie

This river's catchment is in the mountainous area of the Cape Wrath peninsula to the north of the Durness–Rhiconich road. It flows in an easterly direction and discharges its waters into the western side of the Kyle of Durness. Its neighbour the Dionard, flows into the Kyle at its southernmost point.

The Grudie River's headwaters consist of a maze of small feeder tributaries, and the main river itself is comparatively short. It flows through a flattish area of moorland before descending a formidable falls and then running steeply through a series of rocky pools and pots into the Kyle. The Grudie has an early run of heavy fish in June, averaging 12 lb, some of which are as large as 18 lb. These fish are very distinct from the Dionard fish, being long and narrow in shape as opposed to deep and short. This run is followed by runs of grilse in July, August and September. Very few sea trout run this river.

There is a useful angling potential in the rocky section below the falls and again in the flats above the falls before it splits into many small burns. It is, however, entirely a spate river and, although a small loch called Loch na Craige Ruabach is on its headwaters, it is not of any real significance. The Grudie has a wealth of useful spawning and feeding areas in the many burns which form its headwaters.

The fishing is in the hands of the proprietor of Cape Wrath Hotel and is fished by anglers staying in this hotel.

The Daill

This river, like its neighbour, is also short and drains an area of the Cape Wrath peninsula to the north of the Grudie's catchment.

It rises on the east slopes of Fashven, a steep rugged mountain below which is Loch Airigh na Beinne. This is a sizeable loch on the Daill's headwaters and the river flows north-east out of this loch through a stretch of boggy peat land and then enters Loch Bad an Fheur-loch which is a much smaller loch. From here to the sea the Daill's passage is steep and rugged with a series of cascades and small pots forming its course as it tumbles into the sea on the western side of the Kyle of Durness, just on the seaward side of the sandbar which defines the northward boundary of the Kyle.

This river too has a small run of heavier salmon in June, followed by runs of grilse in July, August and September which average 5–7 lb. Very few, if any, sea trout frequent this river.

Angling is very limited, owing to the nature of the river. Fly fishing is mainly confined to the lower loch, the bottom section of the river being too rapid and broken and the upper section above Loch Bad an Fheur-loch being too reedy to allow freedom to fish it. Loch Bad an Fheur-loch does, however, fish well if an angler is willing to venture forth on a day when a stiff south-west wind is blowing.

The Daill has useful feeding and spawning areas on its headwaters, below the upper loch and in some of its tributary burns. The fishing on the Daill's right bank is in the hands of the proprietor of Cape Wrath Hotel and the left bank is owned by the proprietor of Balnakeil Estate.

The Kearvaig

This short north coast river rises in the mountains of the north-west corner of the Cape Wrath peninsula and flows almost due north to discharge its waters into the sea to the east of Cape Wrath lighthouse. It rises on the slopes of Fashven, Cnoc na Glaic Tarsuinn and Beinn Dearg under which three lochs, on it headwaters, nestle. These are namely Loch na Gainmhich, Loch na Glaic Tarsuinn and Lochan na Glamhaichd, none of which are really of significant size. The burns flowing out of these lochs join and send the Kearvaig on its journey of approximately $2\frac{1}{2}$ miles to the sea.

This river, like its neighbours, has a small run of salmon in June and after that a grilse run which covers the period July–September when water conditions are suitable and allow fish to ascend the river. The Kearvaig is very much a spate river. Few sea trout ascend this river system.

The river has a limited angling potential during the summer months. There are useful spawning and feeding areas on the headwaters and tributary streams.

The lower section of the river and best pools are owned by Balnakeil Estate and the upper part of the river is in the hands of Cape Wrath Hotel, but is of little consequence and rather inaccessible. This river system lies within the area of a Naval Gunnery range and is barred to the public when there is an exercise taking place.

The Shinary

This is another short river, which is the most northerly of the rivers flowing into the west coast of Scotland. It drains the south-west part of the Cape Wrath peninsula and flows down Strath Shinary into Sandwood Loch and from thence over a sandy bar into the sea.

Access from the sea into the loch in recent years has become very silted and fish can only ascend freely into Sandwood Loch during spate conditions or on certain periods of extreme high tide.

This river is essentially a spate river draining rugged rocky ground without any loch of any size on its upper catchment, therefore it rises and falls very rapidly.

Sea trout, salmon and grilse ascend this river system throughout the summer months entirely according to water conditions, and in the very driest summers few fish are able to ascend until the drought breaks in the autumn.

Spawning and feeding areas on the Shinary are adequate and can be found on the headwaters of the river and its main feeder burns.

The Shinary fishing is shared between private proprietors and one bank is in the hands of the Garbet Hotel at Kinlochbervie. Angling both on the loch and in the river has declined over the years since the access into the river system has silted up. However, good sport can still be had on the dropping river after a spate once fish have come into the Shinary, but the whole river system is in an isolated part of the peninsula and because of that is rather more inaccessible than its neighbours.

26

THE RIVERS OF NORTH-WEST SUTHERLAND

The Inchard

The Inchard of Rhiconich lies just to the north of the mouth of the Laxford. It rises on the western slopes of Arkle and flows north-west through Lochs Garbet Mohr and Garbet Beg (the anglicised names of Lochs a' Gharbh-bhaid Mor and Beag) and their short connecting channel and gathers water from the chain of small lochs beneath the eastern slopes of Foinaven on its way. The river falls steeply from Garbet Beg over a boulder-strewn course until it discharges into Loch Inchard and the sea a mile and a half downstream. Both Garbet Mohr and Garbet Beg are small lochs, one (Mohr) being just over a mile long and the other (Beg) being just under a mile in length; neither are more than 250 yards wide.

The river, like its neighbours, has only a few early fish and has the main runs in June–August. During this period a surprising number of grilse, salmon and sea trout ascend the river and enter the loch system. The river itself is short, fast-flowing and very rocky. It has few deep holding pools and these are mainly pots and short runs. Although some fish can be caught in the river the main angling potential is in the two lochs.

Garbet Beg is an excellent salmon and grilse fishery. It is for the most part a shallow loch with many bays and, being narrow, has a long length of shoreline for its size. A large part of it, including the neck of the connecting channel with Garbet Mohr, can easily be fished from the shore, and this often causes less disturbance to the fish than boat fishing. However, certain parts of the loch do have to be fished by boat. If two rods are fishing it often pays for one to land on the shore and leave the other to fish from the boat.

Garbet Mohr is the larger of the two lochs both in length and width and it is considered to be better for sea trout than salmon as the former seem to run straight through Garbet Beg into the larger loch. Both these lochs depend very largely on spate water in June, July and August to draw the fish into the loch system. In dry years, such as have been experienced recently, fish are unable to ascend the river and consequently congregate at the mouth waiting for a rise in water. In some seasons, with drought conditions in the summer months, catches are insignificant. However, if conditions are favourable for fish to run freely, few lochs in Scotland can compete with Garbet Beg as a salmon fishery.

UDN has been prevalent in the river system for several years but has never reached epidemic proportions.

The ownership of the Inchard and the two lochs is mainly divided between Oldshore More Estate and the Reay Forest Estate, the former owning the Inchard and most of Garbet Beg and the latter most of Garbet Mohr and part of Garbet Beg.

The Laxford

This river is one of the best west coast rivers in the north of Scotland. Although it is mainly a spate river it is not as flashy as some of its neighbours, having two large lochs, Loch More and Loch Stack, on its headwaters which help to steady and hold the flow of water cascading steeply down the rugged mountains of the Reay Forest. Its course flows north-west from the top of Kinlochbrae, through Loch More, passing Lochmore Lodge, and then into a small lochan before entering Loch Stack. Ben Stack towers above the loch on the south shore and Arkle on the north. At the exit of Loch Stack the real Laxford begins, overlooked approvingly by Lochstack Lodge. The river flows quickly, but not steeply, parallel to the Lairg-Laxford Bridge road, past Laxford Bridge and on to Loch Laxford and the sea. The actual river from Loch Stack to Loch Laxford is about $3\frac{1}{2}$ miles long and the length of the two lochs and their connecting channel is approximately 8 miles.

Although a few salmon and sea trout run up the river in the spring the main run is not until June–August. During these months large numbers of salmon, grilse and sea trout ascend the river and enter the loch system. The Laxford is an excellent angling river, with many varied runs and deep holding pools of widely differing character. Among the most famed are the Top, Duke's, Duchess's, Ridge and Cottage. The 5-year average annual catch of the river (1972–1976) was 115 salmon and 114 grilse. In addition a large number of sea trout were killed.

Loch Stack has for many years been famed for its sea trout catches, as has Loch More although to a lesser extent. Loch Stack has a very peculiar shape, rather like an H with an elongated arm. It is very deep in places but, with its long length of shoreline, it has an abundance of banks and bays which afford ideal fishing water for both sea trout and salmon. In the period 1940–1958 it must have been regarded as the best sea trout fishery in Scotland. Although, like most sea trout fisheries in Scotland, there has been a marked decline in recent years due to a reduction of stock, Loch Stack is still among the best. Sea trout of 5–10 lb are quite common and the record for the loch is 18 lb. Loch More also has these large sea trout but, having fewer bays and inlets, tends to be a deeper loch more suited to dapping than wet fly fishing. The average combined annual catch for the two lochs for the period 1972–1976 was 101 salmon and grilse and 809 sea trout.

The Laxford system is set amongst the most spectacular mountain scenery with the peaks of Ben Stack, Arkle and Foinaven towering above it, while other smaller mountain ridges outline the catchment area. Apart from the beauty of the surroundings to mesmerise the angler, there is also the added thrill of not knowing what size of fish is going to come up to the fly.

Netting in the estuary and river is mainly exercised for management purposes. There is no regular netting, but if fish congregate in large numbers due to low water conditions either in the estuary or the river, then netting takes place. In the late 1950s and early 1960s a fish trap, sited just below Loch Stack, was worked as part of a commercial fishery. This has not, however, been used in recent years. The Laxford system is owned solely by Reay Forest Estate.

A hatchery with a capacity for two million ova is sited on the Achfary Burn beside the village of Achfary. It is managed by estate employees and is stocked mainly with ova stripped from fish netted on the river system. The numbers hatched each year vary according to the availability of ova. Some of the fry hatched are released in the nursery areas on the river while the remainder are sold. UDN has appeared annually in recent years but has never reached epidemic proportions.

There are 6 boats on Loch Stack and 3 on Loch More. These are normally let through Scourie, Garbet and Overscaig hotels. One beat on the river is also let at certain times of the year.

The Duart

The Duart is a small river system immediately to the south of the River Laxford and the village of Scourie. A number of lochs and their tributaries feed into the two main waters, Loch Yucal (Upper Duart) and Duartmore Loch (Lower Duart). From the latter the Duartmore Burn flows into Duartmore Bay. Fish ascend into Duartmore Loch, the upper basin of which is very reedy, and pass on up into the large Yucal Loch. From Yucal Loch they can ascend a steep, rocky half-mile length of river into Loch Allt nan Ramh which is referred to as 'the salmon hole'. The fish can then move on up two tributaries, both of which have insurmountable falls a short distance upstream of Loch Allt nan Ramh which bar their further ascent. The main spawning areas are in Duartmore Burn, the head of Duartmore Loch and the outfall of Loch Allt nan Ramh.

This is very much a spate river system and if flow conditions are right, fish start ascending in June. The catches of salmon are not large and in a good year the total catch will not exceed 20. Hardly any sea trout are caught on this river system.

The fishing is owned by Scourie and Grosvenor Estates and fishing is available to guests at the Scourie Hotel.

THE RIVERS OF NORTH-WEST SUTHERLAND

The Inver

The Inver is the next sizeable river south of the Laxford. It is largely a spate river, though it is more stable than some of its neighbours as it has Loch Assynt, approximately 5 miles long, at its head. This helps to stem the torrents of water which cascade off the steeply sloping mountains of Inchnadamph and Ben More Assynt. The source of the river can be said to be Loch na Gruagaich and Allt Mhic Mhurchaidh Gheir which feed into Loch Awe and from which flows the River Loanan. It flows in to Loch Assynt and below this loch is known as the Inver. The glen south of Loch Assynt through which the Loanan flows is most impressive with Ben More Assynt, Conival and Breabag towering to the east and Canisp overlooking the river from the west. At the head of Loch Assynt is the Inchnadamph Hotel which is a favourite haunt of many anglers, who in the evening can relax over a pint and look down the glen to the mountains of Quinag and Glas Bheinn while behind them towers the massif of Ben More Assynt from which flows the River Traligill cascading down Gleann Dubh and into the loch.

On the north shore of the loch stand the ruins of Ardvreck Castle, and it was to this castle that Montrose was brought after his capture before being transported to Edinburgh for execution.

Below Loch Assynt, and really part of this loch, is Loch na Garbhe Uidhe and a short distance downstream Loch an Iasgaich, below which Allt an Tiaghaich enters the river. It might well be argued that this is the real source of the Inver as this stream drains the lower northerly slopes of Canisp and has a small loch system of its own. However, one thing is certain and that is that the Inver now starts and soon gathers speed and cascades through a woodland gorge of silver birch and more recently planted conifer before entering Loch Inver and the sea at the fishing village of Lochinver some 6 miles south-west of Loch Assynt.

Like most west coast rivers in this area a few early fish run in the spring but, because their numbers are small, there is no serious angling until the main run occurs in June–August. During this latter period a large number of salmon, grilse and sea trout ascend the river and enter Loch Assynt and its headwaters.

The Inver has a good reputation as an angling river, having some excellent holding pools, pots and runs, all of which can afford good sport for the angler. The most productive pools are Loch an Iasgaich, Grassies, Deer, Whirl, Star, Pollan and Ladder, all of which fish well in varying heights of water. The annual catch for the river is about 400 in a good year and 250 to 300 in a bad season. Loch Assynt is mainly a brown trout fishery, although approximately 60 salmon and a few sea trout are taken annually by guests staying at Inchnadamph Hotel, and a good lie is below the ruins of Ardvreck Castle. The River Loanan can also produce a few salmon during times of spate, the Slide Pool being the most productive. Occasionally a salmon is taken in Loch Awe.

In the early part of this century the exit of Loch Assynt was dammed in order that flood waters could be controlled and put in store for use when required. The sluices fell into disrepair but were renovated in 1976. So once again the proprietors are able to use this storage for the benefit of angling and conservation. A fish pass is incorporated into this barrage and sluice to allow the free ascent of fish. Since the last war a lot of improvement work has been carried out, both in the making of new pools and the improvement of existing ones. This has necessitated making groynes and jetties to improve the holding capacity of the pools and increase the flow of water and also improve the fishing stances.

There is a plentiful supply of spawning gravel and abundant nursery areas over the entire river system. However, a hatchery, with a capacity for holding 120,000 ova, is run by estate employees and serves to restock both the Inver and the Kirkaig as required. Ova are normally obtained from these rivers but, if not available, they are bought-in from outside sources. Parr have also been introduced recently as an experiment.

The largest owner of the river is the proprietor of Glencanisp Lodge or the trustees of the same. The remainder belongs to the proprietor of Brackloch. No netting is at present exercised at the mouth of the river, but coastal nets are operated several miles to the north.

UDN has been prevalent in the river system since 1971 and in some years it has reached epidemic proportions. There has been no noticeable decline in numbers of salmon and grilse returning to the river, but angling has been adversely affected by the disease. Sea trout stocks have shown a marked decline recently and everything points to the fact that the disease is at least partly the cause of this decline. It is interesting to note the catch figures for the lower Inver prior to and since the disease outbreak in 1971.

Table 16
Catches of salmon, grilse and sea trout on the lower Inver, 1966–1979

	salmon and grilse	sea trout		salmon and grilse	sea trout
1966	118	65	1973	126	20
1967	227	30	1974	80	8
1968	169	123	1975	100	12
1969	249	38	1976	145	9
1970	225	41	1977	107	No record
1971	129	21	1978	210	No record
1972	156	34	1979	No record	No record

The Kirkaig

The Kirkaig has a very large catchment bordered by Suilven, Canisp and

THE RIVERS OF NORTH-WEST SUTHERLAND

Breabag to the north and Cul Mor and the Cromalt Hills to the south. There is an intricate system of lochs on its headwaters and there are two sources. One of these rises on the western slopes of Breabag and flows west down the Ledbeg River and the other originates in the mountains around the Altnacealgach Hotel and drains into Loch Borralan. South-west of Loch Borralan is the much larger Loch Urigill which receives the streams draining off the northern slopes of the Cromalt Hills. The water from this loch flows north into the Ledbeg. West of Loch Urigill the Ledbeg flows through lochs Cam, Veyatie and Fionn with one loch practically joining on to the next. Below Fionn Loch the river becomes the Kirkaig whose course gradually becomes tumultuous flowing over a sheer 50-foot fall and rushing down a rocky gorge into Loch Kirkaig.

The sheer falls $2\frac{1}{2}$ miles upstream from the mouth bar the ascent of migratory fish so that the splendid scenery and large area of lochs and streams is enjoyed only by the brown trout angler. Even so, the $2\frac{1}{2}$ miles of river which the salmon and sea trout frequent provide excellent sport, and although the excellent spawning and nursery areas which abound above the falls are barred to migratory fish there is a good stock of salmon and sea trout in the river.

The salmon are, on average, heavier than those in other rivers in this area and have a mean weight of 10 lb, with some being taken weighing 40 lb. There are some excellent deep holding pools, some of which are rocky and not very accessible and fish are sometimes difficult to follow when hooked if they decide to leave the pool! The most well-known pools are the Big Falls, Little Falls, Red Pools, Hazel, Heather and Elder. There are 3 beats on the river with two rods to each beat. Two of the above named pools are on each beat.

The main runs of fish are in June, July and August, although a few fish are taken early in the year. The owner of the Kirkaig is the proprietor of Glencanisp Lodge or trustees of the same. The netting rights are owned by the same estate but no netting takes place at the mouth of the river.

As has been mentioned, the spawning and feeding areas of this river are extremely limited and consequently fry from the hatchery, shared jointly with the Inver, are released annually to supplement the stocks.

UDN came to the Kirkaig at the same time, 1971, as it came to the Inver.

Table 17
Catches of salmon, grilse and sea trout on the Kirkaig, 1966–1979

	salmon and grilse	sea trout		salmon and grilse	sea trout
1966	68	10	1973	109	45
1967	91	38	1974	93	3
1968	38	15	1975	61	9
1969	89	9	1976	72	7
1970	157	41	1977	90	No record
1971	79	28	1978	113	No record
1972	71	21	1979	183	No record

The Polly

The Polly is a slightly smaller river than its northerly neighbours, the Kirkaig and Inver. It drains two lochs, the larger Loch Sionascaig at the foot of Cul Mor (2,786 feet) and the smaller Loch Doire na h-Airbhe lying at the foot of Stac Pollaidh (2,009 feet). From these two lochs it descends rapidly over falls and a rocky and gravelly bed until it reaches the Lochinver road where its character starts to change and it assumes a more canal-like appearance. In the last mile of its course it only shows its original form as it tumbles out of the Sea Pool into Polly Bay off Enard Bay. The northern tributary which drains out of Loch Sionascaig runs through a small chain of lochs, Loch Uidh Tarraigean and Loch na Dail. There are falls above and below the latter. The lower falls, which were insurmountable, were circumvented in 1878 when a side channel was deepened and secured a sufficient gradient for fish to ascend. This channel has been further improved recently to facilitate the passage of migratory fish. The fish have since been able to ascend as far as the Upper Falls, which are 25 feet high and also were insurmountable. In 1973 an artificial ladder was constructed to allow the passage of migratory fish through the upper lochs and into Loch Sionascaig. While the number of salmon which have used this ladder has been restricted by the recent outbreak of UDN, salmon are now using this passage in increasing numbers. The management policy of Polly Estates has been to facilitate the passage of migratory fish to the two large lochs at its headwaters and to construct resting pools and provide additional spawning areas, all with a view to improving the runs of fish into the river.

Although a few spring and early summer fish enter the river in May the main run of fish is late June – early August. The fish tend to remain in the lower, deeper stretch of the river where there are good but ill-defined holding pools. The angling is concentrated in the stretch below the road bridge and, while many fish are taken from the Sea Pool, a good number are taken upstream of this lively pool. A short rod is needed and, with a good wind, 'backing-up' the river can be productive of fish. If unused to playing fish in such restricted surroundings the angler may find it a bit difficult to know what to do. The fishing is private but information on lets is available from Polly Estates Ltd, Bloomsbury Square, London. The commercial fishing rights are held by Polly Estates but these are only exercised irregularly and chiefly to obtain fish for the stripping of eggs for the hatchery. The estate now operates one of the largest smolt-rearing farms in Scotland which is situated next to the river and close to the Lochinver-Drumrunie minor road. Its objective is to provide young salmon for the restocking of the River Polly and other rivers. In addition, a large number of salmon smolts are sold to the increasing number of marine salmon farmers who rear the young fish to maturity in sea cages.

The Garvie and Oscaig

The tiny rivers Garvie and Oscaig are really only connecting links in a chain of lochs in the Aird of Coigach, just south of Inverpolly and lying below the Drumrunie-Achiltibuie road.

The Garvie is the lowest river in the chain and flows from Loch Oscaig into and out of the reedy little Loch Garvie and into Garvie Bay. It is too steep and torrential to fish but one can frequently see fish ascending it from the sea into Loch Garvie and from there into Loch Oscaig and it is in these two lochs that most of the fishing is done. They are grilse and sea trout waters and provide good sport in July and August. Fish pass through the River Oscaig and up to Loch Bad a' Ghaill and through into Loch Lurgainn but few salmon are caught in there.

The fishing on Loch Garvie is shared by the Summer Isles Hotel, Achiltibuie and Polly Estates and guests to the above hotel have access to the fishing on Loch Garvie and Loch Oscaig. The commercial bag net fishery around the coast of Rhu More and Rhu Coigach is owned by Mr William Muir of Achiltibuie.

27

THE KANAIRD, ULLAPOOL, BROOM AND DUNDONNELL

The Kanaird

The River Kanaird is a typical west coast spate river. It rises in the mountains of the Rappach and Rhidorroch deer forests and flows south-west down Strath nan Lon, through Loch a' Chroisg and along a flattish glen before cascading into Strath Kanaird and past Langwell Lodge. The last part of its descent is more gentle as it meanders through a quiet backwater of arable farmland before flowing into the estuary at the head of Loch Kanaird beside Isle Martin and overlooked by Keanchulish House. The Kanaird has one main tributary, the Runie, which joins the Kanaird from the north at the Junction Pool about a mile from the estuary.

Although both these rivers descend quietly on their journey to the sea they each have one or two small gorges with formidable falls. On the Runie, one set of falls a short distance above the Junction Pool holds fish back for long periods, and another, on its left bank tributary about 3 miles upstream, is impassable to migratory fish. The Kanaird has a series of falls just above Langwell Lodge which prevent fish ascending above this point.

Although there are a few spring fish to be caught early in the season, the main run occurs in June–August and salmon, grilse and sea trout run both these rivers in reasonable numbers. The Kanaird is the better of the rivers for angling and has many interesting runs and holding pools which allow anglers to spend many peaceful hours fishing in some of the most beautiful scenery that only the west coast of Scotland can produce. Here the corncrake can still be heard in the hayfields and otters are frequently to be seen, either individually or in family parties. Among the best-known pools are the Bridge, Junction and Broken Cottages. The Junction Pool is by far the most productive and interesting and, provided there is a wind, it will fish in all heights of water and from many different angles, having two necks and two tails. The Runie has no definite pools but consists of small runs, pots and flats that can provide interesting fishing under certain conditions.

Agricultural activities, both on The Loops below Langwell Lodge and above South Keanchulish, have necessitated widespread drainage and the removal of gravel from the river bed in recent years. Because of this, several pools have been affected and, with a large movement of gravel in the river system during times of spate, pools will be subject to changes for years to come.

The angling on the Kanaird is shared by Keanchulish and Langwell estates and that on the Runie by Keanchulish and Mr Brammel. The netting is owned by Keanchulish Estate but is not exercised at present.

Both rivers have excellent spawning and feeding areas and also extensive feeding areas which are at present inaccessible to migratory fish. These are utilised by planting fry from hatcheries each year. In recent years the stocking rate has been 100,000 salmon fry annually, with the Kanaird receiving 70,000 and the Runie 30,000. The recent annual catches have been in the region of 100 salmon and grilse, as well as a number of sea trout. Although the river has been affected by UDN for a number of years the stock of fish does not seem to have been adversely affected.

In the 1960s a chain of lochs in the hills above the left bank of the Kanaird were harnessed by the North of Scotland Hydro-electric Board. The pipe line from the lochs can be seen running down the hillside to the power station just above the bridge on the Ledmore-Ullapool road. The water passes through the power station during periods of generation during the day and, during dry weather, this supplement of water is of tremendous benefit to the angler in providing more water for the fish and making conditions more suitable for angling. The power station also plays a useful role during flood conditions as when generation stops in the evening the reduction in flow simulates a 'falling' river, a condition favourable for angling, particularly for sea trout.

Groynes have been placed on certain pools between the road bridge and the Junction Pool to improve the holding capacity of these pools.

The Ullapool

The Ullapool River starts off as the River Douchary, which drains off the hills in Inverlael Forest at the head of Loch Broom, and flows north as far as Rhidorroch Old Lodge where it widens out considerably into a number of large pools and flows west, as the Rhidorroch River, down Glen Achall to the loch of that name. Downstream from Loch Achall the river is called the Ullapool and flows into Loch Broom just north of Ullapool.

The Ullapool River itself is steep and torrential but has some nice holding pools. It is a late river and relies on spates to bring fish in during July and August. The spawning grounds lie both above and below Loch Achall, although a waterfall about 3 miles upstream from Rhidorroch Old Lodge impedes the access of migratory fish to the upper reaches. It is said by some that few fish spawn above the loch. This is rather surprising if it is true and the only reason for this might be the unstable nature of the river bed.

The river below the loch is divided into 3 beats. The upper beat has nearly a mile of fishing with 8 pools and extends from the Loch Pool to the Black Pool.

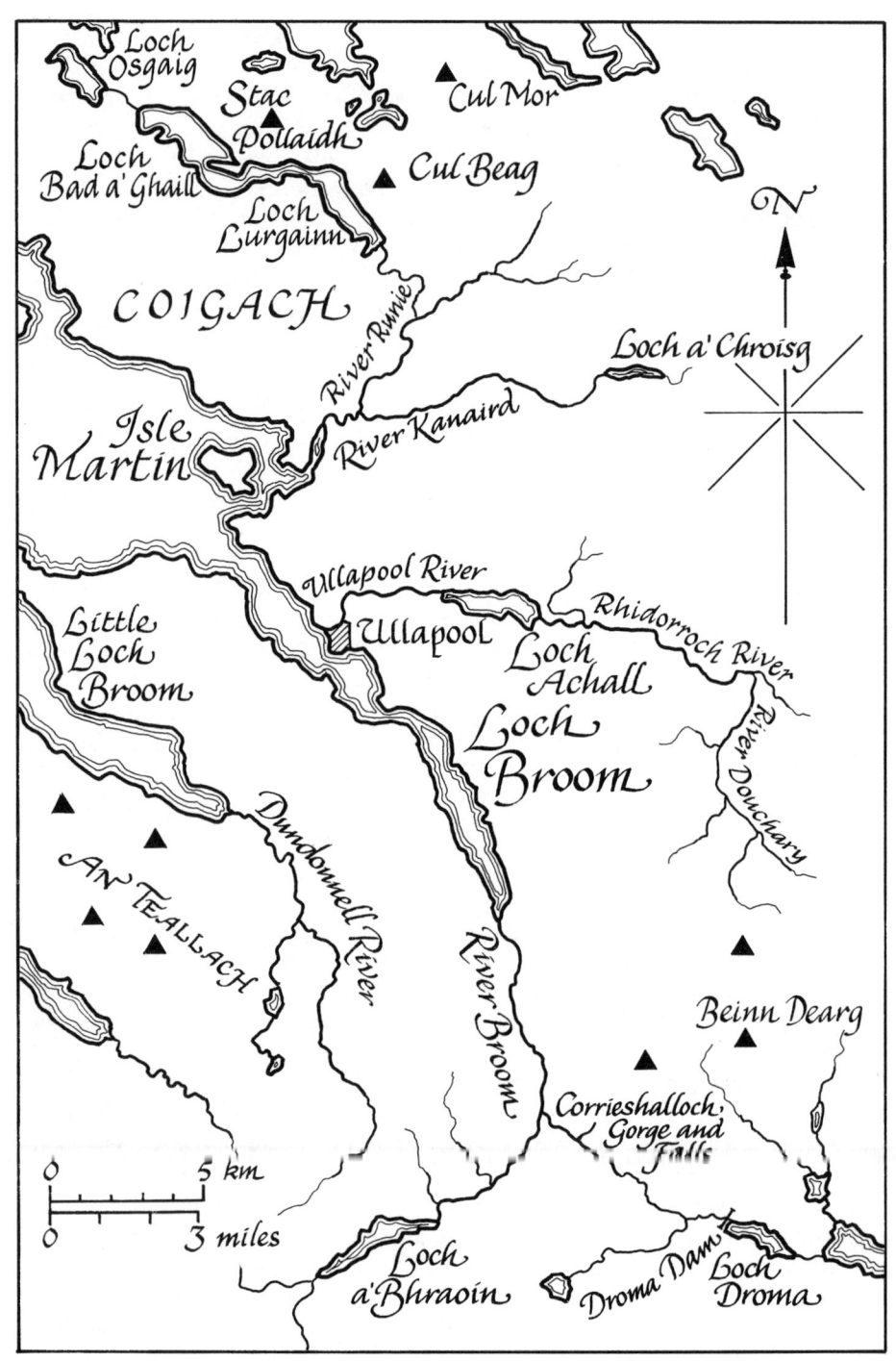

The Salmon Rivers of North-West Ross

The middle beat is from the Black Pool to the Bridge Pool and the lower beat from the Bridge Pool to the sea. The lower beat extends over three-quarters of a mile and has 6 or 7 pools. The middle beat is the best and is let privately by Highland Coastal Estates in Ullapool. The upper and lower beats are also let by Highland Coastal Estates but on a daily basis. The upper beat is only let from 28 May. There is also salmon fishing on Loch Achall but, although an occasional salmon is taken, it is best for sea trout and brown trout.

The Broom

If, on reaching Braemore Junction, one takes the Ullapool road after a drive over the moors from Garve past Glascarnoch Reservoir and along the side of Loch Droma, one drops down into the sheltered valley of Strath More through which flows the River Broom. Before the days of hydro-electric development the sources of the Broom were Loch Droma and Loch a' Mhadaidh whose outflowing streams formed Abhainn Droma which became the Broom on passing through the Corrieshalloch Gorge. This area is vividly described by R. MacDonald Robertson in his book *Angling in Wildest Scotland*. However, the Conon Basin scheme diverted Allt a' Mhadaidh into Loch Droma which, with the aid of a dam, was in its turn diverted east into Glascarnoch Reservoir. Only a compensation flow now passes down the Broom from Loch Droma and the falls upstream from the Braemore-Gairloch road, and the Measach Falls in Corrieshalloch Gorge are only a shadow of their former selves except during times of flood.

To see Strath More at its finest, take the Braemore-Gairloch road and stop at a lay-by just where the road starts to bend away south. From this vantage point one looks out on an incredibly peaceful scene with the whole strath laid out below, stretching out into the distance to Loch Broom. The east side of the strath has been afforested by the Forestry Commission and is known as Inverlael Forest, the west side is only slightly wooded, but it is not all spruce as there are some giant pines and monkey puzzles close to the road and also rhododendrons. The river valley is farmland and it is almost as though one has gone back in time as one passes along it. The hay is still dried on wooden ricks and the oats and corn are still cut with the binder and the sheaves set up in stooks. Perhaps it is this sense of the past which makes it so peaceful.

The Broom is a spate river with salmon and grilse coming up in July. At one time salmon entered much earlier but like a number of west coast rivers this early run has disappeared. It is a good river for sea trout but not as good as it was 15 or more years ago, when catches were high and fish of up to 12 lb were frequently caught. Nowadays it is rare to catch a sea trout of more than 7 lb.

The fish do not go up to the Corrieshalloch Gorge but turn right and ascend Abhainn Cuileig in Gleann Mor.

Inverbroom Estate own the whole of the left bank of the river with the exception of a small stretch at the estuary which is owned by the glebe (the Church of Scotland). Most of the right bank is owned by Foich Estate with the exception of two pools owned by Braemore and a small stretch owned by another proprietor. Fishing is by fly only.

The commercial fishing rights in Loch Broom are owned by the Church of Scotland, which lets the fishing, and by the proprietor who has a small stretch of the right bank of the river.

Inverbroom Estate puts salmon eggs and fry into the river each year in the hope of maintaining the stock although, like so many estates, they are concerned about the sea netting for salmon along the coast.

The Dundonnell

This is a charming little river in Wester Ross which flows through Dundonnell Forest past the eastern slopes of the An Teallach massif and into the sea in Little Loch Broom. It is very much a spate river with fish entering from the end of June, depending on adequate water.

There are two high waterfalls on the river which effectively bar the upper reaches to ascending fish. The upper falls are the ones most frequently seen by tourists travelling on the Braemore-Gairloch road. They are steep and most spectacular, particularly during periods of high water, and would be virtually impossible to open up for migratory fish. The lower falls are much further downstream nestled in Corrie Hallie. These lower falls reduce the length of river available to salmon and sea trout to about half.

Some restoration work along the river has recently been carried out by the Department of Agriculture and Fisheries for Scotland, but during heavy floods much of the gravel and rubble used in this work was washed into the pools which have now to be cleared before they can hold fish. While this is the fault of no one in particular, it does go to show how careful one must be in carrying out any river or bank improvements.

The Dundonnell is owned by Eilean Darach Estate and Dundonnell Estate. The former let the fishing from the mouth of the river to Ivy Cottage and tickets for this stretch can be obtained from Dundonnell Hotel. There is another small stretch from Ivy Cottage to Eilean Darach retained by the estate. Dundonnell Estate have the fishing from just above Eilean Darach to the falls, and permits can be obtained from Dundonnell Estate Office.

28

THE GRUINARD AND LITTLE GRUINARD

The Gruinard

Although the Gruinard and Little Gruinard are about the same length up to the lowest loch on their respective systems, the Gruinard, or Big Gruinard as it is sometimes called, has a slightly larger catchment. The Little Gruinard has virtually no tributary streams above Fionn Loch while the Gruinard has a large network of tributaries above Loch na Sealga (known locally as Loch na Sheallag) and also a large tributary entering the main river just below Loch na Sealga.

The Gruinard has two main tributaries above Loch na Sealga draining the hills of Dundonnell and Fisherfield Forests, namely Abhainn Strath na Sealga and Abhainn Gleann na Muice. These two sizeable streams meet just above the head of Loch na Sealga which lies close under the An Teallach massif in Strathnasheallag Forest. The loch is therefore set in the most impressive surroundings, and with the steeply sloping hills on either side the angler has a most spectacular backcloth to his sea trout fishing which is some of the best in the country, even though it has declined to some extent in recent years.

Immediately below the loch and just upstream of the junction with the Ghiubhsachain Burn there are excellent spawning fords extending over a considerable area, and the extent of the spawning and nursery ground available to both salmon and sea trout is impressive. This is in contrast to the Little Gruinard where the spawning, particularly for sea trout, is limited. The Ghiubhsachain Burn, too, is a good spawning tributary and sea trout ascend it to reach Loch Ghiubhsachain, where they can be caught readily on dry fly, and carry on up to Loch Beinn Dearg.

Below the Ghiubhasachain Burn junction the river has a fairly gentle course before passing into a rocky gorge known as The Rockies. Below the gorge the river levels out again and passes through several pools, some bouldery and some flat and gravelly. Downstream from the Bridge Pool at the main road the river becomes rocky and torrential on its last half mile to the sea in Gruinard Bay. The names of the pools on the river, from the loch to the sea, are: Admiral's, Charlie's, Matheson's, Ghiubhsachain Runs and Flats, Shepherd's, Craigower Stream, Craigower Flats, Tree; Upper, Middle and Lower Rockies, Turn, Silver, Rosalyn's, Colonel, Bothy Flats, Bothy, Miss Baring's; Upper, Middle and Lower Gibralter, Murray's Flats, Otter, Peat, Bank, Iron House Flats, Bridge, Craig, Pot, Garden and Sea.

The salmon run mainly in June and July but this depends on water conditions. Clean fish can be caught well on into August and even September, although there has been no evidence of an autumn run in recent years. However, there is a small run of spring fish about the second week of April and some big sea trout of up to 16 lb can also be caught at this time.

UDN has occurred in this river but, rather surprisingly considering it was so rife in the Little Gruinard, not to any great extent.

The fishing is owned by Eilean Darach Estate, and Gruinard Estate have the right of one rod. The river is divided into 3 beats by agreement between the two proprietors, of which Gruinard have one beat and Eilean Darach has two, and the beats alternate during the week. Both estates have boats on Loch na Sealga.

Little Gruinard

This attractive little west coast river flows out of wild Fionn Loch lying beneath the mountain range of Fisherfield Forest. It receives its water from the numerous neighbouring lochans and streams. The river at first flows slowly downstream and enlarges from time to time into a number of large peaty pools, one of which, the Boat Pool, holds a fair number of fish, particularly in the autumn. For some distance the river alternates between short lengths of steeply-flowing stream and wide, flat pools. There are 3 areas with particularly good holding pools and they are known as the Upper, Middle and Lower Flats. The Lower Flats are very canal-like and salmon lie in some numbers in the deep, clear water which would entice many hot and thirsty anglers in for a swim in the summer if the water was warmer. There is much bird and insect life to interest the angler in this moorland area of heather, deer grass and bog myrtle, and peat hags and sphagnum bogs are guaranteed to make the angler's progress far from easy.

Below the Flats the river becomes far more torrential and the angler who is used to east coast and less torrential rivers may have difficulty in deciding where fish lie, as the pools are small and ill-defined. Coming out of the gorge the first pool below is the Major, with fish lying close into the right bank and down at the tail. Below the Major come a number of other pools, such as the Knoll and the Peat, before the main road is reached. The river now fairly cascades down under the bridge and only slackens its pace as it reaches the Garden Pool. From here to the sea it is a little more gentle, allowing the residents at Little Gruinard to leisurely fish the last few pools — Harry's Run, the Nut Pool and the Sea Pool — before flowing out into Gruinard Bay. This last stretch of water below the bridge provides very pleasant fishing and often affords excitement. For example, there was a time when, under flood conditions, it took the best part of an hour to land a cock fish of 14 lb keen to return

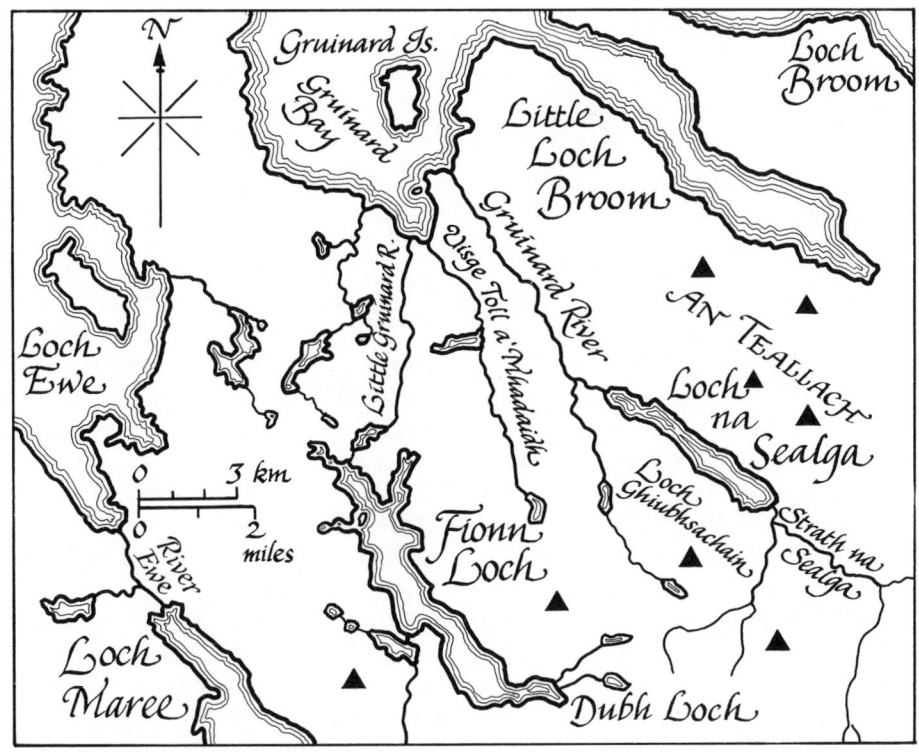

The Gruinard Rivers of Wester Ross

to the sea, and not before the broken rod top of an old Malloch greenheart was banging the fish on the nose. Another occasion entailed being dragged tripping and stumbling over the shingle as a fish decided to take off for the sea and take refuge in the tangle of seaweed.

As can be seen this is a delightful and interesting river. It is owned by Mr James Lawrie of Little Gruinard, with Gruinard Estate having the right of one rod on the river. The average annual rod catch until recently was in the neighbourhood of 100, with more being caught in some years. Unfortunately there has been a decline in recent years which follows the downward trend of many west coast rivers, for which illegal drift net fishing is believed to be the cause. However, a serious outbreak of UDN in 1970 certainly took its toll of fish and many were dying shortly after coming in from the sea. The average annual rod catch is now between 30 and 40. The only local commercial salmon fishery is on the south side of the bay at Laide.

Unlike the Gruinard River, the Little Gruinard holds very few sea trout. Occasionally a large specimen is caught, and in the mid-sixties one of 16 lb was taken. Salmon spawn throughout the length of the river and even penetrate beyond Fionn Loch to Allt Bruthach an Easain at the head of the Dubh Loch.

29

THE RIVERS OF SOUTH-WEST ROSS

The Ewe

The Ewe is a very short river in Wester Ross and flows from Loch Maree into the head of Loch Ewe, a sea loch, at Poolewe close to the famous Inverewe Gardens. What is loses in being short it makes up for in its grandeur, and is rather like the Awe, being fairly steep with fast-flowing water broken up into pools with, in the case of the Ewe, the aid of croys and groynes. This is particularly noticeable at The Narrows.

It is not easy to decide where the Ewe starts and Loch Maree ends as the loch narrows down for some distance. Loch Maree, as well as being fed from the north by Lochan Fada, has a number of tributaries, many of which are useful spawning and nursery areas and also provide some late summer fishing. The Kinlochewe River, which flows into the top end of the loch, has a reasonable run of fish which passes up into Loch Clair and Loch Coulin and, later in the year, on to the spawning fords in this area. The River Grudie, entering the loch further west, is also a good little spawning stream as is the Bruachaig.

Loch Maree is aptly named 'the beautiful loch' as it lies, with its Scots pine clad islands, at the foot of Slioch (3,217 feet) which rises majestically out of the deep waters of the north shore. Further back stands Beinn Lair (2,817 feet) which adds to the splendour of the scenery. It is no wonder that anglers come back to fish this loch year after year when the surroundings are so wild and beautiful. This area is still one of the remaining homes of that now rare Scottish mammal, the pine marten. A nature trail exists near Kinlochewe and the Nature Conservancy Council warden for the area might well help visitors to see many examples of Scottish wildlife.

The salmon fishing on the Ewe has unfortunately deteriorated in recent years and very few salmon are taken nowadays in the early months of February, March and April. A few fish run up in May but they are not easily caught, although angling returns from those trolling the loch confirm that there is some sort of run during that month. The best results for salmon angling in the loch over recent years appear to be at the top end near Kinlochewe. On the whole the numbers of both summer salmon and grilse have declined, although there was a slight improvement in 1977, but in that year there were better flow conditions in the vital months of August and September.

It is pleasant to record a gradual and progressive improvement in the sea trout stocks over the past 2 or 3 years after a very alarming decline which has been pretty general on the mainland and the Outer Isles. There has been quite an increase in the number of sea trout around the 2 lb mark caught in the river which augurs well for the future, but rarely has a large sea trout been taken from the river. However, quite a number of trout up to $7\frac{1}{2}$ lb were taken off the loch in 1977.

The fishing on the Ewe is owned by Scatwell Estate and permission to fish can be applied for through the Scatwell Estate Office, Scatwell, By Muir of Ord. Loch Maree can be fished by application to Loch Maree Hotel which has 9 boats rotating through the beats, together with one from Shieldaig Lodge Hotel, By Gairloch. Scatwell Estate offer a boat on beats 2 and 3 at the extreme bottom end of the loch, and Kinlochewe Hotel and Kinlochewe Chalet Complex both have boats which fish over the top end of the loch down as far as Copachy. The beats include North Shore; Isle of Maree; Weedy Bay; Steamer channel and Slettadale Bay; Grudie Bay; Back of Islands; Black Rock, Salmon Reach and Grudie River; Pig's Bay and Bank's Bay; Ash Island; Sandy Bay and Fool's Rock; Coree; Hotel. To fish Loch Maree is an experience to be remembered, particularly when fishing the 'dap' and it needs a lot of self-control to delay the strike when a big fish rises up to take the dapping fly with a 'boil' like a surfacing whale. *Where to fish on the various beats from the hotel at Loch Maree* is the title of Appendix A in W.A. Adamson's book *Lake and Loch Fishing for Salmon and Sea Trout*, and anglers planning on fishing this loch should endeavour to refer to this excellent guide.

There were severe depredations of fish stocks a few years ago due to UDN, but fortunately it now appears to be declining.

There is no netting at the mouth of the river but there is considerable illegal drift netting on the periphery of Loch Ewe.

The Kerry

The feeder streams of the little River Kerry come off the hills of Flowerdale Forest and out of Loch na h-Oidhche and flow into Abhainn a' Gharbh Choire which flows downstream and tumbles over a fall into Loch Bad an Sgalaig. This loch has a side arm to the south known as Dubh Loch and both lochs are the home of pike which are being kept under control by the efforts of the Gairloch Angling Association. At one time the salmon used to get up to Bad an Sgalaig but, since the Kerry scheme of the North of Scotland Hydro-electric Board, the loch has been dammed and a proportion of the water diverted to the power station lower down the river in the gorge.

This scheme has helped the river as, with compensation water and regular generation flows from the power station, the river is guaranteed an adequate amount of water and is protected from the effects of drought. It is, however, still a spate river and the main run of salmon is after the first flood in July and sometimes continues on into early October; not many sea trout enter the Kerry. Most of the spawning is above Shieldaig Bridge where there are some nice gravelly runs. The best of the angling is from Kerry mouth to Shieldaig Bridge. The lowest pool is difficult to fish and anglers should take care unless they want a ducking. The fishing is leased to the Gairloch Angling Association by Gairloch Estate and the Association has the fishing from the sea to the power station. Permits can be obtained by visitors in Gairloch.

The angling association has been making an number of improvements to the river on a grant from the Highlands and Islands Development Board. The improvements have included increasing the number of pools, and there are now 15 good ones as well as many smaller. There is no serious poaching on the river, although misguided holidaymakers are something of a problem at times. There was one tragic occurrence some years ago when a poacher lost his life one Saturday night while trying to net one of the pools. He was caught up in the meshes of the net and was pulled under by the current and drowned.

The Badachro

Although the Badachro is only a small river in Wester Ross, entering the south side of Loch Gairloch, it could have an exciting future if certain falls are made surmountable to the salmon. As it is at present, salmon can negotiate the first part of the river and surmount the weir at the foot of Loch Badachro (Loch Bad a' Chrotha), albeit with a little difficulty at times, and enter the loch. They can also pass on upstream for $1\frac{1}{2}$ miles to falls which act as a stop to further ascent. If the falls can be eased, and this is being considered at present, then there is nothing to stop the fish moving on into Loch Braigh-horrisdale and even upstream into Loch Gaineamhaich. The river immediately upstream from Loch Badachro is canal-like, being deep and slow-flowing with just a few short gravelly runs alternating occasionally with deep pools, and it is on these runs that the fish have to spawn. Spawning facilities are better nearer the falls and above them the spawning and nursery potential is excellent.

Angling is for salmon only as no sea trout ascend the Badachro. The main run is August – October, although fish have been known to enter the river in April. The average annual catch is in the region of 30 – 40 fish and many of them are taken on the loch, although the canal-like stretch of the river is good if there is a strong wind. The fishing is owned by Gairloch Estate who lease it to the Shieldaig Lodge Hotel and permits are available to hotel guests and the general public.

A number of other improvements to the river are planned, including the construction of groynes.

There has been no evidence of UDN in this river, nor in its neighbour, the Kerry, which is most interesting and makes one wonder what influences the onset of this disease.

THE RIVERS OF SOUTH–WEST ROSS

The Torridon

This little spate river rises in Lochan an Iasgaich at the top of Glen Torridon and drains a mountainous area. On the north side of the river are the massifs of Liathach and Beinn Eighe, well-known to mountaineers, while to the south are Sgurr Dubh and Beinn Liath Mhor. The river flows south-west down this rugged glen parallel to the Kinlochewe to Torridon road for a distance of some 4 miles to discharge into the sea at the head of Upper Loch Torridon. It is very much a spate river but has a few attractive pools where salmon and sea trout can be caught from July onwards. The fishing is entirely dependent on heavy rains but Lochan an Iasgaich holds a number of salmon and big sea trout which provide good fishing. Permits for the river can be obtained from the post office in Torridon.

The spawning is confined chiefly to the main river as its tributaries, particularly those from the north, are too steep for fish to ascend.

The Applecross

This small west coast river lies in Wester Ross and rises in the mountains of the Applecross Deer Forest which forms the promontory projecting out from the mainland opposite the Isle of Raasay and the Inner Sound, with Loch Torridon bordering the northern shore and Loch Carron the southern. Until recently, the village of Applecross was very isolated with only a very hazardous minor road over the mountains connecting it with the mainland. Recently, however, this road has been improved and linked to Shieldaig.

The main source of the river rises on Beinn Bhan and flows north west at first before turning south west down the glen on its 10-mile journey to enter the Inner Sound beside the village of Applecross. It has 3 lochs at its source which feed burns flowing off Carn Dearg, Croic-bheinn, Beinn a Chlachain and Carn Breac. There are good spawning and feeding areas in the lower part of the river and elsewhere in the upper reaches where the river and tributaries are not too torrential. Waterfalls half a mile up the tributary flowing south from Lochan na h-Airidhe Riabhaich into the upper reaches of the river prevent fish ascending further. The stream above these falls could provide additional nursery area provided gravel was imported and laid in the stream as, at present, the stream bed has a rather featureless peat covering.

The Applecross is a typical rugged spate burn. Fish start entering the river from June, and good runs of salmon, grilse and sea trout occur when flow conditions are favourable. In recent years a lot of work has been done on the river in order to make better holding pools, some have been deepened and others altered with the use of gabions to make weirs. In all, about 8 pools have been improved. Large floods in the early 1960s caused severe bank erosion leading to the Department of Agriculture and Fisheries doing a large river retraining and bank strengthening scheme. In 1972 another large flood made further alterations to the river.

In recent years, the average rod catch has been about 100 salmon and grilse and 50 sea trout, with the biggest catches being made in the last two or three years. Salmon range from 5 to 10 lb, occasionally with one over 20 lb being caught, and sea trout weigh from 1 to 8 lb, with quite a few of over 5 lb being taken each year.

Sweep netting has only been exercised at the mouth of the river twice since 1961.

The Balgy

The Balgy is a small short course river in Wester Ross which flows out of Loch Damh nestling between the deer forests of Glenshieldaig and Ben-damph, with the mountain of Beinn Damh rising to almost 3000 feet on its eastern shore. Loch Damh receives the waters of Loch Coultrie and Loch an Loin from the south and those of Abhainn Dearg from two small lochs on Maol Chean-dearg (3,060 feet) to the east.

Loch Damh is a long narrow loch lying north-south. A short distance below the loch the river flows through a steep gorge containing the Falls of Balgy. Below the falls, the river flows more slowly and meanders across flatter ground and under the Torridon-Shieldaig road at Balgy Bridge. Its final descent to the sea from the bridge is over a series of rapids and small falls to Upper Loch Torridon.

The best spawning and feeding areas are at the head of Loch Damh and in Abhainn Dearg. There are also a few useful areas in the centre section of the river. The burns flowing into the sides of the loch are mainly too steep to be of much use for spawning.

Although the distance from the loch to the sea is only a little over a mile this attractive river has a reasonable salmon and sea trout run which begins in June, with the best months of fishing being July–September. During low water conditions the larger fish have difficulty in ascending the two rocky gorges but at such times, particularly in late July and August, finnock can provide good sport. In spate conditions excellent fishing can be had with salmon, grilse and good-sized sea trout in the interesting little pools between the sea and the falls. These falls just below the loch can, as has been said, be a hazard to the free ascent of fish and for long periods fish can be delayed below them, but when conditions for ascent are favourable fish can pass through the river from the sea to the loch in a matter of hours. However, there is a small stream which flows from the top of the Falls Pool, round a hillock, to the top of the Rock Pool, and with a high water a number of fish doubtless use this as a 'ladder', thus by-passing the actual falls.

The river has some very good holding pools and among the best are the Falls, Rock, Wall, Weir and Sea. Geoffrey Braithwaite in his book *Fine Feathers and Fish*, published in 1971, has this to say of the Balgy: 'When fishing the Balgy you must drop your fly in an exact spot either just above a rock or as close under the far bank as possible; then according to the current hang your fly after it has come round. There are some people who think that, owing to the size of the river and when fishing for salmon a ten-foot rod is all that is required, but this can prove disastrous for, at some pools, the fly comes round very quickly and may well get caught in the heather on your bank . . . to avoid such trouble use a 12 or 13 foot rod.' Such advice of course applies to many small west coast rivers.

The average size of salmon in the Balgy is 8 lb and grilse 4–5 lb. Sea trout average 1 lb, but a few heavy sea trout of 5–10 lb are taken each year.

The fishing on the river is private and it is jointly owned by two proprietors who, by agreement, fish the whole river on alternate days. They have recently attempted to improve the holding capacity of the centre part of the river and have improved several pools and replaced ones which were washed away by flood several years ago. Whether these pools will stand up to future winter floods or not remains to be seen. If a small barrage was to be placed across the outfall of Loch Damh to store the winter floods until the fishing season and then the water was used to augment the summer flow, the fishing could well be improved.

UDN has appeared from time to time since 1970, but there has never been a serious outbreak.

Excellent sea trout fishing can be had on Loch Damh, especially dapping, particularly during the months of July, August and September. It is a most attractive loch, about 6 miles long and, in places, a mile wide. Good brown trout can be had in June and July, but while salmon are there in the later months they are not easily caught and invariably only when trolling. The sides of the loch are very rocky with only a few sandy bays, but under normal conditions the whole loch is fishable.

The Shieldaig

Like its neighbour the Balgy, this west coast river rises on the wild rocky rugged mountainsides of Glenshieldaig Deer Forest and tumbles quickly down the glen in a north-westerly direction to enter the sea in Loch Shieldaig some little distance from the village of the same name. Loch Shieldaig is sandwiched between Upper Loch Torridon and Loch Torridon and forms part of this sea inlet.

Unlike its neighbour the Balgy, this river has no loch on its catchment of any size and has a very flashy nature, its catchment being very steep.

Like most west coast spate rivers its season is confined to the period June—mid October and fish can only run this river during spates in this period. Its angling potential is accordingly very limited in dry seasons, but good sport can be had by the angler who is lucky enough to fish it as it drops after a spate.

A few salmon, grilse and sea trout are caught annually, averaging 5–7 lb and 1–1½ lb, with finnock affording good sport on a light rod.

Spawning and feeding areas are limited, as one would expect on a river of this size, and are mainly confined to the main river, as the side tributaries are on the whole too steep to allow fish to ascend. However, they are adequate to produce sufficient stock for a river of this size.

This river is fished mainly by the proprietor and his guests.

The Kishorn

This is a short west coast river which rises on the east side of Applecross Deer Forest and flows in a southerly direction down the glen to enter the sea in Loch Kishorn, not far from the site where one of the largest oil platforms was built in recent years.

The source of the river is high up on the slopes of Beinn Bhan, a mountain nearly 3,000 feet in height. This attractive little river tumbles down the glen in a very picturesque setting.

Once again essentially a spate river, its migratory stock of salmon and sea trout wait patiently in the bay for heavy rain and the resulting spate which will allow them to ascend the river on their journey upstream to their spawning ground.

Like most rivers of this kind the angler who is lucky enough to be able to fish it as it drops after a spate can get good sport catching both grilse and sea trout from June–September. The salmon run normally consists mainly of grilse averaging 5–7 lb, with the occasional heavier salmon. Sea trout average 1½ lb and there are the normal runs of smaller finnock to add to the sport.

Spawning and feeding areas are to be found on the headwaters on a limited scale, but they are quite adequate to assure a reasonable stock for a river of this size.

The river is fished mainly by the owners when it is in order.

The Carron

The Carron rises in Ledgowan Forest only a few miles to the west of Achnasheen and just on the other side of the River Bran watershed. The river flows south-west down Glen Carron, through Loch Sgamhain (Scaven) and Loch Dughaill (Doule) and into the sea at the upper end of Loch Carron. The only steep falls on the river are situated near Glencarron station, but these are surmountable by migratory fish. There are good spawning and nursery areas in most of the burns on the east side of the river and around the top end of Loch Sgamhain. Falls on the little River Lair near Achnashellach Lodge prevent salmon and sea trout from using much of this water, although some sea trout do spawn below the falls in some years.

The main estates owning fishing on the river are Glencarron, Achnashellach (under joint ownership), Arinakaig, New Kelso and Attadale.

The Carron is very much a spate river and the time of ascent of the fish is dependent to a large extent on the availability of water, although after a good flood at the end of May or early June there is usually a stock of sea trout in Loch Dughaill and, a little later, in Loch Sgamhain. There used to be an early spring run of salmon, and fish could occasionally be caught in March, but this run has now disappeared and the first salmon to enter the river now appear in May. Fish continue to enter the river until well into October.

There is usually excellent sea trout fishing on Loch Dughaill and although Loch Sgamhain tends to be dour, some good catches of sizeable sea trout can be had when there is a good west wind with stormy conditions. One of the best drifts on Sgamhain is between the islands at the lower end of the loch. Salmon are taken from both lochs from time to time. Most of the fishing is private, although lets can sometimes be arranged through Bingham, Hughes and Macpherson in Inverness.

There has been no recorded evidence of UDN on this river.

Salmon and sea trout fry, about 20,000 of each, are planted out each year in some of the tributaries by Glencarron, Achnashellach and New Kelso estates.

30

THE OUTER HEBRIDES, SKYE, MULL, ARRAN and ISLAY

ISLE OF LEWIS

When one looks at an Ordnance Survey map of Lewis and Harris one wonders if it is possible to take a step without getting one's feet wet. Most of the waters are lochs and lochans with interconnecting streams and practically all of them hold brown trout and probably every stream flowing into the sea has its run of sea trout. But the number of salmon rivers is relatively small in comparison with the number of sea trout waters. Unfortunately many of the salmon rivers have been bled to death by poaching, which is 'a way of life' on the Island, and many estates have had to give up a losing battle against the poachers. The term 'poacher' tends to suggest a character whose living consists of stealing a fish from the river, a pheasant from the wood or a stag from the hill. Although such characters may still exist, the type described here is really anyone in the community who illegally sets nets along the coast to catch salmon or who puts a net across a holding pool in the river and empties the pools before the anglers have a chance. With such a definition one is referring to an appreciable proportion of the Island's inhabitants and from all walks of life. Some there are who only take one or two fish 'for the pot', but there are many who operate on a commercial basis. For example, there are gangs who use walkie-talkies and, in order to pass messages to one another without being understood by anyone in authority listening in, use a series of coughs to warn of approaching bailiffs and the direction from which they are coming. Frequently they conceal their identity with nylon masks and even threaten the bailiffs' families at times. Many have a constant watch on their hang nets set along the coast and in estuarial water, ready to haul at a moment's notice when the bailiff or fishery cruiser is sighted. The fish they catch are sold to fishmongers and hotels in Stornoway and the mainland and no questions are asked. The poachers tend to receive well below the average market price for the fish and some hotels even pay them in drink, so common is alcoholism on the Island. During Glasgow Fair fortnight each summer, many return to their place of origin for the poaching, while others make it their summer occupation and may even build new bungalows on the proceeds. No wonder then that the one-time salmon rivers such as the Arnol, the Carnaway and the Gress are no longer of use for angling. It has been said that over 100 nets were removed from the Arnol in one day, and that the owners of the Barvas operate the river commercially at the mouth and ignore the sport fishery. Other rivers too, as will be seen, are going the same way. When one looks at the sparse road system on the Isle of Lewis one can see how easy it is for the poacher to operate and, as bailiffs and ghillies are few and far between and have to sleep some time, it is not surprising that he can usually work unhindered. Their brazen nature is shown by the two who parked their car among others standing outside the church on the Sabbath and walked a short distance down to the river to net the pool below the Factor's house.

At present it is difficult to see how this activity can be stamped out. The two district salmon fishery boards on the Island, the Loch Roag and the Creed or Stornoway and Laxay, have met to consider the serious nature of the poaching, and it was suggested that there should be a licensed salmon dealer in Stornoway and that hotels should be asked to buy through him rather than to accept fish at the back door. But who is going to do that when they can get their fish so cheaply and even on the barter system? It is also quite easy now to send them on lorries to the mainland now that a fast and regular car ferry service operates two return journeys to Ullapool every day of the week except Sunday. One suggestion is that fines should be raised from their present puny amounts to some substantial and crippling sum to make it too much of a risk to operate and that cars should be confiscated.

This may seem rather a long introduction to the salmon rivers of Lewis, but the amount of space allotted to it does emphasise the present serious nature of the poaching.

The Grimersta

There is no doubt that the best salmon river system on Lewis, and probably one of the most prolific salmon fisheries of its size anywhere, is the Grimersta. The river itself is very short, being only $1\frac{3}{4}$ miles long, and the majority of the fishing is carried on throughout a chain of lochs extending back into the centre of the Island.

There are five lochs in the main system and from source to mouth they are Loch Langavat, which is 7 miles long and is the largest loch in the Hebrides, Loch Airigh na h-Airde, Loch Faoghail Kirraval, Loch Faoghail Charrasan and Loch Faoghail an Tuim. From the lowest loch the river runs down through a series of well-maintained pools with croys and groynes into the sea lochs, Loch Ceann Hulavig and Loch Roag. There are numerous side lochs on the system of which only Loch an Easa Ghil and Loch an Fhir Mhaoil need be mentioned.

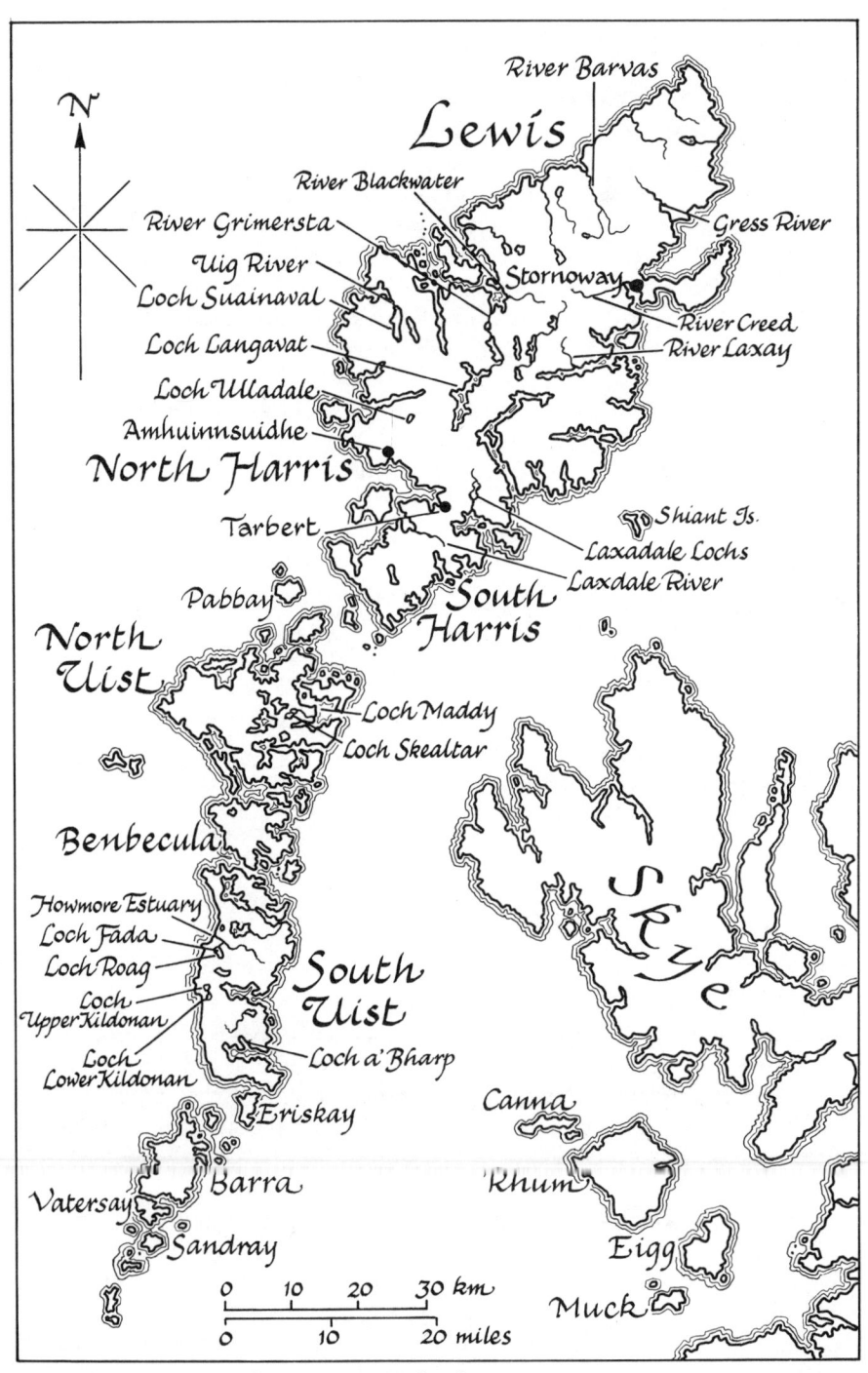

The Salmon Rivers of the Outer Hebrides

THE OUTER HEBRIDES, SKYE, MULL, ARRAN AND ISLAY

Most of the water within the system is controlled by Grimersta Estate Ltd. The march with the neighbouring estate to the south, Scaliscro, goes through Loch an Fhir Mhaoil and Grimersta Estate lease their half, plus a short section of the river below it, to Scaliscro on an annual basis. Grimersta Estate also let Loch Faoghail Charrasan to a Stornoway Angling Club and various trout lochs in the catchment are made available to tourists.

There have been several Grimersta syndicates and the present syndicate was started in 1924 when the Grimersta Estate, which included Garynahine, was bought from Lord Leverhulme. Grimersta sold Garynahine some years ago. The present syndicate has a membership of 19 and members are allowed to invite friends by arrangement. It is an extremely well organised fishery. There is Grimersta Lodge, where members stay, and houses for the Fishery Manager and his assistant, and the fishery employs 25 people, including house staff, during the fishing season.

The fishery is divided into four beats: Beat 1 is the river and the north half of Loch Faoghail an Tuim; Beat 2 is the upper half of Loch Faoghail an Tuim and the stream connecting it with Loch Faoghail Charrasan; Beat 3 is Loch Faoghail Kirraval and Macleay's Stream, which is the stream connecting it to Loch Faoghail Charrasan; Beat 4 is Loch Airigh na h-Airdre and, at certain times, part of Beat 3.

Fishing is by fly only, although trolling with fly is permitted on part of Loch Airigh na h-Airdre. Each loch has boats and there are ferries to take anglers to Beats 3 and 4.

The river is beautifully maintained and has a number of good pools including the Bridge, Captain's, Long and Battery.

Loch Langavat at the top of the Grimersta system is fished by 7 estates and trolling with fly or spinner is the main method of fishing. Grimersta and other estates are opposed to trolling with bait, but it has been impossible to get agreement. A lot of gravid fish are caught by this method in the autumn and it is to be deplored.

Although the main run of fish starts in June there is a very small spring run in April and May and spring fish have been taken as early as March. Fifty years ago a lot of fish were caught in April and May. An interesting feature of the spring fish is that many are not caught until late in the season. Some of these springers are quite big and fish of 19 lb have been taken.

The spawning grounds in the Grimersta system are fairly limited and they are often overcrowded. The fish spawn in many of the interconnecting channels between the lochs and even along the shores of some of the lochs.

Grimersta Estate Ltd has the commercial fishings along the coast in the Shawbost and Carloway areas and these are operated by net and coble.

Records of UDN from Lewis salmon rivers are scarce and it is a pleasure to note that this disease has not been recorded on this river system.

Perhaps one of the Grimersta's greatest claims to fame has been the record catch of fish resulting from the release of stored water as an artificial spate in

1888, and which has been well documented by Calderwood. This practice of releasing artificial spates continues here with varying degrees of success depending on the climatic conditions at the time of release. Dams and sluices have been built on a number of the lochs in the system by the engineer, Macleay, and water is impounded behind them. The lochs so impounded include Loch Sgaire, Loch na Plaide and Loch an Earball.

One of the most time-consuming duties of the estate is that of controlling poaching activities. Students are employed during the summer to help the ghillies patrol the lochs, the river and the coast, and watchers' bothies are sited either on the shores or the islands of the 4 main lochs. Poaching on the coast is rife indeed and an incredible number of gill nets are set out from the shore around Loch Roag, East Loch Roag and Great Bernera. Inland, poachers net the various lochs and even come over the hills to Langavat from Balallan on the other side of the Island.

There are few other predatory animals present, although feral mink are becoming a problem here as in many other parts of Lewis.

The Laxay

With 'lax', the Norse name for salmon, in the name of the river one can be sure that the water holds salmon; and Laxay, like Laxford, is no exception to the rule. Unfortunately this river, like so many in Lewis, is badly poached and its rod catches are dwindling. This is a great tragedy as this is a most appealing salmon river and has a most interesting history. The average annual rod catch during the first three decades of this century were of the order of 140 salmon and 370 sea trout, and between 1930 and 1973 it was in the region of 250 to 300 salmon a year. However, from 1974 the catches have dropped and this is partly attributed to sea netting along the coast as many of the fish caught in the Laxay system since that time have borne net marks.

The Laxay originates from numerous lochs and streams lying immediately to the east of Loch Langavat and draining into Loch Trealaval. The river flows downstream from Trealaval for a distance of 3 miles before entering Loch Valtos and from Valtos it flows a further three-quarters of a mile to discharge into the tidal waters of Loch Erisort.

The Laxay system is owned by Soval Estate, the owners either fishing it themselves or leasing it to tenants. The fishing on the river itself is for one or two rods and most of it is confined to the lower section below Valtos and consists of 3 good pools, the Top, Middle and Lower. The fishing on the river above Valtos is on the Island, Rocky and S-Bend pools, after which there is a series of spawning fords extending upstream for a mile before reaching the Reedy Pool which is very deep and is a good holding area. Above this comes Loch Trealaval. Loch Valtos has 3 beats and there are 3 boats and 3 ghillies.

A run of spring fish used to occur on the Laxay and in 1946 four fish of up to 22 lb in weight were caught as early as March, but this run has now disappeared and the main run is in June and July. There is a run of biggish fish of up to 14 lb in July but few of these fish are caught at that time as they tend to lie up at the top of the loch and only come down in September, when they are caught from a pier running out into the loch (known as The Cast), as they wait to continue their journey upstream to spawn. The largest fish caught on the Laxay system was taken by Richard D'Oyly Carte in September 1933, and weighed $33\frac{1}{2}$ lb.

The Laxay is well provided with spawning fords extending downstream to tidal limits and should be capable of holding a large stock of salmon if an adequate number were allowed to spawn. Unfortunately the depredations of poachers have not always stopped during the spawning season and at one time the villagers of Achmore had a tradition of taking cock fish off the redds and salting them down.

In the past the Laxay had quite a history of management although some of it was a little misguided. At one time a wire net was erected across the inflow to Loch Valtos at the beginning of the season to prevent fish moving upstream. This may have affected the movements of spring fish to their detriment and may even have prevented the free downstream movement of smolts with obvious consequences. On Loch Trealaval another wire net was put across the loch to confine the fish in the lower section. These fences are fortunately no longer installed. On the credit side the river is indebted to 'Sixty-One' — G.H. Hutchinson — (author of *Twenty Years' Reminiscences of the Lews*) who removed an old salmon trap on the lower river, which many years ago was operated by the church, and also got rid of 'foul' nets in the estuary. A further improvement has been the excavation of a channel in the lower part of the river to concentrate the flow and thus enable fish to have a free ascent from the sea. In order to create artificial freshets Hutchinson constructed a dam and sluice at the outfalls of both Loch Trealaval and Loch Valtos between 1847 and 1850 and this may possibly be only the second instance in Scotland of the means of creating artificial freshets in a river system. The first was almost certainly his artificial freshets on the River Blackwater on the other side of the Island.

UDN was first recorded in the Laxay in 1974.

The Barvas

It is rarely that one hears of a salmon river where the resource is harvested almost entirely at the mouth of the river and the stock is maintained almost entirely artificially, but the Barvas is such a river, as is the Oude in Argyll. In the case of the Oude the area available to salmon is not much more than 800 yards, but with the Barvas, which is the longest river on Lewis, it is several miles. However, as the Barvas is very deficient in spawning ground, its angling potential poor and poaching rife, catching fish at the river mouth is the most sensible practice.

Martin Martin, in his book *A Late Voyage to St Kilda* (1698), refers to a practice on this river where a man was sent to ford the river very early in the morning of the first of May each year so as to prevent a woman crossing it first. If this did happen, they believed that it would hinder salmon coming to the river for the rest of the year.

On the lower reaches of the river there is a confined sheltered loch, Loch Mor Barvas, which the sea only enters during storm conditions. Between the loch and the sea there is about 75 yards of river, and near the mouth there is a dam with a fish pass below which are two holding pools. The fish are netted from these pools by the estate and sent to market. During the close seasons some of the fish get up the river and eventually crowd on to the limited spawning grounds. These fish have to be protected and four men are employed for this duty and also to net.

In the region of 75,000 eyed salmon ova are planted in the small gravelly feeder streams each winter and the operation, judging by the netting returns, has been most successful.

The Creed

The River Creed or Greeta River is the most accessible salmon river on Lewis for the holiday angler, not only because of its close proximity to Stornoway, and the main roads, but also due to its waters being available on a daily let basis at a very modest price. There are 5 miles of river fishing ranging from the narrow peaty pools and rapids in its upper reaches and the long gravelly flats below Loch a' Chlachain to the torrential runs and short deep pools as the Creed flows swiftly through the rhododendron-clad gorge on its last mile to sea in Stornoway Harbour. There are two main lochs in its course, Loch an Ois and Loch a' Chlachain, the former being the furthest upstream.

The main run of salmon is usually in July, while sea trout enter a little earlier, usually in June or early July. Like many Lewis rivers the Creed has not been affected to any extent by UDN and there has been only one minor outbreak, in 1974.

The river has not been affected by any man-made developments but it has an excessive poaching problem because of the length of the river, its proximity to the main roads and to the main centre of population and the fact that it runs through a public park in the lower part of its course. Partly for this reason the Stornoway Trust, which owns the river, has very recently installed a trap at the mouth to catch all ascending fish, a proportion of which are released upstream for the anglers and for spawning. A hatchery was also established in 1972 and fish are stripped at the back end of the year and the ova are hatched out in the hatchery and put in the river as fry in quantities ranging from 25,000 to 70,000.

The Creed has 5 miles of fishing on both banks from the estuary to the lochs. There are 13 specific holding pools including the Junction, Long, Falls, Peatstack, Bridge, Sheriff and Bend. The river is divided into three beats with one rod per beat and is fished on a daily rotation. Loch a' Chlachain has two beats with one boat per beat and one rod fishing from each boat. Loch an Ois also has two beats with one boat per beat. Fishing on the river is by fly only, but fly, spinning and bait are permitted on the lochs.

The Blackwater

This river is probably second to the Grimersta in importance as a Lewis salmon river, although the Laxay and Creed are close runners-up. A number of lochs, including 'Sixty-One's' New Loch and Loch Dismal, feed the Blackwater, but they are not arranged in a chain as on the Grimersta. They feed two separate streams which, on uniting some 6 miles from the sea, form the Blackwater. From this junction there are two or three miles of rough water before one comes to any sizeable pool, but from this point onwards there are a number of delightful, although peaty, pools, including the Major's. The river is owned by Garynahine Estate and is private.

Probably the first description of arrangements for the creation of artificial freshets in Scotland is that given for this river by Sixty-One in 1871 in *Twenty Years' Reminiscences of the Lews*:

'I bethought me of the Costello in Galway, by whose pleasant side I had, in former days, killed buckets-full of fish; and, in imitation of what I had there seen practised, I dammed up Loch Dismal. Across the mouth of this loch I erected a dam and sluice similar to the common mill-dams of the country, taking care of course, not to shut the sluices so close as to run the branch of the river dry. I thus kept back water enough to create an artificial spate, which I let go exactly in time to meet the high spring tides that bring the fish up to the rivers' mouths, which they take, wind and water permitting.

'I found the experiment answer perfectly, and over and over again I ascertained to demonstrate that the fish took the river with my artificial, just as they would with a natural, spate.'

As well as the rivers described in detail there are a number of others of lesser importance although, with a stricter control on poaching, some could achieve a better status. For example, the Gress River on the east coast and north of

Stornoway was, at the beginning of the century, reputed to be as good as the Grimersta and had 15 man-made pools on its course. Anglers used to make expeditions to Loch Gress on ponies and stay by its remote shores for some days. Now these pools have been destroyed and only one remains. Happily, in the case of this river, the writing on the wall has been seen and the river has been taken over by the Gress Angling Association and the pools are being rebuilt under the Job Creation Scheme.

The Arnol and Carnaway have also been mentioned as being beyond immediate salvation.

Other rivers have been affected by man-made activities and the Gisla scheme of the North of Scotland Hydro-electric Board has diverted the flow from the River Todall, a tributary of the Red River, above Loch Chroisteam into Loch Grunavat on the Gisla system, and the lower Gisla flowing out of Loch Grunavat and Loch na Ciste has been completely piped to Gisla Power Station on the south shore of Little Loch Roag. In this way the scheme has completely destroyed the Gisla as a salmon river and all that remains is a dry water course. The scheme is reputed to have affected the River Morsgail. This river and Loch Morsgail formed a useful salmon fishery, but it has declined in recent years as it is thought that salmon destined for the Gisla used to ascend the Morsgail before dropping downstream to ascend the Gisla nearer spawning time. The Red River itself, flowing from Loch Chroisteam, has a good run of salmon in late July and is a good angling river, although it suffers from the depredations of the poachers. It is a rocky river but has sand banks at the mouth which make the river outlet shallow and hence hinder the ascent of fish at low river flows.

Another small salmon river in west Lewis is the Uig. Fish ascend the river in August and enter Loch Stacsavat but are prevented from moving on into Loch Suainaval by a grid at the top of Stacsavat. This grid is removed near the spawning season and the length of river between the two lochs is used extensively by spawning fish, as are the streams running into Suainaval.

HARRIS

The North Harris Fishery

The North Harris Fishery is now owned by a private company and comprises the rivers and lochs within the 30,000 acres of the estate. It is bounded to the north by Loch Resort and to the south by West Loch Tarbert, both sea lochs.

North Harris is the most mountainous area of the Outer Hebrides and forms a backcloth of steep, craggy hills, rising to 2,400 feet and running from east to west through the centre of the area. There are two major catchments within the North Harris Fishery, one which drains north into Loch Resort and one whose waters flow south into West Loch Tarbert. The rainfall from the north face drains down two small rivers, the Ulladale and the Voshimid, into Loch Resort. These are the two most important salmon and sea trout systems in the fishery.

THE VOSHIMID

The Voshimid is without doubt, and for its size, one of the finest salmon and trout streams in the United Kingdom. It is not much more than 4 miles long and the angling is mainly carried out on Loch Voshimid, about one square mile in extent and approximately 3 miles from the mouth of the river at Kinloch Resort. The loch is fed by two tributaries, one entering the loch on the east shore and the other at the south, through a shallow, weedy loch (the 'Weedy Loch'), Lochan Fheoir, which, when fish are able to get up the rather steep 'fall' from Voshimid, is an exceptionally good little loch for 'free-taking' fish. Loch Voshimid is shallow over the greater part of its area and there is little of the loch which does not yield fish. There are some excellent named fishing areas, including Richard's Bay, Seal Rock, Sopwith's Bay, Green Bank and, of particular interest, Marie Rose Island — one wonders whether this is the island which James Barrie thought of for his character Marie Rose who vanished into the Land of Fairy while resting on an island in a Hebridean loch.

The two burns which feed the loch have limited spawning areas within a few hundred yards of the loch, after which they are mountainous torrents. Most of the fish which run into the loch drop downstream to spawn, but even so, in a good year, there is little doubt that there is insufficient spawning ground for the enormous run of fish in this small system.

THE ULLADALE

The Ulladale river rises to the west of the Voshimid from a deep craggy corrie. In dry weather its source is a stony desert, but after rain it is a streaming mass of white water passing down into Loch Ulladale and its feeder burn. From Loch Ulladale to the sea at Kinloch Resort the river twists for 4 miles through low-lying bogland broken up by several weedy tarns. The gradient is easy for ascending fish, but the weed growth in the tarns constitutes a major obstruction except during flood conditions.

Loch Ulladale is the most important angling section. It is a small loch divided into two sections by a narrow shoal. The upper section, with a mass of rocky points and shallows is the haunt of salmon, while the lower section is very shallow and mainly a sea trout area. The loch can be productive and most exciting, but it is very much influenced by wind and weather as it lies under a

SALMON RIVERS OF SCOTLAND

great and dramatic cliff of an overhanging mountain, Strone Ulladale (1,398 feet), at its southern end, the haunt of golden eagles. It is a 'feast or famine' loch, with erratic and very squally winds. Loch Ulladale is an exquisitely beautiful loch and is well worth the long rough walk even if fishing conditions are poor.

Midway between Loch Ulladale and the sea there is a small weed-infested loch known as the 'Reedy Loch', although its correct name is Loch a' Cheivla, and below this there is a holding pool referred to as 'Mugg's Pool'. Both these waters hold large numbers of fish and can be very productive given right conditions of wind and water. Below Mugg's Pool is another small loch which is no use for fishing, being shallow and choked with weed.

The principal spawning area is in the last half mile of the main feeder burn running into the south of Loch Ulladale, which is an excellent spawning ground; there is also a minor tributary with limited spawning ground running into the south-east of Loch Ulladale.

The Ulladale system is rather inaccessible and to reach Loch Ulladale involves a foot and pony trek of one and a quarter hours over a very steep gradient, and to reach 'Reedy Loch' and 'Mugg's Pool' involves rowing the length of Loch Voshimid from the road head at the Voshimid fishing hut, followed by an hour of hard slogging over mountain and bog.

SCOURST RIVER

In the West Loch river system there are 3 small rivers running southwards from the central mountain range into West Loch Tarbert. The most important of these is the Scourst or Meavaig River at the eastern end of the estate. The total length of the Scourst is about $3\frac{1}{2}$ miles at the head of which, under steep hills, is Loch Scourst. This is a deep and often dour loch approximately half a mile long and a quarter of a mile broad. There are some excellent fishing shallows at the north end, where the only major feeder burn enters, and a number of good rocky points round its shore. The middle of the loch is very deep and no doubt the dour reputation of this loch is a result of the tendency of the fish to move into the deep water except during and after a flood.

It has a special and well-merited reputation for large sea trout (with fish of 11 lb being recorded), but on good days it is a very fair salmon loch. Running north to south through a very steep valley between high hills it can be very rough and squally. There is, as on Ulladale and Voshimid, a very limited stretch of spawning ground upstream of the loch, but two long stretches of good spawning ground occur between the loch and the sea.

CASTLE BURN

Coming west from the Scourst River, the next, and the largest river system of the fishery, is designated the Castle Burn (although its proper name is the

River Eaval) because it enters the sea, after a very steep fall, at Amhuinnsuidhe Castle. Despite its size—and in watershed area and volume of water it must be by far the largest 'river system' on the estate — it is not a major salmon producing water.

At the head of the system is Loch Chliostair where a dam has been built by the North of Scotland Hydro-electric Board to supply a power station. This, together with the major obstruction of the Amhuinnsuidhe Falls, no doubt adversely affects the fishing potential. Large numbers of salmon and sea trout collect in the bay at Amhuinnsuidhe, but the yield of the river is poor. The fishing is virtually confined to two pools, the Gate and the Gorge, in the river just upstream of the falls, and to a very small weedy loch, the Ladies' Loch, about a quarter of a mile above the falls.

The unproductive nature of this system may be due to the exhausted state of fish after they have negotiated the falls (but many fail to do so and are battered to death on the rocks), and to the erratic river flow consequent on the effect of varying flows from the Loch Chliostair Power Station above Loch Leosaid.

The most productive fishing on Ladies' Loch is during and after late summer and autumn floods, and the best area is in the current where the burn enters the loch. Fish which have lain low in the loch are then moving upstream. Also, for some peculiar reason, a strong wind stirs them up.

Loch Leosaid is virtually unproductive due to its great depth and steep contours. The River Leosaid running into this from the west is now the major spawning area, since the hydro-electric scheme when completed dried out the river upstream. There are also some spawning beds between the falls and the Ladies' Loch and at the mouth of Lochan Beag.

This system is one which would repay development work, especially improvement of the passage over the very formidable falls, and perhaps the controlling of the outflow from Loch Leosaid by sluices to give a more stable flow into the Ladies' Loch.

HALLADALE BURN

Just west of the Castle Burn, and running into the same bay, is the Halladale Burn. This is a very small river system draining a small and rather low-lying area. There are two lochs, upper and lower Loch Halladale. A grid prevents fish from running into the upper loch. The only major feeder burn runs into the lower loch from a steep hillside to the north. The lower few hundred yards of this have some good spawning ground, as do parts of the half-mile stretch from lower Loch Halladale to the sea.

There is a run of salmon and good sea trout into this river system and they tend to run later than in the other systems. While regarded as a very secondary system, compared with Voshimid, some good catches of up to 5 salmon a day and some large sea trout, have been recorded occasionally.

SALMON RIVERS OF SCOTLAND

LOCH A' GHLINNE

Finally, running westward into the entrance of Loch Resort, is Loch a' Ghlinne. This is a tiny system. The loch, which is terminal, drains a steep valley and empties itself over a shingle bed into the sea. It has a small population of late running, and sometimes large, sea trout, but no salmon.

About 95 per cent of the salmon in the North Harris fishery are either grilse or fish which have spawned as grilse and returned for a second or subsequent spawning. In some years, especially in the very prolific Voshimid and Ulladale rivers, a number of fish are taken which appear to have failed to spawn in the previous winter, have spent two or three months or so at sea and returned for a second attempt. They are easily recognised by their kelt-like appearance, even though they may have sea lice on them. The scales show a spawning mark with very slight regeneration at the edge. At present the average weight of grilse is 5–6 lb although fish of 8 lb are quite common. A very few small summer fish are caught, perhaps one or two per cent of the total.

The salmon run starts in mid-June and reaches its peak in mid-July when the best catches are made.

Sea trout, from finnock up to very large fish of 6 lb and more, run at the same time as, or very slightly later than, the salmon. Many sea trout with 5 or more spawning marks have been taken. The average weight of sea trout, however, is $1\frac{1}{2}$–$1\frac{3}{4}$ lb.

Heavy and prolonged spells of rain are essential in these small systems. The lochs must be well filled to get at least 48 hours of flood water in the rivers before any significant number of salmon can run into them. The sea trout will creep up in small numbers as long as the streams are not completely dried out.

The average catch for the fishery is between 200 and 250 salmon and 600 to 800 sea trout.

The record catches for the fishery were made in 1974, when 10 rods fishing from 5 boats for 8 days from 10–18 July caught 102 salmon and 103 sea trout; and in 1977 when the same 10 rods fishing from 5 boats for 4 days from 25–28 July caught 100 salmon and 53 sea trout. Out of the 100 salmon caught in this period in 1977, 70 were taken from Loch Voshimid.

Fishing is by fly only. The best flies are Black Pennell, Goat's Toe, Black and Silver, Peter Ross, Connemara Black, Invicta and Elver. Dry fly and dapping with large bushy artificial flies account for a number of the large sea trout.

Although the proprietors have sea netting rights it is not known if they propose to exercise them; the previous proprietors did not.

Seals are believed to take a considerable number of fish in Amhuinnsuidhe Bay.

The Laxadale Lochs

On the east side of Harris and just to the east of Tarbert lies a chain of three lochs known as the Laxadale Lochs. The chain runs from north to south and discharges directly into Urgha Bay and East Loch Tarbert. The Top Loch is fed by three streams flowing down Glen Laxadale and into the top of the loch, and by the Dibidale River flowing in from the west and the Laxadale Burn coming in from the east, both entering near the upper end of the loch. At the lower end of the loch the Londavat River comes in from the east. The next largest of the three lochs is the Middle Loch. The Lower Loch has one major feeder stream coming in from the east. The outfall of the Lower Loch is fairly steep and flows only 100 yards before entering the sea. The Top Loch is sluiced at its lower end so that an artificial spate can be created if the weather remains dry.

The main spawning areas are in the rivers between the lochs, at the top end of the Top Loch and in the tributary streams.

The main run of salmon and sea trout is usually at the end of June but angling does not start until about 10 – 15 July in the hope that sufficient water is available to allow fish to run from the sea. Occasionally fish enter before the end of June but, as the catch ratio is one fresh-run fish to about 10 mended kelts, no fishing is permitted. Fishing over the past few years has been better towards the end of the season and fresh-run fish with sea lice have been caught at the end of September and the beginning of October. Salmon average 5–6 lb and sea trout 1–2 lb.

The fishing is owned by the Harris Hotel at Tarbert. The hotel is an 'angling hotel' built over a century ago and has been in the Cameron family since 1904. Fishing is available to all, but first preference is given to hotel guests.

The hotel started a small hatchery in 1970 and up to 60,000 salmon and sea trout eggs have been hatched each year. In recent years the sea trout numbers have been declining, as in so many other sea trout waters in Harris and North and South Uist. At the same time the numbers of salmon have been increasing. As salmon spawn later than sea trout, and in the same area, the situation is likely to continue to favour the increasing numbers of salmon that probably dislodge the sea trout eggs deposited in the gravel a few weeks earlier.

There has been no evidence of UDN in this loch system.

Laxdale River

The Laxdale originates from a number of lochs lying in the central spine of hills in South Harris and flows north-west through Loch Laxdale and down to the artificial Fincastle Loch with its barrier isolating it from the sea. On the seaward side of Fincastle Loch the river, at low tide, flows out of Luskentyre

Bay through two miles of sand and sea pools.

For most of its length the Laxdale is a ditch of peat-stained water with dark, still pools and as Hamish Stuart says in his *Book of the Sea Trout*: 'It is rather a startling experience to see salmon leaping in the manner usual to their kind in this narrow ditch-like river, which is often not more than six feet across, although here and there you find a fair-sized pool where the river widens.' Loch Laxadale is believed to be the smallest salmon and sea trout loch in the world. It is a deep, weedy water and fishes best when there is a good breeze.

The salmon tend to enter the river about the second week of July while the sea trout come in a few weeks earlier, about the middle of June. It is interesting to find that kelts stay in this river system for quite a long time and can be caught in Fincastle Loch as late as April and May. As elsewhere in the Western Isles and on the west coast of the mainland, the sea trout numbers are declining and the salmon numbers increasing. Not only are the numbers of sea trout dwindling but so also is their average size. Ten years ago the average sea trout catch on the Laxdale was 200 with an average sea trout weighing $2\frac{1}{4}$ lb; at the present time the average catch is down to 140 and the sea trout now only average $1\frac{1}{2}$ lb. The average weight of the salmon is 7 lb. The majority of the sea trout are caught in Fincastle Loch while about 60 per cent of the salmon are caught in this loch and 40 per cent in Loch Laxdale.

Spawning takes place on spate conditions because none of the tributary streams are capable of holding adult fish at normal flows. The fish tend to lie in the lochs and move up the small feeder streams to spawn quickly while flood conditions last. There is little overlap in the spawning areas of the salmon and sea trout, as the latter tend to go to the higher lochs above Loch Laxdale and spawn in the spate burns in that area. So the reason for the decline in sea trout on this river system cannot be attributed directly to the competition between the two species for available spawning area. However, the sea trout in the upper reaches do tend to spawn in areas which dry out when the spates subside. It is felt that one of the reasons for increased salmon numbers here may be due to an imbalance in the relative numbers of unfed salmon and sea trout fry planted in past years.

A hatchery by the riverside incubates about 100,000 sea trout and salmon eggs in wooden troughs each year and the ratio of sea trout to salmon eggs is about 3:1. The young are released in the streams at the unfed fry stage.

The main threat to salmon and sea trout stocks is from poaching at sea and in the tidal section of the river on the seaward side of Fincastle Loch. The river itself is well watched by estate employees but many fish enter the river bearing net marks.

The Highlands and Islands Development Board own the fishing rights throughout the whole river system and it is planned to operate the fishery on a day ticket basis. The commercial netting rights are not exercised.

It is most interesting to note that while the initial symptoms of UDN have been officially recorded on fish taken in the sea pools no infected fish have been recorded from the river. It is believed that fish coming in with the early symptoms of the disease recover after entry. A great deal of speculation surrounds the reasons for this and one theory is that the acidity of the water (pH 5.8) could be responsible.

Horsaclett

The Horsaclett system is more a series of narrow lochs connected by short sections of river than a river. It lies just south of Tarbert and its course runs from near the west coast of Harris across to the east coast in a south-easterly direction. The lochs include Sheep, Horsaclett, Collam, Grosebay and Craobhag. Because of the maze of small side lochans and tributaries lying in an area of moorland and bog, the Horsaclett system appears most complex.

The system tends to be a grilse and sea trout water and in recent years the numbers of both have shown a marked decline. In addition, the average size of the sea trout has shown a noticeable drop. There is no doubt that poaching and illegal netting is partly responsible for this decline. Salmon are caught in Sheep Loch and Horsaclett, and sea trout in the others.

The fishing is let, with Horsacleit Lodge, to tenants by the fortnight. Tenants may, if they so wish, issue day tickets to visiting anglers.

The commercial fishing rights along the coast are not exercised.

UDN has not been recorded in this river system.

NORTH UIST

At the end of the last century the only river system in North Uist in which salmon occurred was the Skealtar system on the east coast of the island. Now, however, according to Campbell and Williamson, salmon are relatively abundant and occur in some waters draining to the west, such as Loch Horisary, and also in the north-flowing Geireann system. In the case of Loch Horisary the salmon rod catch is limited to one or two grilse each season. It is interesting to note that in the Geireann estuary sea pools salmon can be caught on artificial fly, which is most unusual.

Another unusual feature of salmon in North Uist is the significant spring run on the Skealtar system with its chain of lochs — Loch na Ciste, Loch Guerrean and Loch Skealtar. Angling on the Skealtar begins in late February and in recent years by the end of May as many as 43 salmon have been taken, although the average number taken over this period during the last 25 years is

12. The Skealtar spring salmon weigh on average about 10 lb, with occasional fish weighing up to 14 lb while some of over 27 lb have been taken. The regularity of this run and the comparatively large size of the salmon make the Skealtar system unique in the Outer Hebrides, and probably also in western Scotland north of the Firth of Clyde. A run of grilse also occurs in the Skealtar, with peak angling catches being made from late July to mid-August. Campbell and Williamson also record a run of small fresh salmon into the Skealtar during late November. According to some, Loch Skealtar fishes best in a south wind, Guerrean in a west, and na Ciste in a west or north.

Most of the angling on North Uist is owned by North Uist Estate and application to fish the various waters can be made to the North Uist Estate office in Lochmaddy. However, Lochmaddy Hotel has fishing on all the waters within the North Uist Estate and anglers intending to visit this island may wish to write to the hotel.

SOUTH UIST

The two main salmon waters in South Uist are Loch a' Bharp and Loch Lower Kildonan. Between 1882 and 1937 Loch a' Bharp produced very few salmon, usually less than 5 annually and in some years none at all, while the sea trout catches, particularly during the earlier part of this period, were prolific. However, during the period 1961–1965 the average annual catch of salmon rose to 32, while the corresponding figure for sea trout was only 31. Then during the period 1972–1976 the average annual catch of salmon remained the same at 28 but the average annual sea trout catch had dropped to 17. This increase in salmon stocks and apparent corresponding decline in sea trout stocks noted by Campbell and Williamson has occurred more recently at Lower Kildonan, as during the period 1961–1965 the average figures were less than one for salmon and 104 for sea trout, while in the period 1972–1976 the average annual catch of salmon had risen to 13 and the sea trout catch had fallen to 16. It is interesting to note this changeover in the relative abundance of sea trout and salmon on North and South Uist as it has also been recorded elsewhere in Scotland (see Chapters 38 and 39).

There is another loch, the 'Mill Loch' above Loch Lower Kildonan in which salmon have also been seen, although it is unlikely that more than the occasional fish has been taken from it. The other system holding salmon in South Uist, and to an increasing extent, is the Howmore system, particularly lochs Roag and Fada. In these lochs, too, the sea trout catches have plummeted to a very low level.

Fishing on most of these waters is controlled by a syndicate which rents the fishing from South Uist Estate. Most anglers stay at the Lochboisdale Hotel.

An excellent history of angling in South Uist is given in the book by Major R. A. Chrystal entitled *Angling at Lochboisdale, South Uist*.

ISLE OF SKYE

Most of the rivers in Skye are spate rivers and are little more than streams at normal flow but the variation in flow is extremely large, and the rise and fall in levels rapid, due to the ease of run-off which results from the impervious rocks of the mountain ranges, the small drainage basins and, recently, the improved drainage for forestry.

The rivers are for the most part similar in nature. The larger ones, with the exception of the River Sligachan, have numerous deep pools near the mouth but in the middle and upper reaches pools become separated by ever-increasing lengths of shallow streamy water. Many of them drain off the peat-free central massif of the island and for this reason their waters are very clear and do not become peat-stained in flood conditions. The rivers in this category include the Broadford, Camasunary, Coruisk, Drynoch, Brittle, Kilmarie and Sligachan. Salmon run up all these rivers except the Coruisk. Other rivers such as the Snizort, Varagill and Ose (or Ullinish) do become peaty at times, particularly the latter.

The most important salmon rivers on the island are the Drynoch, Kilmartin, Snizort and Varagill. The fish tend to be mainly grilse and do not enter the rivers until the end of July or early August. However, the exact timing of the runs depends on the flow in the rivers. Due to the rapid rise and fall in river levels fish often become trapped in small pools and this makes the job of the poacher much easier. Sea trout appear in the tidal pools of most of the rivers in June. There is no record of UDN from any of the rivers in Skye.

Angling is not one of Skye's main attractions as the late runs limit the angling season to less than three months on the Snizort, which is considered the best salmon river, and most other rivers. Furthermore, the rivers are of such a size that while the largest can cater for about 12 rods, most can only hold no more than 4. Of the main rivers the River Varragill and the River Drynoch are owned by private individuals for their own use, while the Department of Agriculture and Fisheries allow visitors to fish the River Kilmartin. The River Ose is available to visitors to the Ullinish Lodge Hotel and the River Snizort can be fished by visitors to this hotel and the Skeabost House Hotel who also sell tickets to non-residents. Permits to fish on the River Sligachan can be obtained from the Sligachan Hotel.

While all the rivers of Skye are free from pollution they are, alas, not free from poaching. As Alan Souter says in his article *The Salmon Fisheries of Skye* published in *The Salmon Net* in 1966: 'The physical nature of river and countryside and the relation of the roads to the rivers make it an ideal terrain for the poacher. Without exaggeration it would take several 'fishery wardens' to watch each river properly. Any returns that would accrue as a result of improved angling due to reduced poaching would be unlikely to cover the cost of improvement.' There is a ready market for salmon on the island as they can be bought discreetly at a cheaper price than that asked at the salmon netting station. Protecting these rivers from the poacher is at present an almost impossible task as there has been no local District Salmon Fishery Board since 1912, although some proprietors are at present taking steps to resume one.

There are two or three commercial salmon fishing concerns on Skye. One is a net and coble fishery which operates at the mouth of the River Snizort and another is centred on Portree with bag net stations on the coast to the north and south of the town.

MULL

The Forsa

The Forsa flows into the Sound of Mull, one mile east of Salen. It is 10 miles long and fast flowing, draining the high ground to the south. It has some 30 or 40 good holding pools which have a good stock of salmon and sea trout from July onwards, providing there has been heavy rain to increase the flow in the river to allow fish to ascend the falls at the river mouth. Sea trout tend to enter the river first, appearing in May and June, while salmon enter from July to mid-October. Most of the spawning areas are in the main river.

The river is unaffected by man, although there is some occasional gravel extraction for road building. UDN has not been recorded in this river. Poaching is a problem on this river as on most of the Mull rivers as, like the rivers in Skye, they flow through remote areas where there is little chance of poachers being disturbed by the pitifully few river watchers that can be employed.

There is no intensive commercial netting along this part of the coast, although net and coble may be used very occasionally.

Permits for fishing can be obtained from the Glenforsa Hotel in Salen.

The Aros

The Aros River is only about 5 miles long, rising in the hills as a series of burns draining off the hills on the south side of the river and flowing into the Sound of Mull about a mile north of Salen. About $3\frac{1}{2}$ miles up from the estuary the Aros is joined from the north by the Ledmore River which flows from Loch Frisa. Salmon and sea trout run up into this loch. There are two waterfalls on the Tenga stretch of the Aros above the Ledmore confluence, and it is thought that bigger fish do not get up the upper falls. The small burns running into Loch Frisa provide good spawning areas, and other good spawning and nursery areas occur in the streams flowing into the Aros.

If there is heavy rain during the last 10 days of June, a run of sea trout of $1\frac{1}{2}$ lb–3 lb is expected. Salmon will run any time during late June, July and August providing there is sufficient water in the river. There is sometimes an October run, especially if there has been a drought in preceding months.

There are some excellent pools on this attractive river flowing through some of the best of the Mull countryside and these include the Yellow, Garden, Bucket, Sandmartin, Ash Tree, Corner and Stonechat pools.

From the estuary to 3 miles upstream the north bank of the Aros belongs to the White House of Aros, while the south bank is owned by Glenaros. Upstream from the Ledmore River the north bank of the Aros is in the hands of Tenga Estate and the south bank, Killichronan.

Over the last 5 years very few fish suffering from UDN have been seen. The main source of mortality is from poaching. There is no commercial netting, and although White House of Aros has estuary netting rights these are not exercised. Many years ago it used to be a practice in this and other small salmon rivers, to spear salmon in the pools when the water was low and the weather bright.

Day permits to fish the river can be obtained from Killichronan Estate, while Glenaros let their fishing to tenants of their holiday cottages. Glenaros and White House have a mutual agreement to fish fly only.

Loch Frisa holds many good little brown trout and there is always a chance of a salmon or sea trout. The loch is best fished from a boat and boats can be hired by arrangement with Lettermore.

The largest salmon recorded from this river was a cock of 45 lb which was taken on worm from the Ash Tree pool in August 1911 by Mr James Greenhill of Edinburgh. This aroused much interest at the time and the general opinion seemed to be that it was a fish originating from the River Awe which had lost its way. The scales of this fish were read by Arthur Hutton. The fish had spent 2 years in the river and just over 4 in the sea and was returning to spawn for the first time.

The Ba

The Ba is a very short river, being about $2\frac{1}{2}$ miles long. There are no falls on the river and it makes a very gradual descent from Loch Ba to the sea in Loch na Keal. The upper part of the river winds considerably before straightening out and running parallel to the coast. It is a very attractive river with good glides and pools and having its east bank lined with trees. The main spawning areas are in the rivers Clachaig and Glencannel which drain into Loch Ba. Salmon and sea trout run the Ba from the end of June until October and, if conditions are right, excellent fishing can be had on a number of attractive pools including Benmore, Garden, Corner, Oak Tree, Drumlang and the Sea.

UDN has not been recorded in the Ba and it is considered that this is because the water is too acid. As with the other Mull rivers, poaching, chiefly at the river mouth in this case, is a problem.

Over a period of 5 years The Viscount of Massereene and Ferrard, owner of Benmore Estate, put many thousands of young salmon into the streams at the top of Loch Ba. In addition many croys were constructed on the Ba, but unfortunately most of these have been washed away.

Benmore, Gruline and Killichronan Estates are allowed to fish the Sea Pool three days per week with splash nets, and net up to 100 salmon and 200 sea trout. Benmore Estate has netting rights on the south shore of Loch na Keal, but these are not exercised. There are, however, bag nets round much of the coast of Mull.

The Ba is let by the week, month or for whatever period a tenant wishes. In addition day tickets are available for the sea pools and also Loch Ba when not tenanted.

Loch Ba is a very good loch for big sea trout and salmon. The largest sea trout caught in recent years weighed 19 lb but fish of 10–12 lb are quite usual and are caught to a great extent on the dap. The average salmon weighs from 10–14 lb but salmon of up to 20 lb are caught on occasions. Benmore Estate owns two-thirds of the loch and Gruline Estate the other third.

The Coladoir

The Coladoir River lies in the south-west corner of Mull. It flows from Loch Fuaron for a distance of 4 miles to enter the sea at Loch Scridain. It is very much a spate river and consists of good pools and glides. Some of the best salmon pools are the Sea, Bridge, Black Bank, Elbow, Brigadier, Brigadier Glide and Farm House. There are falls on the river about $3\frac{1}{2}$ miles from the sea but migratory fish are able to surmount them. The main spawning areas of the river occur in the upper river and its small tributaries, some of which drain Ben More (3,171 feet).

Providing there is adequate rain the fish start moving into the Coladoir from the end of June through to October, with the main part of the run coming in July.

The Lussa

The Lussa rises in Glen More close to the upper reaches of the Coladoir and flows west and enters Loch Spelve shortly after passing Strathcoil. Loch Spelve is a sheltered sea loch with a narrow arm opening into the Firth of Lorn. The Lussa is fed by two lochs in its upper reaches, Loch Airdeglais and Loch Sguabain and the main spawning areas are in the vicinity of these waters. The Lussa is very much a spate river and fish only ascend during flood conditions. It is an attractive river with falls alternating with pools. Much of its lower course flows through forestry plantation. There is a large waterfall, Tor Ness, $3\frac{1}{2}$ miles up the glen from the sea where salmon congregate. However, the fall is surmountable and fish readily pass upstream. There are some good pools on the lower river, including the Sea Pool and the Pedlar's Pool. The latter consists of 50 yards of still, deep water and is the last pool of any size before the river valley steepens and the river becomes a series of small cataracts with deep potholes.

The main run of fish is in June and July, with a few fish entering in August.

As on so many of the rivers of the Inner and Outer Isles, poaching is on the increase. Fortunately there is no commercial netting on the river and UDN has not been recorded.

The fishing is in the hands of three private owners and the Forestry Commission and permits can be obtained on application to the owners.

ARRAN

Machrie Water

The Machrie Water rises amidst the mountains in the centre of the island and drains such peaks as Torr nam Freumh, Beinn Tarsuin and A' Chruach. As its small tributaries flow swiftly off these green bracken-clad mountain sides, the river grows in size and flows south-west to discharge into the sea at Machrie Bay. The start of the river is a rough, rugged rock-strewn gorge in the bottom of the valley. No migratory fish ascend this far up, but at Monyquil farm the Garbh Allt joins the Machrie and from this point the river becomes gravelly with a few nice pools occurring in this stretch extending down as far as the first road bridge. From this bridge to the main road bridge above the mouth there are a number of interesting pools and pots as well as some gravelly runs and a few small falls. From the main road bridge to the sea there are few more nice pools before the Sea Pool is reached. The fishable part of the river amounts to about 4 miles and this is divided into 3 beats and there are in all about 30 named pools. The beats are normally let on a weekly basis and the lets are open for booking during January and February through the Estate Office at Killiechassie at Aberfeldy in Perthshire.

There is a plentiful supply of good spawning gravel throughout the main river system, although above the top road bridge there is a section which is unstable due to bank erosion but further upstream in the vicinity of the Contractor's Pool there is an excellent spawning area. Some of the tributary spawning streams also have good spawning and nursery areas. There is a particularly good sea trout spawning burn entering the right bank of the middle beat between the two bridges.

The average annual catch is about 20 salmon and 85 sea trout. Salmon used to average about 10 lb and sea trout 2 lb, but in the last few years the average weight of salmon has dropped to 6–7 lb. The season is 1 June–15 October and the best of the fishing occurs between July and October.

The river was restocked with salmon and sea trout over a 5-year period in the late 1960s and early 1970s and there was a marked improvement in catches after this.

Iorsa Water

The Iorsa rises in the mountains of north and central Arran, with its tributaries flowing off the slopes of Beinn Bhreac and Ben Tarsuinn. The river flows south at first until it is joined by Allt Tigh an Shiorrain flowing out of Loch Tanna. It then turns south-west and winds through a flat glen until it reaches Loch Iorsa. From the mouth of this loch to the sea it flows swiftly over a boulder-strewn course, with few pools, for about a mile before it is joined by Allt na h-Airidhe on its right bank just upstream of Dougrie Lodge. There are one or two pools below this junction and in front of the lodge, just below which it flows under the road bridge and into the sea.

Although at one time there were a number of man-made pools on the Iorsa these were destroyed by an enormous flood. Now, apart from a few pools in the first few hundred yards above the estuary, there are no resting places until Loch Iorsa is reached. Salmon and a few sea trout enter the Iorsa but most of them run straight up to the loch and it is difficult to assess the stock in the river. Spawning and nursery areas are plentiful above Loch Iorsa but below they are very limited. Between 1968 and 1972 salmon and sea trout ova were planted in the river to try and strengthen the stock of fish. The river has been fished very little in recent years, the previous owners preferring to fish the Machrie when they were in residence at Dougrie.

According to Hamish Stuart, in his *Book of the Sea Trout*, published in 1916, Loch Iorsa is an artificial loch which was in existence as long ago as 1875. It used to be the scene of an annual meeting to which the tenants were invited and the day of the meeting was a festival celebrated in the usual 'highly convivial Highland fashion'. According to Stuart's recollection it was of old standing even in 1875 and was at that time described as a very ancient and 'sporting' institution, so that Loch Iorsa may be regarded as the first artificial or semi-artificial loch frequented by salmon and sea trout.

ISLAY

This is a delightful island with some charming little salmon rivers and, as Dugald Macintyre says in *Memoirs of a Highland Gamekeeper* 'the little rivers of Islay are full of salmon and sea trout from July onwards.'

The Sorn

The Sorn is a small spate river in the centre of the Island. It has its source in two lochs, Loch Finlaggan and Loch Ballygrant and it does not become the Sorn until the tributaries from these two lochs unite about $3\frac{1}{2}$ miles from the sea, which it enters at the head of Loch Indaal near Bridgend. The river flows through alluvial soil and, as Hamish Stuart says in his *Book of the Sea Trout*, 'finds its placid way to the sea in all its lower and salmon-haunted length, through romantic meadows whose turfy smell might grace the fairest land in England.' It is rarely a dirty river except during very heavy floods.

Salmon do not appear in the Sorn until the end of June, but fresh fish have been recorded entering the river in November and clean fish can be taken right up to the end of the season at the end of October. Unfortunately the stocks of salmon and sea trout have declined in this river in recent years, and in the case of the salmon the catches have shown a marked drop from 107 in 1950 to one fish in 1976. As a result of the decline in stocks the river has been restocked with salmon parr for the last 3 years. There is some pollution of the river with silage effluent, but this is unlikely to reach serious proportions. UDN has occurred in recent years.

Fishing can be quite good on this river and it is said to fish best in dull weather, unlike the Laggan which fishes best on a bright day. However, the colour of the water may have a lot to do with this, as the Sorn is a clear river while the Laggan is very peaty.

Some notable people have fished the Sorn, and in 1930 none other than Harry Lauder caught a salmon in Loch Finlaggan. This is the only record of a salmon being caught in Loch Finlaggan.

The fishing is private and is retained by the family owning Islay Estate.

The Laggan

The Laggan lies in the south-east arm of the Island and is more of a moorland river than the Sorn although Hamish Stuart says that while it is essentially a Highland river in colour 'some of its reaches are meadow crowned, and few of its pools are of the wild tumultuous character one associates with the rivers in the land of the Gael'.

The salmon enter the Laggan earlier than the Sorn, coming in from Laggan Bay about the middle of June. There are two good tributaries, the Duich and the Torra, in which fish spawn.

The best of the fishing is in the lower 4 miles of river, from the sea to the minor road from Bridgend to Port Ellen. This section of river holds a lot of fish and in recent years over 300 fish have been caught in a season. This part of the river is owned by Laggan Estate and is let by the week to tenants. Application for lets can be made to the Estate Secretary, Laggan Estate, Bridge House, Bowmore. The Islay Estate and another proprietor each own one bank of the river over the two miles upstream from the Laggan Estate water.

UDN has not occurred in this river.

The commercial fishing rights in Loch Indaal are owned by Islay Estate but are not exercised.

Uisgn Tuigh (Uisk-an-Dhuie)

This little river is sometimes called the Blackwater due to the dark, peaty nature of its water. It is very much a spate river, and is small in size, with an average width of 12–15 feet, but very deep.

The salmon congregate off the mouth of the river in mid-June and enter after then if flow conditions are favourable.

The river is rarely fished nowadays because of the amount of weed present and even in the past only the occasional fish was taken, and usually with the worm.

31

THE LOCH ALSH, KINTAIL, MALLAIG, SHIEL AND MORVERN DISTRICT

Ling

The Ling is a small spate river in south-west Ross draining the Forests of Attadale and Killilan and flowing into Loch Long. It is fed by two streams, Allt Coire nan Each from the east and Amhainn Loch an Laoigh from the north which join at Poll-eisq to form the main river. Allt Coire nan Each drains Aonach Buidhe (2,949 feet) and flows through Loch Cruoshie which lies at the head of the valley running between Beinn Dronaig (2,612 feet) and Aonach Buidhe and Faochaig (2,847 feet). Amhainn Loch an Laoigh, or the River Blackwater as it is called locally, is the larger tributary and flows out of Loch an Laoigh. Although there are good spawning areas in both these tributaries they are inaccessible to migratory fish because of insurmountable falls in their lower reaches, and unfortunately it would be too expensive to improve them.

The Ling is rather unusual for a west coast river in that it has a fairly early run of salmon with fish being caught as early as 17 February, and April is particularly good. There is also a fairly late run of grilse, but their time of entry is very dependent on the occurrence of spates. There is also a good run of sea trout which, over the last three years, has started much earlier in the season with fish being taken by 20 May.

The north bank of the river is owned by Attadale Estate and the south by Killilan Estate. Attadale Estate lets its fishing to tenants who also take the Lodge.

A commercial fishery, using sweep nets, is operated on Loch Long by Conchra Estate.

UDN has not been recorded in this river.

Elchaig

The Elchaig is an attractive little river running west through Glen Elchaig and entering Loch Long just to the south of the mouth of the River Ling. The Elchaig drains the southern slopes of Aonach Buidhe, Faochaig and Sguman

Coinntich and the northern slopes of A' Ghlas-bheinn (3,006 feet) and Sgurr nan Ceathreamhnan (3,771 feet). Two lochs feed the river, Loch Mhoicean and Loch na Leitreach. Just below the latter a small stream, Allt a' Glomach, enters from the south on which are the well-known 300-foot Falls of Glomach.

There are three falls on the main river. The lowest ones are $2\frac{1}{2}$ miles up from the mouth at Coille-righ. The next falls are at the junction with a stream draining Loch nan Ealachan (the Swan Loch). These are in two steps, consisting of an 8-foot sheer wall of rock followed by a series of cascades extending over 40 or 50 feet. The third set of falls, much smaller, occur just below Loch na Leitreach. Salmon and sea trout can ascend all these to enter the loch and pass upstream. The main spawning areas are on the flats just above this loch at Carnach and extend upstream to Iron Lodge.

Like the neighbouring River Ling, the Elchaig has a run of early fish which ascend as far as the first set of falls, which they start to ascend in May, depending on water temperature.

There is a good run of sea trout which in recent years has started running in the early summer.

Four or five years ago 10,000 salmon fry were released in the river, but there has been no stocking since.

UDN has not been recorded in this river.

Fishing on this river is private.

Croe

The little River Croe is a short spate river in Wester Ross. It winds through its 4-mile course down Gleann Lichd and unlike the Elchaig is not a torrential river but has a gently sloping gradient with long sluggish stretches and deep, peaty pools. There are no falls on the river and the main spawning areas are in the upper reaches and side streams draining off the back of the Five Sisters of Kintail which make up the Beinn Mhor massif: Sgurr na Moraich – 2,870 feet; Sgurr nan Saighead; Sgurr Fhuaran – 3,505 feet; Sgurr na Carnach – 3,270 feet; Sgurr na Ciste Duibhe – 3,370 feet.

The Croe is a peaceful river with no man-made developments to disturb it, and the silence of the glen is only broken during times of spate.

The salmon enter this river much later than fish in the Ling and Elchaig, and the run does not start building up until July, continuing well on into October. In fact fish have been caught on the last day of the season (15 October) fresh in from the sea with sea lice. The runs, if anything, are tending to get later each year. Sea trout enter the river slightly earlier, and start ascending in June. There has been a decline in both salmon and sea trout in recent years and the catches in 1977, a drought year on the west coast, were extremely poor. However, judging by the abundance of young fish in the river it may well be that fish are entering the river during the close season, and this is most likely if spates do not occur until this time.

Unfortunately there is a fair amount of poaching on the river and it is all too easy for the poachers to use nets at the deep pools in which the fish lie.

UDN has not been recorded in the Croe.

The river is owned by the National Trust for Scotland and Inverinate Estate and the fishing is so arranged that each has the fishing on both banks on alternate days. There are some good pools on the river including the Morvich, Elbow, New and Road. Fishing is by fly only. Day, half-day and weekly permits (i.e. three days) can be obtained from the National Trust for Scotland through Mr Maclean of Morvich Farm. Fishing permits can also be purchased from Mr Carr, the gamekeeper for Inverinate Estate.

Commercial fishing by sweep nets is exercised along the shore of both sides of Loch Duich.

The Shiel of Duich

The River Shiel rises in the hills of Cluanie Forest and flows north-west down Glen Shiel, beneath the Five Sisters of Kintail which rise nearly sheer from the river, and enters the sea at Loch Duich.

The river is about 10 miles long but has a fall which is inaccessible to migratory fish about $4\frac{1}{2}$ miles from its mouth. The lower half-mile of the river is rough and rocky and lined with alders; above this the river runs more slowly among reeds and rushes. For 3 or 4 miles above little Loch Shiel the river is a series of slow-running deeps connected by shallows, with no well-defined pools. At the end of this reach of dead water, rocky pools are again in evidence. The main spawning areas lie upwards of $1\frac{1}{2}$ miles from the river mouth and it is in these lower reaches that the best of the angling is to be had and in which there are 4 good pools. The Bridge Pool is nearest to the sea and holds more fish than any of the others; above this is the Half Pool and then, above a small stream which comes in from the south and which is a good sea trout water, the Captain's Pool. A short distance higher up, the river expands into Loch Shiel, a small and very weedy sheet of water. Immediately below the loch is a peaty stream called the Inkpot which is good in high water. Loch Shiel is particularly good for sea trout but salmon, although present, are less keen to take the angler's lure.

The main runs of both salmon and sea trout are in July and August. There has been a decline in the numbers of salmon caught, largely due to the river being fished rather less than in the past. However, the sea trout catch has increased. UDN has not been recorded in this river. The fishing is owned by Dochfour Estate and is normally let to those who stay in either the Shiel or Cluanie Lodges, and is not normally let to the day ticket public. However,

The Glenmore and Glenbeg

The Glenmore and Glenbeg (its Gaelic name is Abhainn a' Ghlinne Bhig) are two delightful spate rivers draining the range of mountains to the south of Loch Duich. The Glenmore drains Sgurr Mhic Bharraich (2,553 feet) and Glenbeg, Ben Sgriol (3,196 feet). Both rivers enter the sea a short distance apart in Glenelg Bay in the Sound of Sleat between the mainland and Skye.

The Glenmore is the larger of the two rivers and is beautifully described, although not by name, by Ian Chalmers in his delightful book *Salmon Fishing in Little Rivers* published by A. & C. Black in 1938. His descriptions are so vivid that they deserve quoting:

'I have one lovely little river in mind with a course of nine miles to the sea, a nine miles full of incident and with three distinct changes of character in them. The first few miles are through high open moorland, and here the river is just a busy little burn. It twists in and out among the heather-covered mounds, the mountain sheep cross it where they will, while the small trout in its shallow pools dart for safety at the slightest sign of danger. It is just a young thing and from a fishing point of view of no great value, but the time taken in making its acquaintance will not be wasted. The scenery, away in the heart of the deer mountains, alone will repay you.'

This is a beautiful paragraph which will conjure up many Highland streams to a great number of readers. He then goes on:

'Then comes the first change. For the next two miles the river rushes down through a series of gorges, alder-clad and difficult of access, small waterfalls alternating with little foaming pools of no great depth, but here and there you will find dark pot-holes almost hidden by the trees, holes which later in the year fill with red and black salmon, many of which, alas, fall victims to the hayforks and "snigglers" of the crofters . . .

'In these last two miles the river has grown appreciably in size. It begins to develop runs which look as if they might hold fish, and pools which certainly do, and after emerging from the gorges, heading for the sea, it winds its way through the rough farmland till about five miles further on it reaches its destination. All through this pasture-land, snatched from the moor, this little river is strengthened every here and there by small mountain streams; streams which in fine weather are mere trickles but which, after a day's rain, swell into torrents showing up like white scars where they pour down the misty hillside and fill the main river banking with golden-brown peat water. This is the best

DISTRICTS FROM KINTAIL TO MORVERN

fishing part of the river and here you will find pool after pool of every possible variety, all of them containing fish . . .

'Close to the little village [Galltair] it forces its way through the shingle bank and enters the sea, leaving behind in the last few hundred yards two fascinating sea pools, so tempting to look at but so disappointing to fish.'

The Glenbeg, although not such a large river, almost mirrors this description, as do so many other West coast rivers.

Providing there is water, fish enter from June to August, or even later. In a good year 12–30 salmon are taken from the Glenbeg and probably double that number from the Glenmore.

There have been some improvements made to the Glenbeg in the form of croys and both rivers have excellent holding pools. Unfortunately both rivers are still poached particularly at their mouths. Eilanreach Estate has the netting rights on the Glenbeg but these are not exercised. On the Glenmore the netting rights are owned by Dochfour Estate and are exercised.

The angling on the Glenbeg is private and is retained for the family of the estate, while that on the Glenmore is leased privately by Dochfour Estate.

The Arnisdale

The little River Arnisdale rises on Sgurr na Sgine (3,098 feet) and runs west through beautiful mountainous country before flowing into the sea on the north shore of Loch Hourn opposite the Sound of Sleat and Skye. There are steep falls about 5 miles upstream which bar the further ascent of migratory fish. However, there are good spawning and nursery areas in the lower 5 miles of river which help to maintain the production of both salmon and sea trout.

Salmon and sea trout rarely enter this river before June but from then onwards there is a good head of fish in all the many pools, providing there has been sufficient rain.

There has been no record of UDN in the river but furunculosis has been a problem at times. However, seals are a problem in Loch Hourn and the neighbouring Loch Nevis. It is gratifying to learn that poaching is not a problem on the Arnisdale; this is probably due to the proprietor generously allowing the locals to fish the river in his absence. There is no netting on either the river or along the neighbouring coast.

The Guseran

The Guseran rises on Ladhar Bheinn (3,343 feet), runs through Knoydart

Estate and falls into the Sound of Sleat after a run of 10 miles. It is, therefore, very much a short torrential spate river. The fish can run upstream for 6 miles before being stopped by insurmountable falls.

Fish start entering the river in May, but June and July are the best months. The Guseran was a much better river at the beginning of the century than it is now, and while salmon and grilse are still to be had it is much more of a sea trout river.

There has been no sign of UDN in this river or the rivers Inverie and Carnach also on Knoydart Estate. However, poaching is a problem on all three of these rivers, particularly at the river mouths, as their isolated position makes it difficult for them to be adequately watched. The seals, too, are a nuisance and fish travelling along the coast into Loch Nevis have to run the gauntlet of these animals.

The river is let, by the estate, to tenants, on a weekly or fortnightly basis and the river is divided into an upper and lower beat with the change-over being at midday.

The Inverie

The Inverie River is the best of the three rivers on Knoydart Estate. Its tributaries rise on the slopes of Luinne Bheinn (3,083 feet) and Meall Buidhe (3,107 feet) and drain into the Dubh-Lochain. From the outlet of this small dark loch the river has a further run of 3 miles before entering the salt water of Loch Nevis a little to the east of Inverie House. The Dubh-Lochain acts as a reservoir for the river and consequently a good water level is maintained for a much longer period than on the Guseran and Carnach. There is a small private hydro-electric scheme which uses a tributary of the Inverie flowing from a small loch above Choineachain.

Fish enter this river much earlier than the Guseran, and large sea trout come in as early as the last week of March or the beginning of April. Salmon appear a little later, at the beginning of May. Many of the fish move up into the Dubh-Lochain which is a good holding water.

There is commercial netting at the mouth of the river where sweep nets operate for two hours either side of high tide. Bag nets are also set along the shore at the mouth of Loch Nevis.

The estate has recently set up a hatchery at Inverie and rear fish to the smolt stage, when they are released in the Guseran and Inverie. At present salmon eggs are bought in for rearing at the hatchery, but it is hoped that in time there will be sufficient fish in the river to allow some, surplus to the natural spawning requirements, to be caught and stripped.

The fishing is let on a weekly or fortnightly basis to tenants taking the lodge and the house. The river is therefore divided into two beats, an upper and lower with rods changing over at midday. There are two boats on the Dubh-Lochain, one for each of the beats.

The Carnach

The Carnach is a small stream which runs into the head of Loch Nevis and is reached from Inverie House by boat. Unfortunately it is heavily poached and there are few fish in it. It is unlikely that poaching is entirely responsible for this lack of fish; heavy predation by seals in Loch Nevis is believed to be the main reason.

The Morar

The Morar is the shortest river in the British Isles and it runs out of the deepest loch (1,017 feet). The river is only 600 yards long but the fishable part is confined to the lower half of its course below the Falls of Morar. There are three pools in this stretch, of which the Falls Pool is generally considered the best as fish tend to congregate there. There is a streamy pool below the Falls Pool and below this the Island Pool, just above the road bridge. In this pool fish pause after leaving the sea creek immediately below. In the narrow gut into which the river empties, large numbers of fish may be seen.

Loch Morar is of little use as a salmon fishing loch, although an occasional fish is taken in the summer and autumn, but it is very good for sea trout.

Loch Beoraid drains into Loch Morar from the south by way of the River Meoble, but it is inaccessible to salmon because of a fall a short distance from the outlet. The Meoble and two small streams at the head of the loch are the main spawning areas in the catchment.

The river was the first to be harnessed by the North of Scotland Hydro-electric Board, and a low-head power station was built at the falls and a weir added to the top of the falls in order to divert water to the power station. To compensate for this the Board has built a pool pass to allow fish to by-pass the falls. A fish counter is installed in the pass.

The Morar is a very good sea trout river and also holds a good stock of summer salmon. The right bank of the river is owned by Lovat Estate, who lease the fishing privately, and the left bank is owned by another proprietor.

The Ailort

The River Ailort is more renowned for its sea trout than its salmon. The river drains about 26 miles of high ground and after a short run of less than 3 miles flows into the sea at Loch Ailort opposite the island of Eigg. The river flows from Loch Eilt and, shortly after leaving the loch, widens out into a small sheet of water from whence it has a more torrential run of about 2 miles to the sea. Fish spawn mainly in the feeder streams running into Loch Eilt. There is a dam at the foot of the Loch Eilt and during the summer months artificial freshets are released from a gate when conditions for the upstream movement of fish are favourable. The fish can surmount the gate and enter the loch. About 200 yards above high tide mark a weir has been built to retain a large pool to enable the Unilever Research Laboratory based at Inverailort to abstract water by pumps for their research facilities. The water is returned to the river estuary after passing through the fish tanks. Marine Harvest Ltd, a subsidiary of Unilever also has a salmon farm in Loch Ailort where salmon are reared in cages for the market. This was the first of the salmon farms to be established in Scotland and their salmon are marketed under the trade name of Lochinvar.

UDN has not been definitely recorded in this river. However, one source of mortality for adult salmon is predation by seals which are quite abundant in Loch Ailort.

Quite often the stock of young fish in the river is supplemented by the release of surplus salmon fry from the Unilever Research Unit.

Two estates own the fishing on the river and the loch, and this is shared by agreement. The present owners are Mrs Cameron-Head and Mr Sandeman. The fishing is usually advertised in the sporting press. The main run of fish is in July.

There are 8 pools each on both the upper and lower beats and, starting at the outlet of Loch Eilt, these are as follows: Sluice Run, Falls, Stream, Run Out, South Bend, McPherson's, Round, Deep, Monument, Lord Elgin's, Rock, Policeman's, Bridge, Mrs Cameron-Head's, Butts and New Bridge.

The Moidart

The River Moidart lies between the Ailort and the Shiel and has a total length of about 7 miles. It runs off Beinn Gaire, Croit Bheinn and Sgurr Dhomhuill Mor and flows through a remote but pleasant countryside before discharging into the head of Loch Moidart, a shallow and muddy arm of the sea, completely sheltered and 2 miles inland from Eilean Shona. During its course the river passes through a small lochan near Glenmoidart House. The river is fast-flowing with good, well-defined pools and fast runs. Its tributaries are ideal spawning and nursery areas for both salmon and sea trout.

The main runs of salmon and grilse occur late May – July and September – October. The second run, in the autumn, is a more recent phenomenon, as on the Croe. In recent years there has been a definite drop in the catches of sea trout, and fewer have been seen on the spawning grounds. This cannot be attributed to UDN, as this disease has not been recorded in the Moidart, nor to local netting activities as there are no commercial fishings in the district. There is no regular stocking with young fish, but a few years ago 12,000 salmon parr were released into the river.

Fishing on the river is let by the day through the estate and permits can be obtained from Mrs Bley, West Lodge, Kinlochmoidart.

The Shiel

The Shiel catchment, like the Morar further north, consists of a large deep loch drained by a short river.

Loch Shiel is probably one of the narrowest lochs in Scotland for its length ($17\frac{1}{2}$ miles), the mean width being less than half a mile. The top end of the loch is extremely deep, in places over 400 feet, but towards the bottom end it is much shallower. Except for a few small areas such as Polloch Bay and Lady Bay, the loch is of little value for salmon fishing although some salmon are caught by trolling. It is, however, still popular with sea trout anglers who 'fish the dap' with daddy-longlegs or conventional artificial flies during the summer months.

The loch is fed by a number of rivers. Amongst the most important, at the head of the loch near Glenfinnan, are the Callop River and the River Finnan which enter from the south east and north respectively. The Prince Charles Monument, in memory of the raising of Bonnie Prince Charlie's standard at Glenfinnan in 1745, lies between the mouths of these two rivers. The other major river, feeding the loch from the south at Polloch, is the Hurich, or, as it is sometimes called, the Doilet, because it passes through Loch Doilet, which is a good sea trout loch at times. The Doilet has fine spawning grounds but much of the Callop tends to be too sluggish to be of much value for spawning fish. The bed of the Finnan is to a large extent unstable for good spawning although there are some good areas.

The River Shiel flows out of Loch Shiel on its 3-mile course to discharge its waters in the southern arm of Loch Moidart, the sea loch into which the Moidart also flows. The Shiel drops only 23 feet between the loch and the sea and is a wide, slow-flowing river and for this reason has very little torrential water in its entire length. The only rough piece of water is the Sea Pool, when the tide is out. The bed of the river consists mainly of fine sand, mud and small gravel, and most of the holding pools lack any rocks or holding lies. It is said that most of the larger stones were removed from the bed of the river in the olden days in order to make it easier to net the pools — in those days the Shiel was evidently netted very heavily. Another interesting peculiarity of the Shiel is that it has very little camber on its entire length and because of its width this means it lacks, for the main part, fast-flowing runs to the heads of pools. It relies, therefore, on either high water conditions or a good breeze of wind to ruffle the surface of the still pools to make these pools fishable. In many cases deposits of gravel and sand have been formed into heaps throughout the width of some of the quieter sections, and these tend to throw the current in numerous directions preventing the formation of any clearly defined pools. Weed growth at certain times of the year is also very heavy in some parts of the river and seriously impairs the angling potential of some pools.

The River Shiel forms part of the boundary between the counties of Inverness and Argyll. As it flows out of the loch it runs quietly at first over a sandy gravelly section containing one or two useful pools which fish best late in the season; then, a short distance after passing under the new road bridge, there is a section of river which is more gorgy in nature, with deep holding pools and rock outcrops on either bank. In this section are the Boat Pool, Gullet, Ledges, Parapet, House Stage and Grassy Point all of which are very useful taking places under the right conditions. After leaving this gorgy section the river continues its gradual descent through meadowland, flowing at times parallel to the roads which are on either side of the river, until it finally reaches the sea. The best pools in this section are the Cliff, Garrison and Captain's, and, just above its mouth, the Sea Pool.

In recent years attempts have been made to improve certain sections of the river by the use of groynes to concentrate and straighten out the crooked flow of the river caused by gravel deposits. In some places this has been successful and a pool called the Road Pool, which once had a good reputation but became filled in over the years, is again producing fish. There is little doubt that, with careful use of groynes and the introduction of holding lies, certain parts of this river could be vastly improved.

No significant runs of salmon occur in the Shiel until June although at one time there used to be a small run of early fish, some of which were heavier than the normal summer run. This run seems to have died out in recent years. From June to the end of September there are good runs of salmon and grilse in the Shiel, and whereas most of the early fish run straight through into the loch the later runs tend to stay in the river itself.

The River Shiel was also famed for its sea trout but in recent years the strength of these runs and the size of the sea trout have shown a marked decline (which is the usual trend in most of our Scottish rivers). It would appear that most of the sea trout now running the Shiel pass quickly through the river and more seem to be caught on the loch.

Seals can occasionally be a problem on the Shiel and the deep slow-flowing nature of the river allows them to reach the loch up which they range for many miles.

The fishing on the north bank of the river is owned by Dorlin Estate and on the south bank by a syndicate. The fishing on the north bank is leased at certain times of the year.

Throughout the length of the Shiel there are many useful spawning and feeding areas which can accommodate a large stock of salmon. In some cases the weed growth which causes problems in the angling pools serves a useful purpose on the feeding areas, because it not only provides useful cover and protection for the young fish when they are pursued by predators, but also acts as a form of food production for the feeding fry and parr.

It is also quite probable that the peculiar mounds of sand, gravel and silt which are so evident in large sections of the river, have formed originally on old salmon redds.

The Aline and Rannoch

The Aline and Rannoch rivers lie in superb country on the south side of the Morvern peninsula. The River Aline is about 3 miles long between Loch Arienas, from which it flows, and Loch Aline, a sea loch, into which it discharges. Two of its major tributaries join the river below Acharn, a short distance below Loch Arienas, and they flow through Gleann Dubh, the Black Glen and Gleann Geal, the White Glen. In the upper reaches of these glens the rivers meander almost into a water meadow, while nearer the foot both rivers flow through gorges in which are waterfalls which in the past have proved almost complete barriers to migratory fish. Below the two gorges the rivers converge at Acharn and the river then joins the River Aline about 100 yards below the point at which the River Aline flows out of Loch Arienas. When the waters in either the Black Glen or the White Glen or both flood, and the flood reaches a certain level, the water, instead of turning left down the River Aline, turns right up the River Aline and back into Loch Arienas. The Black Glen and White Glen, under these conditions, fill up Loch Arienas which then keeps the River Aline in a moderate flood for a much longer time.

Since the early 1960s, the eggs and fry of salmon and sea trout have been planted above the waterfalls in the White Glen, and in 1969 Ardtornish Estate erected a concrete dam on the pool below the falls, thereby reducing the height by about 6 feet. Since that date there has been a good run of fish right up the Glen. In 1974 a similar dam was built, this time with gabions and stones, on the pool below the waterfall in the Black Glen and the results, although not so good, have been perfectly satisfactory.

The Aline is divided into 3 beats and fishes well from June onwards.

The other river to run into the head of Loch Aline is the Rannoch River, which flows in from the east. This is a small river rising about 5 miles from the sea. About half a mile from the sea it flows through a gorge with steep waterfalls which no salmon or sea trout can pass. There is a very small run of salmon and sea trout up as far as the waterfalls. Some of the sea trout weigh up to about 6 lb, but the majority are finnock and are taken in the tidal stretches.

SALMON RIVERS OF SCOTLAND

The fishing on the Aline and the Rannoch is owned by Ardtornish Estate and is let to visitors renting their holiday cottages. In recent years the fishing has declined slightly, particularly the sea trout fishing. This is most apparent on Loch Arienas which used to be a superb sea trout loch but in recent seasons relatively few have been taken.

The fishing returns for the Black Glen, White Glen, River Aline, Loch Arienas and the Rannoch River are given below.

Table 18

Catches of salmon and sea trout on Ardtornish Estate, 1968–77

	salmon	sea trout		salmon	sea trout
1968	13	221	1973	50	350
1969	59	290	1974	43	414
1970	54	366	1975	32	177
1971	29	248	1976	17	230
1972	27	269	1977	18	111

At the mouth of Loch Aline there is a sand mine which extracts about 200,000 tons of sand per year, most of which is shipped out by sea. It is unlikely that this could cause a significant disturbance to the fishing.

32

THE LOCHY DISTRICT

The Lochy district is an extremely interesting one in that it contains two separate river systems, the Lochy and Spean, which join a few miles from Fort William at the head of Loch Linnhe, the united river being called the Lochy.

The River Lochy flows out of Loch Lochy, the western of the 3 lochs making up the Caledonian Canal along the Great Fault which cuts through Scotland. Loch Lochy extends north-east as far as Loch Oich, being separated from it by lock gates on the Caledonian Canal at Laggan and the Oich is in turn separated from Loch Ness by short stretches of river and canal running from Aberchalder House to Fort Augustus.

Into the lower end of Loch Lochy drain the waters of Loch Arkaig via the short little River Arkaig. The outflow from Loch Lochy is dammed by Mucomir Power Station and barrage on the site of the old falls, so that the flow down the river is controlled. An alternative but unwelcome outflow from the loch is controlled by the canal gates at Gairlochy.

On the eastern side of the River Lochy the rocky River Spean flows down 800 feet from Badenoch and enters the main valley of the Lochy after gathering in the waters of the Roy and the Cour. As Calderwood points out 'there is no other district in Scotland where rivers unite at such abrupt angles from such diverse directions, and in no district, except perhaps in that of the Findhorn, have we such an example of prolonged and deep rock erosion as is to be seen in the course of the Spean.' Certainly the physical features of the Spean remind one of the upper and middle reaches of the Findhorn in miniature, but that is as far as the similarity goes because since the 1920s the position on the Spean has been a tale of woe as its upper reaches and tributaries have been steadily and severely tapped by the British Aluminium Company in Fort William.

The Lochy

The Lochy is the counterpart of the Ness at the other end of the Caledonian Canal, as Loch Linnhe is the counterpart of the Inverness Firth. The Lochy is an open river with fine beds of gravel. Although it is tree-lined along most of its length, casting is not hindered as there are wide-open stony shores. A few of the pools are large and are better fished from a boat. The scenery is magnificent

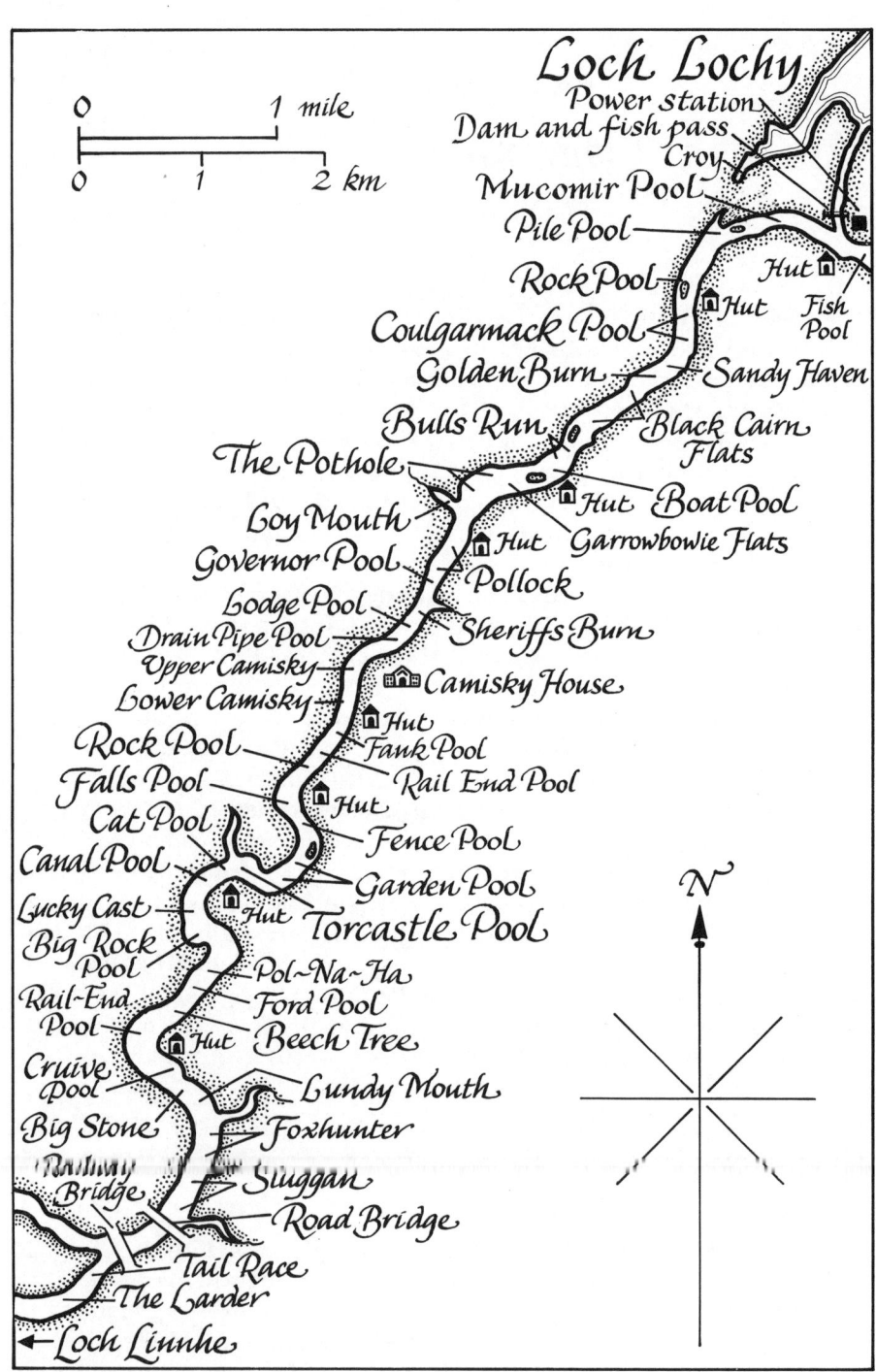

Salmon Pools on the River Lochy

with Ben Nevis to the south making a spectacular backcloth, particularly to the Loy Mouth Pool.

The river is 9 miles long and is managed by the River Lochy Association, their present manager being Vice-Admiral Sir Hugh Mackenzie, who was Director of the Atlantic Salmon Research Trust for 10 years. The river is divided into a number of beats which are let through the River Lochy Association. The beats are as follows: Beat 1 – Croy Pool to Black Cairn Flats; Beat 2 – Bull's Run to Camisky House; Beat 3 – Camisky House to Torcastle; Beat 4 – Torcastle to Lundy Mouth. Fishing on these beats is by fly only after the third week in June. The deep Mucomir Pool, at the confluence with the Spean, is a separate seasonal let.

Below the Lundy Burn there is a stretch called the Sluggan, which is let to the Inverlochy Angling Club and the Fort William Angling Association. A further stretch between the road bridge and the railway bridge is let to the West End Hotel in Fort William. The river between the railway bridge and the sea is known as the Town Water for which daily tickets are available from the Rod and Gun Shop in Fort William; the permit prices vary from month to month. The tailrace from the British Aluminium Company enters the river on the left bank just below the railway bridge and many anglers congregate at this point as often the flow of water from the outfall is considerably greater than that coming down the river.

Although some fish enter the Lochy in April and May the main run is late June–early August. This is different to the situation at the beginning of the century, when Calderwood referred to spring fish congregating in Mucomir Pool: this occurred because when the new water-course for the upper part of the Lochy was cut the Canal Commissioners were allowed to create the Mucomir Fall, and hence the spring fish waited at the fall. They also refused to continue up the Spean as the water temperature was lower than that in Loch Lochy.

There is also a good sea trout run in the Lochy and this can be seen from the counts of fish at the Borland Pass at Mucomir Power Station.

Table 19

Counts of salmon, grilse and sea trout at Mucomir Power Station, 1963–1979

	salmon and grilse	sea trout		salmon and grilse	sea trout
1963	951	2,652	1972	652	2,121
1964	621	4,179	1973	601	2,616
1965	959	1,538	1974	444	2,773
1966	576	4,354	1975	455	2,411
1967	553	3,563	1976	463	1,889
1968	286	1,986	1977	262	1,299
1969	676	1,505	1978	231	804
1970	550	2,143	1979	184	1,088
1971	615	1,217			

The commercial netting rights are owned by the River Lochy Association but are not exercised. However, there is one net and coble fishery at the head of Loch Eil and one bag net station at Corran.

The River Lochy Association has a small hatchery at Camisky capable of holding 300,000 ova and the resulting fry are planted out in the major tributaries and the main river.

The Spean

Up to the early 1920s the Spean had a free run to the Lochy from Loch Laggan and was plentifully supplied with water from this loch and Loch Treig which comes in from the south at Tulloch Station. It received more water from the Roy and the Cour before reaching Spean Bridge and greatly helped to swell the flow down the Lochy. Salmon could ascend the Spean as far as the 23-feet-high Monessie Falls but could go no further, which was most unfortunate as miles of suitable spawning and nursery ground was available above.

However, in the 1920s the crunch came; Loch Laggan was dammed and its water was piped through the hills to the British Aluminium Company in Fort William. The first abstraction was followed by the damming of Loch Treig and the tapping of its tributaries by aqueducts. Furthermore, no compensation flow was passed downstream from Loch Treig. The Spean was now, if not ruined, certainly deprived of its former glory and relied on spates down the Roy to provide a reasonable flow. In fact it is now believed that nearly all the fish ascending are Roy fish, and the big fish that are occasionally caught in the Lochy and Spean (one of 37 lb was caught in the Spean in 1976) are likely to have originated in the Roy. Some fish continue to run up the Cour.

Above Spean Bridge the fishing is owned by the British Aluminium Company and leased to the River Lochy Association. This Association lets the right bank from Roy Bridge to Spean Bridge to the British Aluminium Angling Club and the left bank to the Caol Angling Club and to day ticket holders who can obtain permits from the Rod and Gun Shop in Fort William. The fishing below Spean Bridge is let to the Spean Bridge Angling Club, the Spean Bridge Hotel and the Pulp Mill Angling Club. Fishing is by fly and spinning.

The Roy

The Roy is a natural spate river which, through having no loch on its course, relies on rainfall. It is a rocky river with small but deep holding pools. It has not been touched by man and is a useful little river from late June onwards, and some large fish ascend it.

The river is owned by a partnership of three, including the River Lochy

THE LOCHY DISTRICT

Association and the owner of Braeroy. Fishing is arranged through Braeroy and is let to long-established tenants. Due to the nature of the pools worming is the most frequently used method of fishing.

The Arkaig

The Arkaig is a short river flowing from Loch Arkaig to Loch Lochy. Its flow is kept up pretty well and fish ascend the river from late June onwards. The spawning grounds are at the top of the River Arkaig and above Loch Arkaig in the wild glens of Dessarry and Pean where the commandos did some of their training during the last war.

Pike occur in both Loch Arkaig and Loch Lochy and are netted in the winter months between Loch Arkaig outflow and Mucomir.

The fishing on the Arkaig is owned by Colonel Sir Donald Cameron of Lochiel.

The Loy

The Loy is a small spate river which runs into the Lochy from the north-west. It serves as a water supply to Fort William and has a dam, with a fish pass, across its course. A few salmon and sea trout run it and the fishing is let to Caol Angling Club. It contains good spawning grounds in its upper reaches.

The Nevis

The River Nevis is not strictly a tributary of the Lochy, as it flows directly into Loch Linnhe just east of Fort William close to the mouth of the Lochy. It is a spate river and has a spectacular run down Glen Nevis to the sea, through impressive mountainous country over which towers the Ben Nevis massif.

The fishing is let to the Fort William Angling Association and the fish run this river at about the same time as the Lochy; it is perhaps more of a sea trout river than a salmon river but it is stocked from time to time by the River Lochy Association and by the tenants.

The Leven of Kinlochleven

The Leven rises as the Black Water in the hills of Corrour Forest. However, much of its course is now taken up by the large Blackwater Reservoir, which was formed to supply water to the British Aluminium Company's factory at Kinlochleven. Below the reservoir the river runs for about 5 miles before entering the salt water of Loch Leven at Kinlochleven. Falls about a mile upstream from the river mouth, known as Dan Mackay's Falls, prevent the further upstream ascent of salmon and sea trout. These are sheer falls with a height of about 20 feet, and the cost of making them passable would be too great to make it worthwhile. Because of the torrential nature of the river, its course does tend to change over time but at present it seems to be stable.

A few salmon enter the river in the spring, but the main run is in September. Unfortunately due to the effects of reservoir impoundment, river poaching and sea netting, the salmon runs are nothing like the size of those of 30 years ago, and the days of good catches, as described by Grimble, are things of the past. It is now a rare event for more than three salmon to be caught in a week. Although UDN did occur in 1976, this disease cannot be blamed for the present low numbers. The fishing pools still exist and if the dedicated Kinlochleven Angling Club, which has the fishing, had the money to undertake stocking and police the water, then the Leven could once more attain its former glory. Permits to fish the Leven can be obtained at a very reasonable price from the Angling Club in Kinlochleven.

33

THE ORCHY, AWE, ETIVE, KINGLASS, COE, EUCHAR, NELL, AND OUDE

The Orchy

The Orchy is a wild river flowing through magnificent mountainous country. The river starts from the outfall of Loch Tulla, a picturesque loch with wide sandy shores and isolated stands of old scots pine. On its north shore are Forest Lodge and Black Mount and on the south stands the peaceful old Inveroran Hotel. The loch receives its water from two directions. In the east it collects water from the Water of Tulla which drains the large hills in the Grampian Mountain range, Beinn a' Chreachain (3,540 feet), Beinn Achaladair (3,404 feet) and Meall Buidhe; to the west it gets its water principally from Allt Tolaghan and Allt Dochard which flow through the Black Mount Forest. The latter stream, which is a good spawning area, runs through little Loch Dochard and is larger than the Tulla Water. Its tributaries drain the steep hillsides of Stob Ghabhar (3,565 feet) and Beinn Suidhe. In the early part of the century Loch Tulla was an excellent trout loch, but with the appearance of pike and perch the quality of the trout declined even though the pike are netted regularly by Black Mount Estate.

Immediately below the loch the Orchy flows through flat exposed heathland until, a short distance below Bridge of Orchy, its gradient increases and it tumbles from gravelly pool to gravelly pool over areas of flat bedrock and a series of rocky falls and gorges. The B8074 road follows the river practically the whole way through Glen Orchy until it joins the A85 at the River Lochy confluence. Below the Lochy junction the Orchy starts to widen out and below Dalmally gravel banks and islands occur in mid-stream and the pools are larger and fewer and less well defined. The river then flows into the east end of Loch Awe near the peninsula on which stands the Castle of Kilchurn which was occupied by the Breadalbane family till 1740.

The Orchy is divided into a number of beats. The uppermost beat is owned by Black Mount Estate and extends downstream from Loch Tulla to just above the Junction Pool where the Allt Kinglass joins the main river. The Kinglass itself used to be a useful little salmon river but since the water in its upper reaches has been tapped and transferred by aqueduct to Loch Lyon as part of the Breadalbane hydro-electric scheme it has no longer been seriously fished. This

Kinglass (Allt Chonoghlais on some maps) must not be confused with the Kinglass which flows into Loch Etive to the west of Loch Tulla.

The next beat belongs to the Lord Trevor of Auch Estate and extends from the Junction Pool to the Shepherd's Pool at Invergounan. The beat has a number of useful pools including the Upper and Lower Otter, the Short Cast, the Fank and the Worm Hole. This beat is let on a weekly basis.

Below Invergounan comes the Inveroran Hotel water, which extends as far as the Upper Boat Pool. The fishing is available to hotel residents. A most useful pool on this beat is the Upper Falls.

The Craig Estate Fishings start at the Lower Boat Pool and extend downstream to the Little Colonel's Pool. They include the Dewar, Woodpecker and White Rock pools.

These four upper beats tend to fish from mid-June onwards, depending on the availability of water and water temperature. Generally, however, they are late summer and autumn beats.

After Craig Estate comes another private beat owning both banks from the Little Colonel's Pool to Catnish (sometimes referred to as Sam's Box). This is a good beat from the middle of May and has some delightful pools to keep the angler occupied, including the Witches or Bewitched, General's Rock, Gauge, Yellow Flag and Oak Rock. The first salmon of the season are always taken at the Pulpit and Gut of the Iron Bridge Falls.

The Dalmally Hotel fishings start on the left (south) bank at Catnish and extend downstream to the Railway Bridge. This is a very useful beat with 25 named pools. The most famous pool is Black Duncan and it was here in April 1961 that Mr Chris McLauchlan took a 35 lb fish on a brown and gold devon. The fishing is open to the public and day tickets at £6 per rod can be obtained from Mr Alan Church of Croggan Crafts, Dalmally. There is no limit to the number of rods fishing on any day, so that during the best part of the season, from June onwards, the angler may find himself with company when fishing conditions are right.

On the right (north) bank the Craig Lodge beat is from Catnish to old Dalmally Bridge. The pools in this stretch include Black Duncan, Jubilee, Succoth, Lochy and Craig.

The last beat on the river is owned by Tattersfield Estates and extends on the right bank from the old Dalmally Bridge to the junction with the Strae. This beat is open to let.

The Orchy was at one time an early river, in fact much earlier than the Awe, and started to fish in April and May; however, since the barrage was built across the Awe by the North of Scotland Hydro-electric Board the fishing tends not to start until May, and even this depends on how many fish have passed through the barrage. As a consequence the Awe anglers tend to catch more Orchy fish than before. In addition, the Orchy has tended to become very flashy and this is attributed to drainage operations by the Forestry Commission. The river was also noted for big fish, and two large mounted specimens are to be seen in the public bar of the Dalmally Hotel, one of which weighed 37 lb and was caught on 27 March 1935, and the other 42 lb, caught on 13 October 1923.

There are few sea trout in the Orchy, the majority moving up the River Strae and into the Mhoille Burn.

Few fish enter the River Lochy as falls about a mile upstream prevent further access.

Some stocking of the upper reaches and tributaries of the river with fry is carried out from time to time by the Awe District Salmon Fishery Board.

The Awe

Until the early 1960s the Awe used to start its turbulent course from Loch Awe through the narrows of the forbidding Pass of Brander and storm down its 3 miles to the salt water of Loch Etive in a series of turbulent rocky runs and pools of strong-running water; but since that time the Awe has become a shadow of its former self owing to the erection of a 59-foot-high concrete barrage across the river below a former pool known as the Shallows. The Awe was always renowned for its large salmon which were a constant challenge to the skills of the angler fishing this turbulent water, from the moment of striving to present the fly to the fish in such turbulent water to eventually landing a fish weighing well into double figures. Three fish of particular note caught in 'the good old days' were one of 57 lb (caught by Mr A. W. Huntington in Castledhu Pool on 26 July 1921); one of 55 lb (taken by Mrs G. B. Huntington from the Erract Pool on 19 September 1927) and one of 51 lb (caught by Mrs G. B. Huntington in the Stepping Stones on 22 May 1930). The fish of 57 lb was only 7 lb off the weight of the British record rod-caught salmon taken some years ago on the Tay by Miss Ballantine. Although heavy fish of 30 lb or so are still caught occasionally, none of the very heavy brigade are ever seen now.

However, there have been some benefits to the Awe as well. Prior to hydro-electric development the river did not start to fish until June owing to the early fish passing straight through on their way to the Orchy, but now the Awe starts to fish in early April and May as fish are held up to some extent at the barrage. The best fishing period on the Awe now is from May to July, with fish being caught as early as April and as late as August and September. One says 'as late as August and September' with some feeling, as many Awe proprietors would like to see the angling season closed earlier than the present official closing date of 15 October, which late date allows the anglers in the upper Orchy to catch and keep gravid fish just about to spawn. However, at present the fishing on the Awe is closed, by agreement of the proprietors, on 30 September.

There are now very few sea trout and any taken are caught either at the mouth of the river or in the Stepping Stones Pool in the middle reaches of the river.

Although there are a number of fishing proprietors on the Awe, including the North of Scotland Hydro-electric Board, the fishing is all syndicated and the river is divided into 7 beats. From the barrage to Inverawe they are: Beat 1 – Barrage to the burn at Nether Lorn Hotel – right (north) bank; Beat 2 – Barrage to Oak Pool – left (south) bank, and Shepherd's to Oak Pool – right bank; Beat 3 – Cassan Dhu to Big Otter – left bank; Beat 4 – Cassan Dhu to Long Pool – right bank; Beat 5 – Red Brae to Gray – left bank; Beat 6 – Little Otter to Gray – right bank; Beat 7 – Gean Tree to Power Station at Inverawe – both banks. Fishing on all beats is by fly only.

The netting rights in the river and on Loch Etive are now no longer exercised.

There are agreed compensation flows from the barrage, and the size of these varies with the season of the year and the height of Loch Awe. In dry years when the loch is low it has been known for the flow to be reduced in July to winter compensation flow. Freshet flows from the barrage are usually released on Sundays. The purpose of the barrage is to divert water from Loch Awe down a tunnel to generate electricity at the Inverawe Power Station. Some idea of the size of the runs through the barrage is given in the table below.

Table 20
Annual counts of salmon and grilse ascending the Awe Barrage, 1964–1979

1964	5,070	1970	2,942	1976	4,389
1965	3,831	1971	4,488	1977	2,867
1966	3,117	1972	3,631	1978	2,204
1967	4,471	1973	3,700	1979	3,102
1968	3,619	1974	3,528		
1969	3,719	1975	2,599		

In Loch Awe itself there is some trolling for salmon, but most of the fishing on the loch is for trout, and large specimens of *ferox* trout are taken. The largest 'trout' recorded was one of $39\frac{1}{2}$ lb, but this record has now been rejected as it is thought to have been a salmon. However, trout weighing in the double figures can be caught. Pike and perch are also present in the loch.

There are two other hydro schemes centred on Loch Awe and these are the Cruachan and Nant schemes. Cruachan is a reversible pumped storage development which uses energy from steam generating stations at times when the system load is low to pump water from Loch Awe to a high level reservoir on Ben Cruachan. Pumping is carried out mostly at night and at weekends. The water stored in the high level reservoir is then used to generate electricity to meet daytime peak loads on the Scottish supply system. Because the surface area of Loch Awe is 15 square miles the operation of the power station has little effect on the water levels.

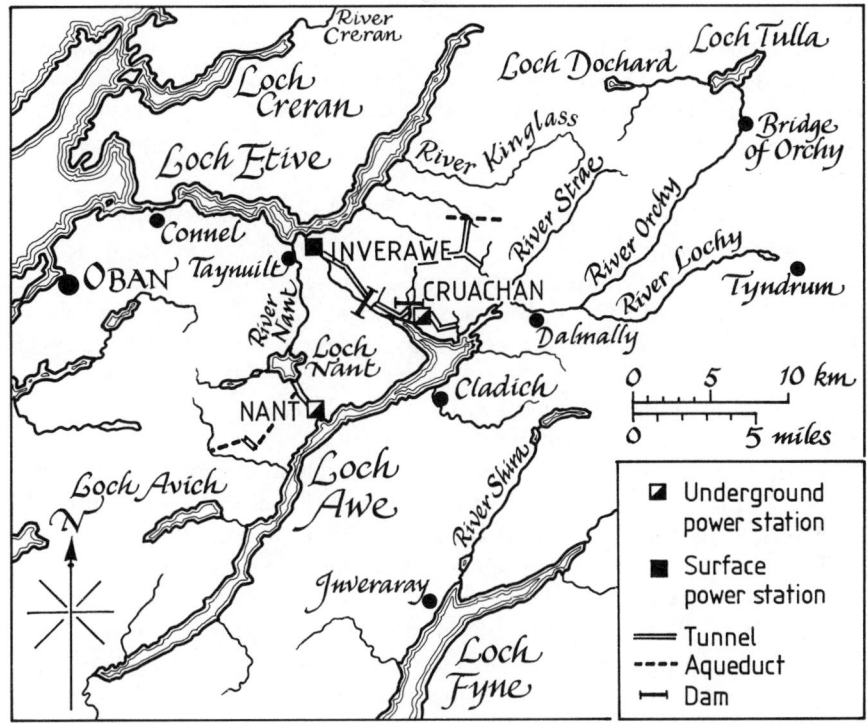

The Rivers Awe and Orchy and the Awe Hydro-electric Scheme

The Nant scheme is a separate self-contained development. Loch Nant is dammed and a system of aqueducts collects water from other streams to supplement the natural flow to Loch Nant. The water from the loch is then fed to an underground power station which discharges into Loch Awe. The River Nant, which flows into Loch Etive in Airds Bay a short distance west of the Awe, therefore has a reduced flow which is supplemented by compensation water during dry periods.

A small river which runs into the long western arm of the loch is the Avich. It drains out of Loch Avich, which collects water from a large catchment to its north which includes Loch Scammadale and Allt Braglenmore. Falls between Loch Avich and Loch Awe have recently been blasted by the Forestry Commission with a view to getting salmon up to Loch Avich. Owing to the nature of the falls it is not yet known whether or not this has been successful. However, the Commission has planted salmon fry in the feeder streams leading into Loch Avich to help increase the number of fish coming to the falls.

Further conservation work is carried out by the Awe District Fishery Board and a salmon hatchery which can accommodate a million eggs has been provided by the North of Scotland Hydro-electric Board near Inverawe House. The adult fish are trapped in the lift at the barrage after 15 October and held in ponds near the hatchery until they are ready to be stripped of their eggs. The fry are later distributed to the various tributaries of the Awe and Orchy.

Unfortunately UDN has been rife in the Awe and Orchy for the last 10 years, and in low water diseased fish are easily seen.

The Creran

The Creran is a short, fast-flowing river which drains an area of Appin between Ballachulish and the Dalness Forest. After a course of about 6 miles it is joined by the Ure, a small river with good spawning and feeding areas and a short distance downstream from this confluence the Creran enters Loch Fasnacloich. It then flows a further 2 miles from the foot of the loch before entering the salt water of Loch Creran, about 20 miles north of Oban.

Loch Fasnacloich is now becoming silted up and requires the regular dredging it used to receive many years ago. Upstream on Allt Eilidh, a tributary of the Creran, there used to be two artificial lochs which provided freshets for the river when required. The dams on both these lochs were breached by floods some years ago and have never been replaced.

There are many good holding pools for salmon and sea trout upstream from Loch Fasnacloich but the banks are lined with dense growths of alder and oak which make casting difficult and as a result worm fishing has to be resorted to. However, with judicious tree felling many of the pools could be fished effectively with fly.

The Ure has few good holding pools and is mainly a spawning tributary. It has a large catchment and is fed by lochs lying on either side of An Grianan. At the lower end of Glen Ure stands Glenure Lodge which Robert Louis Stevenson used in *Kidnapped* as the home of the Red Fox (Colin Roy Campbell of Glenure).

With good management the stocks of salmon and sea trout could be substantially improved. The Estate of Glencreran has recently changed hands and the new proprietors plan to improve the fishing in co-operation with the two other riparian owners. The availability of fishing will depend on the success of the improvement schemes and enquiries regarding the fishing should be made to the West Highlands Estates Office in Oban in the first instance.

The Etive

This little spate river flows through some of the most mountainous country in Scotland. It rises up in the Black Corries on Rannoch Moor and after flowing gently past Kingshouse Hotel it tumbles down Glen Etive through the Royal Forest in a series of deep pools and high falls, with the steep southerly slopes of The Shepherds — Buchaille Etive Mor (3,345 feet) and Buchaille Etive Beag

(3,029 feet)— and Beinn Maol Chaluim coming down to the river's right bank and those of the Black Mount range sloping down on the left side. After passing Dalness, Invercharnan and Glenceitlein it reaches the head of Loch Etive and the sea at Gualachulain. It is not surprising that the river bed is so unstable, and if one takes a moment to look up at the steep slopes of The Shepherds, where the streams cascade down, one can see large mounds of gravel washed down and piled up near the bridges along the Glen Etive road. It is the turbulence occurring in the Etive which results in such severe washouts of the spawning redds in the river and the Lairig Gartain burn and, as the Dalness Falls are insurmountable to the salmon and sea trout, there are consequently no good spawning and nursery areas accessible to the fish. If ever the Dalness Falls were opened up there would be good spawning and nursery grounds available in the Kingshouse area.

Below Dalness Falls the left bank of the river for 3 miles to below Glenceitlein is owned by the Dalness Trust, and thereafter Black Mount Estate. The right bank of the river downstream from Dalness is owned for a quarter of a mile by the Dalness Trust, and from then to the sea by the Black Mount and Glenetive estates. There are 25 named pools in the river between Dalness and the sea and these are divided into 3 beats. The most well-known pools are the Home and the Wall on the top beat, the Luncheon and the Graveyard on the middle beat and the Big, the Fence and the Master's on the bottom beat.

The fish run from late May to early October but there are few fish before the end of June or early July. There is generally a fresh run in late September or early October. The annual catch is of the order of 40–100 salmon and 20–40 sea trout. There is no public fishing nor is there any commercial netting.

There has been some incidence of UDN in the last 4 years and it is felt locally that this is the reason for the absence of fish in the lower pools. Other serious forms of mortality in recent years have been the increase in poaching by skin divers, who not only kill many fish but severely wound others, and hang netting in Loch Etive.

Some efforts have been made to keep up the stocks of migratory fish in this river and a hatchery was operated by Glenetive Estate until the mid-1930s. In the last 10 years Dalness Estate have done it in a small way. Salmon and sea trout fry were stocked in 1950–1957 and, more recently, in 1976.

One of the previous proprietors of the Etive constructed a small loch on the right bank of the river and only a short distance from it. He also built a pass between the loch and the river to allow fish to enter the loch. Sea trout used to run up into the loch and spawn in the streams running into it, but at the moment the main water supply to the loch, which is piped from a neighbouring burn, has failed and the pass has fallen into disrepair.

It is to be hoped that in the future some way will be found of opening up the Dalness Falls and increasing the production of the Etive and, at the same time, increasing the fines from the present derisory ones at present imposed on poachers.

SALMON RIVERS OF SCOTLAND

The Kinglass

The River Kinglass rises in the mountains of Glen Kinglass Deer Forest and its source is in Corrie-na-cain between Beinn nan Aighenan and Glas Bheinn Mhor. As it winds through the floor of this corrie it is joined by a tributary called the Double Bridges Burn and then flows over steep falls in a narrow gorge. It then levels out again for a distance of approximately 2 miles and descends a series of formidable falls consisting of wide slabs of smooth rock. A short distance below these falls it passes under the road bridge leading to Glenkinglass Lodge situated on the left bank of the river.

The river continues its journey down Glen Kinglass for a further 7 miles before flowing into Loch Etive close to the Ardmaddy keeper's house. On its journey down the glen below Glenkinglass Lodge the river flows over gravelly flats with only an occasional holding pool. It then cascades over some small falls into the Dyke Pools. There are no pools for the next three-quarters of a mile but then the river flattens out and runs through a section with a number of good fishing pools amongst the best known of which are the Acharn, Long Run, Ford, Poultoch, Narrachan Rock and the Maiden, which is probably the best known pool on the river. Below the Maiden Pool there are some places where one can catch fish, but from there to Ardmaddy, where a bridge crosses the river, the bed of the river is liable to change. It meanders through a wide gravelly flat, straightening out as it approaches the bridge and then running in a straight line into the sea loch.

The streams entering the river below the lodge are, on the whole, very steep and torrential and many of them are unstable and thus unsuitable for spawning.

The falls just upstream from Glenkinglass Lodge are too formidable for migratory fish to ascend and so the main spawning and feeding potential of the river is almost entirely confined to the main river below the falls and, to a very limited extent, to the bottom sections of one or two burns, particularly Allt Hallater in which a few fish are seen at spawning time.

Fish stocks in the river are fairly limited, and this is probably due to the small amount of good spawning gravel and feeding areas in the section of the river which is accessible to migratory fish. But there is little doubt these could be vastly improved if the feeding and spawning areas at the head of the river were opened up. As the falls are too formidable to ease and thus allow access, the only course open to improve the stock is to plant out fry annually in the headwaters.

At the present time the angling season is confined to July–October and depends entirely on spate conditions to allow fish to enter the river. There is little doubt that in dry seasons the seals that frequent Loch Etive decimate the stocks of salmon and sea trout which congregate at the mouth of the river waiting to enter.

In recent years 10–20 salmon and 20–50 good seatrout are caught on the river annually, but the size of the rod catch entirely depends on water conditions and fishing effort. The water in this river is gin clear and its clarity is exaggerated by the pale straw colour of the gravel and rocks on the river bed.

There is little doubt that the stocks of fish destined for the Kinglass have also been reduced by the recent escalation of illegal hang netting for salmon off the west coast of Scotland, and there is evidence that this also takes place in Loch Etive itself.

City-dwelling anglers should be warned of the remoteness of this river which can only be reached overland after a long and arduous journey by landrover.

The Coe

The Coe starts as a mountain stream rising in the northern slopes of the Buchaille Etive in the Dalness Forest and after a run of 5 miles through the Pass of Glencoe enters little Loch Achtriochtan, 230 feet above sea-level. From the foot of this loch to Invercoe, where the river flows into the salt water of Loch Leven to the east of Ballachulish, there is a further run of 3 miles. Until the 1930s the ascent of salmon to Loch Achtriochtan and the upper Coe was barred by a sheer fall of some 12 feet, but these were opened up when the engineers making a larger road through Glencoe built a fish pass in the falls. Since this time salmon have been able to reach Loch Achtriochtan and the upper Coe, and their main spawning grounds are situated at the outfall of the loch and in the small tributaries above.

Salmon and grilse ascend the falls in late June providing there is enough water. Many of the fish remain in the loch until spawning time. A few sea trout also ascend as far as the loch. Some very good runs of salmon and grilse have occurred in recent years.

The fishing on the upper reaches of the Coe and Loch Achtriochtan is owned by the National Trust for Scotland and permits can be obtained from the cottage by the loch. Most of the fishing rights on the lower Coe are in the hands of the Glencoe Angling Club, a private club which does not issue permits. There are also one or two other proprietors with fishing rights on the lower Coe.

There is no longer any commercial netting on the Coe.

The Euchar

The upper tributaries of the Euchar rise in the hills to the west of Loch Awe and drain into Loch Scammadale. Flowing from the loch the river, for the first 3 miles, hurries between banks of heather, bog myrtle, rushes and bracken. It then comes to a fall several feet in height, from which point it flows with increased speed until it enters the sea in Loch Feochan close to the little village of Kilninver. The falls are not a serious obstacle to migratory fish, except in times of drought.

Some of the spawning grounds in the upper reaches have been lost to salmon stocks. Two square miles of the upper Euchar system have been diverted by aqueduct to Loch Nant as part of the North of Scotland Hydro-electric Board's Awe and Cruachan scheme. Also a dam at the east end of Loch Scammadale, as part of a small private electricity generating scheme, prevents fish ascending to the old spawning grounds in Allt a' Coromaig in Bragleenbeg Glen. However, each year the proprietors stock the feeder streams of Loch Scammadale with sea trout fry and the whole river system with about 30,000 salmon eggs and fry.

Few salmon enter the river until June, although an occasional fish is taken in April and May, and the main run is in July and August. About 60 salmon, averaging 7 lb, and 150 sea trout are taken from the river each year. The main fishing proprietors are Kilninver, Raera and Scammadale. Fishing is available on a large part of the Euchar. Kilninver Estate lets the Barochreal stretch of 2 miles of single bank and half a mile of double bank fishing with one of its holiday houses; Barndromin Farm has one mile of fishing to let on three days a week; Lagganmore lets about a mile of double bank fishing, and Scammadale Estate also has fishing to let on the river and on Loch Scammadale. According to Grimble, writing in 1899, Scammadale is a cold dreary-looking loch about 2 miles long and half a mile wide. Many years ago it had a good reputation for sea trout fishing but this has deteriorated in recent years. Now 4 or 5 sea trout to a rod constitutes a good day.

The Nell or Feochan

The River Nell starts off above Loch Nell as the Lonan and flows through Glen Lonan in a series of gorges and passable falls. At the top end of the glen is a loch which at one time was impounded in order to produce artificial spates, but the dam burst in 1953 and has never been replaced. Below the loch are some good spawning fords but at the top end the area is marshy.

The outfall to Loch Nell is rather sluggish but after a short distance the Nell has a steady run to the sea, meandering through alluvial gravels with no rocky barriers to hinder the ascent of fish. There is one gravel pool which is excavated from time to time. However, there are only a few good pools between the loch and the main road bridge and these are only worth calling holding pools during time of flood. Most of the surrounding land is scrubby woodland but nearer the loch it opens out into arable fields. Below the main Oban to

Lochgilphead road the river is tidal and there are two or three sea pools where salmon lie before making a direct ascent to Loch Nell without settling in along the section of river between the bridge and the loch. The sea trout tend to spawn in the river below the loch.

The occasional large salmon of 10–14 lb enters the river in April, but the main run of fish is not until later. Sea trout are the first to arrive, in May and the first half of June, along with an occasional salmon, and the grilse start to enter after this, usually from the second or third week of July. There is also some evidence of a later autumn run. There has been a marked decline in the numbers of sea trout in recent years.

The little river Feochan Bheag also enters the sea at Loch Feochan, from the east. This is a very flashy spate river and inaccessible falls two miles upstream prevent the further ascent of migratory fish.

Water is abstracted from the Nell under the Loch Nell Water Order, 1969, and pumped to Loch Glenbhearrie, south of Oban, to supply the town. There are provisions for a minimum compensation flow of 4 million gallons per day at all times, but in 1976 and 1977 this flow was not provided and the river below the abstraction point was virtually dry for a long period and resulted in a high mortality of young fish. This lack of water would also have been detrimental to the river environment because of lack of dilution water for the effluent from the sewage treatment works at the new housing estate at Kilmore.

Commercial netting by net and coble is carried out on the south side of Loch Feochan and at the river mouth by Glen Feochan Estate. Other estates also have commercial fishing rights in other areas of Loch Feochan, such as the Kilbride netting station at Dunach on the north shore.

Most of the fishing on the Nell is owned by Glen Feochan Estate, although the Glebe has a small stretch. The major portion of the fishing of Loch Nell is owned by Glencruitten Estate which also has the middle section of the right bank of the Nell. Day tickets for Loch Nell can be obtained from the Oban and Lorne Angling Club, and fishing on the loch also goes with two holiday cottages owned by Glen Feochan Estate.

An interesting development on the tidal section of the Nell in recent years has been the trapping of elvers in May by a commercial company. The elvers are stored in water and ice and transported to the firm's factory to be reared in tanks supplied with warm water.

The Oude

The Oude has been developed by the North of Scotland Hydro-electric Board as part of the Kilmelfort scheme and the length of river now available to salmon is only 800 yards upstream of the tide. After that there is the

SALMON RIVERS OF SCOTLAND

Kilmelfort Power Station and the Oude headpond and dam.

This lower section of the river is owned by the Melfort Farming Company and the arrangements for the salmon and grilse which return between August and October is entirely artificial. The river is used as a breeding station. The fish are caught and stripped and between 30,000 and 40,000 unfed fry are planted out annually in the 800-yard stretch which has had 8 weirs built at intervals along its length.

There is no angling available and the river is only fished privately for a few days in the year. The commercial netting in Loch Melfort is owned by the Company.

34

THE KINTYRE DISTRICT

The Add

The River Add rises from a number of small streams in the hills behind Furnace on Loch Fyne and flows initially south-west. In its upper and middle reaches, down to about Lechuary, the river has a rapid and rocky course, dropping about 400 feet in about 4 miles. A major tributary, the Tunns, joins the Add a short distance above Craigans. At about 300 feet above sea level it turns north-west, and in about a mile and a half it passes out upon the northern point of the flattish moor or Moss of Crinan through which the Crinan Canal is cut. At Kilmichael Glassary the river is only 50 feet above sea level and has still 6 miles to go before reaching the sea at the western end of the Crinan Canal in Loch Crinan. Through this last stretch of flat country the river meanders in deeply-cut loops. The lower 2 miles of this stretch are tidal. If the river is high and there is a spring tide the river as far as Drimvore becomes one long flat. The main spawning areas are in the region of the confluence of the Add and the Tunns.

In 1955 the North of Scotland Hydro-electric Board started the Loch Glashan scheme which involved tapping of the headwaters of the whole Add catchment above Lechuary Glen, impounding of the upper part of the Tunns and diverting the waters of the Add and Tunns into an enlarged Loch Glashan. Water from Loch Glashan is passed to Loch Gair Power Station on the shores of Loch Gair, a small sea loch on the western shore of Loch Fyne to the north-east of Lochgilphead. The scheme was completed in 1961.

The river now exists with a compensation flow régime and relies very much on heavy rain to produce large spates which will provide the extra flow needed to produce good flow conditions for angling and the upstream movement of migratory fish. A fish pass has been installed in Leuchary Glen to facilitate the passage of fish under these reduced flow conditions.

The extensive afforestation by the Forestry Commission is also affecting the flow of the Add and the movement of gravel and silt in the river.

The Add is a late river for salmon and the main run of grilse is from late June or early July to the end of August. The larger salmon tend to enter in August. There are three beats on the river, the upper belonging to Minard Estate, the middle to Kirnan and the lower to Poltalloch. Poltalloch is the best beat on the river, although in some years Kirnan is almost as good, but the upper beats are not fished very hard. The lower point of the Poltalloch beat, around Dunadd and Dalnahasaig, is particularly good and holds a number of excellent pools including Hardy's, Reed, Wood, Bert Lard's, Poacher's Pot, and Horse Shoe. Gathorne-Hardy refers to this beat in his book *Autumns in Argyleshire with Rod and Gun* and mentions that it is only at 'first of flood' that sea trout rise for a short time while salmon stop rising as soon as the ground begins to be covered. As the tide floods, therefore, the angler has to proceed upstream fishing as he goes, casting upstream due to the reversed flow. Details of the salmon catches on the three beats from 1954 to 1962 are given below.

Table 21
Catches of salmon and grilse on the Add, 1954–1962

Year	Poltalloch	Kirnan	Minard	Total
1954	81	22	not rented	103
1955	264	55	not rented	319
1956	121	30	not rented	151
1957	198	44	3	245
1958	165	33	27	225
1959	42	26	16	84
1960	53	65	15	133
1961	63	90	7	160
1962	202	51	4	257

Poltalloch was the most heavily fished of the three beats at this time. Kirnan, the next beat up, was only fished in August and September, and hardly fished at all if there were plenty of snipe and black game around. Minard, the top beat, from the upper end of the Gorge above Lechuary, was hardly fished at all, due to the difficult approach, until the Forestry Commission and Hydro-electric Board built access roads.

The situation was obviously much better in the days of Grimble and he records that in the 19 years from 1857 to 1875, 480 salmon and 7321 grilse were taken by the rods, or an average of 28 salmon and 385 grilse each season. The two best years in this period were those of 1858 and 1862, the earlier one giving 992 grilse and 53 salmon, while the latter showed no less than 1154 grilse and 55 salmon.

Commercial sweep netting is carried out by Poltalloch Estate in the river downstream of Dalnahasaig. There are also netting rights in Loch Crinan, but these are not exercised.

The Barr

The little Barr Water flows through some of the loveliest sheep country in the

Mull of Kintyre and enters the sea on the west side of the peninsula 12 miles north of Campbeltown. The headwaters of this river, Allt Mor, Allt a' Bhlair and Abhainn a' Chnocain, rise 10 miles inland and the bulk of the catchment consists of moor, sheepwalk and peat bog at altitudes of up to 1,400 feet. From Arnicle Farm to the sea, a distance of about 5 miles, the river drops 200 feet as it flows through a narrow strip of arable land. Below the village of Glenbarr the river flows into a steep gorge to reappear at the Sea Pool. Throughout its length the river bed consists of small boulders, stones and gravel, and is ideal spawning and nursery ground.

There are three riparian owners on the Barr. The lowest three miles are owned by Glenbarr Estate, while upstream Amod and Arnicle farms share one mile of fishable river.

A unique feature of the river is the presence of so many man-made pools as a result of the construction of stone weirs. The history of these structures on the Barr goes back at least to the mid-nineteenth century, and the maintenance of these weirs was almost entirely due to the care of the keepers on the Glenbarr Estate. Stone weirs on the Arnicle fishings fell into disrepair after the 1920s when new owners took over the farm. Prior to 1925 these fishings and the farms of Arnicle and Ugadale were part of an historical gift by Robert the Bruce to the descendants of MacKay of Lefnastrath which passed to the Estate of MacNeal of Lossit during 600 years of continuous ownership by the family. However, new concrete dams, instead of the traditional stone weirs, were built at Arnicle by Mr MacArthur, the present owner, and have been in existence for up to 20 years and have required little maintenance. Mr MacArthur and his son Charles are to be commended on the way they have reclaimed the Arnicle fishings from a state of wilderness and dereliction which existed 30 years ago. The value of these man-made pools on such a small spate river cannot be over-emphasised and illustrates the points made in Chapter 4. When the river drops to low summer levels these artificial holding pools ensure a total area of $15\frac{1}{2}$ acres of water which would not otherwise be there and, due to the rocky nature of the river bed, nor would the fish.

The estates have shown a very sensible approach to bank clearance, and tree growth has only been restricted on one side at the fishing pools so as to provide shelter from the other bank, elsewhere there is a thick canopy from alders on both sides.

The main run of salmon and grilse is in July. Poaching is particularly rife in the lower reaches of this river, as in so many other small west coast spate rivers, and the splash net is one of the main instruments used by this fraternity. Because of the high incidence of poaching, there is no public fishing as it is felt that this would allow access to the river to too many people. The fishing is therefore private and is in the hands of the above three riparian owners.

The commercial netting rights at the mouth of the Barr and up the coast at Clachaig, which have not been exercised for about 100 years, are now held by the rod fishers of the Barr in the names of two anglers.

Since the 1950s the Barr has had some of its headwaters diverted to the Lussa system as part of the North of Scotland Hydro-electric Board's Glen Lussa project. The abstraction involves the diversion of the headwaters and tributaries of Abhainn a' Chnocain which flows out of Loch Arnicle and joins the Barr at Arnicle. This abstraction has had the effect of reducing the size of natural spates upon which the Barr depends for its runs of migratory fish.

The future of the Barr and many other small west coast rivers as salmon waters depends upon the untiring efforts of riparian owners and their helpers, not only in maintaining the natural and artificial attributes of the river but also in preventing poaching. Every support should be given to these dedicated conservationists.

The Lussa

Glenlussa Water is a small spate river on the east coast of the Mull of Kintyre flowing into the sea near Peninver, 4 miles north of Campbeltown. The upper part of the Lussa catchment is impounded behind a dam to form Lussa Loch, and some of the head reaches of the lower tributaries are also tapped and led by means of open aqueducts into the pipeline leading to the Lussa Power Station situated lower down the river at Gartgreillan. There is no provision for the release of compensation water from the dam and this means that the section of river immediately below the dam is dry, and during dry weather the $2\frac{1}{4}$ miles of river from the dam to the power station receive only a very small flow from the small burns coming off the rather steep sides of the valley. From the dam to the Upper Falls, about three-quarters of a mile downstream, there are extensive stretches of gravel which were used by spawning fish before the Lussa scheme, but are now of little value due to the lack of water. The Upper Falls were a difficult obstacle for fish to ascend in the days prior to the scheme although some fish were successful and in 1957, after the scheme came into operation, most of the salmon were said to spawn in a $1\frac{1}{2}$-mile stretch of river between the upper and lower falls. However, as there is a lack of compensation water from the dam, there is probably a very high mortality rate among the fry in dry weather. The Lower Falls provide a check to ascending fish at certain heights of water but are accessible at other times. According to Dugald Macintyre* these falls were blasted in the 1930s to allow fish to ascend. From the Lower Falls, immediately above the ford at Drumgarve, the river is fairly flat for about 400 yards and has some pools and a limited amount of spawning; it then runs into a steep rocky gorge half a mile long with deep pools, rough boulders and rocks. Downstream from the gorge to the power station there is a short stretch of rocky water with some pools, but below the power station, with the provision

* *Wildlife of the Highlands*

THE KINTYRE DISTRICT

of a minimum flow of 5 mgd, the river flows at a fishable level through attractive farmland. There are a number of good holding pools providing excellent angling water. After a course of about 5 miles the river flows out to sea in Kilbrannan Sound.

The angling rights over the entire length of the Lussa are held by Inland Fisheries Ltd who also own the Lussa View Fish Farm at the river mouth. The salmon and sea trout run in June – October and ascending fish are caught at a trap built across the river just upstream of the main Campbeltown road. Some of the fish are held in a 40-foot diameter tank, covered with a low shed, and stripped of their eggs in the autumn. The remainder are released upstream. Fry and parr are put into the higher reaches of the river and the surplus eggs are sold for commercial salmon farming.

The commercial sea netting rights by bag net are owned by Inland Fisheries Ltd and extend from Black Bay to the mouth of the river. A lease of rights is also held by them for about half a mile on the other side of Ardnacross Bay. The netting rights at the river mouth are exercised independently. The salmon fishing records for the sea netting, trap and angling are given below. In addition over 200 sea trout are caught each year.

Table 22
Details of salmon caught on the Lussa river system, 1973–1976

	1973	1974	1975	1976
Sea Netting	28	351	380	316
Fish Farm (trap)	238	214	162	184
Angling	70	60	65	70

Day permits can be obtained from the fish farm. When the fishing conditions are good the river can become rather overstocked with anglers.

Machrihanish or Backs Water

Machrihanish Water is sometimes referred to as Backs Water, although the latter is actually the northern tributary which joins the Machrihanish just west of Bleachfield Farm. Although salmon run the Backs Water, which is a rather peaty tributary, Chiscan Water, which flows into the Machrihanish from the south just east of Bleachfield, is the more fertile stream, with very clear water. Unfortunately farmers use it as a source of gravel.

The Machrihanish is just like a canal in some parts and there are no well-defined pools. One of the most popular pools is the Sandy Broo (or Bank) which lies a mile upstream from the Sea Pool and is referred to by Macintyre in his book *Memoirs of a Highland Gamekeeper*. Another pool of some popularity is situated near Bleachfield Farm.

The angling seems to be free to all comers and when the river is in spate in

July and August the majority of the local angling population and holiday anglers are on the riverside fishing with worm in the peat-stained waters. Some numbers of salmon are taken, and fish of up to 20 lb have been taken on occasion.

The river finishes its journey across the lovely sands of Machrihanish Bay on the west coast of the Mull.

The Breackerie and Conie Waters

Two small streams flowing out at the southern tip of the Mull of Kintyre are the Breackerie and Conieglen Waters. The Breackerie lies further west and enters the sea at Carskey Bay while the Conie enters the sea at Brunerican Bay near Southend. Both these waters hold salmon but they are badly poached and netted heavily at their mouths. Permission to fish can usually be obtained from the farmer owners providing it does not interfere with their netting operations!

Carradale

The Carradale is an attractive river which flows gracefully through Carradale Forest, which is now heavily afforested by the Forestry Commission, and enters the sea in Carradale Bay on the east side of the Mull opposite Kilbrannan Sound.

The banks of the river are overgrown with alders and some judicious tree clearing is required. It is very much a spate river and fish enter from July onwards. Unfortunately it is heavily poached. However, spate conditions do provide good angling from time to time and permits can be obtained from the keeper of Carradale Estate at Carradale House just outside Carradale.

Commercial netting is carried out by the estate at the mouth of the river on an irregular basis.

Strathclyde region abstracts 50,000 gallons of water daily from the river to supply the village of Carradale.

The Claonaig

The Claonaig is a small spate river which flows east along the line of the minor road from West Loch Tarbert to Claonaig and Skipness on the east coast of the Mull of Kintyre. There are three major tributaries, two of which are fed by lochs, which join a short distance upstream from Glenrisdell to form the

THE KINTYRE DISTRICT

Claonaig. The little river runs through a steep wooded valley and enters the sea in Claonaig Bay. Salmon and sea trout can travel a long way up the Claonaig, well beyond Glenrisdell, to a piece of land known as Lon Lea. In past years, when otters were plentiful, fish were often found on the banks of the river well inland.

The salmon tend to run up the river from late July, if spate conditions occur at that time. The sea trout tend to run a little earlier, from late June. The angling rights are owned by Skipness Estate which issues permits to visitors who take their holiday cottages in the village of Skipness. This estate also owns the sea netting rights which extend from Allt Romain in the south to Laggan House in the north. The heaviest fish caught in the sea by netting in recent years weighed 22 lb.

Pollution from silage was a problem at one time, but this has now been controlled.

UDN occurred in this river about five years ago but seems to have disappeared.

35

THE FYNE, KINGLAS, ARAY, SHIRA AND DOUGLAS

The Fyne

Up until 1950 the River Fyne flowed untouched by engineers or developers, through the steep narrow glen into the head of Loch Fyne. The river was formed from the meeting of its two upper tributaries, Allt an Taillir and Allt Coir' an Longairt. Further downstream it was joined on the left bank by the waters of Allt na Lairige which cascaded down the steep hillside. In times of heavy rain other small streams tumbled down the crags on either side of the glen, and helped to swell the swirling waters of the main river. But in 1950 Allt Coir' an Longairt and the upper part of Allt na Lairige were diverted to Loch Sloy as part of the Sloy hydro-electric scheme, and other small streams feeding the Fyne in its lower reaches were also tapped and passed into Loch Sloy by tunnel. The flow of the Fyne was further reduced in 1955 with the advent of the Glen Shira scheme, when the river's other tributary, Allt an Taillir, was diverted into the neighbouring Lochan Shira, to return to the Fyne once more just above the tidal limit after passing through the Clachan Power Station via the Shira tunnel. Allt na Lairige was also impounded to form a reservoir to supply a power station on the left bank of the Fyne only a short distance downstream of the now dried-up Allt na Lairige.

Only compensation flow arrangements now remain on the upper two tributaries and the Fyne now has an artificial régime which is further upset by the power stations' generation patterns. The Allt na Lairige Power Station runs from 7.30 a.m. to 7.30 p.m. from mid-June to mid-September in order to maintain a small but steady flow in the river. The Clachan Power Station generation times are now irregular and depend on weather conditions. As a result of these arrangements the river always has some water at all times, although the flood flows are partially creamed off by water being either diverted or impounded. However, after this arrangement catches of fish improved noticeably.

There is a small run of mainly big fish in late April and May, if there is water, but the main run is in late June – late August with the majority of the fish being grilse. There is a small proportion of summer fish (salmon that have spent more than two years in the sea and are returning in the summer) and the largest fish recorded is one of 34½ lb.

The Fyne is owned by the estates of Cairndow (Lord Glenkinglas) and Ardkinglas (Mr John Noble) and is divided into four beats downstream from the falls. Little fishing is done upstream of these falls.

A few fish, mainly sea trout and finnock, are caught below the main road bridge but the first good holding pool in the river is Ballingall's. The Sea Pool just above the bridge used to be good but it has become filled with gravel. To fish well Ballingall's requires a good flow of water and consequently fishes best when the Clachan Power Station is generating. The next mile of river upstream has few holding pools, but the best known is the Whirl. Upstream from here pools are plentiful right up past Glen Fyne Lodge to the falls, the popular ones being Clachan, Black Bridge, Strutt's, Cottage, Swing Bridge and Laraige. All these pools have been improved by the construction of weirs some made of concrete and others of gabions (wire baskets filled with stones). Most of the weirs existed before the hydro-electric schemes, but five were constructed or improved in order to replace three pools whose flow was severely lessened by the Allt na Lairige Dam.

In the last few years the Fyne has often been leased to tenants who have more enthusiasm than skill in fishing, and who do not have a ghillie in constant attendance for advice and guidance. While the amount of fishing measured in rods per day has gone up, broadly speaking the skill or efficiency has sharply deteriorated. Many of the anglers have to be lucky to catch a fish on a worm when this is allowed.

In recent years the rod catches have declined. A number of reasons may be responsible for this decline including the high seas salmon fishing, illegal inshore netting or even too severe a cropping of the river stocks by the rods. Whatever the reason the figures below reveal a marked decline in salmon caught, though sea trout numbers have increased. This returns more nearly to the 1920–1940 figures before the Hydro-electric Board began work. Naturally the two estates are most concerned and have been taking steps to improve matters by stocking the upper reaches with salmon fry and imposing stricter limits on fishing with worm. No spinning is allowed.

Table 23

Rod catches of salmon and grilse on the River Fyne 1962–1975

Year	Catch	Year	Catch	Year	Catch
1962	355	1967	423	1972	131
1963	260	1968	220	1973	162
1964	463	1969	175	1974	95
1965	409	1970	236	1975	130
1966	227	1971	168		

The Kinglas

The Kinglas flows into the head of Loch Fyne at Cairndow. It is a typical small

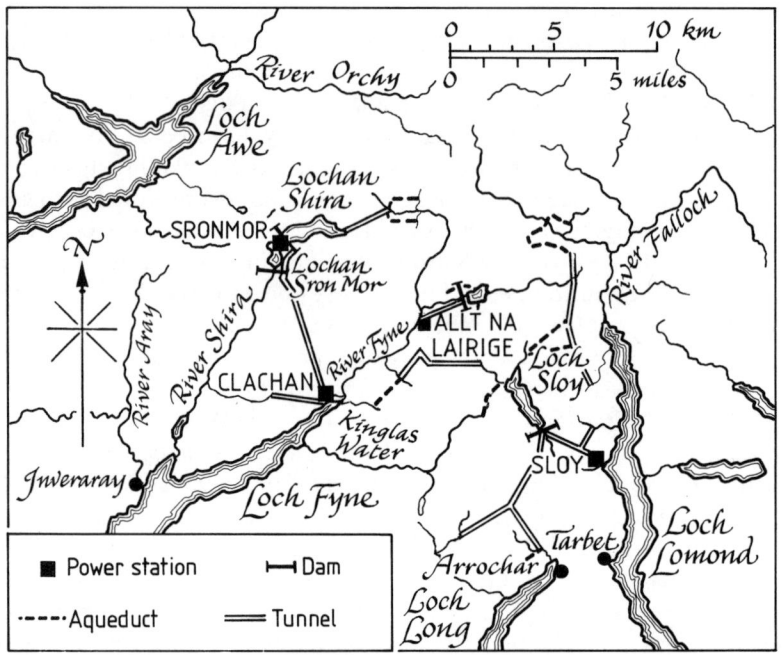

The Salmon Rivers of South Argyll and the Sloy–Shira Hydro-electric Scheme

west coast spate river. It rises at the head of Glen Kinglas, only a short distance from Loch Sloy, and flows through the narrow steep-sided glen past the derelict croft of Abyssinia where it is joined by the little Allt Uaine. This small stream is partly diverted to Loch Sloy so that the flow of the Kinglas, like that of its neighbour, the Fyne, has been reduced by the Sloy hydro-electric scheme. The glen has a forbidding appearance with steep crags on either side with Beinn Chorranach and Beinn Ime towering over the eastern side, while facing one on looking down the glen to Butterbridge is Beinn an Lochain. At Butterbridge the Kinglas is joined by a small tributary which runs out of cold little Loch Restil at the top of the Rest and be Thankful and over a steep cascade of falls barring the ascent of migratory fish. From Butterbridge to the sea the Kinglas flows close to the main road. For about $1\frac{1}{2}$ miles, until it reaches the grounds of Ardkinglas House, it flows through a narrow gorge and forms a series of deep clear pools or pots which, because of the steep banks and overhanging trees, are almost impossible to fish with anything but worm or spinner. In the grounds of Ardkinglas the river has a sylvan air and for part of its time flows past the exotic conifers which grow in this well-known pinetum.

A steep weir lies across the course of the river a short distance from the sea. This was originally built to divert water to produce electricity for Ardkinglas House. Although it still serves this purpose it also conveniently helps to supply water to a recently constructed salmon hatchery built by Golden Sea

Produce Ltd on the banks of the river close to its confluence with Loch Fyne. A fish pass is incorporated in this weir which is therefore no barrier to ascending salmon and sea trout.

The Kinglas is owned by Ardkinglas and Cairndow Estates and fishing is let on a daily basis. The annual catch of salmon is rarely more than 30, but many more sea trout are caught, including large specimens upwards of 10 lb. Most of the fishing is done between the mouth of the river and Butterbridge, with the pools at the weir and in the gorge receiving the most attention. It is planned to improve the angling on this little river by judicious tree-felling to allow easier access for fishing, by pool construction in the upper reaches and by the planting of young salmon and sea trout.

The Aray

The upper tributaries of this small west coast spate river rise in the hills on the west side of Loch Awe and meet near Taynafead. From here the Aray flows south close to the A819 road down Glen Aray and enters Loch Fyne at Inveraray. In the upper part of its course it is a rocky stream flowing through moorland and rough pasture, with ill-defined pools and many good spawning areas. As the river descends the glen, the pools become well-defined and provide good holding water for fish and excellent fishing for anglers. The middle course of the river is heavily wooded with a number of plantations reaching to the riverside. On the right bank near Foal's Bridge a rainbow trout farm belonging to Castle Fisheries takes its water from the river. The lower section of the river passes through the parkland of Inveraray Castle and has a most ornamental appearance with ornate bridges, glistening cascades separating the long slow-flowing pools, and man-made rectangular stepping stones. The river here is overlooked by the steep Dunchuach Hill with its stone tower on top which can be reached by way of a winding track.

There are three runs of fish into the Aray, a run of spring salmon in May, a main run of salmon and grilse from mid-June to the end of July and an autumn run in September. Very few sea trout enter the river and those that do rarely go above the tidal water which extends upstream as far as the Stepping Stones.

Afforestation has affected the nature of the river flow, and the run-off from the hill causes the river to rise fast and fall even more rapidly.

The river is owned by the Trustees of the 10th Duke of Argyll and the fishing is divided into two beats. The upper is taken by a syndicate which has the fishing upstream from Foal's Bridge at the Miller's Linn Pool, while the lower is let on a daily basis, permits being available from the Argyll Estate Office.

The commercial fishing is also owned by the Trustees of the 10th Duke of Argyll and is carried out to the north-east of Inveraray in Loch Shira, which is really a small bay on the north shore of Loch Fyne.

There is no record of UDN occurring in the river and it would seem that the salmon in the rivers in this part of Argyll have been fortunate in escaping this disease.

The Shira

The Shira lies between the Aray and the Fyne. Its upper tributaries drain the same steep hill slopes as those of the Fyne and at some points are no more than a few hundred yards apart. Much of this part of the Fyne catchment has been diverted to Lochan Shira as part of the Sloy-Shira scheme of the North of Scotland Hydro-electric Board. Lochan Shira is the main reservoir of the Glen Shira scheme, and water passes from the main Shira dam through Sronmor Power Station into Lochan Sron Mor. It is interesting to note in passing that Sronmor was the forerunner of the Board's major pumped storage schemes and has a detachable pump on the same shaft as the turbine and motor generator, enabling water to be pumped up to the main reservoir during periods of heavy run-off and when the output of the main station is not required. The lower loch is formed by a dam centred on a rocky knoll in the middle of the glen. In effect there are two small dams, a concrete section being sited on one side of the knoll and an earth embankment on the other. Water from Lochan Shira also flows by tunnel and pipeline to Clachan Power Station on the River Fyne.

Below Lochan Sron Mor a compensation flow passes down Glen Shira into Dubh Loch which is joined to the sea by the Garron or Gearr Abhain, which is tidal throughout its length and flows into Loch Shira, a small bay on the north shore of Loch Fyne.

The Shira, between Lochan Sron Mor and its confluence with the Brannie Burn, a short distance downstream from Rob Roy's House, is fairly rocky, but below the confluence it tends to become slower flowing, has a fairly smooth gravel bed and is overgrown by heavily wooded banks. Much of this section of the river needs clearing to make fishing more comfortable, and there are many branches and tree roots which could be removed. This section of the river as far as Dubh Loch fishes best in the autumn because, although the main run of salmon, grilse and sea trout is in July and August, the fish tend to remain in Dubh Loch until close to spawning time. However, the duration of their stay in this loch is to some extent dependent on the frequency of spate conditions, but it is a good holding water and fishes well when conditions are right. Hamish Stuart in his work *The Book of The Sea Trout* (1916) has this to say of the Shira: 'The Shira itself, whatever it may have been in the past, is not at the present day a very suitable stream for salmon. Here and there in its course there are deep pools; but the absence of sheltering rocks, the rapidity with which the river falls, and, above all, the broad deep waters of the Dhuloch and the easy road to the sea have a most marked effect upon the habits of the salmon. It is only in times of flood or when about to spawn that they ascend the river in any numbers, preferring to lie in the Dhuloch . . . The constant invasion of the lake by the tide seems, moreover, to induce an occasional return to the sea.' Day permits for Dubh Loch and the Garron together, and the Shira, can be obtained from the Argyll Estate Office, the fishings being owned by the Trustees of the 10th Duke of Argyll.

Lastly, a word of consolation to anglers who may be beguiled into thinking that the fish cruising along the shallows of Dubh Loch, occasionally making boiling rises and displaying large dorsal and tail fins, are sea trout which are irritatingly refusing to take any flies presented to them: ignore them as they are grey mullet, a species which abounds in this loch and swims to and from the sea via the little River Garron. If the fishless salmon angler wants to amuse himself let him put a piece of his sandwich on a hook stripped of its feathers and float it out to these stupid beasts. They are good to eat if cooked while still fresh!

The Douglas

The Douglas Water is a small river, not much more than 12 miles long, which flows swiftly into Loch Fyne just over two miles south of Inveraray. It has a rocky channel with an abundance of waterfalls and rocky pools. One of the falls, about 3 miles from the tidal waters of Loch Fyne, prevents salmon and sea trout from going further upstream. Being confined to the lower reaches the fish have to share a limited stretch of broken water and 10 fairly good pools. Few of the pools are deep and while they fill up rapidly during a flood the water subsides very quickly. One of the better pools is the Roman Bridge Pool which is also of interest because of the old Roman bridge which is an ancient and outstanding landmark.

Permits for the limited angling available, chiefly July–September, can be obtained from the Argyll Estate Office in Inveraray.

36

THE RUEL, EACHAIG, LOCH LOMOND, FALLOCH, LEVEN AND ENDRICK

The Ruel

The Ruel is an interesting little river in south Argyll which starts off as a typical small moorland stream at the head of Caol Ghleann and then quickly flows into a steep gorge in which there are insurmountable falls. These are at the Castle Pool and mark the upper limit of migratory fish. After flowing out of the gorge below Dunans the whole character of the river changes and, as it flows through the rich pastureland of Glendaruel, it assumes the appearance of a Hampshire stream with deep smooth-flowing pools and short deep runs. The only difference is in the colour of the water which, in the case of the Ruel, is deeply peat-stained. Unfortunately Forestry Commission plantations are encroaching on this farmland and the Glendaruel Forest is gradually extending up and down the glen. Below the Clachan of Glendaruel the river starts to meander into tidal water and on into the head of Loch Riddon and the Kyles of Bute.

The main run of salmon, grilse and sea trout is from late July to the end of September, and approximately equal numbers of salmon and sea trout are taken by rod and line. The exact time of the run depends on the first spate in this period.

Since the start of afforestation in 1948 the river has tended to become increasingly flashy in nature due to drainage operations. In addition water has been abstracted from the upper reaches by the Cowal scheme of the North of Scotland Hydro-electric Board which has diverted water by aqueduct from the Tamhnich Burn and Allt a' Chapuill direct to Loch Tarsan Power Station at the head of Loch Striven.

The best of the fishing is on the two lower beats of the river. However, day permits can be obtained for two miles of the lower section, a mile either side of Clachan of Glendaruel, with the exception of a small section belonging to the Glebe, from the post office at Clachan of Glendaruel.

The commercial fishing is taken up by the riparian owners but it is only very occasionally exercised so as to conserve the stocks of migratory fish.

This river is one of the few in Scotland in which UDN has not been recorded.

The Eachaig

The Eachaig is a short river with a $4\frac{1}{2}$ mile course from the foot of Loch Eck to the head of Holy Loch and the Firth of Clyde. Loch Eck is a narrow deep loch 6 miles long and with a maximum depth of 139 feet. As well as holding salmon, sea trout and brown trout, it also contains powan and char. It is surrounded by high hills with their lower slopes clad with conifers. The stream which flows into the head of the loch is the Cur which gives its name to the village of Strachur situated on the south shore of Loch Fyne. The Cur is one of the main spawning tributaries of the Eachaig, with salmon spawning near the old sawmill at Strachur and sea trout ascending as far as the waterfall at Succoth. The largest tributary of the Eachaig is the Massan which enters the river near Benmore Gardens.

The Eachaig is more of a sea trout than a salmon river, although the salmon stocks have increased slightly in recent years. The sea trout numbers in this river have shown no signs of decreasing and large specimens are caught each year. In 1977 a sea trout of 15 lb was caught by a young angler, and fish of up to 20 lb have been taken in the nets at the mouth of the river.

UDN has occurred spasmodically. One source of damage to fish entering the Eachaig is from sea lampreys which have been recorded inflicting severe wounds on sea trout.

A water scheme has been developed on Loch Eck and a barrage with a centre notch has been built across the outfall of the loch. Provisions for a compensation flow have been made. There is also another weir a short distance downstream at Eckford. This is a larger structure without a fish pass and which must act as a barrier to ascending fish at low flows.

The fishing on the upper Cur is available by permit from Succoth Farm near Strachur, while permits for the lower Cur nearer Loch Eck are available through the Dunoon and District Angling Association. At one time the fishing on the Massan was let to the Dunoon and District Angling Association by Mr John Younger, but from 1978 the fishing has been made available to the public by Mr David Younger of Benmore Estate on a day permit basis. The Massan is very much a spate river and bait fishing is allowed. Tickets are available from the offices of the Economic Forestry Group in Sandbank. Day tickets are also available for the upper and lower beats of the Eachaig throughout the whole season and for the middle beat up to the second week of June and for the first week of October. From mid-June to the end of September the middle beat is let to tenants at Eckford Lodge, but as from 1980 the whole of the river will be available on a day ticket basis. Fishing on the Eachaig is by fly only and tickets are available from the Economic Forestry Group in Sandbank. A good pool on the Eachaig during low water conditions is the Cauld near Benmore Gardens.

Day tickets for salmon and sea trout are also available from the Economic Forestry Group and nearby hotels for Loch Eck. Boats are also available from

Whittlefield Hotel, Coylet Hotel and Coylet Caravan Park.

Netting is carried out at the mouth of the Eachaig and at the foot of Loch Eck, but only on a restricted basis from mid-June to the end of August. Netting stops during periods of low river flow. As a conservation practice, most salmon caught are returned to the water; only sea trout are kept.

Loch Lomond

Loch Lomond and its tributaries are situated in some of the most breath-taking scenery in Scotland, literally on the doorstep of the most densely populated area in the Strathclyde region. The loch nestles in the valley bottom only 30 feet above sea level, with the steeply sloping mountains rising to heights of between 1500 and 3000 feet on both sides of this large expanse of water. The highest mountains are Ben Vorlich (3,092 feet) to the west at the north end of the loch and Ben Lomond (3,192 feet) about half way down the eastern shore. The loch is about 21 miles long and lies almost due north-south; from the mouth of the Falloch, at the northern end, to Ross Point it is deep and narrow, varying from half to three-quarters of a mile in width. From Ross Point it gradually widens out and the surface of the loch is studded with many islands. It is 4 miles wide at its widest point, opposite the mouth of the River Endrick. From Inchmurrin the loch narrows gradually to its outfall to the River Leven at Balloch.

The main feeder streams of Loch Lomond are the Falloch, running into the extreme northern end of the loch, and the Inveruglas Water, the Douglas, Luss, Finlas and Fruin which enter on the western side of the loch. All these tributaries accommodate a few sea trout at spawning time, but with the exception of the Fruin, they are short, flashy rivers. On the east shore there is only one tributary of any significance and that is the Endrick which is by far the largest tributary entering the loch.

Loch Lomond, its tributaries and the River Leven do not form a fishery district of their own. Under the Salmon and Freshwater Fisheries (Scotland) Act of 1868, when salmon fishery districts were formed, they were part of the Clyde District. The River Clyde in those days was a good salmon river which gradually deteriorated due to the huge quantities of domestic and industrial effluent discharged into the river. It is indeed surprising that the same fate did not befall this fishery, as the River Leven was extremely badly polluted at times. No doubt the fact that most of its spawning and nursery areas are many miles upstream from the polluted area, and that there is a large volume of clean water flowing out of Loch Lomond, has played a large part in saving the migratory fish stocks. Due to the combined efforts of the Clyde River Purification Board and the Loch Lomond Angling Improvement Association, much of the pollution has been eliminated and the migratory fish stocks built up. The

SOUTH ARGYLL AND LOCH LOMOND

Loch Lomond Angling Improvement Association was formed many years ago and it has been able to obtain or rent a large amount of fishing on Loch Lomond, the River Leven, the River Endrick and the River Fruin for its members. The Association's full membership was for some years confined to 950 per annum but is now unrestricted. The Association also issues season, week or day permits for adults, children and old age pensioners. The sale of various classes of permits brings in an income of several thousand pounds each year. This association is also responsible for restocking its waters as required and also employs bailiffs. For several years the association has been considering the possibility of building its own hatchery on one of the tributaries running into Loch Lomond. A stone building has now been converted for this purpose. Brood fish are netted for stripping on the Endrick and other rivers, under the management of the association.

Recently the Central Scotland Water Development Board obtained an order to enable them to abstract, by pumping, up to 100 million gallons of water a day from Loch Lomond. A control works was sited on the River Leven at Balloch to control the flow out of the loch and compensation flows, with freshet allowances, were agreed for the River Leven. The pumping station is near Ross Priory Point and water is pumped from there to treatment works. These works came into operation in 1971 and compensation was paid to the Loch Lomond Angling Improvement Association.

UDN has been prevalent in the fishery since the late 1960s, and, although there has never been a catastrophic outbreak, losses have occurred in most years. Salmon stocks in particular seem to have suffered most.

In spite of its size Loch Lomond is a remarkably good salmon and sea trout fishery. The southern end of the loch is much wider and shallower than the northern and fishing at the south end begins early in the season. There are many bays and banks around the shore of both the loch and its many islands and these afford good drifts for anglers fishing from boats. Other areas of the loch, where the water is deeper, can be trolled with equal success using minnows, spoons and other spinning lures. Many anglers keep their boats at convenient anchorages at such points as Balloch, Balmaha, Luss and Rowardennan. However, with the help of outboard engines, anglers are able to cover large areas of the loch. It is impossible to mention all the best angling spots, but on the west shore fish can be found off the mouths of the inflowing tributaries, and off the mouth of the Fruin fish can be taken both early and late in the season. On the east shore some good points are the mouth of the Endrick and Endrick Bank inside Aber Isle; the net bay in the south-east corner below Endrick mouth to Ross Priory Point; part of the shore north of Balmaha, particularly on either side of the black rock; Milarrochy Bay; Critreach Bay, and from Ross Point to Strathcashel. Later in the season areas around Rowardennan and Ptarmigan Lodge and Inversnaid Hotel produce salmon and sea trout. There are also good fishing banks around the islands, and off these many good sea trout and salmon can be taken. The best areas are Inchmurrin, north shore of Torrinch, Creinch, north-east shore of Inchlonaig, north-west shore of Inchfad, Ellanderroch and the pass between Inchcruin and Inchfad. For the angler wishing to know all the best drifts on the loch and how best to fish them there is no better book than Ian Wood's *Loch Lomond and its Salmon*.

The first salmon are usually caught in the loch in March but July is probably the best month of all. Salmon only start coming to the fly in May. Fish of over 20 lb can be taken but the average weight of salmon and grilse is 8 – 9 lb. The recorded average annual catch of salmon and grilse is in the region of 290 but the best year recently produced 400, and in 1925 465 were caught. Sea trout can be caught from March onwards with the best fishing being June – August. Sea trout of over 10 lb are frequently taken but the average weight is 2 – 3 lb. In recent years the average annual catch has been 625 with the best year producing 950 sea trout. In 1912 1,464 sea trout, weighing 2,544 lb, were recorded.

Netting is still exercised by sweep net off the mouth of the River Luss and on the east side of the loch by the Luss and Montrose estates, and elsewhere in the loch where netting rights are owned.

River Falloch

The Falloch is a most picturesque little river rising in the mountain range to the south of Crianlarich and flowing down Glen Falloch over a series of spectacular falls to Loch Lomond, which it enters at Ardlui. This is purely a sea trout river and it is a rare event to catch a salmon. The sea trout can ascend the lower two sets of falls but are prevented from ascending the upper reaches by the Falls of Falloch. There is, however, a side channel around the left bank of the Falls and if this was breached and properly stepped it would allow sea trout to ascend into a much better spawning and nursery area which extends upstream as far as Derrydarroch. The major part of the river and the fishing belongs to Glenfalloch Estate and is private.

The Leven

This river is some 6 miles in length and for a large part of its length is mainly slow-flowing over a predominantly gravel bed.

There are some useful pools and it is a useful salmon and sea trout fishery. The first fish of the season is normally caught in February although sometimes it is into March before one is landed. Much depends on water conditions and particularly water temperature. When water conditions are suitable any month from April to October can produce good catches, and July is often a very good month.

Salmon and grilse average around 10 lb and some good-sized salmon are normally caught each year, including some of over 20 lb. Recent annual catches are in the region of 230, with 258 being the best season's total in recent years. Sea trout fishing is also good on the Leven. Early in the season, during February and March, only a few finnock are taken, but from April to October the river can produce good sport, with July to September, if anything, being the best period. The annual average catch is around 1,660 with fish averaging just over $1\frac{1}{4}$ lb. The best annual catch in recent years was of some 1,900 fish.

The river is fished by members of the Loch Lomond Angling Improvement Association and their permit holders. Spinning is probably the most popular form of angling on this river. There are some useful spawning and feeding areas in the river itself, but mainly for salmon and grilse. There seems to be no evidence that salmon are being held back at the control barrage on the river.

The Endrick

This river rises in the Gargunnock and Fintry hills in west Stirlingshire and flows south at first before running west, a course it holds for the rest of its journey before discharging into Loch Lomond south of Balmaha. Its journey to start with is rocky and rugged until it reaches the loup of Fintry a spectacular series of falls some 90 feet in height. From this point to the loch is roughly 20 miles, and for the first part of the journey the Endrick flows through a section with many fine pools intermingled with excellent spawning ground. In the vicinity of Gartness village the river takes a distinct dogs-leg in the shape of a sharp loop. Above the village there is a weir, which used to divert water to a small wool mill, above the weir is a famous pool named Craigbell. Over the years the weir became dilapidated and a number of years ago eventually collapsed during one frosty winter. The proprietors called in expert advisers from the Freshwater Fisheries Laboratory at Pitlochry and after one abortive attempt, eventually replaced the weir with a fish pass in the centre of it. This now works very well, but the Loch Lomond Angling Improvement Association have recently modified it by removing the top 6 inches of the crest. Below this weir is a small fall and about a mile below this at the other end of the loop is another formidable fall known as the Pot of Gartness. This fall is passable in certain heights of water, but fish do find it difficult to ascend. A major tributary, the Blane Water, enters the river from the left bank some distance below the Pot. The junction pool is known locally as the 'Meetings Lynn' and is a very popular angling spot.

From Drymen to Loch Lomond the river flows through flat meadow land and some beautiful woods surrounding Buchanan Castle, a derelict residence belonging to the Duke of Montrose. This section of the river is wider, more sluggish and abounds with pike and coarse fish, but it still has a certain potential for migratory fish angling. The spawning and feeding potential of the Endrick and many of its tributaries is extremely high, especially between the loup of Fintry and Drymen. No migratory fish ascend the loup.

The angling potential of the Endrick is good, provided that there are spates to allow fish to enter the river. In recent years the dry summers have curtailed any good angling until September and October, but in normal years fish ascend the river from June onwards.

The average weight of salmon is 6–7 lb, and a few good fish over 20 lb are caught, mostly below the Pot of Gartness. An average year's catch on the Endrick is around 100 fish between the Angling Improvement Association water and the private beats.

Sea trout fishing on the Endrick can be very good when suitable water conditions draw the fish out of the loch. Night fishing for sea trout can bring good baskets and many catches with fish averaging 4 lb having been taken at this time.

Recently the average annual catch of sea trout has been between 450–500 fish over all the angling waters. The average weight of the fish is $2-2\frac{1}{2}$ lb, but some of over 10 lb have been taken. There are many excellent angling pools both above and below the Pot of Gartness. UDN on the Endrick seems to have had more of an adverse effect on the salmon than the sea trout stocks.

37

THE GRYFE, IRVINE, GARNOCK, AYR, DOON, GIRVAN AND STINCHAR

The Gryfe

In the early 1800s this river was well-known for its runs of salmon. The last known record of salmon in the river was in 1860 when *The Scotsman* reported on the presence of 40 salmon in the Coalbog Pool just downstream from Bridge of Weir.

The river has had a bad history of pollution from industrial sources since the Second World War, particularly from the tanneries in Bridge of Weir. This has been further aggravated by pollution of the Black Cart, which the Gryfe joins near Blackstone Mains, and the White Cart which the Black Cart flows into near Renfrew. The White Cart joins the River Clyde a little way upstream from Clydebank and the Clyde too has had a bad pollution record.

Continuing attempts to reduce pollution on all four rivers are meeting with success, and over the last 8–10 years there have been reports of salmon seen in the Gryfe. These reports, however, could never be substantiated by reliable witnesses. On several occasions dead salmon were found but they had been dead so long they were useless as reliable evidence. However, some 6 years ago two salmon were taken from the water immediately below the disused Bridge of Weir tannery weir and placed in the clear water above it, but nothing was ever heard of these fish again. With the subsequent cleaning up of the Clyde, the White Cart and the Black Cart, together with the linking of the two remaining tanneries at Bridge of Weir to the sewer to Linwood, the water conditions have improved.

In late September 1978 a report was received of a single salmon being seen; this report was considered to be reliable, so a watch was maintained on the river and in late October the first salmon was seen. This was quickly followed by more sightings of other fish and in the first week of the run at least 10 separate fish were identified. These were all very 'red' fish but seemed to be in reasonable condition. Four fish were netted and placed over the falls 200 yards below the road bridge at Bridge of Weir and three other fish were seen to surmount the falls unaided. By November a further 20 fish were noted. These were clean-run fish, bright silver and in very good condition. At least 6 were known to have got over the falls. In all, 60 fish were recorded during this three-week autumn period. During the first week of November a number of sea trout were also seen but it is not known whether or not they ascended the falls.

In early September 1979 more salmon were seen and at least 40 separate fish were recorded. Judging by the number of salmon parr in the river, spawning has been successful.

The only major hazard to returning salmon in the future will be the amount of water abstraction which is made from the upper reaches of this river where a number of small reservoirs are sited. This results in the river rising and falling very rapidly, and salmon are only going to be able to ascend during extended periods of high river levels.

The Bridge of Weir Angling Club (River) has rented the salmon fishing rights from the local salmon proprietor.

The Irvine

The River Irvine rises on Loudoun Hill on the Ayrshire – Lanarkshire border. It flows in a westerly direction for 26 miles to Irvine where it enters the harbour, Irvine Bay and the Firth of Clyde. It is joined in its estuary by the River Garnock. The river, in its upper reaches, is moorland in character and at Darvel, 4 miles from its source, it is joined first by the Gower Water and then by the Glen Water. Many smaller tributaries join the river as it flows through the villages of Newmilns and Galston. The Irvine then flows through Kilmarnock, the largest town in the catchment and with much heavy industry. At Kilmarnock the Irvine is joined by Kilmarnock Water, a tributary made up of the Fenwick and Craufurdland Waters which unite $1\frac{1}{2}$ miles upstream from the Kilmarnock Water–River Irvine confluence. The Carmel Water joins the Irvine $5\frac{1}{2}$ miles downstream from Kilmarnock, then the major tributary of the Irvine, the Annick Water, enters just south of Irvine. Although the Annick has a greater gradient than that of the Irvine, neither has the rush and turbulence of a highland salmon river.

Only a few salmon and sea trout spawn in the lower reaches of the river and the only ones that do are fish entering late in the season. The main spawning areas are near the source of the river at Darvel, Newmilns and Galston. A fair number of fish also spawn in the tributaries and connecting burns. Until recently a large number of salmon and sea trout ran the Annick to spawn in the upper reaches around Dunlop and Stewarton and in the main tributary, the Glazert, but due to large scale pollution from Drumgrain Moss refuse tip, the numbers of fish running the Annick have been drastically reduced, although the water quality in the Annick is relatively unaffected by the Glazert Water pollution.

The main run of salmon, depending on water levels, is during late July and

August. There is a small run of spring salmon in May, with fish in the 8–18 lb class. The fish in the summer run are mainly grilse. In October there is another small run of grilse and salmon, and during the close season a number of salmon in the 20–30 lb class run the river, although it is difficult to say whether or not they occur in large numbers. A large number of sea trout enter the Irvine and Annick throughout the season, from April onwards. The large numbers are attributable to the stocking of the upper reaches of the Irvine with sea trout ova by the River Irvine Angling Improvement Association. It is said that the runs of salmon and sea trout have declined since the mid-1960s but there was a marked increase in the numbers of both salmon and sea trout in 1978.

UDN was recorded in the Irvine in 1972 and again in 1975, but few have been recorded with this disease since then.

There are in the region of 30 weirs on the Irvine and many of these are the main sites for large scale poaching. The two weirs in Irvine have fish passes but the Girtridge Mill Weir, the Lawe Saw Mill weir within the Dreghorn Angling Club's boundaries and the Drybridge Dam are the main targets for poaching. During the period of the main run of fish poachers can be seen from the main road which runs through the village of Drybridge, gaffing salmon and large sea trout ascending the dam.

There is a considerable amount of pollution on parts of the Irvine and some of its tributaries. The upper reaches are periodically contaminated by surface water from Loudoun Hill Quarry. Further downstream some of the smaller tributaries are occasionally polluted by organic farm waste, particularly silage liquor during the summer months. In the Kilmarnock area there are 12 storm water outflows, mainly sited on spur sewers, which often discharge crude sewage into the river before the rainfall is reflected in an increase in river flow. The upper reaches of the Annick are affected slightly by the discharge from the new sewage treatment works at Stewarton. Further downstream, the Annick is joined by the Glazert, which is grossly polluted near its source by the drainage from Drumgrain Moss tip, and further downstream still it is polluted by the effluent from the overloaded and outdated Dunlop sewage treatment works. At Irvine there are more storm water overflows which cause localised pollution because they come into operation much earlier in wet weather than they should.

While there are several riparian owners on the river, individual clubs usually hold the salmon fishing rights and leases and there are very few stretches which are not fished by angling clubs. On the Irvine, from the mouth to source, the main clubs are – Irvine and District, Dreghorn Angling Club, Kilmarnock Angling Club, Hurlford and Crookedholm Angling Club, Galston Angling Club, Newmilns Angling Club and Darvel Angling Club. Tickets for most of these club waters can be had from local fishing tackle shops.

The main clubs on the Annick from mouth to source are the Irvine and District Angling Club and Dreghorn Angling Club, who share the lower reaches to the confluence of the Irvine, the Kilmaurs Angling Club, the

Stewarton Angling Club and the Dunlop Angling Club.

All clubs on the Annick and Irvine are members of the River Irvine Angling Improvement Association. The commercial netting rights on the estuary and river are owned by this association and, needless to say, the rights have never been exercised.

The Garnock

The River Garnock rises at The Sprout in the open moorland of the Kilbirnie Hills and flows south through Dalry and Kilwinning to enter the estuary of the River Irvine in Irvine Bay. Downstream from Dalry the river is joined by the Water of Caaf and Dusk Water. The main tributary, however, is Lugton Water which rises at Loch Libo and flows south-west to its confluence with the Garnock just upstream of the estuary.

The Garnock is a fairly long river with stretches of fast water alternating with long pools. The main spawning areas are in the upper reaches of the river in the neighbourhood of Dalry and Kilbirnie. There are a number of weirs and dams along its course but, given the water, fish have no problems in surmounting them. Unfortunately, as on the Ayr and the Irvine, poachers gather at these vantage points. Poachers that are convicted find that they are faced with such puny fines imposed by the Sheriffs that they continue undeterred. Steps must be taken to rectify this deplorable situation.

The main run of salmon and sea trout is in August but a smaller run occurs in late May or early June depending on the river flow.

The Garnock, like the Nith, is a success story as, up to 14 or so years ago, few salmon ascended the river because of the polluted conditions. However, with the advent of the Garnock Valley sewage scheme the water quality improved tremendously and salmon began to ascend. Unfortunately there is still some pollution in the Garnock estuary from a number of trade and sewage discharges, but these should be phased out soon and replaced by a single outfall which will discharge directly into the Firth of Clyde. In April 1978 there was severe pollution on the Dusk Water as the result of a fire at a tyre dump on which cyanide wastes had been illegally tipped. The cyanide and phenols washed into the water were responsible for a very severe fish kill in the Dusk and the Garnock and countless numbers of salmon parr, as well as trout, were killed.

The fishing on the Garnock belongs to the Kilwinning Angling Club and the Dalry Angling Club and both are members of the River Irvine Angling Improvement Association. The Kilwinning anglers have good sport during spate conditions but as the spate subsides and the salmon ascend the dam the Dalry stretch comes into its own where good holding pools provide excellent angling water.

THE RIVERS OF RENFREW AND AYR

The Ayr

The River Ayr is the longest of the Ayrshire rivers, being 39 miles long. Its upper tributaries rise in the Leadhills and flow into Glenbuck Loch near Muirkirk. From Glenbuck Loch the Ayr flows in a westerly direction to enter the Firth of Clyde at Ayr. In its upper reaches the river flows through moorland and has a gravelly bed as far as Sorn, $11\frac{1}{2}$ miles from source. On reaching Sorn, where there is more arable land, the river becomes more rocky and red sandstone, much used for building in the past, forms the bed and banks of the river. The rocky character of the river continues for some miles through Catrine and Mauchline down to Failford. This is perhaps the most beautiful part of the river, with its deep pools and gorges. The gorge at Barskimming, the house of Lord Strathclyde, is really spectacular where an Adam bridge spans the river. Downstream the river passes the village of Stair where a grey stone is found and used for building houses. The river continues through Enterkine Estate, down to the mining village of Annbank, past Tarholm and then through the lands of the West of Scotland College of Agriculture and on to the town of Ayr. For the greater part of its course red sandstone forms the bed of the river, and this also applies to its main tributaries, the Lugar, which joins the Ayr at Mauchline, and the Coyle which enters the river near Tarholm.

The main spawning areas are in the main river around Mauchline and in the Lugar Water.

At Catrine there is a fall or weir which few fish are able to negotiate. The river is comparatively wide at this point for the flow of water and consequently the covering, even in a spate, is quite thin. A number of angling clubs contributed to improve an existing pass to allow fish access to the upper reaches but it has met with little success, and fish are taken here by illegal means. A similar state of affairs has occurred at Ochiltree on the Lugar. Poaching is such a problem that there exists an Ayr Association for the Suppression of Poaching!

The main run of salmon and sea trout begins in early August provided there is heavy rain. Few fish appear before then, as the spring run of fish is now almost non-existent. On both the River Ayr and the River Doon the tidal high water mark occurs at a weir and the fish are unable to ascend when there is little flow. If they cannot ascend they fall back with the tide to again be at the mercy of the netting in the estuary.

The netting rights on the river are owned by Ladykirk Estate who let the fishing to a commercial firm. Nets are set along the coast north of the estuary towards Prestwick, and a net and coble fishes the dock basin where fish lie should they manage to come directly from the sea by the shipping channel.

The Ayr is badly affected by pollution. In its upper reaches the river is polluted with ferruginous mine water which emanates from the disused coal mine at Kames. The discharge reaches the river via the Garpel Water and much of the bed of both rivers is covered with a heavy accummulation of iron sludge. The river is affected for 7 miles, despite receiving two major tributaries within a short distance, the Greenock Water and the Whitehaugh Water. In the Muirkirk area, the river receives a grossly polluting effluent from Kames Hill sewage treatment works via the Linky Burn. Below Mauchline the river receives effluent from Barskimming sewage treatment works which receives a very large organic loading from the Mauchline Creamery. The production at the Creamery is at its peak in the summer months and there is then a marked deterioration in the quality of the effluent. The discharge badly affects the river downstream, where pools containing solid material from the sewage works putrify. There are a number of active coal mines in the Ayr catchment and these cause the river to be contaminated by suspended solids, particularly during wet weather. The main sources of this type of pollution are the opencast mines at Auchengilsie, the deep mining at Killoch colliery, Ochiltree, and also the Barony Power Station, which uses coal slurry for fuel.

As the migratory fish stocks have been declining most clubs have been restocking the river, according to their means, with brown trout. A few clubs have small hatcheries which rear fish to the unfed fry stage, but the mortality is so great that larger fish are now introduced.

There are a number of angling clubs on the river at Ayr, Ladykirk, Annbank, Mauchline, Catrine, Sorn and Muirkirk. There are also a number of syndicates who rent their stretches from neighbouring estates. Permits for certain stretches may be obtained from Annbank and Cumnock while in Ayr the local authority issues permits for the Craigie Fishings for which the Ayr Angling Club has a block permit.

The Doon

The Doon rises in the hills on the borders of Kirkcudbrightshire. Some of these headwaters spring from Loch Enoch, a desolate loch about 1,700 feet above sea level, whose waters flow into the head of Loch Doon. Loch Doon is part of the South of Scotland Electricity Board's Galloway scheme and some of its waters are now diverted into Kendoon Reservoir via the Water of Deugh. This has been possible as a result of the construction of a 44-foot-high dam at the foot of Loch Doon which has consequently raised the level of the loch. Below the dam the river passes through a rocky gorge and into Ness Glen. A long time ago a fish pass was incorporated in the gorge to allow fish to ascend into the loch. Now at Loch Doon, as a result of the hydro-scheme, there is a unique type of fish ladder arranged in an ascending spiral inside a circular tower to enable the fish to cope with the wide range of water levels in the loch which can vary by as much as 40 feet.

Below Ness Glen the Doon runs for about a mile through meadowland, and passing Dalmellington, it widens out into Bogton Loch, which is about half a mile long and full of pike. From there it has a run of 16 miles until it enters the sea two miles to the south of the mouth of the Ayr. In its lower reaches the river meanders through attractive farmland in the heart of Burns country and, shortly before reaching the sea, flows under the famous Brig o' Doon near Alloway, the birthplace of Rabbie Burns.

The Doon is not a spring fish river now and the main run does not start until July, with the peak of the run being reached in August and September. However, if one gets a spate in May or June, which is seldom the case, some fish will run. Some sea trout ascend the river, although it is not a sea trout river of any consequence.

At one time the Doon was badly polluted by the wastes from collieries bordering the river, particularly in the Dalmellington area, but this source of pollution has now almost cleared up. There is, however, some pollution from the sewage disposal unit at Dalrymple. At the present time many inhabitants in the Doon valley are most concerned by the proposals to use the Loch Doon area as a dumping ground for nuclear waste. In addition to the water taken from the river system by the Galloway hydro-electric scheme there are a further four abstraction points on the river system for the purpose of water supply and industry. This results in the river having rather complicated compensation flows which do not help to provide a good flow régime for migrating fish.

There is some planting out of salmon fry in the small tributaries. Other improvements have included modifications to the fish passes on the two weirs near the river mouth.

The main salmon fishing proprietors are Craigengillan Estate near Dalmellington; the National Coal Board who let their fishing to two angling clubs; Smithston Farm; Casillis Estate (belonging to the Marquis of Ailsa); Monkwood; and Rozelle. There are two particularly good pools on the two last-named stretches and these are Turn Wheel on Monkwood and Rumbler on Rozelle. Salmon fishing is available on the Drumgrange and Keirs Angling Club water between Bogton Loch and Patna, and tickets can be obtained from Mr M. MacDonald, Palace Bar, Waterside Stores, Duneskin.

There are commercial netting rights at the river mouth which are exercised most energetically.

The disease UDN was first recorded in the Doon in 1967 and unfortunately it shows no sign of abating. An examination of the fishing log for a $1\frac{1}{2}$-mile beat on the lower Doon for the period 1946–1975 shows a decline in the rod catch of salmon, and the 10-year averages for the three decades is 19, 35 and 8. Since 1967 the catches were only into double figures in three years.

A River Doon Improvement Association has recently been formed to endeavour to restore the river to its former glory.

SALMON RIVERS OF SCOTLAND

The Girvan

The Water of Girvan has a number of sources, including those rising in the hills of Tairlaw Ring by the Big Hill of Glenmount and in Loch Bradan. Loch Bradan was developed as a water supply scheme for Irvine in 1905 and its area was increased in 1977 with the construction of a new dam in order to raise the water level. The river at first flows north-west as far as Kirkmichael but then turns south-west and enters the sea at Girvan. In its upper reaches above Straiton it is very much a moorland river, but from Straiton to Crosshill it has a series of attractive holding pools and fast runs which make this stretch a pleasant angling area. Below Crosshill, due to land improvement, the river is deep and sluggish until it reaches Dailly, after which it becomes quite rocky. Probably the loveliest part of the Girvan is centred round Blairquhan, where attractive views of the open countryside and river valley can be had from the mixed woodlands in Blairquhan Estate which were planted from 1800 onwards by the landscape architect Sir David Hunter Blair.

The main spawning areas are from Milton Bridge to Blairquhan Castle and upstream from Blairquhan to Tairlaw Linn whose 100-foot falls bar further upstream ascent of migratory fish.

There are three major riparian owners with salmon fishing. These are Bargany Estate which extends from Cairnhill Bridge to Dailly Bridge; Kilkerran Estate from Carsloe to Kilkerran, and Blairquhan Estate from Blairquhan to Cloncaird. There are also a number of angling clubs and associations with salmon fishing rights including Carrick, Dailly, Maybole and Straiton. The latter club was granted salmon fishing rights by Captain Sir Edward Hunter Blair, 6th baronet, in 1920.

The netting rights on the coast are in the hands of two owners, one operating on the south side of the river mouth and the other on the north side, who both use bag nets.

The main developments affecting this river are the Loch Bradan water supply scheme and the abstraction of water from above the weir, upstream from the main coast road, for the nearby alginate factory. At one time there was some pollution of the river from the Killochan colliery. However, the greatest threat to the future of the salmon in this river is the acid mine water which, since late 1979, has been entering the river from the Dalquharran colliery which the National Coal Board closed down in 1977. After the closure of the colliery the toxic waste built up in the shafts and in August 1979 began to discharge into the river about 6 miles upstream from Girvan at the rate of more than 500,000 gallons a day. Not only did this affect the salmon fishing but it also disrupted the production at the Alginate Industries factory and created problems for the Grant's Whisky distillery.

The angling clubs of the river, with the support of the Girvan District Salmon Fishery Board, have set up a small salmon hatchery on the Blairquhan Estate for the purpose of restocking some of the tributaries.

At one time there used to be an early run of fish into the river with fish being caught as far upstream as Blairquhan in March, and the earliest date on which a fish was taken was 10 March. Some fish are still caught in the spring, but the main run does not start until late May or early June, and there is also a good autumn run.

There appears to have been a decline in the catches of salmon in the last few years and the figures, kindly supplied by Mr James Hunter Blair from his fishing log book for the Blairquhan Estate, from 1965 — the first year in which the river was leased to permit holders — reveal this trend quite well.

Table 24
Catches of salmon on Blairquhan beat, River Girvan, 1965–1979

Year	Catch	Year	Catch	Year	Catch
1965	133	1970	156	1975	26
1966	366	1971	85	1976	30
1967	266	1972	70	1977	19
1968	72	1973	14	1978	33
1969	86	1974	17	1979	55

There is a large amount of salmon fishing available to the public on the Girvan and, as well as the angling clubs noted, salmon fishing is let on a daily basis from the three major estates. Bargany has four beats providing 8 tickets a day on a number of excellent pools such as Brunstone Wheel, Colonel's Pool, Lady Wheel, Stepping Stones, Pantry, Laird's Cast and Allan's Stream.

Kilkerran Estate lets fishing on a daily and weekly basis and a few concessionary permits are given to estate employees. Not more than 10 visitors' permits will be in use at any one time. Kilkerran also lets waters to the Dailly and Maybole Angling clubs and Kilkerran permit holders may also fish these waters with fly provided that they show proper consideration for club members already on the river.

Blairquhan Estate leases 10 day-permits on delightful water with a large number of pools providing sport under a variety of conditions. The better pools are Black Wheel, Goat Wheel, Witch Wheel, Lynn, O'Malley's, Sir David's, Ash Tree Hole and Kirstie's.

The Stinchar

The Stinchar rises on the moorlands of Carrick Forest and at first flows north as far as the Black Hill from which point it flows west as far as the Mull of Miljoan. It then changes its course again, to south-west, and flows past Barr, Pinwherry and Colmonell, finally entering the sea at Ballantrae after a run of some 30 miles. It is the most attractive of the Ayrshire rivers, is gravelly and fast-flowing and is well sheltered by woodlands. The main spawning areas are above Barr. The Stinchar has one major tributary, the Duisk River, which salmon and sea trout can ascend as far as the Linn at Barrhill. It is a very peaty water and for some reason is not a very good salmon river.

The Stinchar is a spate river but unfortunately its headwaters are tapped and led to Loch Bradan on the headwaters of the Girvan. It is felt that this abstraction, together with the effects of the extensive afforestation by the Forestry Commission in the upper reaches, is greatly reducing the time that the river is in good fishing order.

There is only a small amount of pollution, most of it emanating from farm effluents. Gravel extraction from the river at Pinwherry causes occasional problems, the main one being dirty water resulting from the workings. There is some gravel movement in the river and this is very apparent at the river mouth where the movement of gravel banks sometimes changes the river's course and the point at which the river enters the sea. UDN has occurred in this river but it has never reached serious proportions.

Knockdolian Estate, belonging to the Duchess of Wellington, has carried out a number of river improvements and, with the judicious siting of croys and logs anchored into the river bed, a number of additional pools and lies have been created. In addition, Knockdolian and Stair estates, which constitute the Stinchar District Fishery Board, have restocked some of the tributaries with salmon eggs.

The Stinchar is an excellent salmon and sea trout river. The sea trout run chiefly in June–September, but the salmon are a little later entering the river. The best months for salmon fishing are August, September and October. The total monthly catches of salmon and sea trout on the Knockdolian beat for the 10-year period, 1965–1974, reveal this very clearly.

―――――――――――――――――― Table 25 ――――――――――――――――――
Total monthly catches of salmon and sea trout on the Knockdolian Estate, 1965–1974

	salmon	sea trout
May	18	78
June	48	132
July	220	158
August	487	202
September	772	104
October	543	34

The average weight of the salmon is $8\frac{1}{4}$ lb and sea trout 2 lb. There is reputed to be a run of greybacks in November, but there is no rod fishing for them as the close season starts on 1 November.

There are a number of riparian owners with salmon fishing on the Stinchar. The four major owners of salmon fishing, starting upstream, are the estates of Dalreoch, Bardrochat, Knockdolian and Stair. The fishing on Stair Estate is let through the Stair Estates Office in Rephad, Stranraer, while the Knockdolian and Bardrochat beats are let through Michael Barne & Partners, 14 Alloway

Place, Ayr. Knockdolian beat has five fishing huts and 26 named pools including Ducat, Minister's, Maggie's Wheel, Corbie Stairs, Dalni Prunn, Shaksiston, Black Stone, Mermaid, Twins, Lynn Paeth and Sallachan. Most of the fishing is by fly only and, while most of the well-known patterns are useful, the Black Stinchar is recommended. The Colmonell Angling Club also has half a mile of fishing in the Colmonell area and the Daljarrock Hotel in Pinwherry can arrange fishing.

The commercial fishing is owned by Stair Estate and is leased to Knockdolian Estate. The fishing is carried out by net and coble and is limited to 500 fish.

38

THE SOLWAY RIVERS: 1

The Luce

The Water of Luce is a spate river rising from two streams whose sources are in the moorlands of Ayrshire. The westerly stream is the Main Water of Luce which is fed by a number of burns including the Penwhirn. This has now been dammed to form Penwhirn Reservoir which serves as the main water supply for Wigtown and only a compensation flow comes to the Main Water from this one time fruitful tributary. The easterly stream is the Cross Water of Luce which extends well into Ayrshire as far as Strawarren Fell which it drains. Because of its large catchment the Cross Water can rise very rapidly. Apparently 'cross water' refers to a tributary which joins the main stream at a cross or abrupt angle. The junction of the two streams is at New Luce, 6 miles from the sea and from here to Luce Bay the river runs fast over first a rocky bed and then gravel. Perhaps the main criticism of this lovely river, which rises and falls so rapidly, is the general scarcity of good holding pools. At one time the Puddle Hole, immediately below the railway viaduct and less than a mile from the mouth of the river, had a reputation for holding large numbers of fish, particularly sea trout, and this was probably earned through it being the first holding pool for fish running up the straight and rather shallow stretch of water from the sea. However, the reputation of the Puddle Hole is now of less importance and one wonders if it is because there are now fewer sea trout in this river than there used to be.

Salmon run up both tributaries but sea trout tend to go up the Main Water. There is good spawning throughout the whole of the river, particularly above New Luce, and in the feeder streams. However, the construction of holding pools would ensure a better distribution of fish and provide them with more shelter during drought periods.

The major run of fish is from July, although occasionally fish are caught in May and June but usually below New Luce. The main period for sea trout is July and early August and there is some good night fishing to be had in the lower reaches. The best of the fishing is from New Luce to Penwhirn on the Main Water and from New Luce to Glenwhilly on the Cross Water.

The fishing is owned almost entirely by Stair Estates but some fishing is available to the public through Stranraer and District Angling Association, who have fishing on a section of the Cross Water upstream from Quarter Bridge. Some stretches of the river are also let through the Stair Estate Office at Rephad, Stranraer.

There is no commercial netting in the tidal part of the river but there is a sweep netting station on the east side of the river mouth near Stairhaven which is on lease from Stair Estate.

UDN reached this river in 1968 and has appeared every year since then until 1976 when no disease was recorded. It is not known whether this is the reason for the decline in the sea trout stocks, but what is certain is that the Luce has, in recent years, become a very much improved salmon river.

The Bladnoch

The Bladnoch is a gentle little river flowing out of Loch Maberry and down through the Galloway countryside and the top of The Machars to the sea at Wigtown. The river can be conveniently divided into five sections. The first, from Loch Maberry to Glassoch consists of gravelly runs with some deep holding pools and is a good spawning area; from Glassoch to Barhoise Dam the river becomes deep and sluggish and very peaty and there are only a few small runs. In this part pike and, more recently, perch abound and the pike undoubtedly create havoc among the migrating smolts. This section is, however, a good holding area for fish but is not good for fishing barring one pool at the dam. Just above the dam there are falls at the Linn of Barhoise which fish do not ascend until April. The third section, from Barhoise Dam to Crows, is fast with gravelly pools and rocky runs; it is the best section for fishing and is excellent fly water. There are good brown trout in this part of the river as far up as Spittal Bridge and it is felt that this is because of the smaller number of pike present — possibly because it is not pike habitat and because the pike that were there have been caught. From Crows to Torhouse Mill the river reverts to a sluggish nature and again pike and perch abound. However, it is good for salmon in the spring and when there is a fair wind fly fishing can be good. The last section from Torhouse Mill to the top of the tide consists of fast-running water with gravelly and rocky stretches with pools. In the tidal area the river wends its way over the Wigtown Sands and at low tide its channel can be seen joining that of the Cree.

A number of burns join the Bladnoch along its course and the three main ones are the Black Burn, the Tarff Water and the Malzie. The Black Burn joins the river a mile above Shennanton and is basically a spawning tributary. The Tarff is a major tributary and joins the Bladnoch just below Kirkcowan. It is basically a grilse river and the grilse run appears to be shared equally between the Tarff and the Bladnoch. Some salmon, however, are taken from the Tarff from late April. The Tarff is a good spawning tributary and consists of gravel and bedrock with deep holding pools. The Malzie flows out of Mochrum Loch, which is the only freshwater nesting site of the cormorant in the British Isles, and joins the main river just below Dalreagle. It is a good spawning burn and fish enter it in late October and November. Perch have been found in it in recent years which does not augur well for the young salmon.

Unlike many south-west coast rivers the Bladnoch has a good run of spring fish. Some fish are caught in February but the run is chiefly from the third week of March to the end of May. The spring fish average about 9 lb and big fish are scarce, although fish of up to 34 lb have been taken. The grilse run is from the end of June to the end of July but this depends on the availability of water. Some anglers maintain that there is an autumn run of 'greybacks', but others point out that these fish are rather too coloured to be considered clean fish recently in from the sea and also that they are gravid and ready to spawn. Virtually no sea trout are caught in the river although a few finnock or herling are caught in the estuary.

UDN first appeared in 1968 but has been of no consequence since then.

It is noticed that the river runs off much more rapidly after a spate than it used to do and the ploughing carried out by the Forestry Commission has been blamed for this. It is also blamed for the high peat content of the water as a result of this drainage.

A Bladnoch River Board has now been set up and fully constituted, and the secretary is Messrs McCormack and Nicholson in Newton Stewart. The main concern of the Board is the conservation of the river's salmon stocks and the general river environment. One big improvement it has been considering is the removal of the coarse fish, particularly the pike, which are so prolific. Spinning for these brutes has helped but, because of the extent of suitable water available to them, more effective control measures are necessary. An interesting phenomenon which has occurred in recent years is the appearance of grey mullet in the tidal waters of the river. It may be that the warmer water temperatures prevailing during the summer months, as a result of summer drought flows in recent years, has attracted these fish into the river from the Solway.

The angling on the Bladnoch is almost entirely privately owned, except for a 3-mile section below Loch Maberry at Waterside Farm which is leased by the Newton Stewart and District Angling Association.

The commercial fishing consists of a net and coble fishery operated below Torhouse Mill by Shennanton Estate and stake nets in the estuary belonging to Innerwell Fisheries.

The Cree

The Cree rises in Loch Moan and has a large catchment area extending out over the high ground in south Ayrshire and west Kirkcudbright. Its reputation for rising rapidly, with the result that it has flooded the low ground near Wigtown Bay, is due in fact to its steep rocky tributaries. These tributaries are the Minnoch, Trool, Penkiln and Palnure, and they drain an extensive area which covers Carrick and Glentrool Forests in the north and Kirroughtree Forest and the Cairnsmore of Fleet in the south and west. The Minnoch is the largest tributary of the Cree and extends further into Ayrshire than the Cree itself and its western feeder streams drain off Brandy Well and Rowantree Hill, two hills overlooking the Nick of Balloch; while to the east the Pilnrark Burn comes into the Minnoch a little way south of Waterhead and the Shalloch Burn, draining off Shalloch Craig Face, enters the Minnoch near Shalloch on Minnoch. The Cree flows west from Loch Moan, turns south and picks up a side arm of the river draining out of Loch Dornal on Drumlamford Estate.

The Cree is at first a stony stream with broken rocky runs and long thin streams with occasional deep pools, but about $2\frac{1}{2}$ miles upstream from Bargrennan there are steep falls a short distance above Birch Linn. The fish congregate in the deep pools below these falls, which are only surmountable at certain heights of water. The fishing in this area tends to be good, but between Bargrennan and the Minnoch confluence at Clauchaneasy there is a long stretch of even, shallow water where the fishing is poor. Below Clauchaneasy the river becomes deep and sluggish and widens out into what is known locally as 'Loch Cree' which extends downstream as far as Penninghame Open Prison. This part of the river is the home of pike and one can imagine the toll they take of migrating smolts. One pool on this stretch, known as Cunningham's Ford, is considered the best pool on the whole river. Below Penninghame the river is still deep but it has a faster flow and is good fly fishing water all the way to Linloskin. The area from Linloskin, a mile above Newton Stewart, downstream to the tide is fast and shallow with rocky runs and occasional pools and is good water for fly fishing.

The season on the Cree is 1 March – 30 September; there is a good run of fish in the early part of the season and a much greater run of grilse from July to the end of the season. Salmon do not reach the upper Cree above the falls until late in the season and it is unusual for anglers to catch fish in the upper reaches well above Bargrennan until August. Sea trout only ascend the Cree as far as Linloskin and the main run is in June and July.

The Newton Stewart and District Angling Association have the majority of the fishing on the lower Cree around Newton Stewart and permits can be obtained locally. Upstream from Newton Stewart the Galloway Estate has the fishings up to Clauchaneasy and these are divided into four beats. Starting from the furthest upstream they, and their pools, are: Beat A — Junction, Island, Cunningham's Ford; Beat B — Burnfoot, House, Garden; Beat C — Barclye, Island, Learie's; Beat D — Stepping Stones, Challoch, Challoch Run.

These beats are let through the Galloway Estate Factors, G. M. Thomson & Co, 10 Victoria Street, Newton Stewart. The average annual catch on these

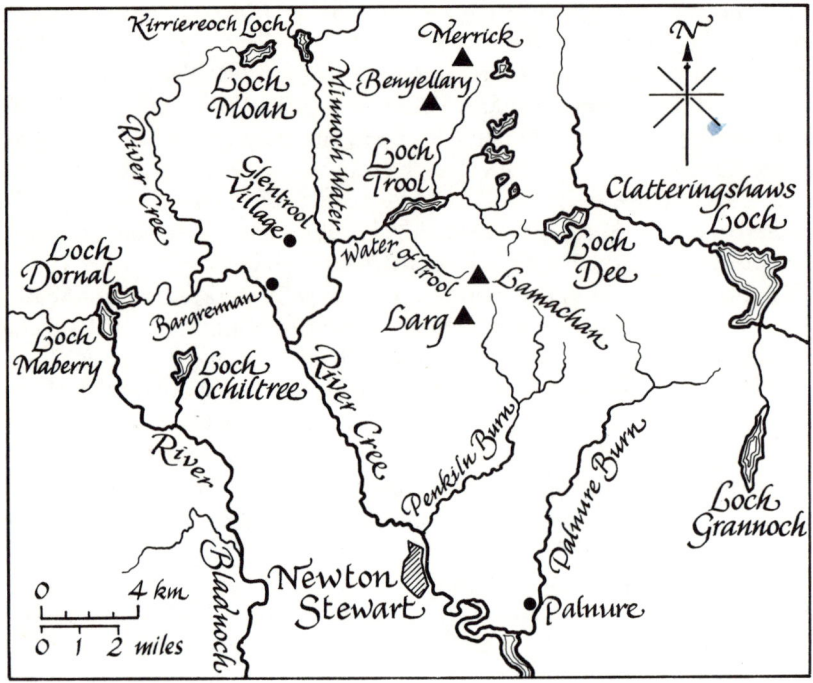

The River Cree

beats is approximately 200.

A small section of the upper Cree near Loch Dornal, owned by Drumlamford Estate, is available for let from Michael Barne and Partners, Ayr.

There are net and coble stations near the mouth of the river, one being half way between Newton Stewart and Creetown, one by the mouth of the Palnure Burn and a third just above Creetown. Below Creetown for some distance there are sets of stake nets.

The three main tributaries, the Minnoch, Penkiln and Palnure are all good salmon streams and are worthy of mention.

The Minnoch throughout most of its length is a steep rocky stream. Below Glencaird there are fine banks of gravel as the stream slows down and just before reaching the Cree it becomes quieter and deeper. Three miles upstream from its confluence with the Cree the Minnoch is joined by the Water of Trool which descends from Loch Trool through a really beautiful glen. Glen Trool and the line of the Minnoch converge from either side of a spur of hills named the Rig of Stroan, which rises in a succession of eminences culminating in the mountain of Merrick (2,764 feet) which commands a view over a very wide area.

The Minnoch has an early run of fish. The largest and best part of the Minnoch is owned by Messrs Moore of Littlewood's Pools who reside at Glen

THE SOLWAY RIVERS: 1

Trool Lodge. Through their generosity this lovely home is made available to their employees when they themselves are not in residence. Higher up the Minnoch, above the Trool confluence, the Newton Stewart and District Angling Association have two miles of fishing from the right bank. At this point the fishing is best from June onwards.

The Penkiln joins the Cree from the east, just upstream from Newton Stewart. This is a steep fast-running stream draining off Kirroughtree Forest but is not blessed with an early run of fish as is the Minnoch, and the main run starts in June. However, it has a good run of sea trout. The Newton Stewart and District Angling Association have the fishing on both banks of this stream above Mattie White's Bridge. The fishing is best from July onwards, depending on availability of water.

The Palnure Burn drains off the Cairnsmore of Fleet and is a fast river with a rocky and gravel bed. It is largely in forestry ground and rises and falls quickly. In its lower and tidal reaches it flows much more slowly and it is quite sluggish as it enters the Cree below the village of Palnure. The river is tidal some distance upstream and the fish have access on the tides. Unlike the Cree the Palnure has no spring run, and the main run for salmon, grilse and sea trout does not start until mid-June. The best of the fishing is from the top of the tide upstream for 4 or 5 miles. Until recently the Newton Stewart and District Angling Association had some of the fishing on the Palnure but this stretch has now been leased privately. There is sweep netting on the tidal reaches of the stream.

The Cree river system is a healthy one and perhaps the main improvement required is the construction of more pools, particularly in the lower beat in Newton Stewart and perhaps in the stretch between the Minnoch confluence and Bargrennan.

It says a lot for the Newton Stewart and District Angling Association and Galloway Estate that so much salmon and sea trout angling is available to the public. Perhaps the one thing that could be controlled by them more effectively is the sniggling, snatching or foul hooking of fish during periods of low water, but this is a deplorable practice carried out on some Scottish rivers by people who should know better.

The Cree is one of the very few rivers in Scotland which has a large run of smelt from the Solway Firth into its tidal reaches in late March and early April.

39

THE SOLWAY RIVERS: 2

The Fleet

The Fleet is one of the most attractive of the smaller Solway rivers. It has two tributaries, the Big Water of Fleet and the Little Water of Fleet, which rise high up in the lovely Galloway hills. The Little Fleet comes out of Loch Fleet, lying between the Fell of Fleet and Craigwhinnie, and flows down through the moors and the Forestry Commission plantations. After passing under the Little Water of Fleet railway viaduct, which is unfortunately now closed to rail traffic due to the misguided policy of axing the railway service to Stranraer and so throwing an intolerable burden on the westbound roads, the river reaches Craigie Linn and impassable falls at Burnfoot. Below Burnfoot the river continues down a narrow valley overlooked by the Doon of Culreoch and the Scrogs of Drumruck and joins the Big Water of Fleet at Aikyhill. The Big Water of Fleet and its tributaries drain off the eastern slopes of the Cairnsmore of Fleet and the southern side of Craigwhinnie. The Big Fleet then flows south past the interesting rock formation of the Clints of Dromore, close to the Big Water of Fleet railway viaduct, and down to join the Little Water of Fleet to become simply the Fleet.

The main river flows through a charming woodland area made up of a number of oakwoods of which Carstramon is the largest and most interesting. In the springtime this wood is virtually carpeted with wild hyacinths, and people come from miles around to see this natural display of wild flowers which can rival any man-made garden. Perhaps this wood's greatest claim to fame in recent years was the temporary sanctuary it gave to some wild boar which escaped in 1970 from a local landowner's estate. This caused considerable concern to the neighbours, to the Forestry Commission and to the Department of Agriculture. The animals were eventually destroyed but a survivor of the first round-up and shoot, who became known as 'Fred', was only eventually killed in 1974 some 42 miles away; he weighed 274 lb and measured five feet in length.

There are some nice pools on the river from Aikyhill to Gatehouse of Fleet including the Bridge, which is the best on the river, Barbara, Battery, Standing Stone and Stranger's.

Below Gatehouse the river is sluggish and includes a long straight stretch.

THE SOLWAY RIVERS: 2

This section is the old canal which was made in 1924 to enable vessels to navigate up the river as far as Port MacAdam.

The course of the Fleet can be traced at low tide right out of Fleet Bay and into Wigtown Bay. As on the Bladnoch, grey mullet are now seen up as far as Gatehouse.

The ownership of the River Fleet is shared mainly by Cally and Rusko estates, but by arrangement the whole is controlled by Cally Estate; all of it is available by ticket to the public. The Fleet and the Big Water of Fleet are divided into a lower, middle and upper stretch. The Lower Stretch extends $2\frac{1}{2}$ miles on both banks and season tickets are available. The Middle Stretch consists of 2 miles on both banks; it is split into six beats and, working upstream, they are 1, 2, A, 3, B and 4. This is the best of the fishing and is more expensive, but still very reasonable as prices for salmon and sea trout fishing go nowadays, and is let by the day. The Upper Stretch covers both banks for $4\frac{1}{2}$ miles and consists of beats 5 and 6, both of which are in the Big Water of Fleet and are separated from Beat 4 by a blank stretch of water which yields few fish. The Upper Stretch is also let by daily tickets. Beat 5 extends up to the railway viaduct and contains a good pool at the falls known as the Pool of Ness. One of the biggest fish to come off this river was one of 20 lb caught recently by a River Watcher in the Wire Fence Pool on this beat. Beat 6 is from the railway viaduct upstream. Although rod fishing on the Fleet is officially from 25 February to 31 October, the proprietors in fact do not open the river to angling until 1 June. This would seem to be early enough, unless by any chance there is an unrecorded spring run, as the Lower and Middle stretches yield sea trout but only an occasional grilse in June and the main run of salmon, grilse and sea trout is from July to mid-August. On the Upper Stretch the run is that little bit later.

The Little Water of Fleet is let by the day and the main run is at about the same time as that in the Upper Stretch on the Big Water of Fleet, but this depends on the availability of water. Details of all the fishings can be obtained from the Cally Estate Office in Gatehouse of Fleet.

The Fleet is more of a sea trout river than a salmon river, although in recent years the number of salmon and grilse caught on rod and line have shown a slight tendency to increase, as can be seen below.

Table 26
Catches of salmon, grilse, sea trout and finnock on the Fleet, 1971–1976

	Salmon	Grilse	Sea Trout	Finnock
1971	4	5	133	87
1972	2	1	45	25
1973	7	3	55	16
1974	8	14	31	21
1975	5	6	45	41
1976	12	17	72	15

There is no commercial netting in the river but there are stake nets in the bay fished by Cardoness Estate.

The spawning grounds are in the upper reaches of the Big Water of Fleet and in a number of burns running into the middle reaches of the river. These include the Pulcree Burn, the Barley Burn (known also as the Fleuchlarg Burn) and the Castramont Burn. The latter is a beautiful spawning stream with clear water and a gravelly bed and, although running through a fairly dense deciduous wood, shows none of the signs of silting, erosion and lack of life so characteristic of streams now blocked off from the daylight by the new coniferous forests sprouting up all over Scotland.

Cally Estate maintains the sea trout stocks by planting sea trout fry annually. Until recently these came from the Danish island of Bornholm.

There is considerable concern for the river environment from the effects of afforestation, and the river now rises rapidly and falls even more quickly as a result of hill drainage. Many of the better pools are becoming shallower as a result of gravel and silt deposits. Furthermore, there has been a marked increase in the acidity of Loch Fleet and Loch Grannoch, which is attributed to the surrounding land being planted. In Loch Fleet the pH value in 1975 was 4.4 compared with a more alkaline value of 6.6 in 1961. The erstwhile considerable brown trout stocks in both these lochs has declined dramatically, and are now virtually non-existent.

The Dee

Prior to hydro-electric development the Dee drained a catchment of about 360 square miles. Its main branch, the Ken, rises among the hills where the counties of Kirkcudbright, Ayr and Dumfries meet, and flowed as a fast, gravelly stream for 20 miles to the head of Loch Ken. Here, its nature changed and it became a deep and sluggish water, moving through 13 miles of weedy lochs infested with pike and perch. For the last 6 miles of its course it gathered speed and raced down a steep-sided gorge to the head of tide at Tongland. The principal tributary, the Black Water of Dee, drained an area of moorland to the west of the Ken. Much of it was fast flowing and gravelly but it traversed lochs and smaller pools, all of which held pike. It joined the Ken at Parton, about half way down the slow-moving section, and from there the combined river was called the Dee.

The Galloway Dee power project, to harness the waters of the Dee system, was proposed and started in 1927 by the Galloway Water Power Company (now the South of Scotland Electricity Board) and completed in 1934. Starting from the lower reaches, the largest power station on the system is at Tongland. A little less than a mile upstream the gorge was dammed to a height of 72 feet so that the whole of the gorge became a head pond and the whole river is diverted down a tunnel and aqueduct to the power station. A compensation flow passes downstream from the dam to lead fish to the pass. The problem of securing a supply of water from the reservoir to the fish pass with every variation in the surface level has been solved by a system of automatically operated sluices constructed in the wall of the dam and placed in a regular descending series, each sluice communicating with its corresponding pool in the pass and opening as the water level in the reservoir falls or, conversely, closing as the water level rises again. The sluice openings are designed to operate as submerged orifices and are all of the same area as the orifices in the cross walls of the pools in the fish pass below which consist of 25 small pools and four resting pools. Lessons learned from this scheme, and experience from other schemes, have enabled modifications to be introduced and some of the pass has been changed to a pool and overfall construction. A needle valve was also introduced to add compensation water at the foot of the pass without increasing turbulence in the pass. This provides additional incentive to draw fish up to and beyond the ladder. About 7 miles upstream at Glenlochar an eight-foot barrage was built across the Dee, which impounds about 9 miles of slow-moving water, including Loch Ken. A one-chamber fish pass is provided for when the barrage is closed.

On the Black Water of Dee a large dam was built at Clatteringshaws to impound more than half the watershed of that river in Clatteringshaws Loch reservoir from which water is passed eastwards by tunnel to the Ken at Glenlee Power Station. No compensation flow is provided on the Black Water below the dam so that the river relies entirely on water from inflowing tributaries below the dam.

Above Loch Ken the river Ken is dammed at Earlstoun, Casfad and Kendoon, each dam having a headpond above and a power station below. Fish passes are installed in the Earlstoun and Casfad dams, but not in the dam at Kendoon.

The natural flow of water down the Ken has been greatly increased by the damming of Loch Doon (see under River Doon) and diverting some of the water from Loch Doon into the Ken basin.

According to King-Webster in his article in the 1969 issue of *Salmon Net* entitled *The Galloway Dee — A Short History of a Salmon River*, the loss of potential spawning area in the Dee and Ken watershed as a result of these developments amounts to about 50 per cent of the total available. King-Webster also considered that the hydro-electric developments reduced the salmon stock as a result of the experimental design of the fish passes, in particular the pass at Tongland which, built on the pool and oriface system, deterred the ascent of fish, as a result of the violent jets of water and the unnatural turbulence in the pools.

A further reason for the decline of the salmon stocks after this power scheme was the increase in the amount of deep and sluggish water which became infested with pike and perch, as well as large brown trout, which were already present in Loch Ken and which is famed for the Kenmure Pike, a monster fish caught many years ago and reputed to weigh 72 lb.

In 1959 plans were made to restore the runs of salmon, and since 1960 the South of Scotland Electricity Board, the Dee District Salmon Fishery Board and the Dee Salmon Fishing Association have carried out a number of remedial measures. These have included reconstruction of the fish passes, removal of pike, perch and large trout, planting nursery areas with eggs and fry and experimenting with the volume and timing of compensation water releases. The fish passes were converted from the pool and orifice to the pool and overfall type and the chambers have been re-shaped. By 1966 the run of fish had increased about tenfold. Unfortunately as a result of the advent of UDN in 1966, the Dee was the first river in Scotland to record it, and offshore netting, the stocks again declined and only started to show signs of recovery in 1977, although low flows in 1976 and 1977 may have made it difficult to draw an accurate conclusion.

The main salmon proprietors on the river are the South of Scotland Electricity Board, the National Trust for Scotland, Nether Hall, Balmagie, Colonel Forbes of Earlstoun and Lord Sinclair at Knocknalling.

Salmon fishing on the River Ken is available to the public through the New Galloway Angling Association, who have rights on certain parts of the river. Salmon fishing is free to residents at Ken Bridge Hotel. Below Glenlochar barrage the salmon fishing is in private hands.

There has been no spring run of salmon since the advent of the Galloway scheme and it is not until May that salmon start to run the river. The average weight of salmon is in the region of 11–12 lb and that of grilse 5 lb.

The Dee is not a good angling river and even when fish are present they are loath to take the angler's lure. Very few sea trout run up the Ken, as those entering the Dee tend to go up the Tarff which enters the Dee at Tongland.

The commercial fishing which existed in the lower Dee at Tongland prior to the scheme was most interesting and quite unique. The fishing methods used were doachs, ladle nets, shoulder nets and draught nets. The doachs were rather like cruives and consisted of a masonry wall joining various outcropping rocks, and extending right across the bed of the river from bank to bank. In it were three gaps which let the water through, but which could be closed to the larger fish by removeable hecks. These hecks were wooden gratings with vertical bars a minimum of 3 inches apart. They were only removed during the weekly close-time. For the rest of the season all fish too large to pass between the bars were held back. Fish so held back were caught with ladle nets and shoulder nets. Ladle nets were outsize landing nets with 20-foot shafts which were used for scooping fish from immediately below the doachs. Shoulder nets were used in small pools among the rocks lower down the river. In addition draught or drag nets were worked in the Linn and Draught Pools at the foot of the rapids. This combined fishing was owned and fished by the St Mary's Isle Estate until it was purchased by the Galloway

Water Power Company under sanction by Parliament.

Other net fishings in operation in the estuary were those using yair nets which are unique to the Dee. Since 1931 the only commercial fishing below Tongland Dam has been two yairs, at Bishopton (Gibb Hill) and Castlesod, operated by the Dee Salmon Fishing Association, under licence from the South of Scotland Electricity Board. This helps to finance the association which is doing its utmost to rehabilitate the salmon stocks of this river.

The Urr

Although the Urr Water, which lies just to the east of the Dee, seems an insignificant river even in its lower reaches it has in fact quite a large catchment area and is approximately 35 miles long, from its source in Loch Urr to its mouth in Rough Firth. A number of burns join the Urr a short distance below Loch Urr, including the Craigenputtock Burn which flows past Craigenputtock of Thomas Carlyle fame. The Urr is a moorland stream for a large part of its length but becomes more sluggish as it reaches Dalbeattie and the tidal waters. Unfortunately it suffers from the effects of drainage, both forestry and agricultural, with the result that it rises and falls rapidly. This has disastrous consequences for angling as the Urr is a river which does need a good flow of water before the fish will run.

There used to be a good run of spring fish into the Urr in March and April before UDN occurred in the river in the late 1960s. Although UDN is of no consequence nowadays, the best months for salmon angling are now September and October, and the local anglers maintain that the fish entering the river at this time are 'greybacks'. Not very many grilse enter the Urr unless there is a wet summer. Unlike the Fleet to the west of the Dee, the Urr is not a sea trout river; it is most interesting to see how so many neighbouring rivers in this area vary in their apparent ability to support sea trout, and how the size of the sea trout stocks has changed in recent years. Research in this field might well produce interesting findings.

An appreciable part of the salmon fishing on the Urr is available to the public through the Dalbeattie Angling Association and the Castle Douglas Angling Association. The Dalbeattie club has the fishing on the lowest 4 miles of the river from the tidal waters to the old railway viaduct, while the Castle Douglas Angling Association has $4\frac{1}{2}$–5 miles of fishing from East Logan at the Urr viaduct to Nethertown of Croys. There are some good pools on this stretch including the Well, Baron, Step End, Cauls, Davie Craig, Red Braes, Spottes Dam, Battery, Jeans and Grange Water.

Commercial netting with haaf nets is carried on in the tidal part of the river at Palnackie, while stake nets occur along the coast.

40

THE SOLWAY RIVERS: 3

The Nith

The Nith is the largest of the Dumfriesshire rivers. It rises in south Ayrshire in the hills to the east of Dalmellington, drains 435 square miles of moorland and arable farmland and throughout its course receives numerous tributaries. The Cairn, entering 3 miles above Dumfries, is the most important of these. The upper section flows in a south-easterly direction to New Cumnock, just north of the Dumfriesshire boundary, and then takes an easterly course to Kirkconnel and Sanquhar, all three being within the coal producing area. Between New Cumnock and Sanquhar the river meanders considerably and the flow is sluggish for several miles at average water levels. Downstream from Sanquhar the river enters the most picturesque part of the valley of Nithsdale and touches several communities on route to the county town of Dumfries. Here at the top of the tidal water a cauld, 400 feet in length, about 5–7 feet high and having an efficient fish pass, crosses the river and marks the divide between fresh water and the tidal channel. The latter extends about 6 miles before merging in the waters of the Solway, approximately 50 miles from its source in the Ayrshire hills.

Up to the early 1950s the value of the Nith as a salmon river was seriously affected by extensive pollution. In the upper reaches colliery pollution was of very large proportions and the bed of the river was smothered in coal 'gum' to a depth of anything up to 10 inches. With every rise in the river level the vast accumulation of this material was carried in a black suspension downstream for the whole breadth and width of the river. In the tidal reaches there was further pollution from the discharge of crude sewage from the Burghs of Dumfries and Maxwelltown, and this section of the river was virtually an open sewer which no fish could penetrate except during flood conditions.

With the constitution of the Nith Fishings Improvement Association in 1934, and the subsequent affiliation of the Dumfries and Galloway Angling Association, the Mid-Nithsdale Angling Association, the Upper Nithsdale Angling Association, the Dumfries Town Council and the Nith Estuary Proprietors of Salmon Netting, steps were taken to control the pollution. The endeavours of this Association were given the full support of Mr P. R. C. Macfarlane, the then Inspector of Salmon Fisheries for Scotland, and with the co-operation of the National Coal Board the upper section of the river gradually improved and is now a healthy environment. On the tidal reach new purification installations were gradually brought into use after pressure from the Solway Purification Board, constituted in 1953 in terms of the Prevention of Pollution (Scotland) Act, 1951, was applied. It says a great deal for the Nith Fishings Improvement Association and the Solway Purification Board as, due to their efforts, the Nith is now a clean and pollution-free river, and a glance at recent issues of Annual Report of the Nith Fishings Improvement Association reveals no mention of pollution. Pollution was not the only phenomenon which was affecting salmon stocks and netting also had a great effect on these. At that time the tidal waters right up to the Cauld Pool were systematically and extensively netted on the ebb tide. A full account of the recovery of the Nith as a salmon river has been given by David Lawrence in an article in the September issue of the *Salmon and Trout Magazine* for 1965. The annual catches of salmon, grilse and sea trout for the years 1934 to 1979 speak for themselves.*

Table 27

Catches of salmon, grilse and sea trout on the River Nith, 1934–1978

Year	Salmon	Grilse	Sea Trout	Notes
1934	188	11	273	Formation of the Nith Fishings Improvement Association
1935	359	7	378	
1936	288	7	446	
1937	215	13	422	
1938	349	22	1,112	
1939	168	19	408	
1940	173	10	449	
1941	139	8	265	
1942	194	9	758	
1943	277	14	604	
1944	190	11	298	
1945	130	7	914	
1946	167	23	874	
1947	238	53	854	
1948	599	49	1,489	Suspension of netting in all Burgh Waters
1949	158	21	760	Stocking programme started
1950	396	51	738	
1951	246	113	923	

---

* These must be considered as minimum figures due to incomplete returns being made by anglers.

Year	Salmon	Grilse	Sea Trout	Notes
1952	230	21	741	
1953	377	61	1,681	
1954	609	67	1,983	
1955	608	133	1,814	
1956	968	333	3,329	
1957	1,205	292	2,439	
1958	1,338	302	3,847	
1959	1,185	170	4,266	
1960	1,219	161	2,988	
1961	1,418	214	4,024	
1962	2,026	559	6,411	
1963	2,357	408	6,499	Some limit to haaf netting achieved
1964	2,611	637	8,256	
1965	2,279	333	6,471	
1966	2,251	559	9,502	UDN appears
1967	1,072	267	5,646	
1968	830	266	3,377	
1969	997	497	2,753	
1970	1,444	666	2,812	
1971	902	380	3,615	
1972	637	252	3,488	
1973	1,166	423	5,386	
1974	1,312	576	4,386	
1975	1,078	423	5,470	
1976	750	308	4,816	Drought year
1977	1,020	316	3,451	
1978	968	367	3,426	
1979	1,072	608	3,896	

The increase in catches of salmon, grilse and sea trout was not entirely due to pollution abatement, but also to suspension of netting in Burgh Waters, the prohibition of angling in the Cauld pools, stocking with eyed salmon and sea trout ova, the removal of pike and grayling, a limitation to the amount of haaf netting in the tidal channel and the demolition of obstructions to migratory fish on tributary streams. Such an exercise in rehabilitation on a river the size of the Nith is to be applauded and all those involved in the task congratulated. As Lawrence said: 'For the greater part of its length the Nith is an example of a beautiful river which invited and certainly merited the protracted treatment which was applied.'

Over the last 14 years there has been a change in the seasonal catches of salmon on the Nith, and in recent years there has been a decline in the number of spring fish, even though running conditions have in some years been suitable, and an increase in the number of fish caught in the autumn. In 1975 and 1976 the increase in the numbers of fish caught in the autumn was almost

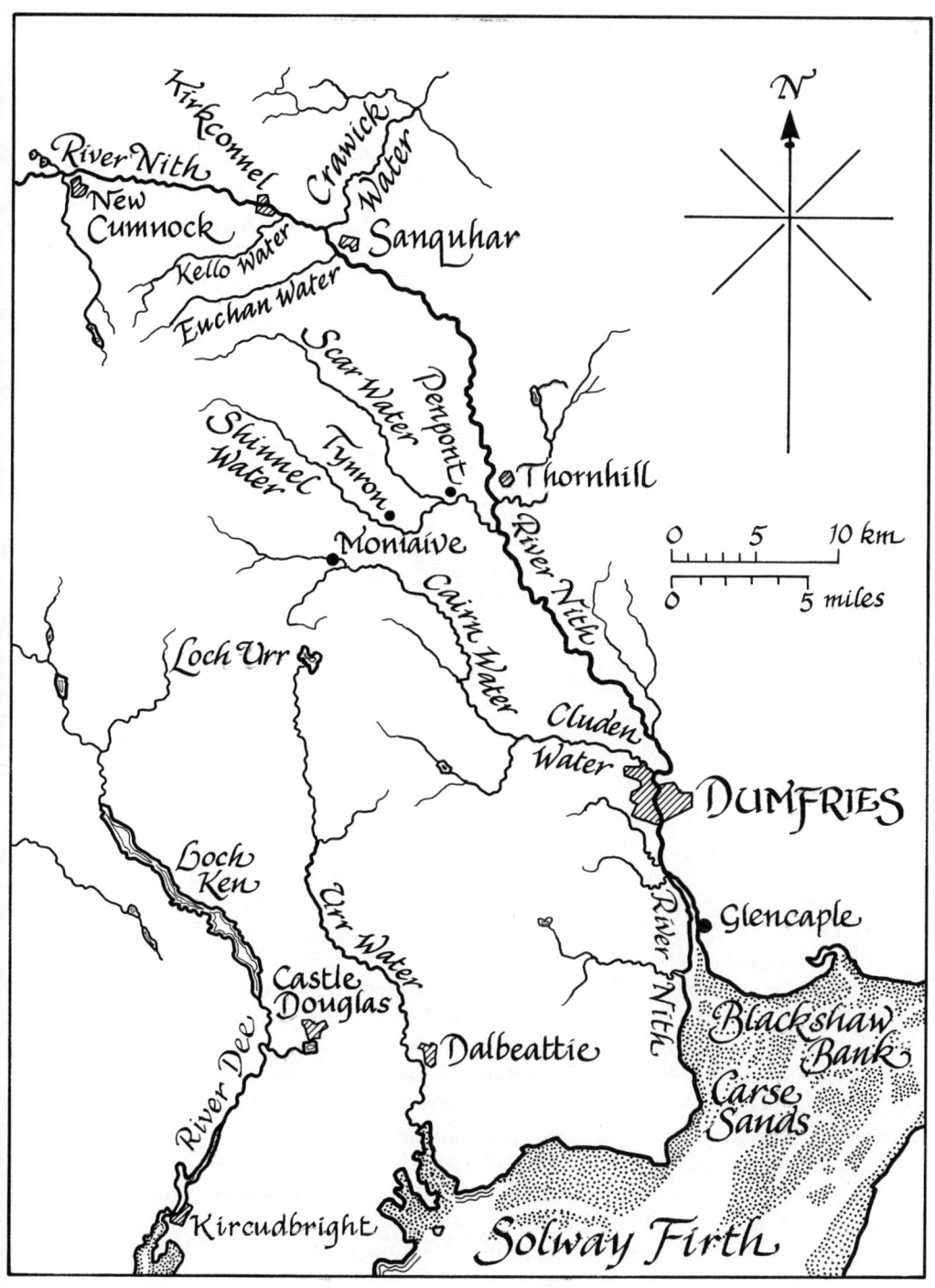

The River Nith

certainly due to the drought conditions which had prevailed for most of the summer. The seasonal catches of salmon for the years 1964 to 1979 are given below.

Table 28

Seasonal catches of salmon, expressed in percentages, on the River Nith, 1964–1979

	Spring	Summer	Autumn
1964	14	34	52
1965	23	35	42
1966	27	34	38
1967	25	35	40
1968	20	41	39
1969	12	49	39
1970	9	56	35
1971	11	62	27
1972	18	54	28
1973	12	36	52
1974	6	46	48
1975	10	16	74
1976	9	17	74
1977	16	19	65
1978	10	30	60
1979	7	32	61

It can be seen that there has been a drop in the percentage of spring fish since the advent of UDN in 1966, although it should be stressed that UDN may not be the only reason for this decline.

The average weight of salmon is about $9\frac{1}{2}$ lb, grilse $4\frac{1}{2}$ lb and sea trout 2 lb. Large salmon of up to 30 lb are occasionally caught.

The Nith was one of the first of the Scottish rivers to be affected by UDN, the disease first being recorded in 1966 and reaching alarming proportions in 1967. Although there has been some abatement in the extent of infection since then, the disease is still present.

Restocking of the Nith continues with salmon and sea trout fry from the Eccles Hatchery — which has a capacity of 240,000 salmon and sea trout ova and is operated by the Mid-Nithsdale Angling Association.

There is a certain amount of poaching on this river, as on many others. One of the main problems in this connection occurs at the Cauld Pool where small groups of youngsters 'snatch' waiting salmon by foulhooking with various types of spinning lure. More than one juvenile poacher has been seen, when the alarm has been given by his lookouts, running full pelt across the Whitesands with a salmon trailing behind him.

Wild mink are fast creating a problem throughout the Solway area, and the

Nith Fishings Improvement Association give a bounty of 50p for each mink tail received. In 1976 they paid out the sum of £62.50 for these tails.

One continuing problem is that of haaf netting, which appears to be proliferating, and in 1977 there were 140 permits issued for haaf netting in the Nith estuary from Kelton to beyond Glencaple.

Another type of net over which there is some concern is the Paidle (or White Fish) net which bears a close resemblance to the certificated salmon stake net and is normally operated within the tidal channel and estuary of the river. While they are ostensibly set to capture white fish, which they have a right to do, it has been suspected for a long time that the operators are more interested in salmon, to which they could claim no title. A test came before the court some years ago when this type of net, as constructed (to take salmon), was declared illegal. Some of these nets have since disappeared but others remain, presumably modified!

A considerable amount of salmon and sea trout fishing on the Nith is available to the visiting angler and much of this is in the hands of the Upper Nithsdale Angling Club, the Mid-Nithsdale Angling Association and the Dumfries and Galloway Angling Association. It has been said that the salmon on the Nith do not 'take' readily compared with neighbouring rivers such as the Annan, but, judging by the catch data, the occasions on which these non-taking moods occur must be few.

The Cairn

The Cairn Water is strictly speaking called the Cluden in its lower reaches, and only the upper part, from where three head streams — the Dalwhat, Craigdarroch and Castlefern waters — unite at Moniaive, is called the Cairn Water. However, from long usage the whole of this lengthy and important Nith tributary is known as the Cairn. From the source of the Dalwhat Water to Lincluden Abbey, at the confluence with the Nith, the Cairn is about 25 miles long.

At one time a cruive and a number of dam dykes hindered the ascent of migratory fish on the Cluden. The falls at the dangerous Cluden Rocks, a hazard for many anglers, are a gathering point for salmon and sea trout during low water, where they are vulnerable to poachers and boys with high-velocity air rifles.

The Dumfries and Galloway Angling Association have done a lot to improve the sea trout fishing in this river and have planted sea trout fry from the Danish island of Bornholm over a number of years. This association has the salmon and trout fishings over a considerable length of this river and visitor's tickets are available from David McMillan, 6 Friar's Vennel, Dumfries.

SALMON RIVERS OF SCOTLAND

The Annan

The River Annan rises in the high fells bordering the Devil's Beef Tub, only a short distance to the south of the source of the River Tweed at Tweed's Well. It is quickly swollen in size by a number of tributary streams including the Birnock Water and Moffat Water which drain Swatte Fell and White Coomb respectively. The approximate length of the Annan is 35 miles. From Moffat the river flows south through Dumfriesshire, firstly through wild highland country and then rich agricultural land, passing Newton, Hightae, Brydekirk and Annan before discharging into the Solway Firth. It is interesting to note the origin of Solway which seems to come from the name of Sulwad or Sulwath — 'sol' or 'sul' being from the Anglo-Saxon and Norse meaning mud and 'wad' or 'wath' meaning a ford. The Annan is said to derive its name from an old Gaelic word meaning 'slow flowing', but it does not accurately describe the upper waters, as for the first 15 miles of its course it is a swift, strong stream, which only begins to flow more quietly after passing Johnstonebridge. It is in this slow moving part of the river, particularly in the Dalton area, that grayling, chub and pike abound. The chub in particular are renowned for their size and occasionally fish are caught which weigh into the double figures.

The flow of the Annan used to be hindered by a number of caulds across its channel and, although a number of them, such as those at Brydekirk, Murraythwaite and Dormont are now breached, several still exist. These include the weir at Annan and the Milnbie Cauld which was reconstructed to allow water to be diverted to the Atomic Energy Authority Power Station at Chapelcross. Another weir has been reconstructed at Johnstonebridge to divert water to a trout farm on the banks of the river. There is no doubt that the Milnbie Cauld causes much controversy, and anglers blame the poor fishing upstream on what they claim is a badly-designed fish pass in the centre of the weir which the fish are unable to ascend at low flows.

There are a number of good tributary streams which join the Annan in the Lockerbie area and these are the Dryfe Water, the Water of Ae and Kinnel Water, the latter two joining before entering the main river. Another good tributary which joins the Annan just downstream from Dalton is the Water of Milk. This otherwise good tributary is badly affected by three poorly-designed weirs all in the Middleshaw Bridge and Castlemilk area.

The Annan is fairly free of pollution and is well maintained by the Solway River Purification Board. Some industries nearer the coast discharge straight to the Solway Firth rather than to the river, and these include the Atomic Energy Authority.

The main run of salmon in the Annan tends to be late in the year and the best fishing is during September – November. The spring fishing has tended to be rather poor, but in 1978 there was a very good run of spring fish with excellent catches in the Milnbie Cauld area. A few grilse enter the river in June – August

THE SOLWAY RIVERS: 3

but it requires spate conditions to draw them in. There is a fair run of sea trout in the Annan but there have been signs of a decline in recent years. Unfortunately UDN is still present in the river.

There are 47 salmon proprietors on the Annan and its tributaries, but the main proprietors are Newbie Salmon Fisheries, Kinmount and Hoddom Estate, Castlemilk, Halleaths and the Kindly Tenants. The Kindly Tenants are an interesting body as they consist of the tenants of the Royal Four Towns Association of Hightae, Greenhill, Heck and Smallholm, who were granted the salmon fishing over 4 miles of the Annan by Robert the Bruce for the support they gave him during his battles. The tenants have the right to free fishing for salmon but, let it be noted, people who come to live in the area do not have this privilege unless they are on the voter's roll for that area. This was made statutory under a recent Act of Parliament. Property owners who are on the Kindly Tenants roll and who pay rent to the landlord, the Earl of Mansfield, are also entitled to this privilege.

A considerable amount of salmon fishing is available on the Annan and estates and angling clubs letting salmon fishing include, from mouth to source, Newbie Estates (permits from T. Nelson, Newbie Mill, Annan); Hoddom (permits from P. Helm, 22 Fernlea Crescent, Annan); Halleaths Water (a limited number of weekly and season tickets from Messrs McJerrow and Stevenson, Lockerbie); Annandale and Egremont Fishing Club (per Annandale Estates Office, Lockerbie); Upper Annandale Angling Association (J. Black, 1 Rosehill Grange Road, Moffat), and Applegirth Estate (A. Wright, The Clock House, Lockerbie). In addition fishing can be had on the Milk Water from Castle Milk Estates Office, Lockerbie.

Commercial fishing for salmon on the Scottish side (Annan district) of the Solway is carried out mainly by legally certified fixed engines which stem from titles held for foreshore fishing rights. Certified fixed engines are in the form of stake nets and poke nets. Another form is by haaf nets but these have not been granted certificates and the legality of haaf netting has never been tested. In the Annan Fishery Board area there are four Solway proprietors who, between them, hold certificates for 34 stake nets, not all of which are set in any one year, and 610 'clouts' of poke nets. Stake nets, with regional variations, are used in other parts of Scotland but poke nets (effectively a series of bags or 'pokes') are peculiar to this part of the Solway. The main proprietor of poke nets is Annandale & Eskdale District Council who have 500 of the 610 'clouts'. All four Solway fishery proprietors hold their titles by Royal Charter dating back to the sixteenth century.

One Solway Fishery, Annan District, is west of the River Annan and the other three are east of the river and therefore adjacent to the channel of the Border Esk and Eden rivers. Haaf netting permissions are granted to individuals by only two of these fisheries and, to give unhampered access to salmon entering the Annan, haaf netting is not permitted in or close to the mouth of the Annan — nor in the Annan low water channel west of the river mouth.

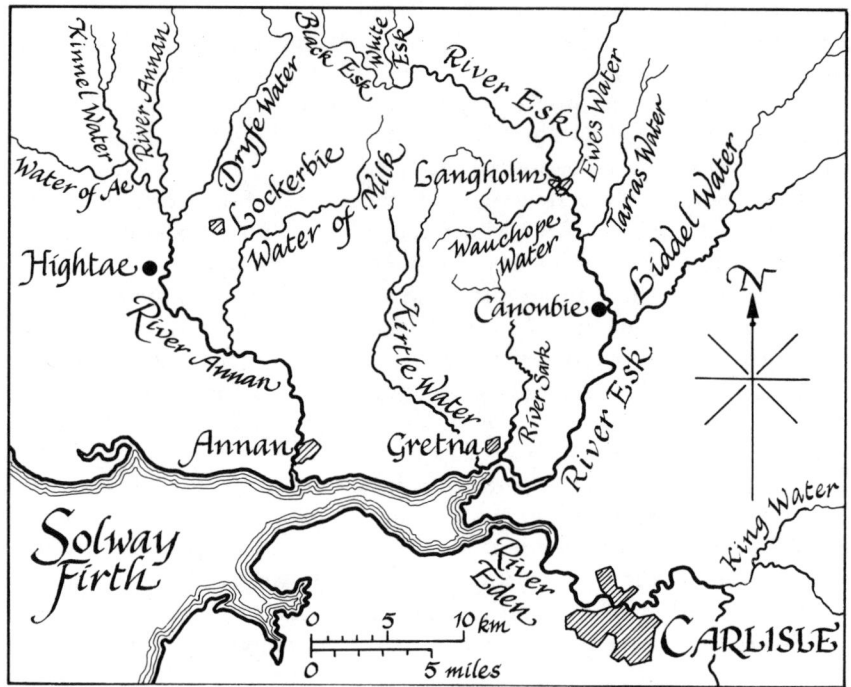

The Rivers Annan and Esk

Drift netting, from boats, is practised in the combined channel of the rivers Annan, Border Esk and Eden under licences issued by the North-West Water Authority.

The Border Esk

The Border Esk is formed from the meeting of the White and Black Esk a short distance to the south of Castle O'er. The White Esk rises in the Ettrick Hills, while the Black Esk flows from the Black Esk Reservoir in east Dumfriesshire. On its journey to Langholm the Esk is joined by a number of tributaries including the Meggat Water, and, in Langholm itself, by the Ewes Water and Wauchope Water. A little to the south of Langholm the Tarras Water enters the river opposite Irvine House. The Esk's main tributary is the Liddel Water which flows south-west down Liddesdale through Newcastleton to join the river a short distance below Canonbie. The Esk enters England a little above Longtown and flows into the Solway at Sarkfoot Point only a few miles to the north of the Eden.

Although the Esk is renowned for its sea trout more than for its salmon the latter do occur in fairly large numbers. There are a few fish taken in the early spring around Longtown and Canonbie, but the main run is from late August to October, and the fishing is usually best in the latter month. Fishing for both salmon and sea trout is said to improve once the commercial netting on the Solway, with poke nets and haaf nets, has closed for the season. However, be that as it may, sea trout tend to run in late May or early June, and in some years they can be present in large numbers around Langholm by the end of June or in early July.

In recent years it has been noticed that the river rises and falls much more rapidly than it used to, and this is attributed to improved hill drainage and extensive afforestation in the upper part of the catchment. A large proportion of the river banks are overgrown with alders and willows. Anglers more familiar with Highland rivers may, therefore, find fishing a little frustrating due to impeded access to the water and tackle getting caught up in overhanging branches.

The greater part of the Esk and its tributaries is in the hands and under the protection of the Esk and Liddel Fisheries Association which was formed in 1863. The proprietary member of the Association is Buccleuch Estates Ltd. There are some excellent pools on the part of the Esk which is in the hands of the Association. Around Langholm there are Caul Pool, Skipper, Sowie, Island and Crannel Holm, while in the Canonbie area there are Grey Stane, Dub, Tommy's, Mill, Jock's, Dead Neuk, Long, Burn's, Willow and Cauldron. Details of the Association fishings can be obtained from the Secretary, Stevenson and Johnstone, W.S., Langholm, Dumfriesshire. Buccleuch Estates also lets stretches of the river, and details of these can be had through their estate office in Langholm. Farms also have fishing rights and these are sometimes let along with their holiday cottages. The river is under the jurisdiction of the North-West Water Authority but a Regional Water Authority fishing licence is not required.

An interesting development has recently occurred in the law governing net fishing rights in the Solway. Some time ago the channel of the rivers Esk and Eden, where they flow into the Solway, shifted towards the Scottish border. The English haaf net fishermen, who had been issued with permits to fish by the North-West Water Authority, followed the shift and began fishing in what had been previously recognised as Scottish Waters. After discussions with the Regional Water Authority it was decided that the only way to resolve the matter would be to raise an action in the Court of Session.

This action was raised under two basic heads, the first was for Declarator that the waters being fished in were in fact Scottish waters, the second was for Interdict to prevent the interference with Scottish fishing waters.

The Annandale and Eskdale District Council claimed that they had been granted an inalienable right to the land containing the waters by Royal Charter granted by King James VI of Scotland and I of England. The North-West Water Authority argued that the international boundary followed the channel of the Esk and Eden no matter where it shifted to. The Court of Session granted Declarator that the waters were in fact Scottish by virtue of the Royal Charter but refused to grant Interdict on the grounds that by the time the action appeared in Court the channel had shifted back again. But the Court did explain that having granted Declarator, the correct procedure would be for the Council to take out an action of Interdict if ever the channel shifted again. This interdict, which would be immediately granted, would then prevent the Regional Water Authority from issuing tickets granting permission for their fishermen to fish in Scottish waters, and would make transgressors subject to punishment in the Scottish Courts.

Epilogue

The 200 or so salmon rivers described in this book contributed, for the 10-year period 1968–1977, to an average annual commercial and rod catch of 431,378 salmon and grilse. This present level of, or any increase in, production is very much dependent on the future availability and state of the spawning and nursery areas in these rivers, and the environmental conditions in the rivers during the ascent of returning fish.

In recent years there has been a reduction in spawning areas on some of the major river systems as a result of hydro-electric and water abstraction schemes. Hydro-electric development schemes in Scotland increased after the Second World War with the passing of the Hydro-electric Development (Scotland) Act in 1943. Since that time around 25 schemes have been developed by the North of Scotland Hydro-electric Board and the South of Scotland Electricity Board. Some of them have been very extensive schemes involving the formation of reservoirs, the raising of the water levels of existing lochs and the diversion of rivers and streams by pipeline and aqueduct. Scotland's most important salmon river, the Tay, and its major tributaries, the Tummel, Garry and Lyon, were the first to be harnessed for power. The development of other salmon river systems followed, including the Awe, Beauly, Conon, Garry, Moriston and Shin in the north and the Galloway Dee and Doon in the south west. Due to the impounding and tapping of the headwaters for these schemes, some of the rivers have lost an appreciable amount of their spawning and feeding areas. Fortunately both these Boards and the Salmon District Fishery Boards have put a great deal of care into looking after the welfare of salmon in these affected rivers. By the construction of fish passes and fish screens, the opening-up of previously inaccessible spawning grounds, the construction of salmon hatcheries, and the provision of compensation flows and freshets, the stocks of salmon have been satisfactorily maintained in these waters.

However, with an increase in industry and population there is an ever-growing demand for water and, according to the government publication *A Measure of Plenty* (1973), the total water consumption in Scotland is likely to double from its 1971 figure of 2,130 megalitres per day (Ml/d) to one of 4,414 Ml/d by the year 2001. This is perhaps not a lot of water when one considers the extent of Scotland's water resources. Over Scotland as a whole the average rainfall is around 1,400 mm a year. Making an allowance for evaporation and other effects, it is calculated that the total quantity of water which runs off the surface of the mainland and down our streams and rivers to the sea is some 73,000,000 Ml a year, or an average of 200,000 Ml/d. That being so, with a population of about 5.1 million the total quantity available is equivalent to about 40,000 litres per head per day. The average consumption from public supplies in 1973 was about 400 litres per head for all purposes, domestic and trade— about 1 per cent of the available supply. However, the rainfall varies over the year and winter storage is necessary. The development of Scotland's water resources for public supplies up to 1971 has resulted in a total of 380 reservoirs and lochs being developed and 259 river intakes being built. Since then Castlehill Reservoir on the River Devon has been completed and the large Megget scheme on a tributary of the River Tweed is under construction. On the completion of the Megget scheme and the development of neighbouring St Mary's Loch there will be 6 major reservoirs on the River Tweed and its tributaries, two of which result in the loss of appreciable salmon spawning areas.

One of the effects of reduced river flow and change in flow régime as a result of water resources development has been removed with the improvement of water quality. The untiring efforts of the Scottish river purification boards, set up by the Rivers (Prevention of Pollution) (Scotland) Act, 1951, have helped to reduce pollution considerably, and with an extension of their powers by the Rivers (Prevention of Pollution) (Scotland) Act, 1965 and the Control of Pollution Act, 1974, many longstanding polluting effluents have been eliminated. Unfortunately pollution is still a problem on some existing salmon rivers and also on some rivers that, were it not for pollution, could quickly become salmon rivers. In the first category comes the River Don, which is still polluted by paper mill effluent; in the second category are rivers in Scotland's Central Belt which are affected by iron waters from disused mines and opencast coal sites, in Fife and the Lothians in particular. Potentially viable salmon rivers such as the Leven in Fife and Carron in West Lothian are at present devoid of migratory fish, while the West Lothian Almond and Musselburgh Esk are only occasionally visited by salmon which would soon establish themselves if the iron waters were treated and the numerous weirs removed. Although salmon are on Glasgow's heraldic coat of arms it is many years since salmon have spawned in the Clyde, because of industrial pollution.

The effects of hydro-electric development, water abstraction and pollution on stocks of migratory fish are well-known and can, with effort, be alleviated. In the future, however, there are likely to be other more insidious effects on the salmon nursery areas, and ones, although less easily measured, perhaps more serious. These are associated with land drainage and afforestation, for Scotland is becoming rapidly afforested; open moorland is being purchased, drained and planted by the Forestry Commission and private woodland owners. For example, it is estimated that 60% of the Mull of Kintyre will soon be afforested. The total area in Scotland at present afforested is 0.75 million hectares, or 9.7% of Scotland's total land area, and an afforested area of 1.6 million hectares could be achieved. It has already been shown that the planting of conifers has seriously affected the productivity of some Scottish streams,

EPILOGUE

leading to a paucity of invertebrate and fish fauna in streams flowing through mature forest with a dense tree canopy preventing the sunlight from encouraging algal growth and ground vegetation. While this effect can have direct repercussions on the value of nursery areas, the effects of rapid run-off from drainage channels can cause serious erosion leading to the silting of spawning and nursery areas and the in-filling of holding pools with gravel. While drainage channels may at first prevent flooding, due to a smaller surface run-off with the land being better drained, they will, during periods of heavy or continuous rain and when the surrounding land is saturated, produce flash floods resulting in serious scouring. Due to the temporary nature of these spates they are often of little value for fish ascent and do not keep the stream bedload in suspension for any length of time. So in drought years, with some rivers experiencing lower minimum flows as a result of land drainage, there is a tendency for salmon holding pools in the upper reaches of rivers to become shallower, the gravel more compacted and the stream beds more silted. This change in flow régime in afforested areas is further accentuated by water loss from the tree canopy interception of precipitation, and transpiration. Work by the Institute of Hydrology on Plynlimon in mid-Wales has shown quite conclusively that the trees intercept substantially more water than open moorland, and this could have adverse effects in long dry periods with irregular rain. From work in England, it has been shown that high rainfall in areas in the west of the country (which corresponds climatically to the west of Scotland) are expected to have a greater interception loss than the rainfall in areas such as East Anglia. It was shown that out of a total rainfall of 2,770 mm, 780 mm were lost as interception and 310 mm as tra-spiration, producing a total water loss of more than twice the potential open water evaporation. It is unlikely that nursery streams can afford the water losses that these afforested areas will incur.

There is evidence that drainage in some afforested areas is making the neighbouring waters more acid. Furthermore, there is growing concern that this increase in their acidity is being hastened by rain that has become acid as a result of sulphur dioxide carried by the wind from industrial areas. This is a phenomenon which has already had serious repercussions in salmon rivers in southern Norway. Work on the effects of acid precipitation in Scotland has now started at the Freshwater Fisheries Laboratory at Pitlochry. Analyses of precipitation collected during the years 1973–75, from various sites in Scotland, were compared with results obtained ten years previously. The results showed a gradual decrease in precipitated acidity with increasing distance away from the large industrial belt around Glasgow, and an increase at individual sites from 1962 to 1975. The weighted average pH values for Loch Ard, on the headwaters of the River Forth, were very similar for the period 1973–1975, being 4.19, 4.20 and 4.26 respectively and the values for total acidity (precipitated) for these three years were 122, 139 and 112 microequivalents per square metre. Unless a salmon proprietor was aware that low pH values of less than 4.5 were detrimental to young salmon, he might plant salmon ova or fry in waters with these low values to no avail.

There are a number of other activities which from time to time have threatened salmon stocks in Scotland, but these have been of a more local nature. The recent development of the North Sea oil and gas resources has resulted in the construction of a number of pipelines through eastern Scotland which have crossed the tributaries and main channels of rivers such as the Ugie, Don, Dee, North and South Esk, Tay, Earn and Teith. In some instances spawning and nursery areas were temporarily affected. Spraying activities, too, have caused local concern and parts of the catchment of the rivers Helmsdale, Naver, Brora, Shin and Strathy in Sutherland and the Wick in Caithness were in an area sprayed with Fenitrothion in May 1978 by the Forestry Commission in order to combat the Pine Beauty moth which was ravaging plantations of Lodgepole pines.

Predation of young and adult salmon by birds and mammals has always been of concern to Scottish salmon proprietors. The goosander, red-breasted merganser and cormorant are periodically controlled, but it is the grey seal which is the centre of attention in this respect and present estimates show that these seals take the equivalent of the Scottish salmon catch. This has resulted in seal culls which are opposed by many wildlife conservation bodies and in the future it is likely that these bodies will have a greater influence on predator control policies. One mammal whose control they are unlikely to oppose, because of its depredations on bird life, is the mink. Since 1961 there has been a dramatic spread of feral mink which have escaped from mink farms, and they are now known to be present in nearly all Scottish mainland counties and on some of the Islands. It has been found from an analysis of mink scats from three Scottish rivers that salmon are a major food item, and predation by this animal in the future could well be serious.

Introduction of alien fish species have not always had a beneficial effect on indigenous fish stocks, and the concern shown over the possibility of the escape of a confined batch of young Coho salmon into a Scottish river demonstrates the fears existing in many people's minds of the effects such an introduction might have on Atlantic salmon stocks, so much so that an Act, The Import of Live Fish (Scotland) Act, 1978, has been passed to 'restrict in Scotland the import, keeping or release of live fish or shellfish or the live eggs or milt of fish or shellfish of certain species'. Rainbow trout, which can be migratory, are now being widely introduced to Scottish lochs and rivers and there are a number of records of the capture of sea-run rainbow trout in Scottish commercial salmon catches. The lack of control over the widespread stocking of Scottish waters with rainbow trout is to be deplored, as is the uncontrolled stocking of salmon rivers with brown trout due to misguided policies of trout angling clubs.

There are now over 150 salmon and trout farms in Scotland, many of them sited on salmon rivers and diverting clean water through their farm and

EPILOGUE

returning it to the river contaminated with drugs, antibiotics, disease organisms, copper salts and malachite green as well as organic material. While the river purification boards can lay down consent standards for these discharges, as far as is known no regular check is made on dissolved substances in the farm outflows. There are also instances during drought conditions of fish farmers draining off practically the whole flow of a river, so that the section of the river between the inflow and outflow of the farm becomes virtually dry.

With the number of constraints on the future production of salmon it is important that the rivers are managed wisely and effectively. The Salmon Fisheries (Scotland) Act of 1862 and 1868 set up salmon fishery districts and district boards for their administration. A board consists of not more than three upper proprietors and three lower proprietors together with, as chairman, the proprietor having the largest annual valuation. In addition a superintendent is usually appointed to actively manage and police the rivers in his district and is helped by a number of bailiffs who have certain powers of search and arrest which were extended under the Salmon and Freshwater Fisheries (Protection) (Scotland) Act, 1951. A total of 107 districts were established. At present only 47 of the districts have fishery boards, in the remaining 60 no boards have been constituted. The River Tweed is a Special Area and is administered by Tweed Commissioners. These district boards have only powers pertaining to migratory fish (salmon and sea trout) and are not responsible for other freshwater fish. Only the Tweed Commissioners have this extra control, which was obtained through the Tweed Fisheries Act of 1969. At the beginning of the century the largest of these districts, such as the Tay and the Spey, had a large complement of bailiffs. The Tay had in the region of 26 and the Spey had 50. Comparable numbers today are 6 and 5. At the present time the whole of the River Tweed area has only 9, and the Forth District has none. It is therefore very evident that, however conscientious the staff, it is physically impossible to effectively manage and police the river. The duties of these bailiffs is now almost entirely anti-poaching, patrolling not only the estuarine and coastal waters but also all parts of the river against increasing attention from gangs using nets and Cymag poison. The only other duties for which they have time is hatchery operations — the collection of fish for stripping, the maintenance of the hatchery and the planting out of eggs and release of the young. In the 60 districts with no boards all these duties fall on the shoulders of individual proprietors who must call on the overworked police to help them with poaching incidents. Any major biological work on these rivers, outside that which is carried out by the staffs of the river purification boards, whose brief is one of pollution prevention, is done by the staff of the Freshwater Fisheries Laboratory, Pitlochry or the universities.

The only official published information on salmon rivers is that produced annually by the Department of Agriculture and Fisheries for Scotland in their annual fisheries report. This information is brief and of a general nature. The reports of district boards are only duplicated for limited circulation but the

River Tweed Commissioners do publish an annual report for their members which gives a general account of the state of the Tweed salmon fishing for the year, although individual catch figures for separate river beats or for commercial fisheries is not given. There is only one river, the Nith, for which the type of detailed information the salmon conservationist is seeking is available. This information is provided in the Annual Report of the River Nith Fishings Improvement Association. Fortunately data on river quality appears in the published annual reports of the river purification boards.

If one is to ensure the future of Scottish salmon rivers then it is necessary to have some form of Area Board with a qualified staff as recommended by the Hunter Committee in their Second Report in 1965 (HMSO Cmnd. 2691). It was planned that Area Boards would replace District Fishery Boards and that their revenue would come partly from imposing a licencing system for salmon and trout fishing as in England and Wales. At present serious consideration is being given by the Department of Agriculture and Fisheries for Scotland to this proposal. However, some such arrangement could well go a long way to ensuring the continuance of Scottish salmon stocks in the World of Tomorrow.

Appendix

SALMON FISHERIES

Annual Close Times Applicable to the Salmon Rivers in Scotland
N.B. In the following List the days fixed for the commencement and termination of the Annual Close Time for Net-fishing and for Rod-fishing respectively, are in all cases inclusive.

	Annual Close Time for Net-fishing	*Annual Close Time for Rod-fishing*
Add	Sept. 1 to Feb. 15	Nov. 1 to Feb. 15
Ailort (Kinloch)	Aug. 27 to Feb. 10	Nov. 1 to Feb. 10
Aline	Aug. 27 to Feb. 10	Nov. 1 to Feb. 10
Alness	Aug. 27 to Feb. 10	Nov. 1 to Feb. 10
Annan	Sept. 10 to Feb. 24	Nov. 16 to Feb. 24
Applecross	Aug. 27 to Feb. 10	Nov. 1 to Feb. 10
Arnisdale (Loch Hourn)	Aug. 27 to Feb. 10	Nov. 1 to Feb. 10
Awe	Aug. 27 to Feb. 10	Oct. 16 to Feb. 10
Ayr	Aug. 27 to Feb. 10	Nov. 1 to Feb. 10
Ba and Coladoir (Mull)	Aug. 27 to Feb. 10	Nov. 1 to Feb. 10
Badachro and Kerry (Gairloch)	Aug. 27 to Feb. 10	Nov. 1 to Feb. 10
Balgy and Shieldaig	Aug. 27 to Feb. 10	Nov. 1 to Feb. 10
Beauly	Aug. 27 to Feb. 10	Oct. 16 to Feb. 10
Berriedale	Aug. 27 to Feb. 10	Nov. 1 to Feb. 10
Bervie	Sept. 10 to Feb. 24	Nov. 1 to Feb. 24
Bladnoch	Aug. 27 to Feb. 10	Nov. 1 to Feb. 10
Broom	Aug. 27 to Feb. 10	Nov. 1 to Feb. 10
Brora	Aug. 27 to Feb. 10	Oct. 16 to Jan. 31
Carradale (in Kintyre)	Sept. 10 to Feb. 24	Nov. 1 to Feb. 24
Carron (W. Ross)	Aug. 27 to Feb. 10	Nov. 1 to Feb. 10
Clyde and Leven	Aug. 27 to Feb. 10	Nov. 1 to Feb. 10
Conon	Aug. 27 to Feb. 10	Oct. 1 to Jan. 25
Cree	Sept. 14 to Feb. 28	Oct. 1 to Feb. 28
Creed or Stornaway and Laxay (Lewis)	Aug. 27 to Feb. 10	Oct. 17 to Feb. 10
Creran (Loch Creran)	Aug. 27 to Feb. 10	Nov. 1 to Feb. 10
Croe and Shiel (Loch Duich)	Aug. 27 to Feb. 10	Nov. 1 to Feb. 10
Dee (Aberdeenshire)	Aug. 27 to Feb. 10	Oct. 1 to Jan. 31
Dee (Kircudbrightshire)	Aug. 27 to Feb. 10	Nov. 1 to Feb. 10
Deveron	Aug. 27 to Feb. 10	Nov. 1 to Feb. 10
Don	Aug. 27 to Feb. 10	Nov. 1 to Feb. 10

SALMON RIVERS OF SCOTLAND

	Annual Close Time for Net-fishing	Annual Close Time for Rod-fishing
Doon	Aug. 27 to Feb. 10	Nov. 1 to Feb. 10
Dunbeath	Aug. 27 to Feb. 10	Oct. 16 to Feb. 10
Eachaig	Sept. 1 to Feb. 15	Nov. 1 to Feb. 15
Earn	Aug. 21 to Feb. 4	Nov. 1 to Jan. 31
Esk, North	Sept. 1 to Feb. 15	Nov. 1 to Feb. 15
Esk, South	Sept. 1 to Feb. 15	Nov. 1 to Feb. 15
Ewe	Aug. 27 to Feb. 10	Nov. 1 to Feb. 10
Fincastle, Scourst or Meavaig (Harris)	Sept. 10 to Feb. 24	Nov. 1 to Feb. 24
Findhorn	Aug. 27 to Feb. 10	Oct. 1 to Feb. 10
Fleet (Sutherland)	Sept. 10 to Feb. 24	Nov. 1 to Feb. 24
Fleet (Kirkcudbrightshire)	Sept. 10 to Feb. 24	Nov. 1 to Feb. 24
Forsa and Aros (Mull)	Aug. 27 to Feb. 10	Nov. 1 to Feb. 10
Forss	Aug. 27 to Feb. 10	Nov. 1 to Feb. 10
Forth	Aug. 27 to Feb. 10	Nov. 1 to Jan. 31
Fyne, Shira and Aray (Loch Fyne)	Sept. 1 to Feb. 15	Nov. 1 to Feb. 15
Girvan	Sept. 10 to Feb. 24	Nov. 1 to Feb. 24
Gress, Laxdale or Thunga (Lewis)	Aug. 27 to Feb. 10	Nov. 1 to Feb. 10
Grudie or Dionard	Aug. 27 to Feb. 10	Nov. 1 to Feb. 10
Gruinard and Little Gruinard (Lewis)	Aug. 27 to Feb. 10	Nov. 1 to Feb. 10
Halladale, Strathy, Naver and Borgie	Aug. 27 to Feb. 10	Oct. 1 to Jan. 11
Helmsdale	Aug. 27 to Feb. 10	Oct. 1 to Jan. 10
Hope and Polla or Strathbeg	Aug. 27 to Feb. 10	Oct. 1 to Jan. 11
Horisay and Loch na Ciste (North Uist)	Sept. 10 to Feb. 24	Nov. 1 to Feb. 24
Howmore (South Uist)	Sept. 10 to Feb. 24	Nov. 1 to Feb. 24
Inchard	Aug. 27 to Feb. 10	Nov. 1 to Feb. 10
Inver	Aug. 27 to Feb. 10	Nov. 1 to Feb. 10
Iorsa (Arran)	Sept. 10 to Feb. 24	Nov. 1 to Feb. 24
Irvine and Garnock	Sept. 10 to Feb. 24	Nov. 1 to Feb. 24
Kanaird	Aug. 27 to Feb. 10	Nov. 1 to Feb. 10
Kilchoan or Inverie (Loch Nevis)	Aug. 27 to Feb. 10	Nov. 1 to Feb. 10
Kinloch (Kyle of Tongue)	Aug. 27 to Feb. 10	Nov. 1 to Feb. 10
Kirkaig	Aug. 27 to Feb. 10	Nov. 1 to Feb. 10
Kishorn	Aug. 27 to Feb. 10	Nov. 1 to Feb. 10
Kyle of Sutherland	Aug. 27 to Feb. 10	Oct. 1 to Jan. 10
Laggan and Sorn (Islay)	Sept. 10 to Feb. 24	Nov. 1 to Feb. 24
Laxford	Aug. 27 to Feb. 10	Nov. 1 to Feb. 10
Leven	Aug. 27 to Feb. 10	Nov. 1 to Feb. 10
Little Loch Broom	Aug. 27 to Feb. 10	Nov. 1 to Feb. 10
Loch Duich	Aug. 27 to Feb. 10	Nov. 1 to Feb. 10
Loch Luing	Aug. 27 to Feb. 10	Nov. 1 to Feb. 10
Loch Roag (Lewis)	Aug. 27 to Feb. 10	Oct. 17 to Feb. 10
Lochy	Aug. 27 to Feb. 10	Nov. 1 to Feb. 10
Lossie	Aug. 27 to Feb. 10	Oct. 16 to Feb. 10
Luce	Sept. 10 to Feb. 24	Nov. 1 to Feb. 24
Lussa (Mull)	Aug. 27 to Feb. 10	Nov. 1 to Feb. 10
Moidart	Aug. 27 to Feb. 10	Nov. 1 to Feb. 10
Morar	Aug. 27 to Feb. 10	Nov. 1 to Feb. 10
Nairn	Aug. 27 to Feb. 10	Oct. 1 to Feb. 10

APPENDIX

	Annual Close Time for Net-fishing	Annual Close Time for Rod-fishing
Naver and Borgie, *see* Halladale		
Nell, Feochan and Euchar	Aug. 27 to Feb. 10	Nov. 1 to Feb. 10
Ness	Aug. 27 to Feb. 10	Oct. 16 to Jan. 14
Nith	Sept. 10 to Feb. 24	Dec. 1 to Feb. 24
Resort (Harris)	Aug. 27 to Feb. 10	Nov. 1 to Feb. 10
Ruel	Sept. 1 to Feb. 15	Nov. 1 to Feb. 15
Shiel (Loch Shiel)	Aug. 27 to Feb. 10	Nov. 1 to Feb. 10
Sligachan and Broadford (Skye)	Aug. 27 to Feb. 10	Nov. 1 to Feb. 10
Snizort, Ose and Drynoch (Skye)	Aug. 27 to Feb. 10	Nov. 1 to Feb. 10
Spey	Aug. 27 to Feb. 10	Oct. 1 to Feb. 10
Stinchar	Sept. 10 to Feb. 24	Nov. 1 to Feb. 24
Tay (except Earn)	Aug. 21 to Feb. 4	Oct. 16 to Jan. 14
Thurso	Aug. 27 to Feb. 10	Oct. 6 to Jan. 10
Torridon	Aug. 27 to Feb. 10	Nov. 1 to Feb. 10
Tweed	Sept. 15 to Feb. 14	Dec. 1 to Jan. 31
Ugie	Sept. 10 to Feb. 24	Nov. 1 to Feb. 9
Ullapool (Loch Broom)	Aug. 27 to Feb. 10	Nov. 1 to Feb. 10
Urr	Sept. 10 to Feb. 24	Nov. 30 to Feb. 24
Wick	Aug. 27 to Feb. 10	Nov. 1 to Feb. 10
Ythan	Sept. 10 to Feb. 24	Nov. 1 to Feb. 10

Bibliography

Adamson, W. A. *Lake and Loch Fishing for Salmon and Sea Trout.* A. & C. Black, 1961

Braithwaite, G. *Fine Feathers and Fish.* Privately published and printed by T. & A. Constable, 1971

Brown, W. *The Natural History of the Salmon as ascertained by the Recent Experiments in the Artificial Spawning and Hatching of the Ova and Rearing of the Fry at Stormontfield on the Tay.* Thos. Murray, 1862

Buchan, John. *Scholar Gipsies.* John Lane The Bodley Head, 1896

Calderwood, W. L. *The Salmon Rivers and Lochs of Scotland.* Edward Arnold, 1909

Campbell, R. N. and Williamson, R. B. (1979). The fishes of inland waters in the Outer Hebrides. *Proceedings of the Royal Society of Edinburgh, Series B*

Chalmers, I. *Salmon Fishing in Little Rivers.* A. & C. Black, 1938

Chrystal, R. A. *Angling at Lochboisdale, South Uist.* H. F. & G. Witherby, 1939

Dick Lauder, Sir Thomas. *Scottish Rivers.* Edmonston and Douglas, 1874

Gardiner, M. L. G. (1971). A review of factors which may influence the sea-age and maturation of Atlantic salmon, *Salmo salar* L., *Journal of Fish Biology.* 9, 289

Gathorne-Hardy, A. E. *Autumns in Argyleshire with Rod and Gun.* Longmans, Green & Co, 1900

Grimble, A. *Salmon Rivers of Scotland.* Kegan Paul, 1913

Hutchinson, G. H. ('Sixty-One'). *Twenty Years Reminiscences of the Lews.* H. Cox, 1871

Jones, J. W. *The Salmon.* Collins, 1959

King-Webster, W. A. 'The Galloway Dee. A short history of a salmon river. *Salmon Net*, V, 1969

Lawrence, D. 'The recovery of a Scottish salmon river, 1934–1963. *Salmon and Trout Magazine*, no. 175, 1965

Macintyre, D. *Wildlife of the Highlands.* Philip Allan, 1936
Memoirs of a Highland Gamekeeper. Seeley Service, 1954

Malloch, P. D. *Life History and Habits of the Salmon, Sea Trout, Trout and other Freshwater Fish.* A. & C. Black, 1910

Martin, M. *A Late Voyage to St Kilda.* 1698

Maxwell, H. *The Story of the Tweed.* James Nisbet, 1909

McConnochie, A. I. *The Rivers Oykel and Cassley in Sutherland and Ross.* Witherby, 1924.

BIBLIOGRAPHY

Mills, D. H. *Salmon and Trout: A Resource, its Ecology, Conservation and Management.* Oliver & Boyd, 1971
   Scotland's King of Fish. Blackwoods, 1979
Murdoch, W. 'More Light on the Salmon.' *Fishing News*, Aberdeen
Murray, J. and Pullar, L. *Bathymetrical Survey of the Freshwater Lochs of Scotland*, vols I–VI. Challenger Office, Edinburgh, 1910
North of Scotland Hydro-electric Board. *Power from the Glens.* Perth, 1976
Robertson, R. MacDonald. *Angling in Wildest Scotland.* Jenkins, 1936
Sclater, J. R. P. *The River of Content.* Hodder & Stoughton, 1913
Shearer, W. M. 'Grilse and salmon catches on the North Esk, 1925–1970.' *Salmon Net*, VII, 1971
Smart, G. G. J. 'The practical results of increasing the accessibility of spawning grounds in the River North Esk.' *Salmon Net*, I, 1965
Souter, A. 'The salmon fisheries of Skye.' *Salmon Net*, II, 1966
Stoddart, T. *Angling Reminiscences.* The Edinburgh Printing and Publishing Company, 1837.
Stuart, H. *Book of the Sea Trout.* Secker, 1916
Thornton, T. *A Sporting Tour through the Northern Parts of England and Great Part of the Highlands of Scotland.* Edward Arnold, 1896
Wood, Ian. 'Loch Lomond and Its Salmon.' *Scottish Field*, 1954
Younger, John. *River Angling for Salmon and Trout.* Rutherford, 1864

Index

Aberdeen, 12, 82–3
Aberdeen Salmon Company Ltd, 88
Aberdeen University, 91
Aberlour Burn, 97, 99–100
Abhainn a' Chnocain, 261–2
Abhainn a' Chomair, 122
Abhainn a' Gharbh Choire, 197
Abhainn Cro Chlach, 103
Abhainn Dearg, 200
Abhainn Droma, 191
Abhainn Dubhach (Letters Burn) 139
Abhainn Gleann na Muice, 193
Abhainn na Frithe (River Free of Frithe), 153–4
Abhainn Strath na Sealga, 193
Achall, Loch, 189–90
Achanalt, Loch (and Power Station), 123
Acharole, Burn of, 159–60
Achentoul Loch *see* Ruathair, Loch an
Achfray Burn (and hatchery), 182
Achnabourin Burn, 169
Achnamoine, Loch, 153, 156
Achonachie, Loch, 124, 128
Achray, Loch, 40
Achtriochtan, Loch, 255
Adamson, W.A.:*Lake and Loch Fishing*, 197
Add, River, 259–60
Advie Burn, 100
Ae, Water of, 308
Affric, River (and Loch), 116
Aigas Dam, 119–20
Ailort, Loch, 236
Ailort, River, 235–6
Ailsh, Loch, 140
Airdeglais, Loch (Mull), 225
Airidhe Riabhaich, Lochan na h-, 199
Airigh na h-Airde, Loch (I. of Lewis), 205–6
Akran, Loch, 167
Ale Water, 37
Alemoor Loch, 37
Aline, River (and Loch), 239–40
Alladale River, 137–8

Allan Water (Forth), 40–41, 45
Allan Water (Tweed), 37
Allan Water Angling Improvement Association, 45
Allt a' Bhlair, 261
Allt a' Chraois, 173–4
Allt a' Glomach, 230
Allt Airigh-dhamh, 153
Allt an Taillir, 266
Allt Beithe, 145
Allt Braglenmore, 251
Allt a' Chapuill, 272
Allt Coir' an Longairt, 266
Allt Coire nan Each, 229
Allt Dochard, 247
Allt Forsiescye, 165
Allt Graad, 134
Allt Hallater, 254
Allt a' Coromaig, 256
Allt Kinglass (Chonoghlais), 247–8
Allt Mhic Mhurchaidh Gheir, 183
Allt Mor (tributary of Barr), 261
Allt Mor (tributary of Spey), 97
Allt na Bad, 173
Allt na h-Airidhe (Arran), 226
Allt na Lairige, 266
Allt na Lairige Power Station and Dam, 266, 267
Allt na Luibe, 151
Allt nan Albannach, 145
Allt nan Ramh, 182
Allt na Tiaghaich, 183
Allt Tigh an Shiorran (Arran), 226
Allt Tolaghan, 247
Allt Uaine, 268
Alltain Fhearna, Loch an, 153
Almond, River (W. Lothian), 23, 314
Almond, River (Tay district), 48–50, 53, 67–8
Alness, River, 133–4
Amhainn Loch an Laoigh (River Blackwater), 229
Amhuinnsuidhe Falls (I. of Harris), 215
Annan, River, 18, 28, 307, 308–10

Annan Fishery Board, 309
Annick Water, 280–82
Applecross, River, 199
Aray, River, 269–70
Ard, Loch, 40–41, 315
Ardle, River, 66
Ardoch Burn, 43
Arienas, Loch, 239–40
Arkaig, River (and Loch), 241, 245
Arnicle, Loch, 262
Arnisdale, River, 233
Arnol, River (I. of Lewis), 205, 212
Aros River (Mull), 222–3
Arran, Isle of, 225–7
Ascaign, Loch, 154
Assynt, Loch, 183
Atlantic Salmon Research Trust, 82, 150, 242
Auchness Burn, 102
Aven, Water of, 80
Avich, River (and Loch), 251
Avon, River (and Loch; tributary of Spey), 97–8
Avon, River (W. Lothian), 23
Awe system, 109–10
Awe, Loch, 109, 183, 247, 249–51, 255, 269
Awe, River, 109, 248, 249–52; barrage, 248–50, 256, 313
Ayr, River, 283–4

Ba, Loch (Rannoch Moor), 50, 62
Ba, River (Rannoch Moor), 50
Ba, River (and Loch; Mull) 223–4
Backs Water *see* Machrihanish Water
Backwater Reservoir, 66
Bad an Fheur-loch, Loch, 177–8
Bad an Sgalaig, Loch, 197
Bad a' Ghaill, Loch, 187
Badachro (Bad a' Chrotha), River, 198
Badanloch, Loch, 153, 156
Baddingsgill Reservoir, 30, 32
Balgy, River, 200–201
Ballantine, Miss, 249
Ballinloan Burn, 61
Ballinluig Falls, 62
Ballygrant, Loch (Islay), 227
Balnacoil Falls (Brora), 149
Balnagour, River, 134–5
Balquhidder, Braes of, 40
Balvag, River, 40, 42
Barhoise Dam, 291
Barley Burn (Fleuchlarg Burn), 298

Barr Water, 260–62
Barvas, River (I. of Lewis), 205, 209–10
Beag, Lochan (I. of Harris), 215
Beannacharan, Loch (and dam), 118–19
Beannachran, Loch (Loch Scardroy), 123, 132
Beauly, district, 116–21
Beauly, River, 116–17, 119–21, 313
Beg, Loch, 162
Beinn Dearg, Loch, 193
Belladrum Burn, 121
Benevean, Loch, 116–17
Beoraid, Loch, 235
Berriedale Water, 157
Bervie Water, 77, 83
Bharp, Loch a' (S. Uist), 220
Bhealaich, Loch a', 169
Bhealaich, Lochan a, 145
Big Water of Fleet, 296–8
Birnock Water, 308
Birse, Burn of, 79
Black Burn, 291
Black Cart, River, 279
Black Esk, River (and reservoir), 310
Black Falls (Meig), 123
Black Water (tributary of Alness), 133
Black Water (tributary of Brora), 148–50
Black Water (tributary of Carron), 137–8
Black Water (tributary of Conon), 122, 124–7, 129–30
Black Water (tributary of Deveron), 93–4
Black Water (tributary of Ericht), 66
Black Water of Dee, 298–9
Blackadder, River, 39
Blackwater reservoir, 245
Blackwater, River (I. of Lewis), 209, 211–12
Bladnoch, River, 291–2
Blair, Sir David Hunter, 286
Blair, Sir Edward Hunter, 286
Blair, James Hunter, 287
Blane Water, 277
Bogie, River, 93–4
Bogton Loch, 284
Border Esk *see* Esk (Border), River
Borgie, River, 170, 172
Borralan, Loch, 185
Borthwick Water, 37

INDEX

Bowmont Water, 38
Braan, River, 49, 61–2
Bracklin Falls (Keltie), 42
Bradan, Loch, 286, 288
Braigh-horrisdale, Loch, 198
Braithwaite, Geoffrey: *Fine Feathers and Fish*, 111, 201
Bran, River, 6, 122–5, 128–9, 202
Brannie Burn, 270
Breackerie Water, 264
Breachlaich, Lochan, 53
Breadalbane Hydro-electric Scheme, 52–3, 59, 68, 247
British Aluminium Company, 96, 110, 241, 243–5
Brittle, River (Skye), 221
Broadford, River (Skye), 221
Broom, Loch, 189, 191–2
Broom, River, 191–2
Brora, Loch, 148–50
Brora, River, 14, 18, 148–51, 316
Brown, William, 56
brown trout: control of, 146, 316; in Loch Assynt, 183 in river Ayr, 284; in Bladnoch, 291; in Brora, 149; in Loch Damh, 201; in Dee (Solway), 299; in Don, 87; in Eachaig, 273; in Lochs Fleet and Grannoch, 296; on Isle of Lewis, 204; on Mull, 223; poisoned in Shin, 146; in Whiteadder, 38
Bruar, River, 61
Bruiach Burn (and Loch), 121
Buchan, John, 28
Buchanty Spout, 67
Buchat, Water of, 85
Buidhe, Loch, 151
Burnett, Provost, 77
Burnfoot Falls (Water of Fleet), 296

Caaf, Water of, 282
Cabrach area, 93–5
Caen Burn, 154
Caenlochan National Nature Reserve, 65, 74
Cairn Water, 302, 307
Cairngall Burn, 92
Cairngorm Nature Reserve, 78
Caithness County Council (Loch Shurrery) Water Order, 1955, 165
Calder, Loch, 165
Calder, River, 97, 99
Calderwood, W.L., 44, 47, 72, 75,
90, 153, 208, 241, 243
Caledonian Canal, 108, 241
Callop River, 237
Caluim, Loch, 165
Cam, Loch, 185
Camasunary, River (Skye), 221
Campbell, R.N. and Williamson, R.B., 219, 220
Camster Burn, 159–60
Cannich, River, 116
Canny, Burn of, 79
Cantray Mill Trout Farm, 107
Caoidhe, Loch na, 124
Cape Wrath, 173–9
Carmel Water, 280
Carnach, River, 234–5
Carnaway, River (I. of Lewis), 205, 212
Carradale, River, 264
Carron, Loch (S.W. Ross), 203
Carron, River (Kyle of Sutherland), 20, 137–8
Carron, River (S.W. Ross), 199, 202–3
Carron, River (W. Lothian), 24, 314
Carron Water (Cowie, Dee), 83–4
Cashlie Power Station, 52
Cassley, River, 18, 26, 136, 141–5
Castle Burn (I. of Harris), 214
Castle Fisheries, 269
Castlefern, River, 307
Castlehill Reservoir, 314
Castramont Burn, 298
Cattie, Burn of, 79
Cawdor Burn, 107
Ceann Hulavig, Loch (I. of Lewis), 205
Ceannacroc Power Station, 114–15
Ceann-na-coille Burn, 169
Central Scotland Water Development Board, 275
Ceres Burn, 70
Chalmers, Ian: *Salmon Fishing in Little Rivers*, 232
Chapel Cross Power Station, 308
char, 123, 149, 273
Charnaig, River *see* Torboll, River
Cheivla, Loch a' ('Reedy Loch'; I. of Harris), 214
Chiscan Water, 263
Chlachain, Loch a' (I. of Lewis), 210–11
Chliostair, Loch (I. of Harris), 215
Choire, Loch, 169
Choire Mhoir, Loch a', 139
Chon, Loch, 40

327

Chon, Water of, 41
Chroisg, Loch a' (Conon district), 122
Chroisg, Loch a' (River Kanaird), 188
Chroisteam, Loch (I. of Lewis), 212
Chuilinn, Loch a', 123
Ciste, Loch na (I. of Lewis), 212
Ciste, Loch na (N. Uist), 219
Clachaig, River (Mull), 224
Clachan Power Station, 266, 270
Clair, Loch, 196
Claise Moire, Loch na, 140
Claonaig, River, 264–5
Clar, Loch nan, 153
Clatteringshaws Loch, 299
Clova hatchery, 76
Cluanie, Loch, 113–14
Cluden, River *see* Cairn Water
Clunie Dam (Tummel), 62–3
Clunie Power Station, 65
Clunie Water (Dee), 78
Clyde, River, 24, 274, 279, 314; Firth of, 273, 280, 282–3
Clyde River Purification Board, 274
Cnocglass, River (Torran Water), 165–6
Coats Patents Ltd, 257
Cochill Burn, 61
Cochill, Glen, 67
Coe, River, 255
Coiltie, River, 110
Coirefrois Burn, 150
Coladoir, River (Mull), 224–5
College Burn, 38
Combe, Lt Col, 131
Conglass Water, 98
Conieglen Water, 264
Coniecleugh Dyke (Deveron), 93–4
Conon Basin Hydro-electric Scheme, 125, 129, 138, 191, 313
Conon district, 122–32
Conon District Salmon Fishery Board, 124, 128–9
Conon Falls, 123
Conon, River, 12, 122–5, 126–8, 313
Cononish, River, 48, 58
Contin salmon hatchery, 124
Control of Pollution Act, 1974, 314
Corriemulzie, River (River Mulzie), 139
Corrieshalloch Gorge (Broom), 191
Coruisk, River (Skye), 221
Coulin, Loch, 196
Coulside, Loch, 170, 172
Coultrie, Loch, 200

Coupar, D., 166
Cour, River, 241, 244
Cowal Hydro-electric Scheme, 272
Cowie Water, 83–4
Cowton Burn, 83
Coyle, River, 283
Cracail Mor, Loch, 151
Craggie Burn, 154
Craggie, Loch (Caithness), 170
Craggie, Loch (Sutherland), 140
Craigdarroch, River, 307
Craige Ruabach, Loch na, 177
Craigenputtock Burn, 301
Craighall Gorge falls, 66
Craigo Dyke, 72–3
Craufurdland Water, 280
Cree, River, 292–5
Creed (Greeta) River (I. of Lewis), 210–11
Creed (Stornoway and Laxay) District Salmon Fishery Board, 205
Creran, River (and Loch), 252
Crinan Canal, 259
Crinan, Loch, 259–60
Cro, River *see* Abhainn Cro Chlach
Croe, River, 230–31
Croic, Loch na, 124, 130
Croick Falls, 138
Cromarty Firth, 14
Cross Water of Luce, 290–91
Cruachan Hydro–electric Scheme, 110, 250, 256
Cruick Water, 72
Cruoshie, Loch, 229
Cuaich, Loch, 51, 97
Culligran Power Station, 118
Cur, River, 273

Dail, Loch na, 186
Daill, River, 177–8
Daimh, Loch an, 139
Dalchonzie Power Station, 53, 68
Dalness Falls (Etive), 253
Dalwhat Water, 307
Damh, Loch, 200–201
Dan Mackay's Falls (Leven), 246
Davan, Loch, 79
Dean Burn, 37
Dee, River (Aberdeenshire), 15, 78–83, 97, 316
Dee, River (Solway), 298–301; *see also* Galloway Dee Hydro-electric Scheme

INDEX

Dee District Salmon Fishery Board, 80, 82, 300
Dee Salmon Fishing Association (Solway), 300–301
Dee Salmon Fishing Improvement Association, 82
Deugh, Water of, 284
Deveron, River, 14, 18, 93–5
Deveron District Salmon Fishery Board, 95
Devil's Beef Tub, 28, 308
Devon, River, 40, 45, 47, 314
Dherue, Loch an, 175
Dhu, Loch (Forth), 41
Dibidale River (I. of Harris), 217
Dick Lauder, Sir Thomas: *Scottish Rivers*, 30
Dinnet Hatchery, 80
Dionard, Loch, 14, 174
Dionard, River, 174–5
Dismal, Loch (I. of Lewis), 211
Divie, River, 103
Dochard, Loch, 247
Dochart, Loch, 48
Dochart, River, 48, 57–8; Hydro-electric Scheme, 52
Dochfour weir, 108–9
Doilet, Loch, 237; *see also* Hurich, River
Doine, Loch, 40, 42
Doire na h-Airbhe, Loch, 186
Don, River (Aberdeenshire), 25, 85–8, 314, 316
Don District Salmon Fishery Board, 87
Doon, Loch, 284, 299
Doon River, 24, 283–5; Hydro-electric Scheme, 313
Dorback Burn, 103
Dornal, Loch, 293–4
Douchary, River, 189
Douglas, River (Loch Fyne), 271
Douglas, River (Loch Lomond), 274
Dounreay Atomic Energy Station, 165
D'Oyly Carte, Richard, 209
Droma, River (and Loch), 191
Druie, River, 97, 99
Druim a' Chliabhain, Loch, 153
Drumly Harry, Falls of, 75
Dryfe Water, 308
Drynoch, River (Skye,), 221
Duart, River, 182
Duartmore Burn (and Loch), 182
Dubh Loch (Little Gruinard), 195, 197

Dubh Loch (Shira), 270–71
Dubh-Lochain (Lochalsh), 234–5
Duchray Water, 40–41
Dughaill (Doule), River, 203
Duich, Loch (Lochalsh), 231; *see also* Shiel of Duich, River
Duich, River (Islay), 228
Duisk, River, 287
Dulnain, River, 97, 99
Dunbeath Water, 158–9
Dundonnell, River, 192
Dundreggan, Loch, 108, 114–15
Duntelchaig, Loch, 106
Dusk Water, 282,
Dye, Water of, 80
Dyke, River, 167

Eachaig, River, 273–4
Ealachan, Loch nan, 230
Earball, Loch an (I. of Lewis), 208
Earn, Loch, 68; Hydro-electric Scheme, 52–3, 67–8
Earn, River, 48–9, 55, 68–9, 316
Eas Gobhain, 42
Easa Ghil, Loch an (I. of Lewis), 205
Eaval, River *see* Castle Burn (I. of Harris)
Ebrie Burn, 89–90
Eccles Hatchery, 306
Eck, Loch, 273–4
Eckford Fisheries Association, 37
Eddleston Water, 30
Eden, River (border), 309, 310–12
Eden, River (Tay district), 69–70
Eden Water, 30, 32
eels (and elvers), 3, 162, 172, 257
Egerton, Sir John, 146
Eigheach, Loch 50
Eil, Loch, 244
Eilt, Loch, 236
Einig, River, 139–40
Elchaig, River, 229–30
Elrick, River, 103
Endrick, River, 110, 274–5, 277–8
Enoch, Loch, 284
Eriboll, Loch, 173, 176
Ericht, Loch, 50–51, 98
Ericht, River, 50–51, 98
Erisort, Loch (I. of Lewis), 208
Ernan Water, 85
Errochty, River (and Loch), 51, 61
Esk (Border), River, 310–12
Esk, River (E. Lothian), 24

Esk, River (Musselburgh), 314
Esk, North, River, 12, 14, 18, 71–4, 316
Esk, South, River, 14, 18, 74–7, 316
Esk and Liddel Fisheries Association, 311
Eskin, River, 103
Etive, Loch, 248–51, 252–5
Etive, River, 252–4
Ettrick Water, 30–32, 36
Euchar, River, 255–6
Evelix, Loch, 146–7
Evelix, River, 136, 146–7
Ewe, Loch, 196
Ewe, River, 196–7
Ewes Water, 310
Ey Burn, 78, 80

Fada, Lochan (S.W. Ross), 196
Fada, Loch (S. Uist), 220
Falloch, River, 274, 276
Fannich, Loch, 123
Faoghail an Tuim, Loch (I. of Lewis), 205–6
Faoghail Charrasan, Loch (I. of Lewis), 205–6
Faoghail Kirraval, Loch (I. of Lewis), 205–6
Farigaig, River, 110
Farr Burn, 107
Farraline, Loch, 110
Farrar, River, 117–19, 121
Faskally, Loch, 51–2, 61
Fasnacloich, Loch, 252
Fasnakyle Power Station, 116–17
Fedderate Reservoir, 91–2
Fedderate, Water of, 92
Fender Burn, 65
Fenwick Water, 280
Feochan, Loch, 256–7; see also Nell (Feochan), River
Feochan Beg, River, 257
Fernie Burn, 70
Feshie, River, 97, 99
Feugh, Water of, 80
Fheoir, Lochan (I. of Harris), 213
Fhir Mhaoil, Loch an (I. of Lewis), 205–6
Fiag, River (and Loch), 145
Fiddich, River, 97, 99
Fillan, River, 48, 58
Fincastle Loch (I. of Lewis), 217–18
Findhorn, River, 1, 18, 103–5, 241

Findhorn District Salmon Fishery Board, 105
Findhorn Salmon Fisheries Ltd, 104–5
Finglas see Glen Finglas Reservoir
Finlaggan, Loch (Islay), 227–8
Finlarig Power Station, 52
Finlas, River, 274
Finnan, River, 237
finnock, 90, 200, 202, 216, 267, 277, 292, 297; see also sea trout
Fionn, Loch (Gruinard), 193–5
Fionn, Loch (Kirkaig), 185
Fleet, Loch (Solway), 296, 298
Fleet, River (and Loch; E. Sutherland), 151–2
Fleet, Water of, 296–8
Fleuchlarg Burn see Barley Burn
flies (salmon), 15, 19, 22–3, 159, 216
Fordoun Burn, 90
forestry: effects of, 105, 314–15
Forgue, River, 94
Forsa, River (Mull), 222
Forsinain Burn, 167
Forss Water, 165–6
Forth, River, 24, 40–42, 317
Forth-Teith system, 40–47
Foyers, River, 110
Foyers pump-storage scheme, 108
Free of Frithe, River see Abhainn na Frithe
Freshwater Fisheries Laboratories: Almondbank, 67; Faskally, 65; Pitlochry, 73, 74, 78–9, 277, 315, 317
Freuchie, Loch, 61
Frisa, Loch, 223
Fruid Reservoir, 8, 30, 32
Fruid Water, 30
Fruin, River, 274–5
Fuaron, Loch (Mull), 224
Funlack, River, 103
Fyne, Loch, 259, 266–7, 269–71, 273
Fyne, River, 266–7

Gaineamhuich, Loch, 198
Gainmhich, Loch na, 178
Gair, Loch, 259
Gairloch, 198
Gairn, River, 79–80, 97
Gairney Burn, 47
Gairowen, River, 111
Gala Water, 30
Gallery Burn, 72

330

INDEX

Galloway Dee Hydro-electric Scheme, 284–5, 298–300, 313
Garbet Beg, Loch, 180–81
Garbet Mohr, Loch, 180–81
Garbh Allt (Arran), 225
Garbh Allt (tributary of Cassley), 141
Garbh Allt (tributary of Fleet), 151
Garbh Uidh, River, 145
Garbhe Uidhe, Loch, 183
Gardiner, M.L.G., 12
Garnock, River, 280, 282
Garpel Water, 283
Garron, River, 271
Garry, Loch, 50–51, 61, 111, 113
Garry, River, 1, 12, 18, 48, 61, 63, 108–13; and Hydro-electric Scheme, 51–4, 61, 108, 111–12, 115, 313
Garth, Loch, 110
Garve, Loch, 124
Garvie River (and Loch), 187
Gathorne-Hardy, A.E.: *Autumns in Argyleshire*, 260
Gaur, Loch, 51
Gaur Power Station, 50
Gaur, River, 50, 63
Geireann, River (N. Uist), 219
Gelder Burn, 79
Geldie Burn, 78
Gharbh Choire Burn, 78
Ghriama, Loch a, 145
Ghiubhsachain Burn (and Loch), 193
Ghlinne, Loch a' (I. of Harris), 216
Girnock Burn 79–80
Girvan, Water of, 286–7
Girvan District Salmon Fishery Board, 286
Gisla Hydro-electric Scheme (I. of Lewis), 212
Glaic Tarsuinn, Loch na, 178
Glamhaichd, Loch na, 178
Glascarnoch Reservoir (and Dam), 124, 191
Glashan, Loch, 259
Glass, Loch, 134
Glass, River, 116–17, 118, 121
Glazert Water, 280–81
Gledfield Falls, 137–8
Glen, River, 38
Glen Water, 280
Glen Affric, Strathfarrar and Aigas-Kilmorack Hydro-electric Scheme, 117–19

Glen Finglas Reservoir, 40
Glen Golly River, 173–4
Glen Shira Hydro-electric Scheme, 266, 270
Glenbeg, River (Abhainn a' Ghlinne Bhig), 232–3
Glenbhearrie, Loch, 257
Glenbuck Loch, 283
Glencalvie, Water of (and Falls), 137–8
Glencannel, River (Mull), 224
Glendevon Reservoirs (Upper and Lower), 47
Glendey Burn, 47
Glenfarg Reservoir, 68–9
Glenfenzie ('Fingie') Burn, 80
Glenlee Power Station, 299
Glenlussa Water, 262
Glenmore, River, 232–3
Glenmoye, Burn of, 74
Glenogil Reservoir, 75
Glenquey Reservoir, 47
Glensherup Reservoir, 47
Glomach, Falls of, 230
Glutt, Falls of, 162
Gonar Burn, 92
Goodie Water, 41
Gordon, Lord Adam, 71
Gorm Lochs, 141, 144
Gowan, Loch, 122
Gower Water, 280
Grampian Electric Supply Company 50, 62
Grannoch, Loch, 298
Grassy Loch, 162
grayling, 304, 308
Greenock Water, 284
Gress, Loch (I. of Lewis), 212
Gress, River (I. of Lewis), 205, 211
grey mullet, 292, 297
Grimble, Augustus, 90, 246, 252, 256, 260
Grimersta, River (I. of Lewis), 205, 207–8
Gruagaich, Loch na, 183
Grudie, River (tributary of Bran), 123
Grudie, River (Kyle of Durness), 177, 196
Grudie Bridge Power Station, 123
Grudie Burn, 145–6
Gruinard, River, 193–5; *see also* Little Gruinard River
Grumavat, Loch (I. of Lewis), 212
Gryfe, River, 279–80

331

Guerrean, Loch (N. Uist), 219
Guseran, River, 233–4

Halladale Burn (and Loch; I. of Lewis), 215
Halladale, River, 167
Harewood Glen, 37
Harris, Isle of, 204, 212–19
Helmsdale, River (Ullie), 18, 153–6, 316
Helmsdale River Board, 156
Hermitage Falls, 62
Highland River Purification Board, 121, 160
Hogg, James (the Ettrick Shepherd), 36
Holy Loch, 273
Hope, Loch, 173
Hope, River, 173–4
Horisary, Loch (N. Uist), 219
Horsaclett, River (I. of Harris), 219
Hourn, Loch (Lochalsh), 233
Hourn, Loch (Ness District), 108, 112
Houstry, Burn of, 159
Howmore system (S. Uist), 220
Hunter Committee, 318
Huntingdon, A.W., 249
Huntingdon, Mrs. G.B., 249
Huntly, Marquis of, 82
Hurich (Doilet), River, 237
Hutchinson, G.H. ('Sixty-One'), 209, 211
Hydro-electric Development Act (Scotland), 1943, 50, 116, 313
hydro-electric power *see under* individual schemes

Iasgaich, Loch an, 183
Iasgaich, Lochan an, 199
Idoch Water, 93–4
Import of Live Fish (Scotland) Act, 1978, 316
Inchard, Loch, 180
Inchard of Rhiconich, River, 180–81
Indaal, Loch (Islay), 227–8
Insh, Loch, 97, 100
Institute of Hydrology, Plynlimon (Wales), 315
Inver, Loch, 183
Inver, River, 183–4
Inveran Power Station, 145–6
Inverawe Power Station, 250
Invergarry Power Station, 112

Invergarry Salmon Hatchery, 108, 114
Inverie, River, 234–5
Invermoriston Power Station, 114
Inveruglas Water, 274
Iorsa, Loch (Arran), 226
Iorsa Water (Arran), 226–7
Irvine, River, 24, 280–82
Isla, River (tributary of Deveron), 93–4
Isla, River (Tay), 48–9, 55, 65–6
Islay, Isle of, 227–8
Iubhair, Loch, 48

Jed Water, 37
Jedforest Fisheries Association, 37
Johnston, H.W., 56
Johnston, Joseph, & Son Ltd, 72–3, 76
Jones, J.W.: *The Salmon*, 12

Kale Water, 32, 37
Kanaird, Loch, 188
Kanaird, River, 188–9
Katrine, Loch, 40
Keal, Loch na (Mull), 224
Kearvaig, River, 178
Keltie, River, 42–3
Kelty Water, 41
Ken, River (and Loch), 298–300
Kendon Reservoir, 284
Kensary Burn, 159–60
Kerry, River, 197–8
Kildonan Burn (and Falls), 154
Kildonan, Lower *see* Lower Kildonan, Loch
Kilmarie, River (Skye), 221
Kilmarnock Water, 280
Kilmartin, River (Skye), 221
Kilmelfort Power Station, 258
Kilmorack Dam, 119–20
Kilphedir Burn, 154
Kinard, Loch, 79
Kinardochy Burn, 63
Kincardine Fisheries Ltd, 156, 170
Kindly Tenants, The, 309
King Edward Burn, 93–4
Kingie, River, 113
Kinglas, River (Loch Fyne), 267–9
Kinglass, River (Loch Etive), 248, 254–5
King-Webster, W.A., 299
Kinloch, River, 175
Kinlochewe River, 196
Kinnel Water, 308
Kintyre District, 259–65, 314

INDEX

Kirkaig, River, 184–5
Kishorn, River (and Loch), 202
Knaik, River, 45
Knockando Burn Hatchery, 100
Kyle of Durness, 173–9
Kyle of Sutherland, 136–47
Kyle of Sutherland District Salmon Fishery Board, 138, 144, 146
Kyles of Bute, 272
Kyllachy, River, 103
Kynachan Burn, 63

Ladies Loch (I. of Harris), 215
Ladyburn, 70
Lagain, Loch an, 146–7
Laggan, Loch, 96, 244
Laggan, River (Islay), 228
Laidon, Loch, 50
Lair, River, 203
Laird, Miss Lindsay, 150
Lairg Dam, 12
Lairig Burn, 78
Lairig Gartain Burn, 253
Lairige, Lochan na, 52
Langarat, Loch (I. of Lewis), 205–8
Langwell Water, 157–8
Laro, Loch, 146
Lauder, Harry, 228
Lawrence, David, 303–4
Laxadale Lochs (I. of Harris), 217
Laxay, River (I. of Lewis), 208–9
Laxdale River (I. of Harris), 217–19
Laxford, Loch, 181
Laxford, River, 150, 181–2
Leader Water, 30
Leitreach, Loch na, 230
Ledbeg River, 185
Ledmore River (Mull), 223
Lednock, Loch, 53
Lednock Power Station (and Reservoir), 53, 67–8
Lednock, River, 68
Lee, Loch, 71, 74
Lee Water, 71
Leet Water, 31
Leith, River, 24
Leithen Water, 30
Leny Water, 40, 42, 44; Falls of, 44
Leosaid, Loch (I. of Harris), 215
Lethnot, Glen, 72
Letters Burn *see* Abhainn Dubhach
Leven, Loch, 245, 255
Leven, River (Fife), 314

Leven, River (Kinross-shire), 24
Leven, River (Loch Lomond, Balloch), 274–7
Leven of Kinlochleven, River, 245–6
Lewis, Isle of, 204–12
Libo, Loch, 282
Liddel Water, 310
Ling, River, 229
Linky Burn, 284
Linn of Barhoise, 291
Linn of Dee, 78, 80
Linn of Muick, 79
Linnhe, Loch, 241, 245
Lintrathen, Loch of, 66
Little Gruinard River, 193–5
Little Loch Roag (I. of Lewis), 212
Little River, 161–2
Little Water, 89–90
Little Water of Fleet, 296–7
Livet, River, 98
Loanan, Loch, 183
Loch Nell Water Order, 1969, 257
Loch Ness Proprietors Association, 110
Loch of the Lowes, 36
Loch Roag District Salmon Fishery Board, 205
Loch Turret Water Supply Scheme, 68
Lochay, River, 48, 58; and Hydro-electric Scheme, 52
Lochy district, 241–6
Lochy, Loch, 241, 243, 245
Lochy, River, 108, 241–4, 247, 249
Loin, Loch an, 200
Lomond, Loch, 274–7
Lonan, River, 256
Londarat River (I. of Harris), 217
Long, Loch (Lochalsh), 229
Lossie, River, 102
Loups of The Burn, The (falls), 71
Lower Burn, 72
Lower Kildonan, Loch (S. Uist), 220
Lowes, Loch of *see* Loch of the Lowes
Loy, River, 245
Loyal, Loch, 170, 172
Loyne, River (and Loch), 114
Lubnaig, Loch, 40, 42, 44
Lubreoch Power Station, 52, 60
Luce, Water of, 290–2
Lugar Water, 283
Lugton Water, 282
Lui Water, 78, 80
Luichart, Loch, 123, 129
Luichart Power Station, 123, 128, 131

333

SALMON RIVERS OF SCOTLAND

Lundy Burn, 243
Lungard, Loch, 116
Lurgainn, Loch, 188
Luss, River, 274, 276
Lussa, Loch, 262
Lussa, River (Kintyre), 262–3
Lussa, River (Mull), 225
Lussa Hydro-electric Scheme (Kintyre), 262
Luther Water, 72, 74
Lyne Water, 30, 32
Lyon, Loch, 52, 60, 247
Lyon, River, 48–9, 58–60; Hydro-electric Scheme, 53, 247, 313

Maberry, Loch, 291–3
MacDonald-Buchanan, Major Sir Reginald, 128
Macfarlane, P.R.C., 302
Machany Water, 68
Machrie Water (Arran), 225–6
Machrihanish Water (Backs Water), 263–4
Macintyre, Dugald, 227, 262, 263
McLauchlin, Chris, 248
Macleay's Stream (I. of Lewis), 206
Mahaick, Loch, 43
Main Water of Luce, 290
Mallart River, 169–70
Malloch, P.D.H., 2, 57
Malloch, William, 57, 73
Malzie Burn, 291–2
Manor Water, 30
Maree, Loch, 14, 197–8
Marine Harvest Ltd, 236
Mark Water, 71
Martin, Martin: *A Little Voyage to St Kilda*, 210
Massan, River, 273
May, Water of, 68
Mazeran, River, 103, 105
Meadie, Loch, 169
Measach Falls (Broom), 191
Meavaig, River *see* Scourst, River
Meggat Water, 310
Megget Valley, 32–3, 314
Megget Water, 36
Meig, River, 122–3, 125, 130–31
Meiklie, Loch, 108, 110
Melfort, Loch, 258
Melfort Farming Company, 258
Menteith, Lake of, 41

Menzion Burn, 30
Meoble, River, 235
Merkland, Loch, 145
Mhadaidh, Loch a', 191
Mhoicean, Loch, 230
Mhoille Burn, 249
Mhor, Loch, 110
Mhuillin, Loch, 118
Milk, Water of, 308
Mill Loch (S. Uist), 220
Mill of Newe Hatchery, Strathdon, 87
mink, 3, 207, 306, 316
Minnoch, River, 293–5
Misgeach Burn, 118
Moan, Loch, 292–3
Mochrum, Loch, 292
Moffat Water, 308
Moidart, River (and Loch), 236–7
Monachyle Burn, 42
Monar, Loch, 118
Monboys, Burn of, 83
Moncrieff, Col D., 176
Monessie Falls, 244
Montrose Basin, 76
Mor Barvas, Loch (I. of Lewis), 210
Moral Falls, 137
Morar, River (and Loch), 235
Moray Firth Salmon Fisheries Company Ltd, 104, 121, 126
More, Loch, 161–2, 181–2
Morie, Loch, 133
Moriston, River, 18, 108–9, 112–15, 313
Morlich, Loch, 97
Morphie Dyke, 73–4
Morrison, Mrs, 94
Morsgail, River (and Loch; I. of Lewis), 212
Morven Burn, 80
Muckle Burn (tributary of Findhorn), 104
Mucomir Power Station (and Falls), 241, 243
Mudale, River, 169
Muic Burn, 142, 144; Falls, 141–2
Muick, River (and Loch), 79–80
Mull, Isle of, 222–5
Mullardoch, Loch, 116–17
Mulzie, River *see* Corriemulzie, River
Murdoch, W.: *More Light on the Salmon*, 83
Murray, Sir John, 57

INDEX

Nairn, River, 105–7
Nairn Fishery Board, 107
Nant, Loch, 251, 256
Nant Hydro-electric Scheme, 250–51
Naver, Loch, 168
Naver, River, 18, 161, 168–71, 316
Naver Fishery Board, 170
Nell (Feochan), River (and Loch), 256–7
Ness district, 108–15
Ness, Falls of, 68
Ness, Loch, 108–10, 241
Ness, River, 6, 105, 108–9
Ness District Salmon Fishery Board, 108, 111–13
Ness Glen, 284
Nethy, River, 97, 99
Nevis, Loch, 108, 233, 234–5
Nevis, River, 245
New Loch (I. of Lewis), 211
New Luce, 290
Nith, River, 18, 24, 282, 302–7, 318
Nith Fishings Improvement Association, 302–3, 306, 318
Nochty, Water of, 85
Noran Water, 75
North-East River Purification Board, 83, 87, 100
North Esk (Angus), River, 12, 14, 18, 71–4, 316
North Esk District Fishery Board, 73
North Harris Fishery, 212–13, 216
North of Scotland Hydro-electric Board, 50, 53, 61, 63, 66–7, 108, 110, 112–19, 122–3, 126–30, 189, 197, 215, 235, 248, 251–2, 256–7, 259, 262, 270, 272, 313
North Sea oil, 316
North Ugie Water, 91
North-West Water Authority, 310, 311–12

Ogle, River, 68
Oich, Loch, 108, 110–13, 241
Oich, River, 109–11
Oidhche, Loch na h-, 197
Ois, Loch an, 210–11
Orchy, River, 109, 247–9, 252
Orrin Reservoir (and dam), 124–5, 128–9
Orrin, River, 122, 124–6, 129
Oscaig, River (and Loch), 187
Ose (Ullinish), River (Skye), 221

Oude, River, 209, 257–8
Oxnam Water, 37
Oykel, River, 18, 136, 139–41

Palnure Burn, 293–5
Parker, Maude, 56, 83, 99
Pedwell Fishery, Norham, 35
Peebles-shire Salmon Fishing Association, 33
Penkiln, River, 293–5
Penwhirn Burn (and Reservoir), 290
perch, 250, 291, 298–300
Philiphaugh, 37
pike, 3, 6, 100, 123–4, 197, 245, 250, 285, 291–3, 298–300, 304, 308
Pilnrark Burn, 293
Pitlochry Dam, 52, 63
Plaide, Loch na (I. of Lewis), 208
Plodda Falls (Glass), 116
poachers and poaching: control of, 317; on Ayr, 283; on Barr, 261, on Cairn, 307; on Carnach, 235; on Croe, 231; on Garnock, 282; on Irvine, 281; on I. of Lewis, 205, 207–10; on Mull, 222–3; on Nith, 316; on Skye, 222
Poiblidh Burn, 139
Polla, River, 176
Polly, River, 186
Poulary, Loch, 111, 114
Prevention of Pollution (Scotland) Act, 1951, 303
Prosen Water, 75
Pulcree Burn, 298

Quaich, Glane, 67
Quaich, River, 61
Quair Water, 30
Quharity Burn, 75
Quoich, Loch, 108, 111–12
Quoich Power Station, 112, 115
Quoich Water, 78, 80

Radcliffe, Major, 166
Rangag, Loch, 161
Rankle Burn, 36
Rannoch, River (Loch Aline), 239–40
Rannoch, Loch (and Power Station), 50–51, 62
Rappach Water, 139
Red River (I. of Lewis), 212
reservoirs *see under* individual names

335

Resort, Loch (I. of Harris), 212–13, 216
Restil, Loch, 268
Rhidorroch River, 189
Rickards, Commander, 156, 170
Riddon, Loch, 272
Rimsdale Burn (and Loch), 153
River Doon Improvement Association, 285
River Irvine Angling Improvement Association, 282
Rivers (Prevention of Pollution) (Scotland) Acts, 1951 and 1965, 24, 314
Roag, Loch (I. of Lewis), 205, 207
Roag, Loch (S. Uist), 220
Robertson, R. MacDonald: *Angling in Wildest Scotland*, 191
Rogie, Falls of, 124–5, 130
Rosehall Water, 144
Rothes Burn, 97
Rottal Burn, 74, 76
Roy, River, 241, 244–5
Ruard, Loch, 161
Ruathair, Loch an (Achentoul Loch), 153, 155
Ruchill, Water of, 68
Ruel, River, 272
Rule Water, 37
Rumbling Bridge Falls (River Devon), 47, 62
Runie, River, 188–9
Runsdale Water, 161
Rutherford, John, 154

St Fillans Power Station, 53
St Mary's Loch (Tweed), 33, 36–7, 314
salmon: life cycle, 1–3, 6, 26; nomenclature, 1; homing instinct, 2; spawning, 3, 26, 313–15; sea-life, 3; predators, 3, 316; diseases, 6, 32; commercial fishing of, 6–7, 9, 12–13, 34–5, 41; and environmental factors, 7–9, 24, 313 16; fishing season, 14; angling methods and equipment, 14–15, 18, 22–3, 54; river conditions, 24–7, 315–16; conservation measures (and pollution), 7, 24–5, 316–18; research on, 56, 65, 67
Salmon and Freshwater Fisheries (Scotland) Act, 1951, 12, 24, 317
Salmon Fisheries (Scotland) Acts, 1862 and 1868, 24, 32, 274, 317
Sandwood Loch, 178
Saughs, Falls of, 72
Scammadale, Loch, 251, 256
Scardroy, Loch *see* Beannachran, Loch
Sclater, J.R.P., 96
Scott, Col H.E., 94
Scott, Sir Walter, 28, 30
Scottish River Purification Advisory Committee, 87
Scottish River Purification Board, 314
Scourst, Loch, 213
Scourst (Meavaig), River (I. of Harris), 214
Scridain, Loch (Mull), 224
Scrope, William, 28
Sea Fisheries Conservation Act, 1967, 7
sea trout, 14, 18, 41, 299; in Loch Achtriochtan, 255; in Ailort, 235–6; in Aline, 239; in Allt Graad, 134; in Alness, 133;, in Annan, 308; in Arran, 226; in Arvisdale, 233; in Ayr, 283; in Balgy, 200–201; in Balnagown, 135; in Beauly, 121; in Broom, 191; in Brora, 149; in Cairn Water, 307; in Canny, 79; in Carron, 203; in Carron Black Water, 138; in Claonaig, 265; in Cowie, 83; in Cree, 293; in Loch Damh, 201; in Dee, 81; in Deveron, 94; in Loch Dionard, 174; in Loch Doilet, 237; in Dunbeath, 159; in Eachaig, 273–4; in Earn, 69; in Eden (Tay), 70; in Elchaig, 230; in Endrick, 278; in Esk (Border), 310–11; in Etive, 253–4; in Ewe, 196–7; in Falloch, 276; in Findhorn, 104; in Fleet, 151–2; in Fleet (Solway), 297–8; in Forth–Teith system, 41, 44–5, 47; in Fyne, 267; in Garnock, 282; in Gruinard, 194; on Isle of Harris, 214–18; in Lochan an Iasgaich, 199; in Inverie, 234; in Irvine, 280–81; on Islay, 227; in Kanaird and Runie, 188; in Kinglass, 254; in Kyle of Sutherland, 136–7; in Leven (Lomond), 277; in Ling, 229; in Loch Lomond, 275–6; in Lochy, 242; in Lossie, 102; in Water of Luce, 290–91; in Moidart, 235; in Loch More, 181; in Morar, 235; in

Muic Burn, 144; on Mull, 223–4; in Nairn, 106; in Naver, 169; in Ness, 109; in Nell, 256–7; in Nevis, 245; in Nith, 303–4, 306–7; in Rannoch, 239; in Ruel, 272; in Loch Shiel, 237–8; in Shiel of Duich, 231; in Shieldaig, 202; in Shinary, 179; on Skye, 221; in Spey, 98; in Loch Stack, 181; in Stinchar, 288; in Tay, 55–6; in Tweed district, 37–9; in Ugie, 91–2; on S. Uist, 220; in Ythan, 89–90
seals, 3, 87, 233, 235–6, 238, 254, 316
Sealge, Loch na (Loch na Sheallag), 193
Seilge, Loch na, 167
Seilich, Loch an t-, 50–51, 97
Sgaire, Loch (I. of Lewis), 208
Sgamhain (Scaven), Loch, 203
Sguabain, Loch (Mull), 225
Shalloch Burn, 291
Shearer, W.M., 73
Sheeoch, Burn, 80, 83
Sheep Loch (I. of Harris), 219
Shiel, Loch, 237
Shiel, River, 237–9
Shiel of Duich, River, 231–2
Shieldaig, Loch, 201
Shieldaig, River, 201–2
Shin, Loch, 144–6, 150
Shin, River, 2, 136, 141, 145–6, 316
Shin Hydro-electric Scheme, 144, 145, 150, 313
Shinary, River, 178–9
Shira, Loch, 269
Shira, River, 270–71
Shira, Lochan, 266, 270
Shurrery, Loch, 165–6
Sionascaig, Loch, 186
'Sixty-One' *see* Hutchinson, G.H.
Skealtar, Loch (N. Uist), 219–20
Skinsdale Burn, 150
Skye, Isle of, 221–2
Slaim, Loch, 170
Sletill, Loch, 167
Sligachan, River (Skye), 221
Slitrig Water, 37
Sloy, Loch, 266, 268
Sloy-Shira Hydro-electric Scheme, 266, 268, 270
Sma' Glen, 67
Smart, Graham G.J., 73–4
Smigel Burn, 167

smolts, 1–3, 26–7
Snizort, River (Skye), 221
Solway River Purification Board, 303, 308
Solway rivers, 290–312
Sorn, River (Islay), 227–8
Souter, Alan, 222
South Esk, River, 14, 18, 74–7, 316
South Esk District Salmon Fishery Board, 75
South of Scotland Electricity Board, 284, 298, 300–301, 313
South Ugie Water, 91
Spean, River, 241, 243–4
Spelve, Loch (Mull), 225
Spey, Loch, 96
Spey, River, 1, 15, 50, 96–101, 317
Spey District Salmon Fishery Board, 100
Sron Mor, Lochan, 270
Sronmor Power Station, 270
Stack, Loch, 14, 174, 181–2
Stacsavat, Loch (I. of Lewis), 212
Stansfeld, John de B., 73
Staonsaid, Loch, 176
Stemster, Loch, 161
Stinchar, River, 287–9
Stinchar District Fishery Board, 288
Stoddart, Tom: *Angling Reminiscences*, 29, 129
Strae, River, 248–9
Strath Burn, 159
Strathmore River, 173–4
Strathy, Loch, 167
Strathy, River, 167–8, 316
Striven, Loch, 272
Stuart, Hamish: *Book of the Sea Trout*, 218, 227–8, 270
Suainaval, Loch (I. of Lewis), 212
Suisgill Burn, 154

Talla Water, 30, 32
Tamhnich Burn, 272
Tanar, Water of, 79–80
Tanna, Loch (Arran), 226
Tarbert, East Loch (I. of Harris), 217
Tarbert, West Loch (I. of Harris), 212–14
Tarbert, West Loch (Kintyre), 264
Tarff, River, 110
Tarff, Water of (tributary of Esk), 71
Tarf Water (tributary of Tilt), 65
Tarff Water (Solway), 291–300

Tarland Burn, 79, 80
Tarras Water, 310
Tarsan, Loch Power Station, 272
Tay district, 48–70
Tay District Salmon Fisheries Board, 49–50, 52, 60–63, 66–8
Tay, Loch, 48–9, 57; Hydro-electric Scheme, 52
Tay, River, 1, 2, 12, 14–15, 48–9, 54–7, 313, 316–17
Tay Salmon Fisheries Company Ltd, 49–50, 69, 76
Teachmuick Burn, 121
Teith, River, 18, 40–44, 316
Teviot, River, 30–32, 37–8
Thornton, Col T., 48
Thurso, River, 18, 161–4
Thurso Fisheries Ltd, 161–2, 164
Till, River, 31–2, 38
Tilt, River, 48, 50–51, 63, 65
Tima Water, 36
Tirry, River, 145, 150
Todall, River (I. of Lewis), 212
Tombane Burn, 61
Tomich Burn, 116
Tor Ness waterfall (Mull), 225
Torboll (Charnaig), River, 151–2
Torbreck, River, 151
Torr Achilty Dam and Power Station, 124, 126–8
Torr na Caerdeich, Loch, 165
Torra, River (Islay), 228
Torran Water *see* Cnocglass, River
Torridon, Loch, 200
Torridon, River, 199
Torridon, Upper Loch, 199–201
Traligill, River, 183
Traquair House, 30
Trealaval, Loch (I. of Lewis), 208–9
Treig, Loch, 244
Tromie, River, 96–8
Trool, Water of, 293–5
Trossachs, 40
Trow Burn, 37
Truderscaig, Loch, 155
Truim, River, 96, 98
Tulla, Loch, 247–8
Tulla, Water of, 247
Tummel, Loch, 51, 62–3
Tummel, River, 12, 48–50, 62–5, 127; Hydro-electric Scheme, 50–53, 62, 97, 313
Tummel Bridge Power Station, 51

Tunns, River, 259
Turret Burn, 68
Tweed district, 28–39
Tweed, River: seasons, 1, 14–15, 18, 32, 34; damming of upper tributaries, 8, 314; stock fluctuations in, 9–10; fishing conditions, 15, 18; described, 28–35; pools, 30, 33–4; Commissioners, 31, 35, 317–18; owners and beats, 31, 33; commercial fishing in, 34–5
Tweed Fisheries Acts, 1857 and 1859, 24, 31–2
Tweed Fisheries Act, 1969, 31, 317

Uair, River, 167–8
Ugie, River, 91–2, 316
Uidh Tarraigean, Loch, 186
Uig, River (I. of Lewis), 212
Uisgn Tuigh (Uisk-an-Dhuie; Islay), 228
Uist, North, 219–20
Uist, South, 220–21
Ulbhach Choire, Loch, 145
ulcerative dermal necrosis (UDN): described, 6; occurrence, 32, 54, 81, 90, 92, 94, 100, 108, 121, 126, 129, 133–4, 136, 152, 158, 166, 172, 175, 182, 184–6, 189, 194–5, 197, 201, 209–10, 218–19, 227, 246, 252–3, 265, 273, 275, 278, 281, 285, 288, 291–2, 300–301, 304, 306, 309
Ulladale, Loch (I. of Harris), 212–13
Ulladale, River (I. of Harris), 213–14, 216
Ullapool River, 189, 191
Ullie, River *see* Helmsdale, River
Unilever Research Laboratory, Inverailort, 236
Upper Teviotdale Fisheries Association, 37
Ure, River, 252
Urigill, Loch, 183
Urr Water (and Loch), 301

Vaich, Loch, 124, 138
Valtos, Loch (I. of Lewis), 208–9
Varagill, River (Skye), 221
Venacher, Loch, 40, 42, 44
Veyatie, Loch, 185
Voil, Loch, 40, 42, 44

INDEX

Voshimid, Loch (I. of Harris), 212
Voshimid, River (I. of Harris), 213–14, 216

water supply, 313–15; *see also* individual reservoirs
Watten, Loch, 159
Wauchope Water, 310
weed growth, 90–92, 95, 239
West Water, 72–3
White Cart, River, 279
White Esk, River, 310
White Water, 74

Whiteadder Water (and Reservoir), 31–2, 38–9
Whitehaugh Water, 284
Whyte's Dyke (Don), 85
Wick, River, 159–60, 316
Wood, Ian: *Loch Lomond and its Salmon*, 276

Yarrow, River, 30–33, 36–7
Younger, John, 29; *River Angling*, 33
Ythan, River, 89–91
Yucal, Loch, 182